THE DEMISE OF THE AMERICAN HOLINESS MOVEMENT:

A Historical, Theological, Biblical, and Cultural Exploration

By

Darius L. Salter, Ph.D.

First Fruits Press
Wilmore, Kentucky
c2020

ISBN: 9781621719403

The demise of the American Holiness Movement: a historical, theological, Biblical, and cultural exploration / by Darius L. Salter.
First Fruits Press, © 2020

Digital version at
http://place.asburyseminary.edu/firstfruitsheritagematerial/172/

Salter, Darius, 1947-
    The demise of the American Holiness Movement: a historical, theological, Biblical, and cultural exploration / by Darius L. Salter. – Wilmore, KY: First Fruits Press, ©2020.
        427 pages; cm.
        ISBN: 9781621719403 (paperback)
        ISBN: 9781621719410 (uPDF)
        ISBN: 9781621719427 (Mobi)
        OCLC: 1096280297
        1. Holiness movement--United States--History--19th century.
        2. Holiness movement--United States--History--20th century.
        3. Holiness churches--United States--History--19th century.
        4. Holiness churches--United States--History--20th century.
        5. United States--Church history--19th century.
        6. United States--Church history--20th century. I. Title.
BX7990.H6 S34 2020   **287.6**

Cover design by Jon Ramsay

asburyseminary.edu
800.2ASBURY
204 North Lexington Avenue
Wilmore, Kentucky 40390

First Fruits Press
The Academic Open Press of Asbury Theological Seminary
204 N. Lexington Ave., Wilmore, KY 40390
859-858-2236
first.fruits@asburyseminary.edu
asbury.to/firstfruits

To Kermit Farlow and the little band of Pilgrim Holiness believers, who worshiped together in Atlantic, North Carolina.

Table of Contents

Acknowledgements

Because I am too lazy to re-invent the wheel, much less smart enough to improve on it, I have relied on the superb scholarship of the following persons: Ron Benefiel, Richard Heitzenrater, Kenneth O. Brown, Virginia Brereton, Stephen Lennox, Johan Tredoux, Floyd Cunningham, Samuel K. Biser, Mark Quanstrom, Joseph Thacker, Jr., Kenneth Kinghorn, Scott Kisker, Ronald E. Smith, Wallace Thornton, Ellen Eisinger, Kent Brower, William Ringenberg, John Adams, David Bundy, Cheryl Bridge-Johns, Donald W. Dayton, Grant Wacker, Stephen Gunter, Oran Spindell, Mark Olson, Douglas Mastriano, Rob Staples, Melvin E. Dieter, Margaret Poloma, Frank Baker, Stan Ingersol, Robert Lyon, Alex Deasley, Kenneth Collins, Frank Maser, and Henry Rack. Further information can be found about them in the footnotes and bibliography.

I thank the following persons who took time to offer their perspectives as to what happened to the American Holiness Movement over the last several decades: Melvin E. Dieter, Stan Ingersol, Kenneth Collins, Jeff Greenway, William Miller, John Oswalt, Al Coppedge, Robert Coleman, Stephen Seamands, Daniel Tipton, Thomas Hermiz, William Faupel, Norman Moore, Larry Mason, Sam White, Mike Roorbach, Jesse Middendorf, John Neihof, Jr., and Albert Truesdale. Jeff James, Chip Wood, Mark Nysewander, Jeff Calhoun, Ron Houp, Harvey Brown, Jr. Steve Beard and Steve Seamands were helpful in gaining a perspective on the events connected to the Toronto Blessing which took place in Wilmore, Kentucky, February of 1995. None of the above should be held responsible for my interpretation of their research or of the conversations which I had with them.

Paul Taylor gave me information on his father, Richard Taylor, and Brian Taylor on his grandfather, the same Richard Taylor.

As always, I have had to rely on archivists, among them Grace Yoder at Asbury Theological Seminary, Mark Shenise at Drew University, and Stan Ingersol, as well as Meri Jansen-Bond at the Nazarene Archives,

Lenexa, Kansas. Judy Schwanz pointed to resources for understanding "self-differentiation," and Doug Hardy enlightened me on the academic development of "spiritual formation." Karen Roorbach furnished me with up-to-date statistics from Indiana Wesleyan University.

The following people have read all or a portion of the manuscript and offered helpful suggestions and corrections: William Miller, Albert Truesdale, Stella Harris, and Donald W. Dayton.

I owe a special debt to Steve McCormick, who began with me as a graduate student at Drew University forty years ago, and who is my never-failing source on John Wesley. I am particularly grateful to the late Rob Staples, who left a detailed account of the critical events that took place at Nazarene Theological Seminary, 1979-1985.

A special thanks to Kristi Seaton and Alexandra Duenow for their computer skills and word processing. As in most of my projects I have relied on Debra Bradshaw and her tireless library personnel at Nazarene Theological Seminary. Alexandra, thank you, for what seems to be hundreds of items you have retrieved on my behalf via interlibrary loan. Gratitude to my technological genius son-in-law, Joeseph Jarrett, and equally brilliant, Ed Salter, who have rescued us from the dark black hole of the computer universe and enabled us to complete technological tasks which are so difficult for an alien generation lost in cyberspace. Robert "Robbie" Danielson, has done his normal yeoman's job in guiding me through this project and turning my efforts into a readable product.

As for every book I have completed, no one is more responsible than Brenda who said, "I will," almost one-half century ago. If I had known what followed the "I will," I would have not told her because she would have changed her mind and found someone far less challenging with whom to spend her life. The journey has been above and beyond what either of us would have ever asked or thought, but God has supplied the grace and strength. To Him be all the Glory!

Introduction

Born in 1947, I have lived in two worlds. The first world was pre-cell phone, pre-air conditioner, pre-computer, pre-fast food, pre-microwave, pre-travel, pre-mobility, pre-Walmart, pre-secondary education, pre-secularism, pre-mall, pre-middle class, and pre-consolidation. Most of these are self-evident for anyone my age and perhaps several of them are relevant only to me or the individuals raised in my community or similar communities. For instance, until I was sixteen years old I had never been more than 175 miles west of the small fishing village where I grew up on the coast of North Carolina. Until that time, I would not have been out of the state, except for the fact that as a child of a Navy serviceman, I lived my first seven years in Norfolk, Virginia.

A couple of illustrations suffice for my pre-secularity. In the first grade of my attendance at Francis E. Willard public elementary school in Norfolk, Virginia, I played one of the three wise men in a full-blown biblical Christmas pageant. We had Jewish neighbors who attended the same school; if they complained, I am not aware. Unthinkable to us in 2018, they may not even have been offended. Another memory is of my sixth-grade teacher writing the Beatitudes on the blackboard for memorization. I do not believe she was trying to begin some kind of spiritual awakening or convert anyone. She simply worked within a worldview that literacy had something to do with the most profound utterance from the lips of the world's most influential person.

The "pre-consolidation" needs some amplification. In 2015, I celebrated with my high school graduating class our 50th year reunion. I found it interesting that two months before our reunion the last remaining store in the village had gone out of business. There had at one time been five stores in the community, a high school, a theater, a dance hall, the best baseball team in the county and most importantly Clyde's Service Station, where between 15 and 20 men met every night to swap stories, knives, or whatever, drinking nickel cokes, or maybe even something stronger. After a hard day's work, without any designated schedule, they arrived promptly at 6:30 pm, and with a "I guess I'd better go," left around 8:30 pm. By the time of our 50th year high school reunion, all of the above were gone. The community had lost its identity. I suggested in an article which I, at that time, wrote for the Morehead City *News Times* (the official newspaper of Carteret County), that this downhill slide began with the consolidation of three high schools into East Carteret High School. The plight of Atlantic, North Carolina, was not unique. Thousands of American communities have gone out of existence, or lost their identity, because the one resource, which had supported them had dried up, mined out, or swam off; these communities had been supported by farming, gold, timber, oil, or in our case, fish.

The five stores were displaced by Walmart, if not the ultimate symbol for modernity, a prevalent and ubiquitous symbol. "Modernity is the illusion that believes life is getting better, when in some ways it is getting worse. Modernity is a sociological trend, that trades such intangible qualities as loyalty, community, friendship, tradition, and identity for tangible benefits such as expediency, mobility, technology, and above all, a vast array of commodities labeled 'conspicuous consumption,'"[1] a term coined by the economist Thorstein Veblen, in his classic *The Theory of the Leisure Class* (1899). And in case one might interpret my memories as a reconstruction of utopia, I also wrote, "Nostalgia often clouds memory causing us to forget the path that lead to the two-seater in the backyard, back breaking feather beds, the Sunday morning aroma from incinerating scrap fish, and the necessity of earning 50 cents for filling a bucket with shrimp heads. Only years after leaving home did I realize my existence was so marginalized that the American military placed a bombing range three miles from my house."[2]

---

[1] Darius Salter, "Atlantic High School Class of 1965: More Than Meets the Eye" *The News Times*, Morehead City, NC, May 27, 2015. I do not use the word modernity in any technical or philosophical sense. I am not referencing modernity in contrast to post-modernity. There will be no references to Michael Foucault and Jacques Derrida. I speak of modernity as describing a world that has radically changed since 1960, and continues to exponentially change technologically, demographically, sociologically, politically and religiously.

[2] Ibid.

I am working with the thesis that the American Holiness Movement has lost its identity primarily because it has been unable to negotiate modernity. I am furthering the conversation begun by Keith Drury, "The Holiness Movement is Dead," delivered at a breakfast meeting for the Christian Holiness Partnership in April 1995.[3] Drury was historically astute and prescient. Richard Taylor followed with his own observations, "Why the Holiness Movement Died."[4] Taylor was more optimistic than Drury, but at the same time more inaccurate. "The Christian Holiness Partnership (CHP) represents a constituency of some 11 million people and is comprised of 21 member denominations, 47 educational institutions, 2000 holiness camp meetings, and is affiliated with three missional organizations." Taylor's numbers are inflated. There are between one and two million people that meet in church under the Wesleyan Holiness umbrella on a given Sunday within the USA. In regard to the 2000 camp meetings that were possibly once in existence, less than a tenth of those are operative as of this writing. When I was Executive Director of the Christian Holiness Association (CHA) 1979-1986, I sent the Church of the Nazarene 6,500 convention brochures, a brochure for each of their churches. I less than doubled them for all the remainder of the denominations. There are 4-500,000 people in the American Church of the Nazarene on a given Sunday. Thus, my numbers of approaching two million people in church each Sunday under the holiness banner are generous.

But what Drury and Taylor could not accurately predict, is that the Christian Holiness Partnership would forever close its doors in December 2003. (This must have happened after Drury wrote his retrospective, revisiting his original address ten years later published in 2004.) Drury made no mention of the event; maybe God saved him from gloating that he had been right all along. The organization that had been in existence for 136 years (1867-2003) as the most identifiable symbol of the American Holiness Movement had gone out of existence.[5] As Melvin

---

[3] Keith Drury. "The Holiness Movement is Dead," *Counterpoint: Dialogue with Drury on the Holiness Movement.* ed. D. Curtis Hale (Salem, OH; Schmul Publishing, 2005).

[4] Richard Taylor. "Why the Holiness Movement Died," *God's Revivalist and Bible Advocate*, March, 1999.

[5] The Association mutated through several name changes: The National Camp Meeting Association for the Promotion of Holiness, The National Association for the Promotion of Holiness, The National Holiness Association, The Christian Holiness Association and The Christian Holiness Partnership. The crowds year by year grew

Dieter argued in his seminal *The Holiness Movement of the Nineteenth Century*, the doctrine of Christian perfection and its adherents were centrist and conspicuous within America's religious life 1870-1900. The camp meetings of the National Camp Meeting Association for the Promotion of Holiness spread around the world, drawing crowds of up to 25,000 and popularizing the names of John and Martha Inskip, Walter and Phoebe Palmer, Robert Pearsall and Hannah Whitall-Smith, eclipsed only by the urban evangelist, Dwight Moody, even he being at least half on the holiness band wagon. Along with the Keswick Movement in England much of the Christian leadership around the world bought into "the higher life movement," variegated with subtle theological distinctions. In 1871, the Camp Meeting Association set up its tent in Salt Lake City and blasted away at Brigham Young, who attended the services. A short time later, the famed evangelist Dewitt Talmadge, lighted down in Salt Lake City and commented, "We have never seen the brethren of that religious storming party, but we hail them ... for the glorious work that they have accomplished in Salt Lake City."[6]

The storm has run its course; in fact, the wind has gone entirely out of the sails. For the most part, both Taylor and Drury were right in their assessments, but they gave little of the why, like diagnosing the melting glacier at Lake Louise at Bamff, Canada. Most meteorologists would cite global warming, but there is little agreement as to the why of global warming; human or natural causes, carbon dioxide emissions, holes in the ozone layer, coming out of an ice age, or cyclical climate. Both Drury and Taylor cite the "church growth movement" as having at least partially caused the death of the Holiness Movement. For sure, rampant pragmatism had become more prevalent than theological reflection and proclamation of Wesleyan holiness. But from my perspective, the "church growth movement" was not the cause of death; it was a correlation to death. The "church growth movement" replaced

---

grayer and smaller. The annual Convention became a gathering of bureaucrats from the constituent denominations, who were on expense accounts, rather than a gathering of laity. Dan Tipton, who was president of CHP at the time of its closing, informed this writer that the holiness denominations stopped sending their highest jurisdictional officers. My friend William Miller referred to CHP closing its doors as the "funeral" of the Holiness Movement. From my perspective, the funeral formalized the death of an ideology.

[6] Melvin Dieter. *The Holiness Revival of the Nineteenth Century* (Scarecrow Press: Metuchen, New Jersey) 130.

methodologies which no longer worked. It was a desperate thumb in the dike to save the churches that still to some degree associated themselves with the Holiness Movement.

The "church growth movement" accented church planting. Its methodology for planting a church was far different from the methodology that holiness churches practiced fifty years ago: hold a revival in a tent or storefront, get some people saved, leave them there as the members for a new Nazarene, Wesleyan or Free Methodist Church. When I was in the 8th grade over one half of a century ago, I took my girlfriend for a date to a revival at the Methodist Church. It was the only available entertainment option in town. The revival methodology is passé. The competition is overwhelming. The Sunday night service where "sinners" were saved is no longer in existence. Where do we turn? To "successful" pastors who can give us the principles for seeker services, demographic research, the dynamics for corporate management and the priorities for an efficient pastor. But after the excitement of a seminar featuring a popular church growth specialist, most pastors returned to quotidian duties, sleepy congregations, recalcitrant board members and trying to connect visiting nursing homes with attracting the masses.

Let's take another backward look. In the pre-television and pre-cyberspace age, a pastor could have stayed for thirty years in the same community, peaked out his church at 300, retired with a smile on his face, and an all-expense paid vacation to a Cincinnati Reds game and two nights at a Holiday Inn, meals included. But when he became exposed through (choose your medium) to Jack Hyles, Bill Hybels, Rick Warren, Chuck Swindoll, Robert Schuler (the list seems endless) not to mention David Yonggi Cho in Seoul, South Korea, running 500,000 on Sunday morning, the once successful pastor now shriveled up with an inferiority complex which obscured his vision of God and placed a shroud over a heart of gratitude that no longer delighted in the care of his faithful flock. He could only lament, "If only I was one of those great pastors." After all, what success is there in "laying one's life down for the sheep?"

Drury nostalgically recalls the days of his grandfather attending Bentleyville Camp near Monongahela, Pennsylvania. He stayed in a non-air-conditioned cabin and attended a non-air-conditioned tabernacle without running water and only outhouses for sanitation. At the camp meeting, he did have a pleasant grove in which to sit and enjoy the cool of the day. In fact, it dawned on Drury that his grandfather may have been more physically comfortable when he was at camp than when he was at home in his non-air-conditioned, non-insulated house. Allow me to interject, as someone who preached summer camp meetings for twenty-five years straight, discomfort does nothing to increase spirituality. The air-conditioned chapel with padded pews seating two thousand on the campus of Mount Vernon Nazarene University did nothing to decrease the attendance, enthusiasm, lively worship, fellowship and altar calls. My observation is that comfort and convenience made hearts more pliable and responsive to the operation of the Holy Spirit. (Perhaps my observations can only be understood in the memory of having preached 21 times in an open-air tabernacle, where the temperature reached 106 degrees in the shade.)

The single most used vehicle for propagating the message of entire sanctification was the camp meeting. The platform performances of Beverly Carradine, Henry Clay Morrison, Joseph Smith, Uncle Bud Robinson, as well as scores of others, were nothing less than spectacular. Bud Robinson was the Will Rogers of the Holiness Movement. The camp meeting provided fellowship with old friends, a vast throng of worshipping people, rousing music, a vacation from the routine of farm chores, and an annual spiritual checkup. "Perhaps I can spiritually last, and remain faithful, until I return next year to get recharged." The old tabernacle may still be standing, boards missing and paint peeling, but throngs, music, and demonstrative worship are only a memory. The tabernacle probably no longer remains, the land sold to a corporation for a strip mall, the property too expensive to keep up for a once a year, ten-day event or not being able to raise the money to bring plumbing and wiring up to code, or the property has been condemned because those who built the tabernacle, bless their hearts, did not see the need for a sprinkler system. Why go to camp meeting anyway, when Sunday after Sunday I can get all the religion I need from my favorite TV preacher? In fact, why even go to church?

So diagnosing the diseases of modernity and secularization, such as co-modification, materialism, and the cyclical nature of organizations is like saying a person is lazy which results in the tautology, "He does not want to do what he does not like to do." I bet he is not lazy about everything: sex, X-Box, poker, ESPN or whatever. He may sort of be like me. I do not want to work, at least manual work, at least boring work. We might say that the holiness movement died of natural causes, which is what my scholarly friend Ken Collins wrote. "First of all, there is a natural life cycle to revival movements as so ably argued …. But in time all that unfortunately remains for subsequent generations, is the former religion without the inner power. Some scholars contend that the upper length of the cycle is forty years; others argue for a figure considerably less; we are, therefore, well into the 'institutional phase' of things."[7] But that analysis does not seem to apply to the Southern Baptist Convention, the Church of Latter Day Saints, the Seventh-Day Adventists, and many Pentecostal sects.

A Sociology of Religious Movements

I think it is safe to assume that fewer people attend an American church because of specific theological commitments, than say fifty years ago. Not if theological commitments mean Calvinist or Arminian. This observation is even more true if those theological stances are more narrowly defined such as dispensational Calvinist or Wesleyan-Arminian holiness. Theological perspectives, even if given consideration, would sound more like, "This preacher preaches salvation," or "He preaches the Bible." But even allowing for these criteria, such components as music, youth programs, children's programs, accessibility to the church, take precedence over theological convictions. Likely at the top of the list is comfort. Not meaning air-conditioning and padded pews, but congruence and acceptance, a feeling of at-homeness, "These people like me, I am a significant other." Within the last week, I heard about the ultimate criterion for choosing a church. A Nazarene couple moved to Kansas City. Obviously, there were a dozen Nazarene churches from which to choose. After visiting several Nazarene churches, they found it difficult to make a decision. Thus, they left the choice to their two-year-old son. He named the church, or at least, described it. When asked why he desired to attend that particular church, he answered, "The potty is close to my Sunday School classroom." Case closed.

---

[7] *Counterpoint*, 58-59.

The present-day church attendee in America is less attuned or one might even say "tone deaf" to theological nuances, phases or statements in song, sermon, and script. And since we no longer sing hymns with specific theological content, aesthetic catechism through both worship act and art has all but disappeared. This is not to discredit or belittle the liturgical banners that hang in the chancel at special times of the year such as Christmas, Easter, and Pentecost. These would be common to almost all faith traditions. But the following words from Charles Wesley would be unique to a Wesleyan Church, and if the pastor quotes them, there are increasingly fewer lay persons who would immediately recognize them, much less be able to reflect on them.

> Breathe, O breathe Thy loving Spirit Into ev'ry troubled breast!
> Let us all in Thee inherit; Let us find that second rest.
> Take away our bent to sinning; Alpha and Omega be.
> End of faith, as its Beginning, Set our hearts at liberty.[8]

More important than theological perspectives are ethical issues such as abortion, or homosexuality, and political alignments such as red-blue, Democrat-Republican. Probably less explicit and definable, but no less important, is where the church fits on a liberal-conservative continuum. All of this is influenced by education, income, race, as well as other socio-economic factors. In the Church of the Nazarene, the West and Northeast are more liberal on issues such as entertainment, gun control, and the environment than are the Mid-west and the South. In a Ph. D. dissertation done for the University of Southern California in 1986, Ron Benefiel hypothesized and demonstrated by way of statistical research that higher incomes and education made a Nazarene less sectarian; or to put it another way, less likely to adhere to ethical and theological distinctives, which have traditionally defined the Church of the Nazarene. The "sectness," of an individual would be more influenced by education and income in the 35-50 age group as opposed to those older. In developing a trajectory for his research, Benefiel asked the question,

> The most striking feature about both Age and Education is that the respective effects are full of implications for the future reduction in tension between the members of the

---

[8] Charles Wesley, "Love Divine, All Loves Excelling," *Sing to the Lord* (Kansas City: Lillenas Publishing Company, 1993) 507.

organization and the dominant culture. The secularization forces they measure are emerging forces. If Age is the most important single predictor of sectness with younger leaders being considerably less sectarian than older leaders, what does that say about the future secularization of the organization?[9]

For our purposes, the main results of increased secularization and decreased sectarianism is less emphasis on holiness as it has been traditionally understood and taught. Sectarianism means an adherence to distinctives that have defined that denomination and separated it, at least by definition, from other denominations. The distinctive that stood out above all others, was "Entire sanctification as a second work of grace subsequent to regeneration." This formula with all of its rules, regulations, and statements of faith, as well as other accouterments, defined the Church of the Nazarene as a holiness denomination.

In considering the demise of the Holiness Movement, if there be such, the sociology of religious movements must be considered: accommodation to, assimilation into, and acceptance by the wider culture cannot be avoided. This has been especially true for the Church of the Nazarene. The peculiarities of worship practices, ethical beliefs, and the esoteria of its doctrine have been fine sand-papered for frictionless entry into the generic and cultural assembly line of American religious options. Our parts are interchangeable. They are now on the secondary after market, no longer characterized and defined by the primary convictions which at one time provided energy and momentum.

Within this sociology must be considered the generational gap, millennials attracted to churches with black walls, strobe lights, fog dispensers, and music without a melody line, coming from speakers larger than the churches their parents used to attend. The preacher has on a hat, appears to have spent his life in a tattoo parlor, and is wearing a T shirt and shredded jeans, attire suited for an afternoon brake job or tire change. The place is packed, while in my own church I am listening to Wesleyan hymns, expository sermons, surrounded by respectable upper-middle class people with whom I can have an intelligent conversation after the worship service which will end right on time. To put it another way, what I like, they don't; by "they" meaning the people

[9] Ron Benefiel. *The Church of the Nazarene: A Religious Organization in Change and Conflict* (unpublished Ph.D. dissertation, University of Southern California, 1986) 167.

who need to hear the Gospel, that need to be freed from drugs or other addictions, that need to listen to someone, or be with some people who understand them, empathize with them, listen to them, and show some evidence by word or deed, "I understand who you are and where you have been."

The Holiness Movement faces the perennial problem of the immigrant-Italian who founded a pizza restaurant in Chicago in the 1950s. His way of making pizza was the classical Italian way. His ingredients were the proper ingredients, and his crust demanded hours of spinning it an exact amount of times for an exact amount of time. Making pizza represented his tradition and his identity-wrapped pride and nostalgia; his restaurant was filled with the sounds and smells of Grandmother's kitchen. He was always back in Italy, an Italy which he would never leave, at least mentally and spiritually. It worked for a while, until Pizza Hut and Papa John's came on the scene. You have to admire him for his conviction to remain the same, whatever the consequences. But he went out of business. His sons had no interest in making pizzas. They became doctors and lawyers, or got a job on the Chicago Stock Exchange.

During the last third of the nineteenth century, upwards of twenty-five thousand people flocked to such places as Vineland, New Jersey; Manheim, Pennsylvania, and Des Plaines, Illinois. Yes, as Taylor and Drury pointed out, holiness was the "main issue." I have never ceased to be amazed by a newspaper report on a Texas holiness camp meeting given in 1897:

> Whatever may be said of the beliefs of the Holiness people or of their relations to other worship, the simplicity of their nature, their profound belief in the actual presence of the Spirit of God in their midst, the intensity of their piety, and it may be safely said the integrity of their lives, make them a pleasing study and the hours spent with them are profitable ones. To escape from the arid doubts and sneers and materialism of daily life and sit among a people who whether in reality or imagination walk and talk with God, is, as if one, lost in an arid desert, should suddenly find himself on the banks of a great river, amid the umbrageous shade of laughing trees and the aroma of singing flowers.
> The exercises of the first day or two are devoted to prayers for the appearance of the Holy Spirit....There is hardly

a moment when from the quivering voice of holy women, grizzly good men and even children, the throne of God is not dynamited with burning and fiery supplications, all of one tenor and one purpose, that of the coming of the Holy Ghost. It seems as if heaven could not stand the bombardment. "The kingdom of heaven suffereth violence and the violent take it by force."

The Holy Ghost does come or seems to come. There is no doubt of the presence of an afflatus, weird, powerful and overwhelming. It comes as the sound of a mighty rushing wind....The presence lasts for days in a mad, spiritual, but always beautiful revel and one so full of bliss and rapture and inexpressible glory that, if it be God, one day with God is worth a thousand years of mundane life.[10]

All of the above was wrapped in a particular and well-defined cultural package. Note the words "simplicity," "intensity," "burning," "fiery," "bombardment," "weird," "mad," and "spiritual." None of these people were on their cell phones, none had a TV hooked up to a generator, and the camp ground did not have WiFi so that everyone could catch up with their friends on Facebook. They were there, fully there, with no golf clubs, no Rook cards, no volleyball sand pit, and no ice cream social in an air-conditioned dining hall. How hot was it at that summer camp meeting location in Texas? The lives of these holiness camp meeting attenders were indexed in entirely different ways than a society riding on a laser beam through modernity with little thought of eternity. Holy people cannot be separated from holy convocations, sacred spaces, and spiritual practices. We, in holiness denominations such as the Church of the Nazarene, believe we can continue to maintain a holiness lifestyle while our sacred space and time are eroded by the world's technology, the world's entertainment, and the world's priorities. It cannot be done. In a sense, to be holy in today's world demands a more radical commitment than that of our holiness forefathers. In a world of cyberspace, never did the ancient language of the "Prince of the powers of the air," make more sense.

The Texas camp meeting reporter closed his article with the invitation: "To the curious in recondite and abstruse studies, the phenomena of the holiness camp meeting is worth going a thousand

---

[10] Melvin Dieter. *The Holiness Revival of the Nineteenth Century* (Metuchen, NJ: The Scarecrow Press, Inc., 1980) 116-117.

miles to observe."[11] Abstruse means "thrust away, concealed," and, recondite means "hidden."

James Hunter argues: "The history of the conservative faith tradition over the last one hundred seventy-five years has been one of declining influence. These faith traditions have moved from the center of cultural influence to the margins. In some areas of American life, they are not even in the game and exert no influence at all."[12] He then quotes his mentor, Peter Berger, who stated, "Ideas don't succeed in history because of their inherent truthfulness, but rather of their connection to very powerful institutions and interests."[13] Hunter cites several examples: Luther linked to Melancthon and Theodore Beza; the French enlightenment thinkers with the "Salon" movement; Wilberforce in the "Chapman Circle;" Freud within his influential Vienna cohort; James Joyce endorsed by financial donors; Marx funded by Herman Weil, a wool and grain capitalist; and the best example known to us, Billy Graham, touted by the scandalous and ego-manical William Randolph Hearst. On the day that I wrote this, Graham's funeral took place in Charlotte, North Carolina, after he had lain in state for three days in the nation's Capitol, one of only four private citizens to be accorded that honor. None of them were from the Holiness Movement.

None of the above is to depreciate holiness people. The final balance scales, the only scales that count, sit just outside the "Pearly Gates," if there be any balance scales at all. But the above does raise the question: If we have been so "recondite" and "abstruse," why even bother with a post-mortem? Who cares? Well, I do, and nothing that I have ever written has been more subjectively driven. This is a selfish project, because there is no way that I can define myself, outside of the Wesleyan Holiness Movement, as it manifested itself in a small Pilgrim Holiness Church in Atlantic, North Carolina. That small cinder-block church with wood chips for a floor propelled me through five educational institutions from which I received diplomas, all of them with some connection to the Holiness Movement. And I continue to be an Elder in the Church of the Nazarene, a denomination filled with members who

---

[11] Dieter, 117.

[12] James Davison Hunter, "To Change the World," retrieved at https://www.disciplinations.org/media/to-change-the-world_Hunter.pdf

[13] Ibid.

know little of our theological history. Even more critical is the question, "Do we have leadership who are willing to give themselves to careful historical analysis or would rather live within the illusion that our present theological stance is as it always was?"

If not already noticed, the reader will quickly observe that much of this book is about the Church of the Nazarene. This choice is more than a subjective arbitrariness dictated by the fact that I am an ordained Elder in the Church of the Nazarene, and thus know my own denomination better than I do sister denominations with which I have had much less contact. The origins of the Church of the Nazarene differ from the other two major holiness denominations founded on American soil. The Wesleyan Methodists came out of the Methodist Episcopal Church in 1843 over the slavery issue. The Free Methodist church 1860, was a reform movement within Methodism, generated by the conviction that the Methodist Episcopal Church had lost its original vitality. There were other sociological issues for Free Methodism such as slavery and rented pews.

Unlike the above two denominations, the Church of the Nazarene was a concerted effort to unify all holiness denominations and associations. Thus the 1908 Pilot Point, Texas, formation of the Pentecostal Church of the Nazarene was a result of uniting the Pentecostal Church of the Nazarene and the Holiness Church of Christ, the former group a result of joining the Church of the Nazarene with the Association of Pentecostal Churches of America. In 1915, the new denomination would be further augmented by the Pentecostal Mission led by J. O. McClurken in Nashville, Tennessee. By this time, the Pentecostal Church of the Nazarene was truly a nation-wide Protestant Church, and I would argue the quintessential holiness denomination. For instance, Southern Nazarene University in Oklahoma City, is an amalgamation of eighteen different schools, all of them rooted in the American Holiness Movement. They were scattered throughout Texas, Oklahoma, Missouri, Louisiana, Arkansas, Kansas, and New Mexico. Almost all of them were founded by independent holiness associations, which had come out of Methodism, or had been given birth by itinerant holiness evangelists and independent camp meetings. I suspect that

Southern Nazarene University is not only unique within the American Holiness Movement, but in all American Protestantism.[14]

I would also point out that the Church of the Nazarene is by far the largest of the American Holiness denominations. At the time of this writing, average Sunday morning attendance in the Church of the Nazarene is 417,000; making it approximately four times as large as the Free Methodists (107,050) and twice as large as the Wesleyans (233,825).[15] Of course, this could change rather quickly as the Wesleyan Church has grown by almost 20 % over the last ten years, and the Church of the Nazarene has flat lined, if not decreased over the last decade. In my conversations and reading, nothing tells me that the trend moving away from a holiness distinction is not the case for Wesleyans and Free Methodists. For instance, Daniel LeRoy, a former Wesleyan District Superintendent, bemoans the loss of the doctrine of holiness, confessing that "the sanctified American dream became the promise we pursued, and even the preaching throughout the entire American Holiness Movement was immersed in it."[16]

I have also focused on Richard Taylor whom I present as the "patron saint" of the conservative Holiness Movement. Taylor does not deserve the criticism that has been dished out on him by present day scholarship, neither is he without flaws and contradictions. I focus on Mildred Wynkoop because she, more than any other person, offered a new paradigm, a new way to not only talk about, but experience holiness without throwing the baby out with the bath water. Taylor was correct in identifying Wynkoop as the "enemy," and the enemy would win but not for the reasons Taylor suggested. Taylor and Wynkoop are almost pure types of the older formulaic paradigm and the new relational paradigm. Both of these would come to a cataclysmic showdown in

---

[14] Loren P. Gresham and L. Paul Gresham. *From Many Came One in Jesus' Name: Southern Nazarene University Looks Back on a Century* (Virginia Beach, VA: The Donning Company Publishers, 1998) 33.

[15] Numbers provided by the U.S. and Canada Regional Office, Church of the Nazarene, Global Ministry Center, Lenexa, Kansas; the General Secretary's Office of the Wesleyan Church, Indianapolis, Indiana, and Department of Communications, The Free Methodist Church, Indianapolis, Indiana.

[16] Daniel E. LeRoy. *Rediscovering Our Holiness Heritage: How the Wesleyan Church Can Get Back What We Gave Away* (Kernersville, NC: Old Blue Truck Publishing Company, 2018) 29.

1979 – 1980, within both the Church of the Nazarene and the Wesleyan Theological Society. At the time of this writing, a relational, progressive interpretation of holiness has almost completely displaced the two works of grace formulation, the supreme distinctive of the Holiness Movement. It was this ideology that brought together as many as five to ten thousand people for the CHA Convention in Cadle Tabernacle, Indianapolis, IN, during the 1950s, and the gradual loss of the ideology which steadily decreased the crowds and ultimately closed the doors of the CHA.

My two chapters on Wilmore and my treatment of Dennis Kinlaw are self-explanatory. Asbury College and Asbury Theological Seminary made the small community the epi-center of the Holiness Movement. My treatment of Wilmore is bookended by an examination of the influence of Kinlaw and Henry Clay Morrison, the two most powerful personalities in Wilmore, if not the entire American Holiness Movement in the 20th century.

This book is divided into two parts: first, a historical and theological treatment of "holiness" and second, a somewhat arbitrary examination of five areas which I believe the American Holiness Movement has not been able to sufficiently navigate and still remain problematic. Certainly the list and my treatment are not exhaustive and I would find no fault with someone who chose five completely different issues or categories in which Wesleyan Holiness needs to be understood or examined. My last chapter is sermonic, a ray of hope from my perspective or vantage point for the future.

But this project is about far more and other than the Church of the Nazarene. Thus, we begin with John Wesley.

PART I

Chapter 1:
John Wesley

John Wesley is a spiritual father for whom we can be grateful. His accomplishments with a horse for his transportation and a quill pen as his writing instrument staggers the imagination of us moderns with commercial flight and word processers at our disposal. Wesley was both a thinker and a doer; no reformer between the sixteenth and eighteenth century gave a better effort to incarnating both orthopraxy and orthodoxy. His social holiness model, which was far more than talk, is worth pondering and emulating. Then there were unique insights into prevenient grace, universal grace without universal salvation, and freedom of the will which can only be freed by divine assistance. Above all, Wesley believed and preached a Gospel that could and did transform the most ignorant and crude of humanity into triumphant trophies of redemption, exemplifying what Christianity means in a "vile world which is no friend of grace to help us on to God." I am often reminded of Wesley's interchange with a judge before whom he was hauled into court:

> "But I hear," added he, "you preach to a great number of people every night and morning. Pray, what would you do with them? Whither would you lead them? What religion do you preach? What is it good for?" I replied, "I do preach to as many as desire to hear, every night and morning. You ask, what I would do with them: I would make them virtuous and happy, easy in themselves, and useful to others. Whither would I lead them? To heaven; to God the Judge, the lover to all and to Jesus the Mediator of the new covenant. What religion do I preach? The religion of love: the law of kindness brought to light by the gospel. What is this good for? To make all who receive it enjoy God and themselves: To make them like God; lovers of all; contented in their lives; and crying out at their death, in calm assurance, 'O grave, where is thy

victory! Thanks be to God, who giveth me the victory, through my Lord Jesus Christ.'"[17]

But in the American Holiness Movement's pride and rush to claim a Wesleyan heritage, there has been the tendency to uncritically and hagiographically claim Wesley as our spiritual father for the answer to our theological and experiential problems, if we only understood him correctly. And we in the American Holiness Movement have tended to blame our spiritual disillusionment on the nineteenth century founders and exponents of holiness as propagated on the American side of the pond rather than the British side: "If we can only get back to Wesley our spiritual problems both in heart and doctrine will be solved." But I will contend that in his doctrine of Christian perfection, Wesley passed down to his spiritual children a paradigm that has major deficiencies, if not massive contradictions.

Wesley's Definition of Sin

Wesley's first problem is his minimalist definition of sin as a "voluntary transgression of a known law of God." On June 16, 1772, he wrote to Mrs. Bennis,

> Nothing is sin, strictly speaking, but a voluntary transgression of a known law of God. Therefore, every voluntary breach of the law of love is sin; and nothing else, if we speak properly. To strain the matter farther is only to make way for Calvinism. There may be ten thousand wandering thoughts, and forgetful intervals, without any breach of love, though not without transgressing the Adamic law. But Calvinists would fain confound these together. Let love fill your heart, and it is enough![18]

Admittedly, there are many passages in Wesley that explicate and define sin as something far more complex than a simple act of the will, such as breaking one of the Ten Commandments. But this bracketed and outward definition of sin is the only way that a claim to Christian perfection can be maintained. As W. E. Sangster assessed: "To this definition (a voluntary transgression) he holds firmly through all

---

[17] John Wesley. *The Works of John Wesley*. Third edition. Vol. 8 (London: Wesleyan Methodist Book Room, 1872) 8-9.
[18] *Works*, vol. 12, 94

the movement of his argument and the view of Christian perfection for which he contends can only be understood in its light."[19]

Thus, with a second trip to the altar, many in the Holiness Movement obtained a check list for maintaining a testimony to holiness, rather than a greater sensitivity for the tendency of the self to defend its own ego. This is not to say that persons were not entirely sanctified. It is to say, along with Sangster that, "There is no man with the modicum of ability at introspection but has marveled at the artful stratagems and rationalizations of his own mind. He sees that sin ensnares him in subtle ways."[20]

Wesley himself realized the problem with his definition, and we could fill scores of pages with his disclaimers and qualifiers. "Sinless perfection I do not contend for, seeing it is not scripural. A perfection, such as enables a person to fulfill the whole law, and so needs not the merits of Christ, --I acknowledge no such perfection; I do not, and alwalys, did, protest against it."[21] But Wesley did not protest the word "sinless" as loudly and clearly as he thought. Four years after his above disclaimer he wrote, in his "Brief Thoughts on Christian Perfection," "And I do not contend for the term sinless though I do not object against it."[22] Wesley explained the difference between voluntary transgressions and involuntary transgressions:

> To explain myself a little farther on this head: (1) Not only sin, properly so called (that is, a voluntary transgression of a known law), but sin, improperly so called (that is, an involuntary transgression of a Divine law, known or unknown), needs atoning blood. (2) I believe there is no such perfection in this life as excludes these involuntary transgressions which I apprehend to be naturally consequent on the ignorance and mistakes inseparable from mortality. (3) Therefore *sinless perfection* is a phrase I never use, lest I should seem to contradict myself. (4) I believe, a person filled with the love of God is still liable to these involuntary transgressions. (5) Such

---

[19] W. E. Sangster. *The Path to Perfection: An Examination and Restatement of John Wesley's Doctrine of Christian Perfection* (Nashville; Abingdon Cokesbury Press, 1943) 71.

[20] Ibid., 75.

[21] Works, Vol. XII, 257.

[22] *Works*: "Brief Thoughts on Christian Perfection" Vol. XI, 446.

transgressions you may call sins, if you please: I do not, for the reasons above mentioned.[23]

No doubt Wesley understood and taught that sin is a matter of the heart, an inward attitude that produces an outward act. Rob Staples in his insightful and careful investigation, *John Wesley's Doctrine of Christian Perfection: A Reinterpretation,* admits to the confusing aspects of Wesley attempting to balance sin as both an inward principle or condition, but primarily defined as an outward act. "However as Wesley used the term, inward sin means an unholy desire or attitude of the heart, while outward sin means the manifestation of that desire or attitude in word or deed. . . .In many of his writings, however, the neat distinction is not always so easily maintained."[24]

A Voluntary Transgression

To identify the problems in John Wesley's definition of sin, let's examine the phrases "voluntary transgression" and "known law." The word "voluntary" implies volition, and Webster defines volition as the act of "choosing" or "resolving."[25] The key to volition is choice; choice implies options and if there is real freedom, I have the ability to choose one of those options. Am I going to steal today or not steal, am I going to commit murder or not commit murder, am I going to commit adultery or not commit adultery? For most Christians (even most people), these choices do not preoccupy his or her mind. Wesley's primary definition of sin implies a premeditated act. It also implies a temptation or desire to carry out an act. Without desire, there is no temptation, and thus no real choice. I can claim for myself and most Christians that I've never been tempted or given even a fleeting thought to whether I am going to shoplift at Walmart. Most, if not all Christians, with a superficial reading of the Ten Commandments, can use them as a checklist, and say, "I came off looking pretty good today."

[23] John Wesley. *A Plain Account of Christian Perfection* (Kansas City: Beacon Hill Press of Kansas City, 1971) 54.
[24] Rob Staples. *John Wesley's Doctrine of Christian Perfection: a Reinterpretation* (Unpublished Ph. D. dissertation, Pacific School of Religion, 1963) 33.
[25] *Merriam Webster's Collegiate Dictionary* (Springfield, MA: Merriam Webster Inc, 2004) 1401.

When teaching seminars or classes, I have asked on at least a dozen occasions, "What was the greatest sin in David's life?" With the exception of one occasion, I have never failed to get the same answer: his adultery with Bathsheba. After all, tabloid sins are far more interesting than more subtle sins, such as arrogance, pride and greed. All of these no doubt played into David's lust for another man's wife. With the caveat that God does not rate sin, or in other words, "sin is sin," there must be some relationship between the gravity of the sin and the consequences. As a result of adultery and murder, David making sure that Bathsheba's husband was killed in battle, only one person died, the son born of David and Bathsheba's illicit liaison.

In II Samuel 24, as a result of David's census, God slew 70,000 people. There was only one question on the census form, "Do you own a sword?" Our first impression is that this particular sin was a willful transgression, a premeditated act, which was the result of days of consideration and giving orders to Joab to carry out the consideration. But the command to Joab could also have been a panic attack, a momentary overwhelming fear that if the army of the Philistines was not right outside the door, it soon would be.

Nine months later the census report came in, 1,300,000 men owned swords. Immediately the prophet Gad knocked on David's door with the message of God's condemnation. The root of all sin is the very subtle invasion of distrust, a conviction that God is not sufficient for my needs. David, like most of us, believed that it was better to rely on an army than on God. The ultimate insult to God is that He is inadequate to meet my needs. The ultimate compliment to God is that he is sufficient to meet my needs. Thus, the ultimate question in life is, "Is God enough?" Rather than a willful transgression, David's sin may be best described as an angst, a fear, or a propping up of one's ego with significance and security. David's sin was that he never learned to do God's math, God's way. One sword plus God equals God. A million swords plus God equals God. The math is always the same. Only one part of the equation matters, God.

David's sin was a psychological condition, before it was a premeditated act. David probably could not have informed someone of the day he accepted this psychological condition, when he allowed himself to be gripped by an overwhelming angst. One wonders if the choice was even his, but it was nonetheless a sin. If one assesses the two sins, tabloid or the census, by the penalty which was pronounced and carried out, the latter has to be gauged the greater sin.

Americans are obsessed with counting, and no one vocation does more counting than pastors. The constant obsession with numbers is probably best described not as a willful transgression, but the primal temptation to prove one's self to his fellow pastors, or to the denominational bureaucracy. Proving himself was the primal temptation Jesus faced in the wilderness: "If you are the Son of God, turn these stones into bread." Sin is not primarily a willful transgression, but a condition most accurately designated as pride, lust, angst, envy, etc. All of these conditions are an argument for the necessity of entire sanctification, but ironically, Wesley's minimalist definition of sin negates the need for being made holy. If I can get through the day with my checklist intact, why do I need a deeper and further work of grace?

As Jonathan Edwards argued, a person is free to act only according to his affections, or one might say, his character. A person always acts according to his strongest desire, as tautological and circular as the argument may seem (a person did what he wanted to do because that's what he wanted to do). I do not believe that this argument has ever been successfully refuted. Wesley read Edwards and had abridged his *Treatise on Religious Affections* for his Christian library.[26] And though Wesley would have not believed with Edwards that the non-elect were predisposed to sin because of his or her unconverted nature, he would have, at the same time, believed that the affections created the desire for sin, or at least made the person more likely to overtly sin. Edwards wrote, "A man never in any instance, wills one thing contrary to his desires, or desires anything contrary to his will."[27] In his perspective, desires were the same as motives. In his *Treatise on Religious Affections,* he wrote, "The affections are no other than the more vigorous and sensible exercises of the inclination and will of the soul....The faculty is called by various names; it is sometimes called the inclinations and as it has respect with

---

[26] Gregory S. Clapper. "True Religion and the Affections: A Study of John Wesley's Abridgement of Jonathan Edwards' *Treatise on Religious Affections.*" Wesleyan Theological Journal, Vol. 19, No. 2 (Fall 1984) 77-89.

[27] Jonathan Edwards. *Freedom of the Will,* 2. JonathanEdwards.www.ntslibrary.com/ PDF%20Books/Jonathan%Edwards%20Freedom%of%20the Wil.pdf

regard to the actions that are determined and governed by it, it is the will and the mind, with regard to the exercises of this faculty, is often called the heart."[28]

There doesn't seem to be total agreement among Wesleyan scholars as to how Wesley used such terms as disposition, tempers and affections. Kenneth Collins claims that for Wesley, the affections (passions) are fleeting and expressions of the will.[29] Richard Steele charges that Wesley did not understand Edwards: "He never came to grips with Edwards's argument that the will cannot be regarded as a self-determining principle separate from the affections without begging the very question at issue, namely how a perfectly indifferent will could ever 'choose' one course of action over another."[30] My own perspective is that the will for both Wesley and Edwards is not self-determinative, but enabled by grace and consistent with character. The difference between Edwards and Wesley is how one arrives at right character, resistible prevenient grace or irresistible elective grace.

Wesley often argued that sin is far more than a conscious decision. Or to put it another way, sin is a condition before it is an act; being comes before doing. Certainly Wesley understood sin as a disposition, and not just a conscious act. In his sermon on "Sin in Believers," Wesley wrote concerning the regenerated: "They are daily sensible of sin remaining in their heart-pride, self-will, unbelief; and of sin clinging to all they speak and do, even their best actions and holiest duties. Yet at the same time, they know that they are of God; they cannot doubt it for a moment."[31]

Notwithstanding the above, it is the "voluntary transgression" phrase identifying sin as a conscious, decisional, volitional, identifiable, temporal-spatial act that persists for Christian perfection exponents. R. Newton Flew condemned Wesley's definition: "But the word (sin) has too long a history behind it for such a limitation to be possible. Indeed

---

[28] *Treatise on Religious Affections*, 6. www.jonathan-edwards.org/Religious Affections. Pdf

[29] Kenneth Collins. "John Wesley's Topography of the Heart: Dispositions, Tempers and Affections," *Methodist History* Vol. XXXVI, No. 3 (April 1998) 171.

[30] Richard Steele. *"Gracious Affections" and "True Virtue" According to Jonathan Edwards and John Wesley* (Metuchan, NJ: The Scarecrow Press, 1994) 310.

[31] John Wesley. *Wesley's Standard Sermons* Vol. II (Grand Rapids: Francis Asbury Press, 1995) 369.

the narrow sense is not even desirable. Our worst sins are often those of which we are unconscious. The stress on the consciousness and the deliberate intention of the agent is the most formidable defect in Wesley's doctrine of the ideal."[32] Admittedly, we all make choices that are rational, moral decisions. But most of life (who can say what percentage?) is given to involuntary decisions, with little to no rational thought such as driving a car, or repairing a computer, at least, if one has done either for a long period of time.

The more morally mature a person is, the less reason or deliberation plays into decisions, particularly split-second decisions. A mother that runs into a burning house to save her children or a person who jumps off a pier (even if he cannot swim) to save a drowning person, does not do much thinking. Moral psychologist Jonathan Haidt writes, "Intuition is the best word to describe the dozens or hundreds of rapid, effortless moral judgments and decisions that we all make every day."[33]

In January of 2007, Wesley Autrey threw himself on the tracks of a New York City subway, and saved a man who had fallen on the tracks in front of an on-rushing train. Autrey saw nothing "heroic" about his act; it was a clear cut normal act of moral responsibility. In examining this particular incident, Donald Pfaff argues that all humans possess a brain, "wired to propel us toward empathetic behavior."[34] Autrey's central nervous system quickly processed 5 steps: 1) An emergency 2) A person 3) The blurring of that person's image with the image of one's self 4) A positive feeling and 5) A decision to act. "Each step takes place below the level of consciousness and is completed within a limited fraction of a second."[35] In arguing for the altruistic brain, Pfaff questions older theological models of original sin. Charles Finney and Nathaniel Taylor would have both agreed, but I find some naivete in Pfaff's optimism. He quotes a parent, "As a mother of four teenagers, I have found it best to trust that the lessons of respect for others, being a good neighbor and being held accountable for your own actions will extend into their

---

[32] R. Newton Flew. *The Idea of Perfection* (London, Oxford University Press, 1934) 332-333.

[33] Jonathan Haidt. *The Righteous Mind: Why Good People are Divided Between Politics and Religion* (Vintage Books, New York, 2012) 53.

[34] Donald W. Pfaff. *The Altruistic Brain: How We are Naturally Good* (New York: Oxford University Press, 2015) 3.

[35] Ibid., 10.

electronic world and guide their behavior."[36] Living as an "accountable good neighbor" is a gigantic assumption which, as Jesus narratively pointed out, is far from automatic.

A Known Law

The second part of John Wesley's definition of sin, "a known law" is as problematic as the first. In the Old Testament the issue of what to do and what not to do is often black and white. Stone adulterers, do not mate two kinds of animals, do not sow a field with two kinds of seed, and do not weave a garment with two kinds of fibers. But it is a mistake to interpret Old Testament law as simply outward conformity to a moral code. An Israelite was not to hate a fellow Israelite; nor was he or she to bear a grudge, but "to love your neighbor as yourself" (Leviticus 19:18). The interiority of spirituality was not an idea invented by Jesus.

Thus, the moral code introduced by Jesus was not something brand new. When Jesus asked the "lawyer," what is written in the law, he correctly and precisely answered, "You shall love your God, with all your heart, and with all your soul, and with all your strength, and with all your mind, and your neighbor as yourself" (Luke 10:27). The lawyer then heard a story that probably left him troubled, which is often the case when we are honest with God. The "Good Samaritan" inconvenienced himself, put himself in danger, and risked being taken advantage of, leaving his open-ended credit card with the innkeeper. Jesus left us a clear picture of a true neighbor, but at the same time, left us an impressionistic painting with fuzzy lines and blurred images. Most of us, who see someone with a cardboard plea (an art form) or are approached by someone who begs for monetary help as soon as we get out of the car at Quik Trip, are placed in an ethical dilemma. There is no clear guideline for a Christian response. If I never help anyone, I am cold-hearted; if I help everyone who promises to work for food, I am a sucker. I am sure I've helped people that I should not have helped, and I have not aided others that I should have.

I have a flashback to an event that took place on a cold winter day in northeastern Ohio when a lady and her children broke down on the freeway and no one stopped to assist for twenty-four hours.

---

[36] Ibid., 15.

Because of that story reported in the newspaper, I have often stopped to aid someone not because of love, but because of guilt. In other words, many if not most of my ethical decisions take place because of some kind of self-serving rationalization rather than issuing from a love of God and neighbor. These unconscious decisions are no less ethical than not breaking one of the Ten Commandments. I've never been tempted to create an image out of wood or stone, but I may have purchased a house much more elaborate and ostentatious than I needed. And if I did, it was no less a sin because I cannot tell you when I made the conscious decision to commit that sin. Again, the righteousness of Kingdom stewardship is not a matter of a singular known transgression, but an attitude towards things conformed to the conviction that everything I have belongs to God. Wesley admonished:

> If he does not keep himself every moment, he will again feel the desire of the eye; the desire of gratifying his imagination with something great, or beautiful, or uncommon. In how many ways does this desire assault the soul! Perhaps with regard to the poorest trifles, such as dress, or furniture; things never designed to satisfy the appetite, of an immortal spirit. Yet, how natural is it for us, even after we have "tasted of the powers of the world to come," to sink again into these foolish, low desires of things that perish in the using![37]

As an ethical response to the Sermon on the Mount, how does one know when he has looked at a beautiful woman for too long? What does it mean to turn the other cheek, or to walk the extra mile, or when someone asks me for my coat, to give them my shirt also? One can shrug her shoulders and say this has no practical application or sincerely try to interpret Christ's sayings and ask in the light of my present situation or predicament what would be the most Christian response? For Christian situational discernment, Wesley's, "known law of God," is inadequate as a Christian ethic. The "known law of God," is a static concept as opposed to the dynamic illumination and guidance of the Holy Spirit. The Holy Spirit writes his law on my heart, empowering me to be a Christian, and providing the willingness to look ridiculous as opposed to a normative response for fulfilling the expected civil code of conduct. Doing God's will is often intuitional, demanding spur of the moment wisdom rather than "Let me see if I can find a verse of Scripture which applies to this

---

[37] Wesley. "The Repentance of Believers," *Sermons*, Vol. II, ed. Edward Sugden (Grand Rapids: Francis Asbury Press, 1955) 383.

situation." Decisions flow out of character formation that is not simply the result of crisis spiritual experiences, but also years of nurture, relationships, conversations, formal training, reading books, and many other influences including the Holy Spirit's gift of discernment. J. I. Packer wrote,

> The fundamental guidance which God gives to shape our lives, the instilling, that is, of the basic convictions, attitudes, ideals, and value-judgments, in terms of which we are to live--is not a matter of inward promptings apart from the Word but of the pressure on our consciences of the portrayal of God's character and will in the Word, which the Spirit enlightens us to understand and apply to ourselves.[38]

Like many classroom professors, I've shown the film *Twelve Angry Men* to my students to demonstrate how perception plays into right judgment. Thankfully most of us will not spend our lives as jurors, requiring overwhelming discussion and investigation in order to render a right verdict. And even with such intense focus, a confident verdict may not be forthcoming. For a judge, years of jurisdiction may not diminish prejudice, but only increase it. Pure objectivity for all of us is, at times, elusive. Wesley wrote, "And it is certain, as long as we know *in part*, that all men will not see all things alike. It is an unavoidable consequence of the present weakness and shortness of human understanding that several men will be of several minds in religion as well as in common life."[39]

In spite of Wesley's above insight, his simplistic definition of sin circumvented dynamic reflection and application to the extent that some persons who are most scrupulous in keeping rules and regulations, which they believe to be Christian, can best be described as moral pygmies (I had better remove the plank out of my own eye while I'm writing this). I Corinthians 13 raises serious questions about Wesley's primary definition of sin. Does sustained reflection on Paul's lofty ideals leave the spiritually sensitive with condemnation or confidence? Are there sufficient illustrations for Paul's love mandates (What does this look like?) in order to translate them into a known law? Are we left with the conclusion that the higher the standard (and there is no higher standard than I Corinthians 13), the less it is concretely spelled out and

---

[38] J. I. Packer. *Knowing God* (Downers Grove, IL: InterVarsity Press, 1973) 214.
[39] *Sermons*, Vol. I, 131-132.

the less God's requirements resemble the directions on a food can or in a refrigerator manual? It could be that epistemological certitude is disproportionate to lofty ethical obligations and aspirations. Bonhoeffer's plot to kill Hitler may not have been accompanied by a good deal of certitude. I have little doubt that I should tithe my money and have some conviction that I should spend some time at the world's largest refugee camp, which I have, but have more doubts about my motives for visiting the refugee camp, than I do remaining sexually faithful to my wife.

Is it possible to read Paul's description of love without being plagued with doubt that my life is completely fulfilling "the most excellent way?" Does remembering a wrong fall short of "keeping no account of wrongs?" Wesley commented on I Corinthians 13:5, "And in every step in overcoming evil with good, it (charity) is kind, soft, mild, benign. It inspires the sufferer at once with the most amiable sweetness and the most fervent and tender of affection."[40] Does Wesley's description account for Christ cursing the fig tree and cleansing the temple? In his comment on "seeketh not its own," Wesley wrote, "Nay, sometimes the love of mankind seeketh not in some sense his own spiritual advantage, does not think of himself so long as the zeal for the Glory of God and the souls of men swallows him up."[41]

The above "swallows him up" lends itself to a dangerous mysticism and union with the divine will that does not allow for healthy tension between self-desire and God's will (Christ in the Garden). This kind of mystical union often denies or represses sinful human urges and emotions, resulting in theological gymnastics which attempt to vault spiritual discrepancies and contradictions without pausing to deal with them, and more importantly, to confess them as sin. However, I think it is possible, at least for some indefinite duration of time, to be so consumed with God's will that self is forgotten. No doubt, that was often the case for Wesley. Unfortunately, his teaching on Christian perfection often resulted in his followers being preoccupied with themselves, rather than losing themselves in doing God's will.

---

[40] John Wesley. *Wesley's Notes on the Bible* (Grand Rapids: Francis Asbury Press, 1987) 518.
[41] Ibid.

All of Wesley's minute distinctions between voluntary transgressions (the known law) and involuntary transgressions (sin improperly so-called) left Methodists giving time and energy distinguishing between the two, because if it was the first (voluntary) one would have to repent, and why needless repentance when it might be the second? Strangely, holiness necessitated a discernment as to what one needed to repent of rather than the attitude that my righteousness is as filthy rags in God's sight. Wesley should have known better. His mother had written him, "Take this rule: whatever weakens your reason, impairs the tenderness of your conscience, obscures your sense of God, or takes off your relish of spiritual things; in short, whatever increases the strength and authority of your body over your mind, that thing is sin to you, however innocent it may be in itself."[42]

Sin described by Susannah is seldom, if ever, spelled out in the New Testament. Her son's definition of sin was static, stuck in the culture of the first century or the rationalism of the eighteenth century. The mother's was organic, applicable at all times and all places, and pliable enough to preserve the uniqueness of the individual as differentiated from a cookie cutter conformity. The son's definition of sin was mostly informed by what not to do rather than what to do. But fortunately, John Wesley's ethical compass was magnetized by not only sins of commission, but also a sensitivity to sins of omission. For Wesley the gospel was far more than a prohibition; it was an authorization. When he was 73, he recorded, "It is true in I travel 4 or 5,000 miles a year....Yet I find time to visit the sick and the poor; and I must do it, if I believe the Bible, if I believe these are the marks whereby the Shepherd of Israel will know and judge His sheep at the great day; Therefore, when there is time and opportunity for it, who can doubt but the matter of absolute duty (December 10, 1777)."[43] At the age of 81, Wesley could be found wading around town in ankle deep snow begging for the poor which resulted in his "being laid up with a violent flux."[44]

Doing good for Wesley was not the result of special revelation, a command found in Scripture and certainly not an ethical code that

---

[42] Susannah Wesley (Letter, June 8, 1725) Home. Snu.edu

43 John Telford, ed. *The Letters of the Rev. John Wesley* Vol. VI (London: The Epworth Press, 1960) 292.

[44] Nehemiah Curnock, ed. *The Journal of the Rev. John Wesley* Vol. VI (London: The Epworth Press, 1938) 43.

had been instilled in him by academia. Wesley's ethics were anything but mechanical, formulaic, and prescriptive. At the heart of perfect love was total life stewardship. For instance, Wesley often denied himself drinking tea. This was not because tea was addictive or was a stimulant; such luxury eliminated the possibility of doing all the good one could possibly do for others who had more basic needs whether food or clothing. Wesley exhorted that after one took care of the needs of his household, he was to "do good unto all men. In so doing, you (give all you can); nay, in a sound sense, all you have." This kind of social holiness cannot be proof texted. Thus, sin is defined as something other than "a voluntary transgression of a known law of God." Wesley wrote, "I do not say, Be a good Jew giving a tenth of all you possess. I do not say, Be a good Pharisee; giving a fifth of all your substance. I dare not advise you to give a half of what you have; no, nor three quarters; but all."[45] Placing sin within this theological rubric challenges the certitude of righteousness.

The Abandoned "Sunday Order of Worship"

The above defect possibly would have been at least partially avoided had the American Methodists kept Wesley's "Sunday Service of the Methodists in North America." This abridgement of the "Order of Worship" from *The Book of Common Prayer*, and delivered by Thomas Coke to the American Methodists in 1784, was an exercise in paradox and/or contradiction. "The Sunday Service" called for a constant and contrite confession of sin. Thus, those who were delivered from sin were publicly to confess sin. The "Sunday Morning Service" begins with a general confession in unison after the minister while kneeling:

> Almighty and most merciful Father, We have erred and strayed from thy ways like lost sheep. We have followed too much the devices and desires of our own hearts. We have offended against thy holy laws. We have left undone those things which we ought to have done; And we have done those things which we ought not to have done; And there is no health in us. But thou, O Lord, have mercy upon us, miserable offenders. Spare thou them, O God, which confess their faults. Restore thou them that are penitent; According to thy promises declared unto mankind in Christ Jesus our Lord. And grant, O most merciful Father, for his sake, That we may hereafter live a

---

[45] Works, Vol. VII, 9-10.

godly, righteous, and sober life; To the glory of thy holy Name. Amen.[46]

And if the Methodist Episcopal Church met on Wednesdays and Fridays which it did not, the congregation was to repeat in unison the following:

> O God the Father of heaven; have mercy upon us miserable sinners.
> O God the Son, Redeemer of the world; have mercy upon us miserable sinners.
> O God the Holy Ghost, proceeding from the Father and the Son; have mercy upon us miserable sinners.
> O holy, blessed, and glorious Trinity, three persons, and one God; have mercy upon us miserable sinners.
> Remember not, Lord, our offences, nor the offences of our forefathers; neither take thou vengeance of our sins; spare us, good Lord, spare thy people, whom thou hast redeemed with thy most precious blood, and be not angry with us forever.[47]

The heart of the Eucharistic liturgy was confession of sin:

> Almighty God; Father of our Lord Jesus Christ, Maker of all things, Judge of all men; We acknowledge and bewail our manifold sins and wickedness, Which we from time to time most grievously have committed, By thought, word, and deed, against thy Divine Majesty, provoking most justly thy wrath and indignation against us. We do earnestly repent, and are heartily sorry for these our misdoings; The remembrance of them is grievous unto us. Have mercy upon us, have mercy upon us, most merciful Father; For thy Son our Lord Jesus Christ's sake, forgive us all that is past; And grant, that we may ever hereafter serve and please thee in newness of life, To the honour and glory of thy Name, Through Jesus Christ our Lord. Amen.[48]

Had Asbury and the American church not scuttled the "Sunday Order of Worship" and within ten years completely abandoned it, spiritual realism and humility may have floated down to Phoebe Palmer

---

[46] John Wesley's *Sunday Service of the Methodists in North America*, Intro: James F. White (Nashville: The United Methodist Publishing House, The United Methodist Board of Higher Education, 1984) 8.

[47] Ibid., 20.

[48] Ibid., 132.

and the subsequent American Holiness Movement. But the liturgical tempering of extravagant spiritual claims was completely lost on those who attended Phoebe Palmer's parlor and the later founders of the National Camp Meeting Association. Where was the need to expressly and openly confess sin by those who had been saved from not only the act of sinning, but also cleansed from original sin? Even more antithetical to the Holiness Movement's claim of power over sin, was Wesley's covenant service used by early British Methodists and eventually American Methodists as a spiritual refocusing liturgy on New Year's Eve, commonly referred to as a "watch night" service. Frank Baker claimed that this particular service was "The one major contribution of Methodism to religious liturgy…"[49] An early statement in the Covenant Service asserts, "No man will regard a Savior, that does not see himself as a sinner."[50] The Covenant later reads, "O Blessed Jesus, I come to you hungry, wretched, miserable, blind, and naked; a most loathsome polluted wretch, a guilty, condemned malefactor…"[51]

American Methodist Independence

Other contradictions were to be found in Wesley's non-empathy for American independence, his misinterpretation of American anti-aristocracy, and the American hatred for liturgical conformity, which had at one time been at the risk of imprisonment. Had not Wesley himself written?

> Religious liberty is a liberty to choose our own religion, to worship God according to our own conscience, according to the best light we have. Every man living, as man, has a right to this, as he is a rational creature. The Creator gave him this right when he endowed him with understanding. And every man must judge for himself, because every man must give an account of himself to God.[52]

---

[49] Quoted in Steve Johnson. *John Wesley's Liturgical Theology: His Sources, Unique Contributions and Synthetic Practices* (unpublished Ph.D. dissertation, The University of Manchester, 2016) 202.

[50] John Wesley and Charles Wesley. *John and Charles Wesley: Selected Prayers, Hymns, Journal Notes, Sermons, Letters, and Treatises,* ed. Richard J. Payne and Frank Whaling, *The Classics of Western Spirituality* (Mahwah, NJ. Paulist Press, 1981) 3.

[51] Ibid., 7.

[52] *Works*, Vol. XI, 37.

Had he forgotten that his grandparents on both his mother's and father's side had been non-conformists and been kicked out of the Church of England? He had not.

> So, by this glorious Act (the Act of Uniformity), thousands of men, guilty of no crime, nothing contrary either to justice, mercy, or truth, were stripped of all they had, of their houses, lands, revenues, and driven to seek where they could, or beg, their bread. For what? Because they did not dare to worship God according to other men's consciences! So they and their families were, at one stroke, turned out of house and home, and reduced to little less than beggary, for no other fault, real or pretended, but because they could not assent and consent to that manner of worship which their worthy governors prescribed![53]

In his introductory letter to the "Sunday Order of Worship," Wesley wrote, "As our American brethren are now totally disentangled both from the state and from the English hierarchy, we dare not entangle them again either with one or the other. They are now at full liberty, simply to follow the Scriptures and the primitive church."[54] Wesley then proceeded to entangle the American Methodists, but they not only rejected his entanglement, but Wesley himself. By 1787, they had removed his name from the Conference "Minutes," led by Asbury's rationale, "I did not think it practical expediency to obey Mr. Wesley at 3,000 miles distance in all matters of Church government."[55] But the distance was far more than geographical. Wesley created an ecclesiastical aberration that became more aberrant than he ever imagined. As I have written elsewhere, "No pre-nineteenth century event better represented the autonomous and populist nature of American religion than Asbury's ordination. It was a new day. Indeed the ordination was far more American than Wesley intended."[56] The American Methodists had not forgotten that Wesley condemned American "democracy." There was an exact correlation in both timing and style between American independence and the independence of the Methodist Episcopal Church. Thomas Coke when at the 1787 Baltimore Conference affronted the preachers

---

[53] Ibid., 39.

[54] White, III.

[55] Francis Asbury. *The Journal and Letters of Francis Asbury*, Vol. II, eds. Elmer Clark, J. Manning Potts, and Jacob S. Payton (London: Epworth Press, 1958) 106.

[56] Darius L. Salter. *America's Bishop: The Life of Francis Asbury* (Nappanee, IN: The Francis Asbury Press, 2003) 94.

with, "You must think you are my equal." Nelson Reed immediately retorted, "Yes, sir, we do; and we are not only equals of Dr. Coke, but of Dr. Coke's King."[57]

As a result of Wesley letting the American preachers "loose… on the great continent of America,"[58] Asbury unleashed a coterie of preachers, Freeborn Garretson, Benjamin Abbott, Henry Smith, and thousands of others who fully adopted his stated purpose to "shake the formality of religion out of the world."[59] That formality included Wesley's abridgement of the Sunday Order of Worship culled from the *Book of Common Prayer.* On the heels of the American Revolution, American Methodism had tumbled into an American zeitgeist that was diametrically opposed to anything that smelled of British aristocracy. Methodism, the dominant religion of the early Republic, was not going to conquer the frontier with a prayer book. In Karen Tucker's assessment, "Accordingly, many of the church's rights and ceremonies fell into the category of adiaphora, for they were merely outward circumstantials of inner religion which, in their stringent use, had caused the suffering of many."[60] Ironically, out of all the American religious sects, Methodism was the least likely to equip itself with liturgy supplied by a European national church.

The irony is that Wesley who preached, talked, and lived within a full-orbed and comprehensive definition of sin, unfortunately passed on a minimalist definition of sin to his American descendants. The "Sunday Order of Worship" would have provided a correction. But from the perspective of those in the American Holiness tradition, this correction appeared and still seems as a contradiction. Theological convictions and traditions, each with their own merit, differentiated the triumphant tone of holiness worship from the confession mode of Episcopal worship. The worship of the Methodist Societies was remarkably different than the worship of the Anglican Church. Wesley was pathetically naïve in foisting the latter on the Methodist Episcopal Church in America.

---

[57] John Vickers. *Thomas Coke: Apostle of Methodism* (New York: Abingdon Press, 1969) 119.

[58] Letter to George Shadford, *Letters*, 6:23.

[59] Salter, 95.

[60] Karen B. Westerfield Tucker. *The Sunday Service of the Methodists: Twentieth-Century Worship in Worldwide Methodism* (Nashville: Abingdon Press, 1996) 24.

Worship in American Methodism rather than British Methodism would prove to be the logical extension of the Wesleyan Revival.

Love Something Less than Perfect

Wesley fails as a model for Christian perfection in two critical relationships, first his relationship with his wife, and second with his relationship to the Church. On February 19, 1751 at the age of 48, John married a wealthy widow, Mary Vazeille. It was the worst mistake of his life; but it was not an isolated incident. It was in keeping with his life-long pattern of misinterpreting the female sex, warped ideas of marriage, an inability to combine romance and wisdom, social awkwardness, a failure to discern God's will, and for want of a better term, just plain stupidity.

In his early twenties, Wesley recorded sexual attraction to several young women, in particular Sally Kirkham, and Kitty Hargreaves. It was in regard to the latter that he resolved to never touch her hand or breasts again. He was not the first or last Christian young man to be conflicted as to how a romantic relationship should physically evolve. In fact, V. H. Green suggested that escaping lust may have been a partial reason for his excursion to the New World.[61] Hardly ever has geographical relocation served as a solution for physical urges and spiritual temptation. The swamps of Georgia would not compare to the spiritual-sexual morass in which the young preacher would find himself.

John Wesley's first serious romantic relationship was to Sophia Hopkey, when he was 33 and she was 18 years of age. On September 2, 1736, the Georgia "missionary" recorded, "In the evening we landed on an uninhabited island, made a fire, supped, went to Prayers together and then spread our sail on four stakes to keep off the night dew." In spite of this very intimate situation, the couple did nothing illicit, at least according to Wesley. "To Him (God) be the praise, that we were both withheld from anything which the world counts evil."[62] For the next three months the couple grew more physically intimate, but the more the relationship advanced, the more conflicted Wesley became. "My greatest difficulty was, when being obliged, as having but one book

---

[61] V. H. Green. *The Young Mr. Wesley* (London: Edward Arnold, 1961) 226.
[62] Richard Heitzenrater. *The Elusive Mr. Wesley: John Wesley His Own Biographer*, Vol. I (Nashville: Abingdon Press, 1984) 80.

to sit close to her, unless I prayed without ceasing, I could not avoid using some familiarity or other which was not needful."[63] Wesley's love for Sophia was an agonizing mixture of sexual attraction and restraining prudery. "Sometimes I put my arm around her waist, sometimes took her by the hand, and sometimes kissed her."[64] But he was conflicted by the possibility of marriage to someone who was becoming increasingly attractive and some vague notion, perhaps wrong-headed, that he was to remain single. "Such was the woman, according to my closest observation, of whom I began to be much afraid. My desire and design still was to live single. But how long it would continue, I knew not."[65] Consulting with friends only added to his confusion.

How did John decide as to his future relationship with Miss Sophia? By the least reliable and most foolhardy way possible. Along with his friend Charles Delamotte, they placed three pieces of paper in a hat, each with a message: "marry," "think not of it again this year," "think of it no more." Delamotte drew the third, which was the end of the romance, but not the end of conflict and regret.

On March 12, 1737, Miss Hopkey married William Williamson, exactly one year after John and Sophia had met. Upon hearing of his first love's intention of marrying another, Wesley recorded, "I quite distressed....confounded. Tried to pray, lost, sunk."[66] His follow up was shameful and embarrassing. He refused his former female companion Communion under the thin rationale that she had not declared intention to partake having missed several Sundays, which was technically correct, but practically wrong. The new husband, Williamson, brought charges against Wesley, and a Georgia grand jury issued an indictment that contained ten accusations of misconduct. Heitzenrater claims that Wesley's defense painted "the picture of the long-suffering, ill, used servant of God (and friend of the Trustees) who has been misled by the wiles of a beautiful woman, confused by the matchmaking of her two-faced aunt and wrongly treated by the maliciousness of the political powers of the colony."[67] The court wasn't buying it and issued the following for his arrest: "You and each of you (constables) are hereby

---

[63] Ibid., 81.

[64] Ibid.

[65] Ibid.

[66] Ibid., 83.

[67] Ibid., 85.

required to take the body of John Westley (sic), clerk, and bring him before one of the bailiffs of the said town to answer the complaint of William Williamson and Sophia his wife, for defaming the said Sophia and refusing to administer to her the Sacrament of the Lord's Supper in a public congregation without cause; by which the said William Williamson is damaged one thousand pound sterling...."[68] Where was John Wesley going to obtain that amount of money?

Over the next three months, the rancor did not subside but only grew more virulent. Wesley's name became anathema to his bewildered and angry constituents until on December 2, 1737, after appearing in court so many times (6 or 7), he literally jumped bail, boarding a ship to Port Royal, South Carolina and hence to England. "I shook off the dust of my feet and left Georgia, after having preached the gospel there with much weakness indeed and many infirmities, not as I ought, but as I was able one year and nearly nine months."[69]

Most Wesley biographers have declared his Georgia sojourn a complete debacle. A more judicial and analytical treatment is given by Geordan Hammond in his investigative *John Wesley in America: Restoring Primitive Christianity.*[70] Wesley was a faithful pastor, demonstrated by consistently visiting his parishioners, sacrificing his own comfort and safety in treacherous conditions, practicing the disciplines of fasting, sleeping on the floor, and other forms of self-denial. He practiced baptism and weekly communion, as well as other means of grace, all the while keeping careful records of his interactions with his parishioners. James Oglethorpe assessed that "The change since the Arrival of the (Methodist) mission is very visible, with respect to the Increase of Industry, Love and Christian Charity amongst the people."[71] But even Hammond suggests that Wesley exhibited a paranoid and divisive style of leadership. Persecution, suffering, and criticism were worn as badges of honor. By enforcing "primitive Christianity" Wesley presumed that his parishioners were not living up to their spiritual potential, thus, polarizing the idealistic pastor from his inferior flock. One finds repetitions of his father Samuel's pastoral foibles. Hammond writes,

---

[68] Ibid., 88.

[69] Ibid., 51.

[70] Geordan Hammond. *John Wesley in America: Restoring Primitive Christianity* (Oxford: Oxford University Press, 2014).

[71] Ibid., 170.

There is no doubt that Wesley's strict conception of ecclesial discipline contributed to conflicts with his parishioners. Confession and penance, in particular, provoked accusations of popery. Like his father before him, he was more interested in obeying the Church rubrics (when they agreed with his conception of primitive Christianity) than in promoting harmony in his parish through compromise. He was faithful to his father's advice to utilize all the 'Coercive' discipline the Church allows.[72]

Grace Murray

In June of 1748, Wesley fell ill at New Castle and was nursed by Grace Murray, a woman 13 years younger than himself. The woman's solicitous and tender care aroused romantic feelings and upon the preacher saying, "If ever I marry, I think you'll be the person," she responded, "This is too great a blessing for me: I can't tell how to believe it. This is all I could have wished for under heaven, if I had dared to wish for it."[73] Before leaving New Castle, Wesley declared his intention to marry Murray. He then took her to Yorkshire and Derbyshire where she was "unspeakably useful both to me and the societies." He then left her at Cheshire with a fellow Methodist preacher, John Bennett. Not long after, Wesley received a letter from both Bennett and Murray requesting his marriage consent. Before the two married, but were in some sort of engagement, Wesley took Grace to Ireland. How strange could it get? There their romantic flame rekindled: "The more we conversed together the more I loved her, and before I returned from Ireland, we contracted by a contract *de prasanti:* all this while she neither wrote to JB or he to her, so that the affair between them was as if it had never been."[74]

Wesley scholar Frank Baker did not agree with the "though as if it had never been," and argued that the formal intent to be married carried with it legal obligations, and could be dissolved only in a court of law. Thus, by marrying someone else, Wesley committed bigamy, and his true marriage for the rest of his life was to Grace Murray. Frank Maser countered that the contract had to be "pure and simple" (of which we do not have a copy), and if there were any stated exceptions, disclaimers, or

[72] Ibid., 130.
[73] Heitzenrater, Vol. I, 175.
[74] Ibid., 176.

conditions, the agreement was not binding. "Had Grace Murray been a vindictive person, she could have hauled Wesley in to court where he would have been forced on pain of excommunication and imprisonment to publicly marry Grace Murray."[75]

John Bennett was not the only fly in the ointment. Grace Murray caught wind that Wesley was having an affair with a Molly Francis. If not a bigamist, John Wesley was a two-timing lover, a fickle vacillating waffler, who could not translate erotic desire into agape commitment. The man who created the Methodist community of faith that involved thousands, could not bring himself to psycho-sexual intimacy with a woman as devout and committed as that woman demonstrated herself to be in both word and deed.

One more time Wesley underestimated the wiles of a woman and the potency of his competition. On hearing of Miss Francis, according to Wesley, Murray "in a sudden vehement fit of jealousy, writ a loving letter to JB. Of this she told me the next day in great agony of mind; but it was too late."[76] The relationship between Murray and Bennett displaced Wesley. The jilted lover wrote Bennett accusing him of betrayal and insubordination. "You rushed forward and by vehement importunity forced her tender and compassionate mind to promise you again.... Oh that you would take scripture and reason for your rule (something that had escaped Wesley some dozen years earlier) instead of blind and impetuous passion! I could say no more,-only this-you may tear her away by violence."[77]

John sent a copy of the letter to his brother Charles who responded, as interpreted by John, "The thought of my marrying at all, but especially of my marrying a servant, and one so low born, appeared above measure, shocking to him."[78] When Charles met John at White Haven he warned, "All our preachers would leave us; all our societies disperse, if I married so mean a woman." John, with the encouragement of George Whitefield, persisted with his plan to marry Grace. Again his

---

[75] Frank Maser. "John Wesley's Only Marriage: An Examination of Dr. Frank Baker's Article 'John Wesley's First Marriage,'" *Methodist History* 16, No. 1 (October 1977) 37.
[76] Heitzenrater, Vol. I, 176-177.
[77] Ibid., 179.
[78] Ibid., 180.

vacillation resulted in the loss of another woman whom he no doubt truly loved. On October 3, Grace married John Bennett. John's grief did not earn his brother's empathy. Charles with something less than perfect love accosted his brother with, "I renounce all intercourse with you, but what I would have with a heathen man or a publican"[79] On that Friday, John met with Murray and Bennett (now Bennett and Bennett). "We sat weeping at each other....she fell at my feet....he (Bennett) fell on his knees too." John confessed, "I knew what not to say or do. I can forgive. But who can address the wrong?"[80]

The Worst Mistake of His Life

A little over a year later, February 25, 1751, John married Mary Vazeille (Molly), a widow of some means. Perhaps the wedding was on the rebound, the next person in line, no matter her disposition, piety, or looks. It was the one time he should have consulted Charles who was "thunderstruck" upon hearing the news. That very day, John preached on his knees because of a sprained foot. Whether he stood for his marriage, or even where he was married, other than in London, is not clear. Two weeks later, he set out for an eight-week journey to London and the North Country without his wife. Wesley penned while traveling, "I cannot understand how a Methodist preacher can answer it to God to preach one sermon or travel one day less in a married than in a single state. In this respect surely, it remaineth that they who have wives be as though they had none."[81] This marriage philosophy exploded into a marital disaster. How could a man who dished out spiritual advice in some 6,500 letters, two-thirds of them to women, make such a colossal and stupendous blunder?

Wesley's non-empathy for his wife's relational needs would make sure that she played second fiddle in every decision he made and everything he did. The theologian of perfect love did not realize that the litmus test for his relationship to God was his relationship with his wife. What should have been his primary witness to the practicality of "perfect love," became an ugly stain which has been difficult for hagiographers to wash away. Thus, they have chosen to ignore the issue. John did

---

[79] Ibid., 183.
[80] Ibid., 184.
[81] Curnock, *Journal*, Vol. III (March 19, 1751) 517.

not realize that his love for "Molly" and for God should have been one and the same. To perceive that his marriage would have no bearing on his vocation personified arrogance and naiveté, a lethal combination. John's insensitivity to his wife's needs, exemplified by his continuous voluminous correspondence with women, may have been motivated by his sincere concern for their spiritual welfare or his own sublimation of unfulfilled sexual urges. This may be a reckless accusation, but it is certainly not an overstatement to assess that if Wesley had any concern for the sanctity of his marriage, his constant writing to women was ignorance run rampant.

By 1757, Molly was physically avoiding John, what may be referred to today as a "legal separation." In 1759, John wrote a 10-point sermonic letter accusing her of plundering into his private papers, stealing his money, and mistreating his servants. "You treat them with such haughtiness, sternness, sourness, surliness, ill-nature, as never were known in a house of mine in near a dozen years. You forget even good breeding, and use such coarse language as befits none but a fish wife." [82]He signed the letter "affectionately yours." Never did affection and Paul's exhortation "Husbands love your wives" seem so distant. Through it all, John was the sanctified sufferer:

> Under all conflicts it might be an unspeakable blessing that you have an husband who knows your temper and can bear with it; who, after you have tried him numberless ways, laid to his charge things that he knew not, robbed him, betrayed his confidence, revealed his secrets, given him a thousand treacherous wounds, purposely aspersed and murdered his character, and made it your business so to do, under the poor pretence of vindicating your own character (whereas of what importance is your character to mankind if you was buried just now? Or if you had never lived, what loss would it be to the cause of God?);-who, I say, after all these provocations, is still willing to forgive you all; to overlook what is past, as if it had not been, and to receive you with open arms; not only while you have a sword in your hand, with which you are continually striking at me, though you cannot hurt me. If, notwithstanding, you continue striking at me still, what can I, what can all reasonable men think, but that either you are utterly out of your senses or your eye is not single; that you married me only for my money, that, being disappointed, you

---

[82] Telford. *Letters*, Vol. IV (October 23, 1759) 75-78.

was almost always out of humour; that this laid you open to a thousand suspicions, which, once awakened, could sleep no more?[83]

In fact, John could be downright cruel. God had punished Mary for not being a more loving and understanding wife. From the husband's perspective, God was chastising his wife for not fitting more into the famed preacher's purposes, revealing an egocentricity that had not been crucified with Christ. "God has used many means to curb your stubborn will and break the impetuosity of your temper....he has taken away one of your sons....he has suffered you to be defrauded of much money. He has chastened you with strong pain."[84] As an empathetic husband, did John weep with his wife or did he use misfortune to beat her into submission? Giving John Wesley the benefit of the doubt, theodicy for an eighteenth century theologian was much more severe than the benign solipsism spilled out by today's mainline American pastor.

Mary Vazeille died October 8, 1781, having been long separated but not divorced from her husband. October 12, Wesley casually penned in his journal, "I came to London, and was informed that my wife died on Monday. This evening she was buried though I was not informed of it until a day or two after."[85]

The Church of England

One understanding of holiness is wholeness, the ability of the ego to maintain integrity with a minimum of defense mechanisms such as rationalization, compensation, and compartmentalization. Often these defense mechanisms are so subtle that they cannot be detected, at least by the individual who manifests them. To completely know ourselves and to be completely honest with ourselves and with others is probably beyond the possibilities of this life. Our purpose is not to psycho-analyze Wesley, but to highlight some glaring contradictions that were apparent, particularly to his brother, Charles, and even more so to recent historians. Wesley constantly maintained his allegiance to the Church of England, while at the same time giving leadership to a movement unamenable

---

[83] Telford, *Letters*, Vol. VI (July 15, 1774) 101-102.

[84] Ibid., 101.

[85] Curnock, *Journal*, Vol. VI (October 12, 1781) 337.

to the strictures and authority of the established Church. As has been said, "Like a good oarsman, he looked one way and rowed another."[86] Of course his rationalization was that God and the Church of England were often going in different directions, and he would row in God's direction while claiming fidelity to both. When questioned about his disloyalty to the Church of England, blatantly evidenced by all kinds of subversion, subterfuge, and insubordination, to stay with our metaphor, God was his coxswain, and not some Anglican bishop, though Wesley was politically astute enough often to avoid confrontation.

In order to hold credentials in the Church of England and at the same time authorize lay preachers to ignore parish boundaries, Wesley developed a neat compartmentalization. He was being obedient to his "extraordinary call," the high call of God, that if it did not displace the laws of the Church of England, the higher call transcended them. After all, Henry VIII used a similar rationalization in 1532 when he parted ways with Roman Catholicism. John would not take such action, allowing the inevitable to take its own course. Did he live in a constant state of denial, a super spirituality, an authority which resided in him alone, an epistemological certitude that whatever he did was best for the growing sect with the hope or illusion that Methodism was the remedy for the multitude of ills which plagued Anglicanism?

None of this is to say that John was indifferent; he was a troubled man. Many of Wesley's preachers, and in particular his brother, Charles, were increasingly alarmed at what appeared to them to be John's plain dishonesty. Henry Rack summarized the evolving question that the new sect could not indefinitely avoid: "On the one hand, the sense of righteous evangelical doctrine and life was contrasted with the defective life of the clergy and of Anglican order and worship. On the other, since the Methodist ways and preachers seemed to be superior, why should they be kept in a position of subordination to and dependence on the Church of England?"[87]

The above came to a showdown in the early 1750s when some of Wesley's preachers began to serve the sacrament. (This exact controversy

---

[86] Henry Rack. *Reasonable Enthusiast: John Wesley and the Rise of Methodism* (London: Epworth Press, 2002) 291.
[87] Ibid., 292.

would repeat itself and almost become the first schism in the "pre-1784 Christmas Conference" period in American Methodism.) Rack claims that "Charles perceived an unscrupulous cabal plotting against the Church and for a separation through ordination by his brother whom he saw as fatally weak-willed."[88] The 1754 Methodist Conference gave three days to the question: "Ought we to separate from the Church of England?"[89] For the time being, according to John's autocratic decision, it was not "expedient" to separate. John and Charles would keep their Anglican credentials. Methodists would be exhorted to continue communion at the hands of Anglican priests, and John would continue to authorize lay preachers. Maybe he was still hoping and praying for a spiritual back-wash into the moribund official church, and his clout would be maintained by his Anglican officialness.

Many of Wesley's preachers made disparaging remarks in public about the Anglican Church, many of them true, but nonetheless, imprudent. When his un-ordained preachers administered the sacraments, John was simply reaping the fruits of his own rationalized irregularities. Semi-order was restored in that Wesley rebuked and reined in his itinerants. Charles, always desiring to contrast his integrity to the dissimilitude of his brother, declared that his "chief concern was the prosperity of the Church of England; my next that of the Methodists, my third that of the preachers."[90] One might question Charles' priorities in that he continued, though under protest, to follow his older brother. But for sure, Charles was more conflicted than was John.

John, the ultimate pragmatist, kept his conscience intact by arguing for his superior results. To the Bishop of London he wrote, "Here are, in and near Moorefield's, ten thousand poor souls for whom Christ died, rushing headlong into Hell. Is Dr. Bulkely, the parochial Minister, both able and willing to stop them? If so, let it be done, and I have no place in these parts."[91] Wesley contrasted himself with the ineptitude of the Anglican Church and its ministers. "I wonder at those who still talk so loud of the indecency of field preaching. The highest indecency is in St. Paul's Church, when a considerable part of the congregation are

---

[88] Ibid., 297.

[89] Ibid., 287.

[90] Ibid., 302.

[91] Stephen Gunter, *The Limits of Love Divine: John Wesley's Response to Antinomianism and Enthusiasm* (Nashville, Kingswood, 1989) 28.

asleep or talking or looking about (there is plenty to look at in St. Paul's Church) not minding a word the preacher says. On the other hand, there is the highest indecency in a churchyard or field (really?) when the whole congregation behaves and looks as if they saw the Judge of all, and heard him speaking from heaven."[92] Stephen Gunter accurately describes the mind of Wesley: "The logic that seems to have prevailed is that if Wesley had been wrong, the Church would have 'increased' while he 'decreased.' Since this did not happen, Wesley must have been correct. Such pragmatism is not, of course, an accurate test of truth."[93]

In an intriguing psychohistory of Wesley, *John Wesley: A Psychological Perspective*, Robert L. Moore argued that John Wesley was bound to the maternal matrix, his mother Susannah, the most influential person in his life.[94] The Anglican Church served as that continuing authority, a source of identity, which he could not do without. Obviously, the totality of one's life cannot be explained or interpreted by a single, over-arching deterministic paradigm, but at the same time, most of us are driven at least partially by impulses and desires which we do not fully comprehend. The father, Samuel, though a hard-working pastor, faithful husband, and affectionate father, never quite measured up as either an ecclesiastical leader or bread winner. In Samuel's absence, Susannah took initiative for spiritually nurturing whomever of the Epworth parish she could gather around her. Samuel rebuked her by letter to which she responded, "If you do after all, think fit to dissolve this assembly, do not tell me that you desire me to do it, for that will not satisfy my conscience; but send me your positive command, in such full and expressed terms, as may absolve me from all guilt and punishment, for neglecting this opportunity of doing good, when you and I shall stand before the great and awful tribunal of our Lord Jesus Christ."[95]

Samuel was not going to take those odds and backed down. Susannah would not overtly rebel against her husband; she appealed to a higher authority, the foremost tactic that her son would utilize from 1738 to the end of his ministry. As Susannah disguised her rebellion

---

[92] *Journal*, Vol. II, 113.

[93] Gunter, 126.

[94] Robert L. Moore. *John Wesley and Authority: A Psychological Perspective* (Missoula, MT: Scholars Press, 1979).

[95] Quoted in Moore, 39.

against Samuel, John would rationalize his allegiance to Anglicanism and his insubordination as being consistent.

A cursory examination of Wesley's writings reveals his firm conviction that his religious innovations were in keeping with the spirit, if not the written law, of the Church of England. Wesley's devotion to the mother Church and his defense of her blemishes, were even too much for the faithful, sensitive, and yet perceptive, John Fletcher, who wrote, "You love the Church of England and yet you are not blind to her freckles, not insensible to her shackles....have you ever explicitly borne your testimony against all the defects of our Church? Might you not do this without departing from your professed attachment to her? Nay, may you not by this means do her the greatest of services? If your mother who gave you suck were yet alive, could you not reverence her without reverencing her little whims and sinful peculiarities (if she had any)?"[96]

On the outside Wesley was an Oxford don, an Anglican priest impeccably dressed with gown and bands, and on the inside he was a fiery prophet, Jeremiad's echoing within his brain, often not knowing which ones to express and which ones to keep to himself. If a historical novice reads Skevington Wood's biography, *The Burning Heart,* and Frank Baker's *John Wesley and the Church of England*, he may not detect that the two narrative accounts are about the same person. Weaving the disparate story lines together might result in a depiction of ecclesiastical schizophrenia.

Moore pits the irrationality of John as over against the rationality of Charles. John could not foresee the logical consequences of independent societies, extemporaneous prayer and preaching, and an itinerant ministry, because of the sub-conscious fidelity to a maternal superego now represented in the form of the Anglican Church. John was careful that the Societies did not meet at Anglican Church times so that they would have opportunity to receive the sacraments from an Anglican priest. (I have often wondered how many of the Society members operated within both of these conflicting paradigms and very different modes of worship). Did John need the orderliness of the Anglican liturgy to balance out the evangelistic enthusiasm that often characterized the preaching of his itinerants? Baker argues that

---

[96] Ibid., 150.

Wesley was a born organizer, and "The responsibility of setting rules, maintaining discipline, settling disputes, presiding over discussion, even the chore of keeping statistical records, seemed to satisfy some deep, emotional need quite irrespective of the service which he then believed himself performing for others."[97]

This "orderliness" may be a clue to John's seeming non-empathy with his wife and his egocentricity in regard to his brother. Haidt argues that high systematizers are low empathizers. "We want to discover how the moral mind actually works, not how it ought to work, and that can't be done by reasoning, math or logic. It can be done only by observation, and observation is usually keener when informed by empathy."[98] If one "observes" or reads the following written to Charles, it might be concluded that John was not the quickest, at least personality wise, to adopt another's perspective. "And yet I may say, without vanity, that I am a better judge in this matter than Lady Huntingdon, Sally (Charles's wife)...or any other, nay than your own heart."[99] I believe Erik Erikson's description of Gandhi to be somewhat true of Wesley:

> His prolonged identity crisis, in turn, may invoke a premature generativity crisis, that makes him accept as his concern, a whole communal body or mankind itself, and embrace as his dependents those weak in power, poor in possessions and seemingly simple in heart. Such a deflection in life plan, in fact, may crowd out his chances for the enjoyment of intimacy, sexual and other, wherefore the great or often mateless, friendless and childless in the midst of veneration and confound further the human dilemma of combining the responsibilities of procreation with those of individual existence.[100]

One has to wonder, if Wesley was a lonely man, a far different person than the "inkling," C. S. Lewis, or "the common life" Dietrich Bonhoeffer, both who loved to throw back a beer and laugh with their friends. His deep longing for intimacy was reflected in his 1757 letter to his mother: "I am so immeasurably apt to pour out my soul unto

[97] Frank Baker. *John Wesley and the Church of England* (London: Epworth Press, 1970) 23.

[98] Haidt, 141.

[99] Quoted in Mabel Brailsford. *A Tale of Two Brothers, John and Charles Wesley* (New York: Oxford Unversity Press, 1954) 243-244.

[100] Erik Erikson. *Gandhi's Truth: On the Origins of Militant Non-violence* (New York: W. W. Norton and Company, 1969) 132.

any that loves me."[101] Perfect love was anything but perfect for the Church he claimed to serve and the women to whom he professed to be faithful. Perhaps perfect love as understood by the Holiness Movement, does not admit to the harsh realities of life, to confusing voices of loyalty, the not-yetness of a better world, a perfection that we cannot even comprehend, much less claim to possess. The irony of Christian perfection is that, the more one seeks it or attempts it, or even trusts God for it, the more imperfect it seems in the light of God's perfection. In 1758, John Fletcher, the Methodist saint of saints, wrote to Charles Wesley, "I find more and more it is not an easy thing to be upright before God; many boast of their sincerity and perhaps they may, but as for me, I am forced to smite my breast and to say, 'From all hypocrisy, good Lord deliver me...'"[102]

On May 14, 1768 John wrote Charles, "I am at my wit's end with regard to two things - the church and Christian perfection. Unless you and I both stand in the gap, in good earnest, the Methodists will drop them both."[103] John was prescient for both English Methodism and eventually American Methodism. The ideal was too difficult to explain and defend, much less experience. Claims to perfection raised eyebrows, and invited accusations of hypocrisy. Honesty and humility precluded such claims. David's confession in the aftermath of his adultery recorded, "The sacrifices of God are a broken spirit. A broken and contrite heart, O God, you will not despise" (Psalm 51:17). Ironically, even if Christian perfection is a this-life-possibility, less awareness of it may be better than more awareness.

Giving the complexities of Wesley's own life, his peculiar and unique Christian experience subjectively interpreted, his inability to practically bring erotic desires to a mutually satisfying arrangement, his ecclesiastical rationalizations that eventuated into a schism immediately upon his death, his controlling temperament, it is clear to an impartial observer that Wesley's teachings on Christian perfection sound much better in theological prose than in the details of everyday life. His doctrine of sin is inadequate, and thus, his understanding of grace. To minimize

---

[101] Frederick C Gill. *Selected Letters of John Wesley* (New York: Philosophical Library, Incorporated, 1956) v.

[102] Quoted in Gunter, 214.

[103] Ibid., 221.

the problem is to minimize the solution, resulting in a simplistic formula that does not do justice to the complexities of life and the richness of the Christian faith.

Chapter 2:
The Exegetical Scalpel

Preaching in Early American Methodism

Francis Asbury's preachers, who traipsed the eastern seaboard and eventually fanned out across the Allegheny Mountains, were almost totally lacking in exegetical and homiletical skills. They usually chose a text, which though it may have been related to the idea of the sermon, had little to do with context or the narrative behind the text. Their sermons had little resemblance to Wesley's finely-reasoned and logical discourses that could be preached at Oxford, (The Circumcision of the Heart, January 1st, 1733,) or before the "Society for the Reformation of Manners," May 30, 1763. Seemingly, Wesley preached a sermon several times, but then wrote the sermon which served as a full orbed treatise or essay on a particular topic. Some of Wesley's sermons were published and sold in tractarian form.

We have no printed sermons from early American Methodist preachers, not even Francis Asbury. With the exception of Asbury's preaching, and possibly a few of the more educated itinerants, sermons consisted of testimonies, exhortations, warnings, pleadings, dreams, and anecdotes. Quality control was almost impossible. Passion was more important than civil discourse, and emotional reaction more critical than thoughtful response. The following, told by James Finley during the 1811 Earthquake, may have not been all that abnormal: "One day while I was preaching a funeral, the house began to rock and the cupboard doors flew open. The people became alarmed and commenced shrieking and running. It was a time of great terror to sinners."[104]

---

[104] James B. Finley. *Autobiography of James B. Finley* (Cincinnati: Methodist Book Concern, 1872) 238.

Though itinerants received little instruction or critique, Asbury was able to rein in and disenfranchise some of his more extravagant enthusiasts such as William Glendinning. While he was preaching, Glendinning exclaimed, "I was certain Lucifer was near; and I told the people that he would be there that night. Immediately there was a loud rap at the door. I opened it, and saw his face; it was black as any coal – his eyes and mouth as red as blood and long white teeth gnashing together."[105] Apparitions were not the norm for Methodist preachers, though Freeborn Garretson, as well as others, put great stock in dreams and visions. However, there was enough ranting and raving incoherency to cause a Zerah Hawley to write of Cadiz, Ohio:

> The place is populated by illiterate itinerant Methodists. From this view of the subject, it will easily be seen, that the situation of the inhabitants of this country is most deplorable with regard to religious privileges. The great body of the people have no better oral instruction, than what they receive, from the most uninformed and fanatical Methodist Preachers, who are the most extravagant Ranters, of which any one can form an idea, who bawl forth one of their incoherent rhapsodies in one township in the morning, in another township in the afternoon, and in a third place in the evening. Their sermons are without plan or system, beginning with ignorance, and ending in nonsense, interlarded with something nearly approaching to blasphemy in many cases.[106]

Methodists preachers were adept at seizing the circumstances, whether a thunderstorm or a public execution, to trumpet the terrors of the Gospel, and the only hope to be found in repentance and faith in Christ. Asbury was particularly aware of his immediate setting, and exhibited a quaint knack for choosing a text to fit the occasion. He chose an appropriate or applicable Scripture almost at a moment's notice, which caused his traveling companion, Henry Boehm, to assess, "No man ever understood adaptation in preaching better than Francis Asbury."[107] For instance, when Asbury preached at a courthouse, he chose II Corinthians 5:11, "Knowing the terror of the Lord, we persuade men," and preached on judgment, listing the kinds of people to be judged. His manner of

---

[105] William Glendinning. *The Life of William Glendinning* (Philadelphia: W. W. Woodward, 1795) 19-20.

[106] Zerah Hawley. *A Journal of a Tour* (New Haven: S. Converse, 1822) 71.

[107] Henry Boehm. *Reminiscences: Historical and Biographical of Sixty-four Years in the Ministry* (New York: Carlton and Porter, 1866) 396.

preaching was often impromptu, determined both by his auditors and the setting: "a paper mill, under a jail wall, in a prison, at an executioner's stand, at a poor house, at a tavern, from the door of a public house, in a courthouse, in a barn, in the woods, standing on a table, from a camp meeting stand, in a school house, in a borrowed church, in a private dwelling, in a state house, and at Yale."[108]

At times, Asbury was faithful to the text by providing an outline, such as on Peter's denial of Christ: I. He was self-confident. II. Followed from a far off. III. Mixed with the wicked. IV. Denied his discipleship and then the Lord.[109] At other times, the text merely provided a launching point, a spring board for what Asbury wanted to say. Given the nature of his ignorant and crude congregations, we should not be surprised that he would choose Ecclesiastes 5:1 to preach on how one should behave in church, though the idea was not the intent of the biblical writer.[110] Asbury hardly ever gave the context of the text, and provided no historical background. He saw no need to build a bridge between a 3,000-year-old narrative and his contemporary audience. To explain cultural disconnects was not his forte. The Holy Spirit would apply that which was lacking in explanation. When Asbury was 68 years old, he recorded a preaching incident: "I was turned into another man – the Spirit of God came powerfully upon me, and there was a deep feeling amongst the people."[111] Three weeks later he recorded, "If the people say it was like thunder and lightning, I shall not be surprised. I spoke in power from God, and there was a general and deep feeling in the congregation: Thine O Lord, be all the glory."[112]

The critical criterion for all Methodist preaching was the result. As I have written in my biography of Asbury,

> A sermon for Asbury could be evaluated only by its effectiveness. Did it do what the preacher intended it to accomplish? The sermon's purpose was always conversion—conversion to life, to holiness, to righteousness, to action, to perfection, and ultimately to heaven. Asbury was continually

---

[108] Salter. *America's Bishop*, 295.

[109] Francis Asbury. *The Journal and Letters of Francis Asbury*, Vol. II, eds. Elmer Clark, J. Manning Potts, and Jacob S. Peyton (London: Epworth, Press, 1958) 562.

[110] Ibid., 118-119.

[111] Ibid., 742.

[112] Ibid., 745.

assessing his own performance in light of the congregational response. He was a life-long student of his listeners. He often noted that they were "dull, insensible, dead, inattentive, inanimate, lifeless, still, a little affected, unfeeling, little devoted, judicially hardened, word proof, marble hearted, cold, mocking, and offended." At other times, he said, they were "feeling, gracious, profited, melting, attentive, alarming, shaking, well behaved, serious, tender," and even "stricken to the ground."[113]

Asbury often imposed the Wesleyan order of salvation on a sermon, and in particular, sanctification. He rarely, if ever, distinguished between "sanctification" and "entire sanctification." On Samuel 10:6, "The spirit of the Lord will come upon me and thou shall be turned into another man." Asbury proceeded with an outline that had almost nothing to do with the text. "Here I took occasion to show ...the operation of the Spirit on the heart of man – to convince, convict, convert and sanctify."[114] Asbury's claim that he attempted to make sanctification the "burden and labor of every sermon," is debatable, but no doubt, this was his intent.[115] Even to approximate this goal, Asbury would have to twist and interpret a text beyond the intent and meaning of the biblical writer.

Albert Outler assesses that Asbury's "primitivism had no speculative basis. He had next to no sense of tradition....It was rather that the Bible served him sufficiently in his personal spiritual hungers and his passion for awakening and converting souls."[116] Outler has underestimated Asbury in that he had read from Thomas Haweis and Edward Stillingfleet on the history and ecclesiology of the Church. But he is essentially correct in that the course was set, a passion for souls directed by a primitive reading of Scripture and the enablement of the Holy Spirit. Methodists for the next one hundred years would be differentiated from Presbyterians, Congregationalists and Episcopalians, in that the followers of Asbury would interpret the Scriptures by the illumination of the Holy Spirit without scholastic apparatus and formal

---

[113] Salter, *America's Bishop*, 296.

[114] Asbury, *Journal*, Vol. 1: 152.

[115] Asbury, *Journal*, Vol. 2: 283.

[116] Albert Outler. "Biblical Primitivism in Early American Methodism" in *The Wesleyan Theological Heritage*, eds. Thomas Oden and Leicester R. Longden (Grand Rapids: Zondervan, 1991) 150.

education. For American Methodism during the floodtide of its growth, a prepared heart was worth more than a prepared head.

Not all Methodists were ignoramuses; they produced some of the most profound and knowledgeable preachers within the nineteenth century American church. Many of them were autodidacts, having mastered both Hebrew and Greek: Valentine Cook, Henry Bascom, Charles Elliott, Randolph Foster, and Matthew Simpson. When it came to getting immediate results, no denomination outdid the Methodists. When Simpson preached at Walnut Street Church in Chillicothe, Ohio, during the Civil War, it was reported that "Ladies threw away their fans and handkerchiefs, men threw their hats in the air; stood erect and mounted the seats....it was if a great storm at sea had suddenly ceased, but leaving the billows still in commotion – requiring some time for them to settle down, to quiet."[117]

One friend challenged another, who had never heard Simpson, that the preacher "would draw him to his feet." The uninitiated protested as if the two men were in a wager. As Simpson scaled several oratorical peaks, the newcomer managed to keep his posterior attached to his seat, though with difficulty. But when Simpson soared to his final climax, "The people sprang to their feet as if drawn by some magnetic force. I forgot all about my promise and ceased to resist the impulse that moved me. It seemed to me that no one with human feelings could withstand the current."[118]

An Esoteric Hermeneutic

As the nineteenth century turned into the twentieth, holiness exponents intentionally removed themselves, or simply drifted from the Wesleyan via media, a theological persuasion that had been cultivated in the rich tradition of the Church universal. Wesley was steeped in the early Church Fathers, the Councils of the Church, the Reformation, sprinkled in with the French, Spanish, and English mystics, and a full awareness of how both his non-juror and juror ancestors had shaped

---

[117] UMA, Drew University, Crooks' papers, "Something Additional," unidentified newspaper.

[118] Darius Salter. *"God Cannot Do Without America:" Matthew Simpson and the Apotheosis of Protestant Nationalism* (Wilmore, Kentucky: First Fruits Press, 2017) 568.

him, not just in the Anglican Church, but his own family. As successive generations of holiness leaders became less oriented to these theological guideposts, they developed a specialized and esoteric hermeneutic that could hardly be respected, much less adopted by someone who was conversant with historical theology. All of the Bible began to be read through a single lens, that of entire sanctification, which rendered exegetical aberrations, disdained by mainstream biblical scholarship, especially reformed theologians, with their own peculiar and reified paradigms ruling American evangelicalism. Both of these positions became unsatisfactory to millions of American church goers who opted for "open Bible" churches and thousands of other independent churches tethered to no particular theological position.

Stephen Lennox has done a masterful job in tracing scriptural irregularities and tortured interpretations by holiness revival and camp meeting preachers. Individuals such as Beverly Carradine, Joseph Smith, W. B. Godbey, and Uncle Bud Robinson, while not well-known in mainstream Christianity, were celebrities, household names within the twentieth century Holiness Movement. They did much good in leading their followers into a deeper experience with God, but also varying degrees of harm that would show up in succeeding generations who could no longer accept the arbitrary mores and warped biblical interpretations of their ancestors. Some of the best evangelists are teenagers, but they are unlikely to invite their friends to their home congregation, that to outsiders embarrassingly resembles a cult.

The above holiness preachers rushed into the Bible with a certitude that not only were the Scriptures inerrant, but they themselves were inerrant as well. Revered holiness preacher and writer, G. D. Watson, claimed that "a plain man entirely sanctified without learning and with the Bible in his hand, has an understanding of divine promises, sees further into the prophesies of God, gets a firmer grasp on God's word, than all the Drs. of Divinity that are not sanctified."[119] W. B. Godbey added that once the "Rocks of depravity were removed," one could "go down into the profound mysteries of revealed truth, flooded with new spiritual illuminations, and progressively edified by fresh treatments of

---

[119] Stephen Lennox. *Biblical Interpretation in the American Holiness Movement, 1875-1920* (unpublished Ph.D. dissertation, Drew University, 1992)140.

Divine Attributes in glory, though you never saw a college nor inherited Solomonic genius."[120]

Unfortunately, "entire sanctification" did not yield the theological soundness and accurate exegesis that these holiness specialists claimed. Spiritualizing and allegorizing biblical texts was of high priority. According to Watson, the dove released by Noah "typified not only the work of the Holy Spirit in the three dispensations of human history, but also the Spirit's work with the individual."[121] For Reuben Archer Robinson (Uncle Bud), the raising of Lazarus represented the Wesleyan order of salvation (a term he did not use), "the new birth, entire sanctification, the joyous life of holiness, and our task as soul winners."[122] When a camp meeting attendee accused Uncle Bud of finding holiness in the Bible where it wasn't, he quickly responded, "If I can find it where it isn't, you should be able to find it where it is."[123]

Beverly Carradine interpreted Psalm 51:7, "As white as snow," to mean justification and Isaiah 1:8, "whiter than snow" entire sanctification. [124]For Martin Wells Knapp, the woman portrayed in Revelation 12 is "the true holiness movement from its beginning to its final triumph." [125]Just about every time the word two was found in the Bible, there was the opportunity to impose on the text a "second work of grace." Watson exuberated that all throughout the Bible, truth is double-barreled: "There are two Testaments, Old and New, two natures of Christ, two elements, blood and water, that flowed from Christ's side, two touches on the eyes of the blind man, the list is almost endless."[126] Godbey exclaimed, "If I were to notice everything in the Bible, setting forth this glorious double salvation, it would take me the balance of my life."[127]

Lennox claims that in interpreting the dual movement of leaving Egypt and entering Canaan, holiness exponents were "certainly the only modern movement in church history to make such extensive application

---

[120] Ibid.
[121] Ibid., 228.
[122] Ibid., 200.
[123] Told to this author by William Greathouse.
[124] Lennox, 201.
[125] Ibid., 203.
[126] Ibid., 207.
[127] Ibid.

of this biblical event to entire sanctification."[128] Such free-wheeling eisegesis of types, symbols and events made it appear, according to Lennox, "that the further the holiness movement moved from the mainstream of society, the more subjective their arguments became. This should not be surprising for, without a critical audience to hold interpretations accountable, the movement had only to convince itself of the truth of its claims and the validity of its often subjective methods."[129]

Leon Hynson opined that the Holiness Movement developed the Egypt-Wilderness-Canaan analogy into an art form. Being raised in the Pilgrim Holiness Church, he recalled such sermons as the second batch of wine being served at the Cana wedding symbolizing entire sanctification. And the two kinds of rest, rest for the weary and those yoked to Christ (Matthew 11:28-29) were the double movements of justification and entire sanctification.[130] Holiness theologians, W. T. Purkiser, and H. Orton Wiley, and even the earlier Daniel Steele, cautioned against these individualistic interpretations of Scripture, refracted through experience or a single doctrine. Steele warned against entire sanctification being "isolated from its connection with the whole system, and magnified out of due proportion by being exclusively dwelt upon. Such treatment of a most vital truth creates error."[131] But error there was to be. As the Holiness Movement lost its momentum and tried to recapture elusive past glories, according to Hynson, the leadership blamed "cultural intrusion, and responded with a decisive separation from the world, expressed through an ethos which incorporated modesty of dress, avoidance of the world in such areas as movies, jewelry, and a sense of alienation and even persecution."[132] Lennox sadly summarizes (with help from Sydney Ahlstrom),

> The American holiness movement of the late nineteenth and early twentieth centuries was a movement in retreat. In many ways, they could still point to successes: the National Camp Meetings, numerical and organizational growth, a passion for the disinherited. Though never intellectually oriented, the holiness movement retreated almost entirely

---

[128] Ibid., 230.

[129] Lennox, 221.

[130] Leon Hynson, "The Wesleyan Quadrilateral in the American Holiness Tradition," *Wesleyan Theological Journal*, Vol. 20, No. 1 (Spring 1985) 22.

[131] Lennox, 197.

[132] Hynson, 25.

from the scholastic and scientific challenges. Its tendency to withdraw from established denominations represented a retreat from the struggles of modernity that Methodism and others were facing. The movement's single-issue theology – entire sanctification – represented a retreat from the theological issues being addressed. Its ministry among those in the lower socio-economic strata represented a continued retreat from the influential and powerful of society. Even when those from the lower strata began the climb to middle class, the holiness movement continued to identify itself as outcasts, retreating still further from the mainstream of thought.[133]

The Holiness Movement which had been characterized by ecumenicity at its inception, became increasingly an in-house operation. The witticisms, eccentricities, and antics of William Godbey, Uncle Bud Robinson, Beverly Carradine, and John T. Hatfield were expected and enjoyed by their admirers, but served to alienate the movement from the evangelical mainstream. Holiness celebrities were not held accountable for outlandish biblical interpretations and prophecies. Godbey claimed that he had "a divine intimation that the Apostle Paul would be president of the United States. I expect we will receive an invitation from him to the grandest holiness convention that the world ever saw, and people will come from all over Christiandom."[134] Godbey further prophesied that all of Africa would be converted:

> When all the negroes in Africa have shouted full salvation a thousand years, the Dark Continent checkered with railroads and illuminated with Holiness camp-grounds and colleges, those grand old Ethiopians will stand flat-footed, throw their big mouths open, and shout the devil out of countenance, till he be glad to retreat crest-fallen from the land of Ham, without a single follower.[135]

As Francis Asbury said, religion does not make Solomons, and we might add, neither does entire sanctification.

---

[133] Lennox, 241.

[134] Quoted in Kenneth O. Brown. *Leadership in the National Holiness Association with Special Reference to Eschatology, 1867-1919.* (Unpublished Ph.D. dissertation, Drew University, 1988) 277.

[135] Ibid., 277.

A Theology of Perspicuity

In January 1915, a Los Angeles court found 21-year-old Harold Lane guilty of stealing a stack of Bibles. The judge allowed Lane to choose his penalty: seven years in San Quentin or 30 days in the County jail, studying the Bible. He chose the latter. As Lane came to the end of his sentence, he may have regretted his choice of punishment. He would have to pass a test on Bible content, and as he pictured himself being interrogated before Judge Wilbur, his anxiety and hypertension became intolerable. Truth is, Lane found the Bible bewildering, especially for an uneducated person who had never been initiated by Sunday school, much less formally trained to understand the language, culture, and history of an ancient text. Lane could be heard repeating, "The Kenite, the Kenizzite, the Kadmonite, the Hittite, the Perizzite, the Rephaim, the Amorite, the Canaanite, the Girgashite, and the Jebusite." As the day of reckoning approached, Lane confided his fear to a reporter. "I only hope that Judge Wilbur will not expect me to remember all the names I have read in it."[136]

Judge Wilbur made the assumption that almost all American Christians have made, that the Bible is a plain text for a plain people. The Reformation doctrine of the priesthood of all believers, coupled with Gutenberg and Tyndale making the Bible a universally available book, in particular to the Anglo-Saxon world, found their confluence in "perspicuity," a word with which most Americans are not familiar, but yet fervently believe in. Perspicuity means "clearness or lucidity, as of a statement." Its synonyms are "clarity, plainness, intelligibility, and transparency."[137] Several intellectual streams flow into this presupposition: pietism, Puritanism, democracy, individualism, anti-intellectualism, common sense realism, and above all, the belief that the more "Christian" one is, the more he or she will be able to understand God's book. If Americans are God's newly chosen people, they will be able to intuit the meaning of Scripture, even as lovers read exchanged letters between the lines.

---

[136] As told by B. M. Pietsch, "Reference Bibles and Interpretive Authority" in *The Bible in American Life*, eds. Phillip Goff, et . al. (New York: Oxford, 2017) 119.
[137] Webster, 1456.

Taking shelter under the Apostle Paul's teaching, that "The man without the Spirit does not accept the things that come from the Spirit of God... because they are spiritually discerned" (I Corinthians 2:14), provides a high degree of security and certitude that my interpretation of a particular verse or passage is correct. "This distinctive feature of American religious life," according to Corwin E. Schmidt, "diminished the authority of educated clergy and fostered the emergence of a populist hermeneutic in regard to biblical interpretation." This hermeneutic augered "the propensity of Americans to adopt a more literal interpretation of Scripture, as without theological training, competency in Old and New Testament languages of Hebrew and Greek, or appreciation for church tradition," which left readers "few tools with which to interpret scripture."[138]

This literalistic certitude (has to mean this and nothing else) called for a defense of one's position or theological paradigm and the myriad strains of fundamentalism, which included the Holiness Movement, had the solution for defending the faith: "Bible schools." Virginia Brereton lists over one hundred Bible schools founded between 1882 – 1945. (I know she missed some because she failed to include the Bible school which I attended, Kentucky Mountain Bible Institute, begun in 1931.) The Bible school movement exhibited several strengths. First, a student learned the Bible, not just about the Bible. Learning included Scripture memorization, the Biblical narrative, Bible geography, and historical background. A Bible school graduate was likely to preach a sermon more pregnant with Scripture than a graduate of Harvard Divinity School and most other highly-touted seminaries.

Second, as Brereton argues, there was a high correlation between the proliferation of manual training schools (technical institutes) and Bible schools. Both were "hands on," which meant on weekends the student was likely to be present at an inner-city mission in Chicago, preaching at a church in a Kentucky "holler," or digging out the basement of a parsonage with mattock, shovel, and wheelbarrow. Being minted by a Bible school, in all likelihood, better prepared one for the realities of pastoring than the speculative abstractions of an Ivy League school. This

---

[138] Corwin E. Schmidt. "The Continuing Distinctive Role of the Bible in American Lives: A Comparative Analysis" in *The Bible in American Life*, eds. Phillip Goff, et.al. (New York: Oxford University Press, 2017) 203-204.

may be an oversimplification, but I do not think that I wrongly advised my seminary students that the best goals they could accomplish in that first struggling church were to cut the grass and paint the front porch of the parsonage.

Third, Bible schools were not just in the knowledge inventory business, but were also intensely focused on character formation. This formation included consecration, and being attuned to the call of God. In 1962, Safara Witmer, an employee of the Accrediting Association of Bible Schools, estimated that at least "50 % of the 27,000 Protestant missionaries then in the field, had prepared at Bible schools. Of these, some 2,700 were Moody graduates."[139]

Fourth, most Bible school campuses were close-knit residential communities. Students observed the highly-committed and sacrificial lives of their professors often working for low salaries, or even without salary. These individuals were provided spiritual leadership by the practice of prayer, devotional Scripture reading, and not afraid to get their hands dirty by doing manual work on campus. Regularly scheduled revivals, normally twice per year, called for deeper commitment and prayer meetings could be heard echoing across the campus. Moody Bible Institute was referred to as the "West Point of Fundamentalism," and I have often referred to my own Bible school experience as "God's boot camp."

All of the above came with a price. Theological entrepreneurs did not start Bible schools solely motivated by a pure love for Scripture, a generic interpretation centrist to the Reformation, and a few essential tenets of Orthodoxy. Instead, they founded schools and hired professors who would teach the Scriptures with a particular slant or under a well-defined and visible theological umbrella. This included dispensationalists, Pentecostals, Seventh-Day Adventists and no less, individuals who desired to indoctrinate their students in the theology of "second blessing holiness." But little indoctrination was needed, in that students attended a particular school because it unabashedly and unapologetically advertized itself as a school with a particular theological perspective. And even if the school professed to teach "inductive Bible

---

[139] Virginia Brereton. *Training God's Army: The American Bible School, 1880-1940* (Bloomington: Indiana Press, 1990) 129.

study," a deductive proposition hung over every assignment, every lecture, every question, and every interpretation. There was little dialogue and scant confession that a verse or issue found in Scripture might be exceedingly unclear. Brereton unfortunately is correct when she speculates that "Bible school institutions and students, with their preference for quick, easy, and fool-proof methods for capsulated knowledge, and for outlines that rendered scripture crystal-clear and readily digestible, reinforced the rhetoric's propensity for slogans, and formulaic phrases."[140] Brereton helpfully elucidates the philosophy which was behind every Bible school curriculum.

> If the enthusiasms that characterized fundamentalism were to be taught to the uninitiated in the present generation and handed down to the next, they had to be contained, preserved, and codified by means of systems and organizations. Among many fundamentalists the urge to codify and, further, the drive to introduce predictability, permanence, and stability into their thought and activity was pronounced. It was this propensity that gave fundamentalists their reputation for stating their theological positions in formulaic and dogmatic terms, the words and phrases apparently fixed and unchanging for all time.[141]

The Formal Challenge to Traditional Holiness Exegesis

In the late 1970s, the biblical relationship between the baptism of the Holy Spirit and entire sanctification came under scholarly scrutiny. Though William Arnett, Systematic Theology professor at Asbury Theological Seminary, could not make a direct connection between Holy Spirit baptism and entire sanctification, he quoted Wesley's comment on Matthew 3:11: "He shall fill you with the Holy Ghost, inflaming your hearts with that fire of love which many waters cannot quench."[142] Arnett referenced a 1771 letter to Joseph Benson, in which Wesley commented on 1 John 1:2, contrasting "babes," and "young fathers." Wesley stated, "I believe one that is *perfected in love* or filled with the Holy Ghost may

---

[140] Ibid., 25.

[141] Ibid., 14.

[142] William M. Arnett, "The Role of the Holy Spirit in Entire Sanctification in the Writings of John Wesley," *Wesleyan Theological Journal*, Vol. 14, No. 2 (Fall 1979) 19.

be properly termed a *father*."[143] (How Wesley made this conclusion is unclear because there is no pneumatology in the 1 John1:2 passage.) Arnett commented: "Here the expressions 'perfected in love,' and 'filled with the Holy Ghost,' are used synonymously, while 'a babe in Christ' or 'little children,' a 'young man' and 'father,' suggest experiential or maturation stages or levels in the Christian life."[144]

Arnett, who knew Wesley's writings extremely well, admitted that Wesley is confusing in his use of "filled with the Holy Spirit." Arnett wrote, "Ostensibly, the Holy Spirit is the Divine Agent who fills the Christian's heart with love. Again, in the two sermons already mentioned, a Christian can be 'filled with the Holy Spirit' yet inward sin remains. Sin cannot remain, however, if the believer is filled with love. It is apparent there is tension in these views."[145] Arnett concluded concerning Wesley, "Although he maintained that he had been consistent in his belief about the doctrine, there are some areas of tension, perhaps ambiguity, in regard to his application of pneumentological phrases such as 'receiving the Holy Spirit,' 'the baptism of the Holy Spirit,' and 'filled with the Holy Spirit.'"[146] To Arnett's credit, though he in all probability believed the baptism of the Holy Spirit to be synonymous with entire sanctification, he did not impose his American holiness perspective on Wesley.

Asbury Theological Seminary Professor Robert Lyon

From my perspective, Asbury Theological Seminary Professor Robert Lyon did the most ground-breaking investigation concerning New Testament pneumatology and the Wesleyan doctrine of entire sanctification in the history of the Holiness Movement.[147] Lyon began with a word study of *baptiso* (baptize and its cognates), and after exploring all of the contexts which reference water baptism, concluded that, "clearly and inescapably that so far baptism language without exception always has reference to a common experience of all believers and of their entrance

---

[143] Ibid., 20

[144] Ibid.

[145] Ibid., 23.

[146] Ibid., 26.

[147] Robert Lyon. "Baptism and Spirit-Baptism in the New Testament," *Wesleyan Theological Journal*, Vol. 14, No. 1 (Spring 1979) 14-26.

into the body."[148] Lyon noted that though "baptized with the Holy Spirit" occurred six times in the New Testament, the phrase "baptism with the Holy Spirit" (using the noun,) does not occur in the NT. The 3,000 who were converted on the day of Pentecost were offered the same experience as the 120 in the Upper Room. "Peter, by his message and invitation has set before them the very same opportunity, which was fulfilled in the lives of the 120.... All the terms -- baptizing, coming upon, filling, pouring out, receiving -- are equivalent expressions."[149]

Lyon admitted that the Samaritan Pentecost is a "sticky" narrative because it does not easily fit the initiation pattern from which he has argued. Under the ministry of Phillip, the Samaritans believed and were baptized. But Lyon pointed out that this could also be said about Simon Magus (Acts 8), and those who believed on Jesus (John 2:23-24), but yet could not be trusted. Lyon concluded concerning the Acts 8 Samaritan revival, "One thing, however is quite certain, viz., that when Peter and John laid their hands upon them and they 'received' the Holy Spirit, it was their first experience of the Spirit, and cannot be counted as a second experience. In the schema of the book (see 1:8) it is the incorporation of the Samaritans into the body. It was, so to speak, the culmination of their conversion."[150]

Paul's Acts 9 conversion, blindness, visit by Ananias so that he would receive his sight and be "filled with the Holy Spirit," according to Lyon is a conversion narrative, an interpretation supported by Wesley. Saul's three days without sight and food are the "pangs of the new birth."[151] Lyon commented, "What we have here, then, is another example of the experience of the Holy Spirit at conversion. It is Paul's initial encounter with the Spirit."[152]

Concerning the Acts 10 account at Cornelius's house, the Holy Spirit was poured out on them (all who were listening according to the text) and then they were baptized with water. (Acts 11 seems to imply the whole household.) "Peter's account of the event in Acts 15, at the Jerusalem council, 'gave them the Holy Spirit even as he did us,'"

---

[148] Ibid., 17.
[149] Ibid., 18.
[150] Ibid., 19.
[151] Ibid.
[152] Ibid., 20.

confirmed for Lyon that "Everything in these narratives requires our understanding the conversion for Cornelius as the occasion for his experience in the Spirit."[153]

Paul asked the Ephesians if they had received the Holy Spirit when (since, KJV) they believed? The answer was "no." Because Paul believed there was something left out of their baptism by John, he re-baptized the Samaritans and upon laying hands on them, "The Holy Spirit came on them and they began speaking with tongues and prophesying" (Acts 19:6). Lyons wrote, "While certainly not free of ambiguities, what we seem to have here is an account of the conversion of some disciples of John the Baptist..."[154] Lyon's overall conclusion: "Apart from the initial outpouring of Pentecost, (Act 2:1-4) all the encounters are first encounters with the Spirit." As to Acts 2, "The two-step experience of the original disciples is the truly unique experience and cannot be repeated, for there is no way to repeat the relationship with the incarnated and earthly Jesus."[155] Critical for Lyon is that all of the conversions by the Spirit *are* a sanctifying experience that does not preclude entire sanctification. Lyon summarized: "From Pentecost on, all believers receive at conversion the Holy Spirit as promised in His fullness. No biblical basis exists for a distinction between receiving the Spirit and being baptized in, or filled with the Spirit."[156]

Rebuttal and Further Clarification

NTS professor J. Kenneth Grider admitted that he was no match for the New Testament exegete Robert Lyon but, nonetheless, as a theologian, he would do battle. Grider's methodology was to treat the same texts which Lyon had traversed, arguing that for the Jewish Pentecost (Acts 2), the Samaritan Pentecost (Acts 8), the Gentile Pentecost (Acts 10), and the Ephesian Pentecost (Acts 19), the receiving or filling with the Holy Spirit is subsequent to conversion. Grider tended to misrepresent Lyon: "If Lyon is correct that no conversion happened out there along the road, a massive amount of Christian comment over

---

[153] Ibid.
[154] Ibid., 20.
[155] Ibid., 21.
[156] Ibid., 24.

a nineteen century period is quite incorrect."[157] Lyon did not argue that no conversion took place on the Damascus Road. Lyon claimed that Paul's conversion was completed at Simon's house by the visit of Ananias and being filled with the Holy Spirit. (I would say that at Simon's house, Saul's conversion was sealed by the Holy Spirit.) There are many of us, when asked when we were born again, can point to several occasions, not really sure which encounter was most important.

One of the most controversial texts as to whether Luke is speaking of a first or second work of grace is the Cornelius event, Acts 10. Of course, Grider interpreted Cornelius' spiritual state before Peter visited as justified, in that Cornelius was described as "devout and righteous." Even though Grider admitted that this same terminology was used in Acts 17:23 regarding the worship of people toward an unknown god, he maintained, "I feel that its use of Cornelius is corroborative of my view that he is a Christian believer albeit, without very much correct understanding."[158] Was Grider claiming that Cornelius was justified, but did not know it?

As to Cornelius being referred to as "righteous," (Acts 10:22) a soteriological term, Grider's argument breaks down when Paul claims that before his conversion as "for righteousness based on law," he was "faultless" (Phil. 3:6). Grider wandered further afield when he argued that Cornelius had already been cleansed, as in Peter's vision of animals, (Acts 10) when the context concerns the elaborate Old Testament dietary laws for clean and unclean animals. Grider was more on target when he claimed that the Ephesians' Pentecost was post-justification, when prior to receiving the Holy Spirit, the recipients are called disciples. But throughout the New Testament, the word disciple seems to be a slippery and ambivalent term. According to John 6, Jesus had thousands of disciples but many of his disciples "turned back and no longer followed him" (John 6:59, 66).

Grider interpreted Peter's promise to the three thousand, "Repent, and let each of you be baptized in the name of Jesus Christ for the forgiveness of your sins and you shall receive the gift of the

---

[157] J. Kenneth Grider, "Spirit Baptism: The Means of Entire Sanctification," *Wesleyan Theological Journal*, Vol. 14, No. 2 (Fall 1979) 33.
[158] Ibid., 36.

Holy Spirit" as a proclamation of entire sanctification. "This as I see it, will be subsequent to their repentance and also to their water baptism. This might not be quite as clear as systematical, theological language is capable of making it. Yet as I see it, it is quite clearly and emphatically what might be described as an exhortation to what I would call both works of grace, one subsequent to the other."[159]

Grider was correct in claiming that Lyon places a large load of spiritual freight on justification (regeneration) at the expense of what is normally credited to entire sanctification, such as the "body of sin has been destroyed." Grider grounded his argument in the American Holiness Movement, which meant that he worked with the presuppositions of the authors and exponents of nineteenth century holiness theology. Both Grider and Lyon were aware that the latter had departed from these presuppositions. Since each was working with such disparate apriori assumptions, it was impossible for them to merge together divergent interpretations on the relationship between the baptism with the Holy Spirit and entire sanctification.

Asbury Theological Seminary Professor George Allen Turner

George Allen Turner set out to answer two questions. First, is the phrase "baptized in the Holy Spirit" a description of initiation into the Christian life or is it a gift of the Spirit for cleansing, and empowering those who are already believers? Second, is this expression as commonly used in the Holiness Movement a derivative from Wesleyan theology or is it a subsequent accretion, that is, without precedent either in Scripture or usage of the Wesleys?

Turner argued that the baptism of the Holy Spirit in the New Testament is not initiation language, but is subsequent to conversion. The disciples were believers before Pentecost (Luke 9:1, 10:20, John 15:3, 17:6). For Turner, rebirth in the Holy Spirit is concomitant with such initiation language as water baptism, repentance, and regeneration. The baptism of the Holy Spirit would provide purity and power both for holy living and ministry. Turner admitted that the evidence in Luke-Acts is ambiguous in places, but the main thrust seems clear: converted

---

[159] Grider, 44.

persons still need the baptism and filling of the Holy Spirit for maximum effectiveness.[160]

Turner believed that Wesley equivocated when linking the baptism of the Holy Spirit with regeneration. "With reference as to whether the baptism with the Holy Spirit comes with initiation into the Christian life, Wesley was not clear." For Turner, "Wesley did not object to linking the baptism with the Holy Spirit with entire sanctification, and sometimes he made the link himself."[161] But Turner did not quote one Wesleyan passage which makes this link. According to Turner, John Fletcher believed equating the baptism of the Holy Spirit with Christian perfection was more aligned with Charles than with John. In November of 1771, Fletcher wrote Charles, "I shall introduce my, why not your doctrine of the Holy Ghost, and make it one with your brother's perfection? He holds the truth, but this will be an improvement upon it, if I am not mistaken. In some of your Pentecostal hymns, you paint my light wonderfully."[162] Fletcher clearly linked Christian perfection and the baptism of the Holy Spirit, but strangely wrote to Charles in 1775, "I am not in the Christian Dispensation of the Holy Ghost and of power. I want for it, but not earnestly enough. I am not sufficiently straightened till the fiery baptism is accomplished....Christian perfection is nothing but the full kingdom in the Holy Ghost."[163]

Turner concluded by claiming that American Methodist leadership, such as Nathan Bangs and Laban Clark, moved away from Wesley's "baptismal regeneration" language. The concept is more in harmony with the New Testament and the implications of Wesley's own position.[164] But Turner did not make clear what Wesley's implications were, and neither did he cite any evidence for early nineteenth-century American Methodist convictions or consistency about the baptism of the Holy Spirit.

---

[160] George Allen Turner, "The Baptism of the Holy Spirit in the Wesleyan Tradition," *Wesleyan Theological Journal*, Vol. 14, No. 1 (Spring 1979) 67.
[161] Ibid., 68.
[162] Ibid., 70.
[163] Ibid., 71.
[164] Ibid., 73.

Nazarene Theological Seminary Professor Alex Deasley

Alex Deasley, in a 1979 paper, "Entire Sanctification and the Baptism of the Holy Spirit: Perspectives on the Biblical View of the Relationship," unlike most authors, promised little and delivered much. "It is not my purpose, or is it in my competence to trace the subsequent history of their significant and in many respects, embarrassing divergents between Wesley and many of his spiritual heirs." Contrary to Turner, Deasley argued that nineteenth century Wesleyan theologians such as Richard Watson, William Pope, and John Miley, did not equate baptism of the Holy Spirit with entire sanctification. Further, Boston University professor Daniel Steele often cited as equating entire sanctification with Holy Spirit baptism, expressed ambivalence about a clear association within the Pentecostal event of Acts 2. Steele admitted that this was not even clear in the writings of John Fletcher. "Steele concludes that the phrase 'baptism or fullness of the Spirit' may mean something less than entire sanctification."[165]

Deasley traced the historical patterns in the Synoptic Gospels, both in symbol and chronology between water baptism and receiving the Holy Spirit. "When therefore one reads a statement like Acts 2:38, 'Repent and be baptized and you will receive the Holy Spirit,' one is witnessing the application to the individual Christian of the pattern of the experience of Christ or to express it differently, the Christianizing of the baptism of John by its being drawn into the age of the Spirit."[166] For Deasley, it is critical to maintain the continuum of Luke – Acts, understanding one in the light of the other, in that they were written by the same author. In his Gospel, Luke emphasized the role of the Holy Spirit at nodal points in the life of Jesus: his birth, baptism, transfiguration, etc. "Jesus speaks little of the Spirit, yet his ministry abounds in the works of the Spirit: exorcism, healing, prophecy, forgiveness of sins, all of which are part of his Spirit-anointed commission in Luke 4:18." According to Deasley, Luke in his Gospel stresses "The Spirit as the sign of the New Age....

---

[165] Alex Deasley, "Entire Sanctification and the Baptism with the Holy Spirit: Perspectives on the Biblical View of the Relationship," *Wesleyan Theological Journal,* Vol. 14, No. 1 (Spring 1979) 29.

[166] Ibid., 33.

following the progress of salvation by ministering prophetic power to those who receive him."[167]

Deasley interpreted that the ministry of the Holy Spirit as narrated by Luke in the Book of Acts needs to be understood by the incorporation of the Gentiles into the Church, the Cornelius event in Acts 10, and the subsequent explanation or re-account of the event by Peter in Acts 11 and 15. The message that Peter preached in Acts 2 and Acts 10 was in salvation terms. But the outpouring of the Holy Spirit in both cases has further implication than simply regeneration or the "interiorizing of religion" and the "purification of believers." The pouring out of the Spirit is for the purpose of mission, the boldness of proclamation and the formation of character, exemplified by the "seven" in Acts 6 as men of "good repute full of the Spirit and of wisdom" or Barnabas as "A good man, full of the Holy Spirit and faith" (Acts 11:24).[168] Deasley summarized that Luke's "basic intent is to show that the Christian era is the era of the Spirit; that there is no Church without the Spirit; no Christian without the Spirit; and wherever the Gospel goes in power, it goes in the power of the Spirit."[169] While the Pentecostal language of Luke – Acts is primarily concerned with a New Age, a new community, a new creation, and new enablement, cannot be construed as a Wesleyan second work of grace. Neither does the narrative rule out that the full realization of the baptism of the Holy Spirit brings a believer into the experience of entire sanctification.

The Aorist Tense

In a second article, Robert Lyon exposed the fallacious and excessive emphasis on the aorist tense, such as in I Thessalonians 5:23, pointing out that Jesus used the aorist tense in John 2:20, "The temple has been under construction for forty-six years." Thus, the aorist is not punctiliar as in a point of time, but that it looks at a whole action as having occurred, without *distinguishing any steps in its progress.*"[170] Lyon encouraged the interpreters to look at the context rather than the

---

[167] Ibid., 36.

[168] Ibid., 39.

169 Ibid.

[170] Robert W. Lyon, "The Baptism of the Spirit–Continued," *Wesleyan Theological Journal*, Vol. 15, No. 2 (Fall 1980) 71.

verb tense, something that most proof texters are not prone to do. "I am, for example, quite certain that the coming of the Holy Spirit upon the believer is a 'crisis experience,' not because in Acts 1:8 the tense is aorist, but because the context in the very nature of the action as it is described there and elsewhere."[171] Lyon asserted that two works of grace, justification and entire sanctification has to be inferred by apriori assumptions, since the events recorded in Acts are the accounts of an "initial receiving of the Spirit, of their coming to profess inwardly the living Spirit of God."[172]

Randy Maddox also argued against assuming that the "aorist tense" automatically denotes punctiliar action. He quoted A. T. Robertson who stated, "As I see it, the aorist preserved the simple action and the other tenses grew up around it."[173] The aorist was the most simple way to express a verb and does not denote "continuity or lack thereof."[174] As did Lyon, Maddox argued that the right meaning of the aorist could be signified only by the context. "Thus, for example, if one were to say, 'I shot the gun,' in Greek using the aorist tense, it would be impossible to determine if only one shot were fired or if more than one, unless the context specified."[175] When Paul uses the aorist for "filled" and "walk" in Colossians 1:9, "Both the meaning of these verbs and the context which spells out all that is involved in walking in a worthy manner suggests strongly that the action of the verb is not conceived of as taking place instantaneously. Rather, it is the product of a growing relationship with God through Christ."[176] Maddox concluded, "Thus, a proper understanding of the aorist tense can be very instrumental in helping to find a balance in the present debate between the crisis and the process of sanctification in holiness thought."[177]

Lyon observed that the Holy Spirit is always involved in sanctification, but that does not necessarily mean entire sanctification as a second work of grace. Never had the two most oft used arguments

---

[171] Ibid., 73.

[172] Ibid., 75.

[173] Randy Maddox, "The Use of the Aorist Tense in Holiness Exegesis," *Wesleyan Theological Journal*, Vol. 6, No. 2 (Fall 1981) 108.

[174] Ibid., 108.

[175] Ibid., 109.

[176] Ibid., 114.

[177] Ibid., 116.

for entire sanctification, Pentecost and the aorist tense, come under such scrutiny. Lyon was especially hard on Grider who misinterpreted him by arguing that in referring to conversion as a "truly" sanctifying event, Lyon was postulating that the converted person is sanctified in a "pretty complete sense." Lyon protested that he was not using the word "truly" as "wholly," but as Wesley used it in his sermon on "Sin in Believers," when he stated that the hearts of the Corinthians "were truly yet not entirely renewed…we allow that the state of a justified person inexpressively great and glorious. He is born again….he is a child of God….he is created anew in Christ Jesus: he is washed, he is sanctified. His heart is purified by faith; he is cleansed 'from the corruption that is in the world.'"[178] Lyon had given traditional holiness exponents much to think about, if they were willing to think.

These authors had questioned traditional holiness theology which equated Pentecost, Acts 2 with entire sanctification. They proved to be harbingers for the theological explosion about to take place in the Church of the Nazarene. Or to use another metaphor, the scholarship created by Nazarene education was about to boomerang on its creators.

Representative Holiness Preaching

In 1894, the National Camp Meeting Association for the Promotion of Holiness published the *Double Cure, or Echoes from the National Camp Meetings*,[179] a compilation of holiness sermons preached by thirty-three different holiness preachers including J. A. Wood, Beverly Carradine, William Taylor, Henry Clay Morrison, Phineas Bresee, and Joseph Smith. Of the thirty-three sermons, six were based on a Gospel text, and nineteen were from the Epistles. In other words, almost two-thirds of the sermons were based on a portion of the Bible which comprises one-tenth of the biblical corpus. I perceive the reason for utilizing the Epistles is the Western syllogistic, logical writing of Paul, which is more easily doctrinalized and systematized than other literary types.

---

[178] Lyon "Continued," 76.

[179] William McDonald. *The Double Cure, or Echoes from the National Camp Meetings* (Boston: The Christian Witness Co., 1894).

Almost none of the preachers told us anything about the historical Jesus. Regarding Matthew 22:37, "Thou shalt love the Lord Thy God with all thy heart, and with all thy soul and with all thy mind," the preacher utilized no incident in the life of Christ. As to the Matthew 5:38 command, "Be Ye therefore perfect," there is nothing of the context in which Jesus spoke, but there is the following exaggerated and incomprehensible statement, "When man is rightly related to God and himself by perfect love, he is rightly related to any other right self, and holds the attitude of rightness toward every other self in the universe of God, Heaven has in it, 'the spirits of just men made perfect.' When man's entire being is perfected, and God perfects the entire man, there will be no temple but his heart, no mediation, no grace; the original plan will be restored."[180]

For John 3:19-21, "And this is the condemnation that light has come in the world, and men loved darkness rather than the light, because their deeds were evil," J. N. Short referenced Peter asking Jesus about John's future; however, no other narrative was given. One would question the following from Short, "All who obey God without respect to what men think, say, or do, always have the witness of the Spirit, that they please God."[181] Martin Luther, as well as Martin Luther King, Jr., was plagued with doubts. Though one preacher took as his text, Luke 1:69, "To serve Him in righteousness and holiness all of their lives," the sermon consisted mainly of spiritual renewal in the Old Testament.

A brilliant exception to the above was preached by A. J. Jarrell from the text Luke 7:19, "Art Thou he that should come?" entitled "John the Baptist, or Holiness Staggering Under Trials." Though most of the sermon narrated the life of John, it effectively treated possibly the most contradictory and unforgivable deed in the life of Christ. The Savior of the world left his cousin, his advance man, in prison to rot and eventually to be beheaded, "Poor John the Baptist! He seemed forgotten of God in Heaven, and deserted of God on Earth. The very day Jesus heard that he was cast into prison he turned his back on Judea and departed into Galilee. John pining in prison and his Lord preaching in glad simplicity

---

[180] Ibid., 154.

[181] Ibid., 115.

among the lilies of Galilee, John perishing for a crumb of comfort, and Jesus feeding the thousands around Lake Genessaret."[182]

As did most holiness preachers, Richard Taylor (whom we will examine more closely in the next chapter) brought the above one hundred years forward. He provided thirty-five holiness sermon outlines in a book, *The Main Issue: The Why and How of Preaching Holiness*, published the year he died, 2006.[183] For the most part, they are typical of twentieth century holiness preaching. The sermons are topical, propositional, and deductive. Allow me to qualify, that none of these descriptors eliminate the potential of a sermon to do good or invalidate the intended truth. I am confident that many persons found spiritual help under Richard Taylor's preaching. He was thought-provoking, and could turn a memorable phrase: "Justification by faith entitles us to heaven: Sanctification by faith fits us for heaven."[184]

Twenty-five of the thirty-five sermons utilized a primary text from the Epistles. In four sermons, Taylor had no text; the sermon simply proof texted a topic such as Hell or Christian perfection. For three sermons he had multiple texts, not being able to determine which one best fit his topic. (They may have all been appropriate for his subject matter.) Most of his topics were supported by a plethora of biblical references, amounting to as many as eighteen.[185] Almost all of the sermons employed elaborate outlines, perhaps with a tangential relationship to the text, but not based on the text. Most of his sermons provided no context, and strangely, though he was certainly capable, Taylor evidenced little to no exegesis. If so, he would have known in his sermon "Distinctives with a Difference," that the Greek language does not support a distinction between "faultless" and "blameless." Not digging into the cultural and textual background, can allow for major faux pas. For his sermon, "Examine Yourselves," (I Corinthians 13:5) Taylor provided no biblical background which led to the following, "We should dress neatly, avoid body odor through careless hygiene and speak politely."[186]

---

[182] Ibid., 284-285.

[183] Richard S. Taylor. *The Main Issue: The Why and How of Holiness Preaching* (Salem, OH: Schmul Publishing Company, 2006).

[184] Ibid., 14.

[185] Ibid., 84-85.

[186] Ibid., 116.

Four of the sermons provided excellent exposition, staying within the parameters of the text. In a sermon on Barnabas, his only sermon which could be described as narrative (which is odd because most of Scripture is narrative or at least has a narrative behind it), Taylor discussed Barnabas by answering the following questions: a. Exactly what did Barnabas do? b. What was Barnabas' instruction as to how they were to stay true? c. Why was Barnabas motivated to persistently keep on encouraging these new converts? Taylor referred to Barnabas, using his name twelve times, and the personal pronoun "he" multiple other times. Thus, we know a lot more about Barnabas at the end of the message than we did at the beginning. Contrastingly, for his sermon on God's choice of David, "Where God Looks," Taylor gave an introductory narrative paragraph, but then proceeded with an outline that never referred to the text or plot line.

Allow me to again say that Richard Taylor was a revered preacher, deeply committed to theological truth, but his model of persuasion using logic and propositional proof texting is incongruent with a post-modern mentality which thinks in picture, symbol, and narrative. The continued use of Taylor's model is mostly geared to camp meeting crowds and congregations who are already in agreement with his presuppositions. (Also, I am only working with outlines, and there may have been some exposition in the actual preaching of the sermons that I have missed.) With the exception of Taylor's four expository sermons, the above was representative of holiness preaching throughout the twentieth century. This was the best of holiness preaching, spiritually challenging, abundant proof texting, decisionally convicting, Christologically promising, Holy Spirit-anointed, and abundantly optimistic, perhaps too optimistic. The ultimate evaluation renders holiness preaching as deductive/propositional rather than inductive/expositional. The latter, though not foolproof, is the methodology which most ensures a correct and honest biblical interpretation.

The Historical Jesus — M.I.A.

For the first half of the twentieth century, the historical Jesus was almost totally missing from holiness preaching. I need to be lenient; Jesus studies were not in vogue. There was no N. T. Wright to say, "If we are to follow Christ, we need to know about the Jesus Christ we are following."[187] It is in attempting to understand Christ that we begin to learn the content of what it means to be Christian. There is no possibility of living a hallowed, Christian life outside of intently listening to what Jesus said and observing what he did. He is God's audio-visual, presented to us by the Father, and anointed by the Holy Spirit. N. T. Wright states, "I would go so far as to suggest that whenever the church forgets its call to engage in the task of understanding more and more fully who Jesus actually was, idolatry, and ideology lie close at hand."[188] The Holiness Movement by not staying in humble contrition before the incarnated Christ as described in Scripture, a Christ who challenged almost all normal patterns of human behavior, may have been left with an ideology defined by a formula rather than a person. There is some truth to the observation that Jesus came to destroy the formulaic God. The above ideology seriously departed from Wesley in this respect; thirteen of the forty-four standard sermons are expositions of the "Sermon on the Mount." Edward Sugden introduced them with, "Their ethical teaching glows throughout with Spiritual fervor; and their appeal to the conscience is irresistible. They are a candle of the Lord, searching the innermost parts of the soul; and in reading them once again I have been driven to my knees for penitence and confession, many and many a time."[189]

The high measuring bar which Jesus set, the gold standard for Christian living, denies claim to any kind of arrival theology, especially that which was often proclaimed by Christian perfectionists. One might conclude from these sermons a compendium of Wesley's theology, a refutation of mysticism, Gnosticism, monasticism, and all false notions of holiness. "I shall endeavor to show first, that Christianity is essentially a social religion; and that to turn it into a solitary one, is to destroy it."[190] This social religion meant that, "it cannot subsist at all without society – without living and conversing with other men."[191] In his exposition of Matthew 5-7, Wesley set the standard so high, no higher than did Jesus, that we are clued in as to why Wesley did not lay claim to so high a state of grace for himself. Love "destroys all high conceits engendering pride;

---

[187] N. T. Wright. *The Challenge of Jesus: Understanding Who Jesus Was and Is* (Downers Grove: Inter Varsity Press, 1999) 53.

[188] Ibid., 21.

[189] John Wesley. *Standard Sermons*, Vol. I, ed. Edward Sugden (Grand Rapids: Francis Asbury Press, 1955) 313.

[190] Ibid., 381-382.

[191] Ibid., 382.

and makes us to rejoice to be as nothing, to be little and vile, the lowest of all, the servant of all."[192] One of the problems for those who would seek holiness as an experience, is the self-centered on a spiritual high. On "seeking and thirsting after righteousness," Wesley comments, "Yea, in some sense, he may be said *not to seek his own* spiritual any more than temporal advantage, for while he is on the full stretch to save their souls from death, he, as it were, forgets himself. He does not think of himself so long as that zeal for the glory of God swallows him up."[193]

It is impossible to read the Sermon on the Mount with any sincerity or honesty and forget our obligation to those less fortunate. This is the social holiness which Wesley exemplified all of his life, and the Holiness Movement seemingly forgot (with the notable and laudable exception of the Salvation Army). Wesley is most stringent on this point, "Whether they will finally be lost or saved you are expressly commanded to feed the hungry, and clothe the naked. If you can and do not, whatever becomes of them, you shall go away into everlasting fire."[194] We are not to give help irresponsibly or without discernment. And yet it is not left completely to us to decide who is worthy and who is not. We may have to err on the side of mercy, that is, be willing to be taken in by some unscrupulous panhandler who presents a completely false narrative of the woes that have befallen him.

We are to be peacemakers. Something is wrong with a spirituality that is contentious. True holiness endeavors to calm the stormy spirit of humanity, "to quiet their turbulent passions, to soften the minds of contending parties, and if possible, reconcile them to each other."[195] This posture does not mean passivity, but a willingness to be at odds with the world. Persecution from the world was for Wesley one of the surest indicators that one was doing God's will. "This cannot fail; it is the very badge of our discipleship; it is one of the seals of our calling; it is a sure portion entailed on all the children of God; if we have it not, we are bastards, and not sons; straight through evil report, as well as good report, lies the only way to the kingdom."[196]

---

[192] Ibid., 348.

[193] Ibid., 348-349.

[194] Ibid., 395.

[195] Ibid., 365.

[196] Ibid., 372.

In the Sermon on the Mount, we discover that true religion is a matter of the heart, a heart that produces right action, but takes no stock in that action: "Be thou little, and base, and mean, and vile (beyond what words can express) in thine own eyes, amazed and humbled to the dust by the love of God which is in Christ Jesus."[197] Nothing was more antithetical than pride and holiness, self-dependence and God dependence, "Wise, therefore, is the man who buildeth on Him; who layeth Him for his only foundation; who builds only upon His blood and righteousness, upon what He hath done and suffered for us. On this cornerstone he fixes his faith, and rests the whole weight of his soul upon it. He is taught of God to say, 'Lord, I have sinned! I deserve the nethermost of hell.'"[198]

As already suggested, I believe Wesley's most outstanding contribution was his dual emphasis on both orthodoxy and orthopraxy. Right belief and right practice, a practice that applied the Gospel to the needs of society. A right relationship to God eventuated in a right relationship to one's fellow being, especially those persons lacking the basic necessities of life. Though Wesley was not an expositor, narrating the events of Christ's life, (he was a topical, logical, persuasive preacher) he was fully aware that close attention needed to be given to what Jesus actually did and said while he was on earth. Thus for Wesley, there is no false dichotomy between the historical Jesus and the Christological Jesus, between inwardly experiencing Jesus, and outwardly expressing Jesus, between the soteriological Jesus and the societal Jesus.

Holiness Hymnody

Soteriology was given primary importance in the hymnody developed by the American Holiness Movement: Phoebe Palmer, "The Cleansing Wave-1839;" Elisha Hoffman, "Are You Washed in the Blood-1878;" Robert Lowry, "Nothing But the Blood-1876;" Fanny Crosby, "Blessed Assurance-1873"; and Haldor Lillenas, "The Wonderful Grace of Jesus-1918." Lillenas was the quintessential hymn writer for the Church of the Nazarene, evidenced by the Church of the Nazarene operating Lillenas Publishing, one of the largest religious printed music producers in the world. He authored such popular camp meeting songs

---

[197] Ibid., Vol. II, 36.
[198] Ibid., Vol. II, 30.

with their emphasis on holiness, "Holiness Forevermore," and "Glorious Freedom," songs decreasingly sung in Nazarene gatherings.

Nothing is more representative of what the Holiness Movement believed than its hymnody, especially during the first half of the twentieth century. Its lyrics emphasized soteriological victory over sin and the full benefits of the Atonement realized here and now. Testimonies in song offered inward confirmation, solidifying assurance by lyrics and a melody line that could be sung every day of the week, a populist poetry that accented both theological truth and subjective experience. Just as in the days of the Wesleys, a theology that could be sung provided a 24/7 spiritual script such as Henry Gilmore's "He brought me out of the miry clay, He set my feet on the Rock to stay, He puts a song in my soul today, a song of praise, Hallelujah!"[199] But the strength of Nazarene hymnody was also its weakness. It was subjective, individualistic, egocentric, and somewhat exaggerated. For instance, in a Lillenas hymn, "Wonderful," while it does exalt Christ and the emphasis of a free and full salvation, Lillenas uses the personal pronoun, "I, me, mine," ten times in the three brief verses. The chorus gives witness to Christ's personal benefits,

> Wonderful, Wonderful Jesus is to Me,
> Counselor, Prince of Peace, Mighty God is He!
> Saving me, Keeping me, from all sin and shame,
> Wonderful is my Redeemer, Praise His Name![200]

The exception to the above was written by Lelia Morris, "Holiness Unto the Lord," which became the anthem of the Holiness Movement and particularly, the Church of the Nazarene.[201] Its lyrics are objective, biblical, ecclesiological, and evidenced the value of hymnody (as opposed to today's contemporary choruses) with a theological plot line. Phrases such as "Church of our God," "Children of Light," "Bride of the Lamb,"

---

[199] *Sing to the Lord*, (Kansas City: Lillenas Publishing Company, 1993) 412.

[200] Haldor Lillenas. "Wonderful," *Sing to the Lord* (Kansas City: Lillenas Publishing Company, 1993) 377. Haldor Lillenas is an outstanding example of the miraculous grace of God. He was born in Norway, raised in a South Dakota sod house and the back woods of Oregon, in abject poverty, who taught himself music and through a series of providential events, founded Lillenas Publishing. He sold ownership to Nazarene Publishing House, on the condition that he would continue to supervise its operation, which he did for twenty years, 1930-1950. See his autobiography: Haldor Lillenas. *Down Melody Lane: An Autobiography* (Kansas City: Beacon Hill Press, 1953).

[201] Lelia Morris. "Holiness Unto the Lord," in *Sing to the Lord*, 503.

emphasize the communitarian aspects of the Gospel, in that God did not become a man primarily to save individuals, but to redeem a Church. In the four verses and the chorus, Morris utilizes eight references or metaphors which substantiate the corporate nature of the Church. The exact correspondence between tempo, tune, and terminology served as a "Call to Arms," for the church militant striving to become the Church triumphant. It has been years since I have heard "Called Unto Holiness" sung in a Nazarene worship service or even camp meeting. I suppose it may still be dusted off for "District Assemblies," or other official Nazarene gatherings.

In a recent "Millennial Conference" in Kansas City drawing together approximately 2,000 pastors, February 2018, the plenary worship service contained nothing of traditional Nazarene hymnody. We seem bent on moving toward a generic evangelical worship experience, modeled by almost all growing mega churches: darkness, strobe lights, fog dispensers, loud music with no melody line and gargantuan flashing, pulsating techno screens. In other words just like a Justin Timberlake concert that my daughters attended last night. In this kind of worship venue there is little cognitive participation other than swaying and clapping. The testimony to holiness which was once learned and retained by poetic verse set to music and given to theological conviction has been left behind. Much of what happens within the "contemporary" worship service is no longer defined by participation but by the theatre of the spectacle. If that be so, then church and worship choices are dictated by whatever spectacle suits one's taste, mainly honed by age and culture rather than trans-generational theology. Even more critical, how does one parse out or distinguish the voice of the Holy Spirit within such an overwhelming appeal to the senses?

The issues involved in the above, "creation of a worship atmosphere," are more critical than simply being co-opted by the world, or providing a wide and user-friendly entrance for sinners, when neither would seem to be relevant to a gathering of Nazarene pastors. The more serious matter is an attempt to simulate the presence of God, or to by-pass the only means to reach God as stated by King David, "The sacrifices of God are a broken spirit: a broken and contrite heart O God, you will not despise" (Psalm 51:17). Contrition and contrivance are two very diverse avenues, the latter possibly equivalent to conjuring up God or approximating the presence of God. Manipulating God's presence, of which all religion including Christianity is occasionally guilty, approaches blasphemy. The human creation of divine ambience seems to be far removed from the power and the glory that overwhelmed holiness camp meeting attendees of a by-gone era, in spite of the heat, humidity, and other primitive conditions.

With the exception of Morris's hymns and possibly a few others, ecclesiology in holiness hymnody was almost non-existent. Also singing about social responsibility would have to wait until the liberal theology of Harry Emerson Fosdick's "God of Grace and God of Glory,"[202] and the Quaker theology of Elton Trueblood. The following by Trueblood cuts across the privatization of spiritual experience. "Save us now from satisfaction, When we are privately set free, Yet are undisturbed in spirit, By our brother's misery."[203]

Now is not the time to stop singing our theology and exalting Christ through song. Now is the time to delve into the life of Christ, giving close scrutiny to what he said and did. Some of the most rewarding and fruitful preaching can be done narrating the life of Christ and pondering some of his most baffling sayings and actions. Why did Jesus constantly violate Jewish law by healing on the Sabbath when he could have utilized some other day? Why did he embarrass a woman when she touched his garment for healing? Why did he curse a fig tree when it was not the season for figs? Why did he tell his disciples to sell their clothes and buy a sword? Why did he command Peter to go hook a fish and by doing so, both of them would be able to take care of their temple tax. You must be kidding. Peter had never used a hook in his life. What a gift God has left us! Homiletical possibilities explored and developed by sustained inquiries under the illumination of the Holy Spirit that will hold the attention of both the saved and lost in every age or place until Christ returns.

The difference between preaching Jesus and entire sanctification, as it has normally been taught, is that the latter is measurable and quantifiable. And, Jesus is not. How do we know when we are sufficiently and perfectly following in the footsteps of Christ? There is abandonment

---

[202] *Sing to the Lord*, 720.
[203] Ibid., 722.

in the Christian journey, but not arrival. Philip Yancey states concerning the Sermon on the Mount that it is an ideal towards which we should never stop striving. "It forces us to recognize the great distance between God and us, and any attempt to reduce that distance by somehow modifying its demands, misses the point altogether."[204] We must live within the paradox that we can know Christ but never fully know Him. As the Apostle Paul recognized his riches are "unsearchable," and his love "unfathomable" (Ephes. 3:8-11). We must be willing to live within the same paradox in which Jesus lived. Yancey writes,

> One day miracles seemed to flow out of Jesus; the next day his power was blocked by people's lack of faith. One day he talked in detail of the Second Coming; another he knew neither the day nor hour. He fled from arrest at one point and marched inexorably toward another. He spoke eloquently about peacemaking, then he told his disciples to procure swords. His extravagant claims about himself kept him at the center of controversy but when he did something truly miraculous, he tended to hush it up.[205]

As Elton Trueblood argued, "Lincoln was willing to live in the land of paradox; there is sternness, yet there is also tenderness, there is melancholy yet there is also humor. There is moral law, yet there is also compassion....The secret of rationality is the maintenance of the tension. The greatest possible mistake is the fatuous supposition that we have resolved it."[206] The no man's land of paradox is a piece of real estate on which Jesus often trod, but a territory which evangelicals and especially holiness types, have rarely frequented. In a world of sloganized sound bite, Tweeting, Instagram, Face Book, and Power Point, paradox may not play all that well. We may have to be content with more spiritually perceptive, howbeit smaller congregations.

---

[204] Philip Yancey. *The Jesus I Never Knew* (Grand Rapids: Zondervan, 1995) 144.
[205] Ibid., 23.
[206] Elton Trueblood. *Abraham Lincoln; Theologian of American Anguish* (New York: Harper and Row Publishers, 1953) 124.

Chapter 3:
Richard Taylor

The Patron Saint of the Holiness Movement

When Calvin Coolidge exited a church service, he was asked by a reporter as to the preacher's topic that morning. "Sin," Coolidge responded. "What did he say about it?" the reporter inquired. "He's against it," was Coolidge's terse reply.

Richard Taylor was against sin, an agenda primarily driven by three concerns. The broader issue was Calvinism's tendency to promote antinomianism via a faulty confidence in imputed righteousness and eternal security. His second concern was what he perceived to be a sinning American church, a cheap grace which did not take sin seriously enough, thus an affront to the holiness of God and a trifling and thankless treading on the blood of Christ. His immediate concern and probably most important to him was his own denomination, the Church of the Nazarene, as well as the wider Holiness Movement, which he believed to be losing its way because it decreasingly emphasized entire sanctification as a second work of grace equated with the baptism of the Holy Spirit. The bottom line for Taylor was that a second work of grace is the only adequate remedy for inbred sin. In 1965, Richard Taylor warned against the "gradual erosion of a clear-cut doctrine of inbred sin."[207] According to Taylor and other holiness exponents, the whole doctrine of entire sanctification rises and falls with the proposition of inherited depravity.

---

[207] Merne Harris and Richard S. Taylor, "The Dual Nature of Sin," *The Word and the Doctrine*. ed. Kenneth E. Geiger (Kansas City: Beacon Hill Press of Kansas City, 1966) 16. Also see George A. Turner. *The More Excellent Way* (Winona Lake, IN: Light and Life press, 1952), 76, and William Arnett, "Entire Sanctification," *The Asbury Seminarian* Vol. XXX (October, 1975) 33.

Taylor was a voluminous writer, producing some twenty-five books.[208] His style was precise, clear, logical, propositional, deductive, and at times, very quotable. Throughout his long productive life, beginning pastoral ministry at the age of nineteen and writing until the time he died at age 94, he served as a college president, seminary professor, editor, missionary, and speaker at countless seminars, camp meetings, revivals, and retreats. I would designate him as the "patron saint" of the conservative Holiness Movement during the latter half of the twentieth century. His colleague, Kenneth Grider, humorously claimed that Taylor was born without original sin, and was "straighter than straight."

Leo Thornton, President of Western Evangelical Seminary, Portland, Oregon, likened Taylor to a "great eagle" as he sat on a camp meeting platform. Others said he was the most like Jesus of any person they knew. Taylor was a man in control, in control of his appearance, speech, actions, mannerisms, and everything about him. Listen to the following advice in his 1962 book, *The Disciplined Life*:

> Shuffling feet and habitual slouch give people the vague, uneasy feeling that your mind shuffles and slouches too. An outward alertness in stance and carriage not only conveys a better impression, but tends to create the feeling of life and sparkle within you. Don't be stiff and starchy, forever standing on your dignity; nobody likes a prig. But stand tall, sit tall, walk tall and then even your laugh will have a wholesome "tallness" about it....Avoid the nervous shiftiness, the vacant look, the restless wandering which advertises a lack of concentration and interest - in fact, an undisciplined mind.[209]

There did not seem to be much incongruity between what Taylor professed and who he was. However, his pen could be somewhat trenchant, especially offending Calvinists, Pentecostals, and perhaps not having the most politically correct gender expressions or explanations to sufficiently please the women who sat under his teaching or preaching. I was the target of a couple of his rebukes. As the editor of *The Sounding Board*, the official publication of the Christian Holiness Association, a figurative position, to which I gave little attention, Taylor granted me full responsibility for its heresy. After the managing editor wrote a feminist interpretation of Genesis 1-3, Taylor approached me with the opening

---

[208] This is a conservative estimate. The NTS Library lists thirty-three book titles, but some are publications in Spanish and others reprints.

[209] Richard Taylor. *The Disciplined Life* (Kansas City: Beacon Hill Press, 1962) 83.

gambit: "When someone is driving a car correctly, I don't say anything, but when they make a mistake, I do." I had a made a mistake and Richard would now say something. (I will save the issue of the second confrontation until later.)

Background

Richard Shelly Taylor was born into a Quaker home in 1912, in Cornelius, Oregon, his father, a Friends pastor. The family became members of the Church of the Nazarene in 1925. At the age of 19, he married Amy Overby, a native of Norway, then living in Portland, Oregon. They had one biological son, David Richard, born in 1934, and adopted a son, Paul Wesley, born in 1944. Amy died in January, 1982, and Taylor subsequently married three times after that. His last wife was still living when he died in 2006. He was converted at age 10 at a Wednesday night prayer meeting in the Piedmont Friends Church, Portland, Oregon. When asked to what he contributed his success in life he answered, "To God's sanctifying grace, received by faith at about 17 years of age, which set my course towards spirituality, obedience, service and a passion for improvement. I early sought to learn to pray and find God's will for my life. Also I began studying the art of writing at about 14 years of age."[210] Taylor further testified, "God is central in my life. I seek to live in the atmosphere of God's consciousness and with his knowledge and approval." In 1984, Taylor recalled that his health had been poor most of his life. "I have had to husband my strength and time penuriously. I have been a strongly motivated person operating on weak batteries. Consequently, many times I have had to cast myself on the mercy of God for strength for the immediate task."[211] At the age of 72, Taylor took a thirty-one thousand mile trip, retracing where he had previously ministered in Australia and New Zealand, speaking 61 times in 46 days.

Taylor was in no way athletic growing up, even though his dad was an avid fisherman. The boy was content with his books and also became an excellent pianist. In later years, his voice always sounded hoarse, his vocal cords and esophagus having been damaged by swallowing some fish bones at the age of 43. According to his son Paul,

---

[210] Nazarene Archives, Richard Taylor Collection, "Personal Resume," 1984.
[211] Ibid.

he was continually gargling with whatever he thought would help or with whatever a doctor or pharmacist would suggest.[212] He never raised his voice while preaching, but instead would punctuate an emphasis by a raised index finger. His weak constitution did not prevent seventy-five years of almost unbroken ministry. A bit of psychohistory lends itself to the possibility that his discipline and perseverance were compensation for his physical limitations. Taylor would have believed with the apostle Paul, that "God's strength was made perfect in his weakness."

A Right Conception of Sin

Taylor may be best known for his book *A Right Conception of Sin*. Interestingly, that treatise was completed before he had earned any diploma beyond high school. He attended Northwest Nazarene College and had to drop out because of health. He did not earn a degree until 1940, a Th.B. in Religion from Cascade College in Portland, Oregon. *A Right Conception* was first published in 1939, at least part of it written some years before. He sent a partial manuscript to H. Orton Wiley, who encouraged him to finish it.

The content of this first publishing effort set a theological trajectory for his next sixty-five years of continuous literary output. On the first page of the first chapter, Taylor wrote a thesis statement that not only provided the cornerstone for *A Right Conception*, but for almost every other book he wrote. "And as Christians, if our conception of sin is faulty, our whole superstructure will be one error built on another, each one more absurd than the last, yet each one necessary if it is to fit in consistently with the whole erroneous scheme."[213] The problem must be understood before the solution can be understood, or confession must be made for the condition, in order for belief to take place for the remedy. Sin, both as an act and a condition, necessitates the one remedy, the atoning blood of Christ. According to Taylor, Calvinists believe in imputation rather than impartation, and once this imputation (salvation takes place), eternal security lapses into moral laxity or antinomianism. Taylor believed that "In the lives of the vast majority of Calvinists,

---

[212] Email from Paul Taylor August 8, 2016.

[213] Richard Taylor. *A Right Conception of Sin: Its Relation to Right Thinking and Right Living* (Kansas City: Beacon Hill Press of Kansas City, 1945) 9.

the general influence of the doctrines themselves has tended more to carelessness than to holiness."[214]

Obviously Taylor had no statistics to support the above assertion. He could only caricature the Calvinists who take a theology of election, irresistible grace and eternal security to its logical conclusion. "He (the Calvinist) does not believe in complete deliverance from all sin. In fact, in his doctrine, he holds that one may have awful sin in his life, but if he has at one time been generally regenerated, such sin will not produce the usual effect, eternal death."[215] But with one swoop of his pen, Taylor crosses out the caricature, with the admission that many Calvinists are better than their theology. "Really, the writer has a strong suspicion that there are many Calvinists who are *not* seeking to avoid the necessity of personal holiness and righteousness and are enjoying a walk with God far higher than their doctrines require..."[216]

At times, it is difficult to discern what definition of sin Taylor is using. The most often used word for sin in the New Testament is *hamartia*, which means "missing the mark." This is much different than Wesley's minimalist definition of sin as a "voluntary transgression of a known law of God." Taylor is well aware that sin can take place in the heart before an outward act is committed. Neither does he limit sin to commission, although "sins of commission" is what most of *A Right Conception* is about. Taylor accurately observed that, "Many feel they are not sinning because they are not actually doing anything that injures another. Their emphasis is all on the outward positive transgression of the law. But when we see that divine love is the standard, we become convicted of the sin of lovelessness."[217] Taylor does not clarify that sins of omission are much more difficult to identify than sins of commission. How much love is enough love for my wife, my children, the homeless, the impoverished in Bangladesh or the Muslim that lives down the street?

Taylor confesses that, "All of us Calvinists and Arminians alike, need to learn that the real quality of a man's spirit is often difficult for us mortals to measure. God is the only one who can judge accurately."[218] It

---

[214] Ibid., 20.

[215] Ibid., 23.

[216] Ibid., 39.

[217] Ibid., 72.

[218] Ibid., 105.

seems that Taylor is speaking concerning our assessment of other people, and does not address our inability to fully know ourselves. Immediately after the above quoted statement he says, "The main thing, then, is to see to it that we have a spirit which is blameless and is transparently pure in his sight. And thank God that we may have such a spirit and know that we have it."[219]

Taylor's Epistemology

Whether Taylor held to the above certitude for the rest of his life is unknown, or at least cannot be ascertained by reading his further writings, and since *A Right Conception* was written before he finished college, it is doubtful that he had analyzed his own epistemology, much less that of John Wesley, or the early Holiness Movement. Taylor never dealt with the historical and theological streams that found their confluence in Phoebe Palmer's parlor and the nineteenth century holiness camp meetings. I know of no one that argues against the assessment that nineteenth century American religious thought was grounded in "common sense realism." Sydney Ahlstrom argued that this philosophical influence popularized by the Scotch philosophers Thomas Reid and Dougald Stuart during the first two-thirds of the nineteenth century at least, was to become among American Protestants the chief philosophical support to theological and apologetic enterprises. "Because they did accord with the 'common sense' of all things, the Scottish philosophers produced in short, precisely the kind of apologetic philosophy that Christians in the Age of Reason needed."[220]

Common sense meant that the human mind could not only know the laws of the predictable Newtonian and Copernican universe, but also know the laws that operated within human consciousness. Taylor's certitude was knowingly or unknowingly grounded in the same philosophy that had provided a foundation for Phoebe Palmer's altar theology. But had Taylor come further along to William James, he would have encountered the possibility that this kind of spiritual certitude which he claimed may be impossible. James wrote, "Faith means belief in something concerning which doubt is still theoretically possible; and

---

[219] Ibid.

[220] Sydney Ahlstrom. *A Religious History of the American People* Vol. I (Garden City, NY: Image Books, 1975) 433.

as the test of belief is willingness to act, one may say that faith is the readiness to act in a cause the prosperous issue of which is not certified to us in advance."[221] Inward certitude concerning both justification and entire sanctification seemed to wax and wane for Wesley. Stephen Gunter perceptively writes that, "Though Wesley's crisis religious experience interiorized the meaning of justification by faith alone, but in his exuberance to communicate the newly found certainty of salvation, his sermons seemed to have induced more consternation then consolation."[222]

Sin and Entire Sanctification

Taylor did much qualifying of what entire sanctification would or would not do. Because of infirmities, diseases and limitations caused by the fall, entire sanctification was not a panacea for the brokenness of life. Much of what ails human existence bears no moral quality for good or bad and, thus, needs to be accepted as the essentials of human existence and the cost of living in a fallen world. The result of Adam's sin and separation from the presence of God was a depraved or degenerate moral nature. "Losing its health and perfection, his nature became diseased and warped and out of line. Inevitably, man's mind and body were greatly impaired because of this spiritual depravity and his continued sinning, so that he has become subject to countless mistakes of judgment, deficiency of knowledge, lapse of memory, faulty reasoning, and perceptive faculties, physical deformities, abnormalities, and peculiarities of temperament, disease, pain and decay."[223]

Such caveats allow much leeway for the sanctified: "In spite of all that's wrong with me, I'm sanctified anyway." But ironically, removing such defects from the moral category intensifies doubts as to whether one has been entirely sanctified. These doubts often lead to disillusionment: "I thought more or better than this was promised." In fact, Methodist Bishop Randolph Foster, who had served as the second President of Drew Theological Seminary, did claim that entire sanctification was a

---

[221] William James. "A Definition of Faith" in *Readings in the Psychology of Religion*, ed. Orlo Strunk, Jr. (Nashville: Abingdon Press, 1959) 196-197.

[222] Stephen Gunter. *The Limits of Love Divine: John Wesley's Response to Antinomianism and Enthusiasm* (Nashville: Abingdon, 1989) 72.

[223] Taylor. *A Right Conception*, 103.

panacea. Unfortunately, the following from Foster characterized much holiness preaching, "Holiness always begets happiness....Here, Christian, is the panacea, the cure for all your grief, for all sins. Take holiness into your bosoms and grief and sorrow and sin will flee from them. You will find rest - a rest, how sweet, how deep, how lasting."[224] To use the word "panacea" was one of the most egregious errors a holiness writer ever made.

This kind of preaching for many holiness preachers and professors ended in intense inner conflict and bewilderment. Though Taylor did at times make overstatements, he knew both himself and others to the extent he was not going to fall into this trap. The "panacea" promise was the credibility gap addressed by Mildred Wynkoop. A central emphasis for Taylor was to separate, unlike Augustine, what is inherent to human nature and what is not. For both Wynkoop and Taylor, concupiscence, being ruled by the flesh is not essential to human existence and can be remedied and removed from this life. Other human tendencies, as ugly as they may be, would have to be tempered and controlled: "True, the nerves lie very close to the moral nature, and must be watched or they will cause us to commit sin; still there is a difference between nerves and morality....Even after having been purified therefore, one may still have temperamental impulses and hence need to be disciplined and physical impulses which are natural and need to be controlled, none of which are essentially sinful."[225]

Taylor did his best to stay away from any definition or depiction of inbred sin (original sin) that suggested materiality or substance; as if a thing was being removed from a person by the Holy Spirit. (As I will later show, he did not do as well on this issue as he believed.) At times, he attempted a philosophically and psychologically nuanced view of original sin as a perversion, ordinate desires which outside of God's grace have become inordinate. The following is one of Taylor's most accurate and helpful passages, "We see therefore that the carnal nature is simply a bloated *self*. The natural instincts of human self-nature have become enlarged and distorted. There is an enlarged sense of one's own importance, a desire to have self-honored, a hyper-sensitiveness to

---

[224] Randolph Foster. *Christian Purity or the Heritage of Faith* (New York: Eaton & Mains, 1897) 315.

[225] Taylor. *A Right Conception*, 104.

injuries, a tendency to magnify the faults of others, and an inordinate tenacious love of one's own will, ideas and plans that causes (sic) him to be deeply depressed or violently rebellious or sullenly stubborn when they are repudiated."[226]

The above condition, Taylor believed as did both Wesley and Wynkoop, split churches, destroyed relationships, and brought contention, betraying the unity that Christ coveted for his followers. Taylor perceived a credibility gap no less than did Wynkoop: "This explains the feebleness and ineffectiveness of Churches today. They are small because the people are small. They are preoccupied with the petty. They move in a tea cup."[227] Taylor, no doubt, believed himself to be describing many holiness folk who claimed to be sanctified.

Taylor's Christology

One of the last books which Taylor wrote was *God's Integrity and the Cross*. This book and *A Right Conception* served as book ends on sixty years of writing. The first addressed the problem, and the second described the remedy, but both books worked with the same thesis: sin is a radical problem which demands a radical solution. The solution can be nothing less than a substitutionary-penal-ransom theory of the atonement. Other theories such as governmental, ethical satisfaction and moral influence hold some truth and are helpful in understanding God and His creation. But only a substitutionary-ontological-objective understanding is sufficient to explain the cross and is essential for our salvation, whether we understand it or not. "The position of this book is that Christ, by His death, paid the penalty for your sins and mine, and that this was inherently necessary. The divine sanctions were not waivered. Nothing is more biblical than the saying: 'The wages of sin is death;' either the sinner must die or a substitute must die. Christ died as our substitute, and his substitutive death was directly related to the penalty we deserved."[228]

---

[226] Ibid., 106.

[227] Ibid., 47.

[228] Richard Taylor. *God's Integrity and the Cross* (Nappanee, IN: Francis Asbury Press, 1999) 19.

A biblical scheme that preserves God's integrity is critical for Taylor: "The soul that sins will die." God must keep his word which preserves his holy character. God can not lie, thus the only way that integrity can be preserved, maintained and demonstrated is for him to accept the penalty and die in human kind's stead. Of course, in the Arminian scheme, the atonement, though universal, is efficacious only through faith and repentance by the individual who accepts God's gift and forgiveness. "[E]fficacy of the atonement is determined by the subject's response in allowing the power of redemption to have its fulfillment in her or him - a response made not as an automatic, but as a free moral agent."[229] Taylor is clear that right choice can only be free as enabled by grace. The individual outside of the willful conscious acceptance of God's gift is eternally lost. The individual is solely responsible for his/her fate either in Heaven or Hell, thus she is captain of her soul and master of her destiny. "This is true for we are the architects of our destiny. Even though God has declared his desire to save all of us, and has a benevolent design for each one, we can reject his plan and bring about our own destruction. For this we are solely to blame. Our eternal loss is a moral consequence of our rebellion."[230]

Taylor postulates several propositions that he believes to be essential to his penal-substitutionary theory, but more accurately he believes that these "truths" *demand* a penal- substitutional remedy.

a) The penalty for sin demands a blood sacrifice. "Sin brought the offender under the death sentence. The sinners' hope was in allowing the animal to bear the death sentence in his or her place."[231] This acceptance must be willful, knowledgeable and intentional. Thus, Christ's sacrifice is a universal provision for salvation, but not a universal actualization of that salvation.

b) God is love and the deepest most profound demonstration of love is that God would die in our stead. Christ is the only person born who did not sin, and since he did not deserve the penalty of death, he can accept ours. God did not deserve to die, but we do. Taylor quotes C.S. Lewis: "The humanitarian theory removes from Punishment the

---

[229] Ibid., 21.

[230] Ibid., 76.

[231] Ibid., 98.

concept of Desert. But the concept of Desert is the only connecting link between punishment and justice. It is only as deserved or undeserved that a sentence can be just or unjust."[232]

c) Sin is deserving of the wrath of God, its punishment. God's wrath has been poured out on us at Calvary around the year 30 C.E., a historical event. This event is the fulfillment, the logical conclusion of God's complete identification with human kind. It is critical for Taylor that God punishes sin; He enacts an eternal torment. This punishment is not passive on God's part leaving the sinner to his own demise or because the sinner is misaligned with God's absolute moral order to the extent that such friction brings eventual death.

d) Love alone cannot draw us to Christ. Pain or the threat of pain has to be real. Thus, those who have been bitten by a snake in the wilderness would be saved by gazing on a bronze serpent on a pole. Jesus used the analogical and historical event to illustrate and proclaim his death, "And as Moses lifted up the serpent in the wilderness, so must the Son of Man be lifted up (John 3:14)." We must not only look on a loving God giving himself for us, we must look on a vile serpent. Why? According to Taylor, "People who are recipients of kindness, feel like they 'have it coming,' that they 'deserve it,' that they take it for granted.... No, love alone will not soften the hard heart and turn people to God.... But pain will ."[233]

e) Christ's death is the purchase price; Satan is real and evil is real. Satan has humanity in bondage, and God on Calvary rescues us from that bondage. Part of the loosening of that bondage takes place in this life, and fully takes place in the next life because God has won the victory over death, hell and Satan. "Satan had not only a real claim to the planet, but access to every human heart to a tyrannical degree. The Son invaded his territory, because a man as exposed to Satan as others, fought him to a standstill in the wilderness, then destroyed his claim on the human race at Calvary."[234]

f) All of Taylor's theology flows into entire sanctification and, no less, the atonement. Entire sanctification is the ultimate accomplishment

---

[232] Ibid., 78.

[233] Ibid., 44-45.

[234] Ibid., 126.

of the atonement, at least in this life. Crucifixion is not simply a metaphor; only through Christ's crucifixion can we be crucified. Only through death with Christ can we become alive in Christ. The atonement of Christ enables the cruciform life. "The cross inspires the devotion; the Spirit internalizes it.... It is this identification and internalization which enables the believer to literally live by the cross 'principle.'"[235] The blood that flows from the cross is the only cleansing agent suitable and sufficient for sin.

The bottom line for Taylor is that the seriousness of sin demands the ultimate sacrifice. The sacrificial lamb would become God himself. Taylor has presented a view of the atonement consistent with both Reformation and Wesleyan theology. As in all of his writings, his Christology is a rebuke to Christianity lite, nominal Christianity that knows little of true repentance and restitution, a hypocrisy professing to follow Christ while at the same time rationalizing self-sovereignty. Taylor's religion has a cross in the middle of it, a cross that is becoming increasingly foreign to or forgotten by a materialistic American lifestyle legitimating Church. The cross is not a worldly symbol accented by floodlights, but the truth that most separates or should separate the world from the Church. As a colleague of mine once said, "Everything looks paltry at the foot of the cross." Without the perspective of the cross, my accomplishments, even my works of righteousness become "hay, wood and stubble." The cross is an uncomfortable place, a vantage point from which many "Christians" are not willing to adopt what it truly represents, death. Taylor's brief book challenges and inspires, and more importantly raises potential questions. Do I abhor sin to the extent the cross demands? Am I crucified with Christ? Am I trampling the blood of Christ by tolerating sin in my life? These are not only optimal questions, but essential for being in and spreading the Kingdom.

Questions and Issues Raised

There are several places that I take issue with Taylor, which are not so much a full frontal disagreement, but possibly areas that he did not fully explore or qualify. In order for him to place full responsibility for one's eternal destiny on the individual, he precludes a confluence of factors that contribute to a person's choice. He fails to raise the question

---

[235] Ibid., 124.

as to why some persons are more likely to become Christian than others. It is questionable that Paul preached the wrath of God before he preached the love of God, as Taylor argues. Do these two truths need to be chronological? Do not most people have a realization of guilt, real ontological guilt which produces fear, anxiety, and a sense that I am due punishment? Taylor states, "Before the sight of Calvary as Hope, must come the sight of Calvary as Wrath.[236] When African children watch the Jesus film, and are moved to tears by seeing the "No Greater Love," than they have ever seen depicted before, are they moved by love or wrath? With all due respect, Taylor's claim that the unsaved are not moved by love is dead wrong. Loving those that do not love us and praying for those who despitefully use us, is Jesus' methodology for saving the world. Paul wrote, "If your enemy is hungry, feed him; if he is thirsty, give him something to drink. In doing this, You will heap coals of fire on his head" (Romans 12:20).

Another point of contention I have with Taylor is his tendency to depreciate justification in order to necessitate entire sanctification. Taylor writes, "Only the inward experience of the new covenant in its full riches can enable us to rejoice in God. Without this fullness, we may believe in God, fear Him, be thankful to Him, and seek to obey Him, but we do not rejoice in Him."[237] Why this needless dichotomy? My mother said that after she was saved, she "walked on air for weeks." No event in life calls for more rejoicing and thanksgiving than passing from the Kingdom of Darkness into the Kingdom of Light.

My main problem with Taylor's atonement theology is not anything that he explicitly says, but the overall tone of the book. I am left with the impression that acceptance and appreciation of the atonement is an American individualist enterprise. There is little in this book which suggests communal salvation so evident on the Day of Pentecost, the Church as described in the latter part of Acts 2 and the familial salvation experienced by the household of Cornelius, Acts 10. There is truth to the concept that society can only be changed one by one, but it is only a partial truth. Systemic problems of race, addiction, class, national identity and political currents certainly play a part as to whether one accepts or rejects Christianity. Two months ago, I was in a refugee camp

---

[236] Ibid., 41.
[237] Ibid., 122.

of almost one million people. All individualism as Americans profess and practice it has been stomped out. The solidarity of evil and solidarity of holiness has been lost on the American church, and Taylor's atonement explication has done little to correct that. What did Paul mean when he said, "For the unbelieving husband has been sanctified through his wife and the unbelieving wife has been sanctified through her husband? Otherwise, your children would be unclean, but as it is, they are holy (I Corinthians 7:14)." Is it likely that one part of the family will go to hell and the other to heaven? This question we will explore in another of Taylor's books.

Taylor's Pentecostal Theology and Entire Sanctification

Taylor's *Life in the Spirit* is his most explicit argument for a holiness ethic, how it is accomplished and applied in the life of the believer. Taylor forthrightly contends that a person can become holy no other way than the baptism of the Holy Spirit which is the second work of grace eradicating inbred sin. This formulation identified Taylor as a conservative within the traditional Holiness Movement and perhaps its primary spokesman and writer within the latter half of the twentieth century. Indeed, Richard Taylor was a household name among those who attended holiness camp meetings, the conventions of the Christian Holiness Association, and in particular those who attended the Inter-church Holiness Convention meeting annually in Dayton, Ohio.

For Taylor, though the word eradication is not used in the Bible, remedial terms such as purify, circumcise, and sanctify suggest the term. These operations of the Holy Spirit will not take place at the point of justification, because of the limitations of the human psyche to reckon with or receive forgiveness and cleansing at the same time. Or to put it another way, in justification, the sinner is asking for forgiveness by way of repentance and faith. In the second work of grace, the person receives the baptism of the Holy Spirit by way of faith and consecration. Taylor writes, "The two phases of redemption available in this life justification and entire sanctification - the pardon of personal sins, and the purging of inherited sinfulness - are so momentous in themselves and so profoundly different, that the accomplishment of both in a single religious experience would be highly improbable as a characteristic norm in the divine plan."[238] Notice that he didn't say impossible and neither did Wesley.

For Taylor, the baptism of the Holy Spirit, Pentecost, and entire sanctification are one and the same event, both in time and essence. Taylor is clear that at the new birth one receives the Spirit, but at Pentecost one is filled or baptized with the Spirit. The secondness of the baptism of the Holy Spirit is predicated on Taylor's primary thesis: "There is not one instance in the book of Acts of Spirit infilling where there is no evidence of some measure of prior spiritual life."[239] (The problem with this statement is that before regeneration there is evidence of prior spiritual life, prevenient grace.) Before Pentecost the disciples were doubting, quarreling, cowardly, and jockeying for power. After Pentecost the disciples "were bursting forth of spiritual vitality, the pushing back of the horizon, the spiritual understanding and insight, the deliverance from the paralyzing fears and tensions, the perfect unity of spirit and fellowship, the clear-eyed, pure-hearted, undivided allegiance to Jesus Christ, the calm courage in public identification, the buoyancy of spirit in facing peril and loss, the disregard of all selfish consideration."[240]

In contrast to the robust-post-Pentecost description of the disciples, Taylor fully admits that there are "sanctified Christians" who do not consistently evidence these qualities. Taylor claims that "the negative traits for the sanctified aren't as 'severe' as they are for only the justified. Unpleasant understandings are still possible. Divine love draws and holds people together, but does not instantly polish the exterior or avoid the pain of sharp edges and rough surfaces that they may feel in their *very togetherness*."[241] Most of the sharpness and roughness is due to temperament. "[I]n spite of grace, discipline and maturity, the basic characteristics of natural temperament will always cling to us as the framework of our style of personality."[242] Temperament may be characterized by volatility rather than cheerfulness, impulsiveness rather than patience, and melancholy rather than joy. These jagged surfaces can only be evened out by mature growth and grace. Immature people, even

---

[238] Richard Taylor. *Life in the Spirit: Christian Holiness in Doctrine, Experience and Life* (Kansas City: Beacon Hill Press, 1966) 86.

[239] Ibid., 83.

[240] Ibid., 81.

[241] Ibid., 154.

[242] Ibid., 157.

the sanctified, often cannot tell the difference between the important and unimportant, the essentials and nonessentials. "Mature people are known as such by their ability to sort the important from the trivial, and to react emotionally as such experience deserves. This maturity is also an ability to keep even justifiable emotion from so unhinging us, so that we are unable to fill our role as responsible adults."[243]

Taylor's Holiness Ethic

From this writer's perspective, Taylor's above observations leave us with a couple of ironies. First, because of culture, education, personal discipline and etiquette some unsanctified Christians may seem more holy than the so-called sanctified. Second, holiness people often display a penchant for not being able to discern the important from the non-important, the essential from the non-essential, which produced rules and regulations (legalism) far more crippling than enabling. Taylor was aware of this liability when he comically but tragically told of a woman in a holiness church who had an affair outside of her marriage, but minimized her sin by claiming at least she did not cut her hair.

To Taylor's credit, in this one book, he does his best job of moving from holiness as something or things we do not do, to a holiness ethic consisting of what we should do, especially in relation to others. What is our responsibility to credible institutions such as government and corporations which provide employment, to whom we pay taxes and give a full day's work? Taylor's questions are penetrating: "Were we completely honest in that car deal, or in the selling of the house, or trading the old washer for the new one, (a bit dated) or giving our medical history when applying for insurance?"[244]

Taylor is also correct that when moral lines are not that clear (There was no speed limit on interstates in the first century,) we are thrown on the law of love. "When the law itself is ambiguous, we can let love take over. After all, love, and love alone is a dynamic of Christian ethics. It is both the motivating drive and the arbiter."[245] But he does confess, "In the world of taxes, corporations, dividends, overtime, fringe

---

[243] Ibid., 157.

[244]

[245]

benefits, coffee breaks, insurance laws, easy divorce, traffic laws, time payments, lawsuits, business protocol, et cetera, life can become very complicated indeed. In the confused array ethical ambiguities can arise which would puzzle a Solomon."[246]

Taylor's social ethic is not escapist, isolationist, or separatist. Sanctified people are conscientious citizens, concerned about those who are materially impoverished, exploited, and economically disadvantaged. Unfortunately, Taylor only gives one paragraph as to how holiness people can be world changing rather than world retreating. He gives no historical evidence as to how nineteenth century social endeavors were grounded in themes of sanctification, which Timothy Smith, Norris Magnuson, David Moberly, Donald Dayton, and a host of others have clearly shown. My present assessment, which I confess may be harsh and judgmental, is that the contemporary Holiness Movement, if there be such a thing, exhibits historical amnesia.

Taylor is helpful in two specific areas which have been troublesome and controversial for those who claim to be sanctified; the essence of temptation and the wholesomeness of sex. In order for temptation to take place, there must be strong and illicit desire, plus the capability of carrying out that desire. The desire to go to Mars is not a temptation, but only wishful thinking for most of us. I suppose that too much time living in a fantasy world would be a sin, but that may cross out the Christianity of C.S. Lewis and J.R.R. Tolkien. Taylor accurately interprets that the temptations that Satan threw at Jesus in the wilderness resonated with Jesus as legitimate desires. But to yield would have been sin because underlying these suggestions was the primal temptation of Christ, proving himself, which would have been yielding to Satan's plan rather than the Father's plan. (Perhaps at this point, we would need to reference Maslow's "hierarchy of needs" to understand why proving oneself is more important to some than others. However, there is not only a pecking order in academic institutions, even in the most primitive tribes.)

I take exception to Taylor's explanation of the difference between lust as temptation and lust as sin. He suggests that temptation becomes

---

[246] Ibid., 172.

sin when the decision has been made, "I would if I could."[247] Certainly in our voyeuristic, pornographic, sex-obsessed world, there is the occurrence of sin in leering, objectifying, and fantasizing before and after, than "If I could have her, I would." This line is very difficult to draw and has been problematic for every male in the history of earth who possesses legitimate sexual desire and even for those the Christian considers illegitimate. Henri Nouwen confessed to struggling with homosexuality all of his life but never yielding to the temptation. It is in this specific area, sexuality, that Taylor demonstrates a sensitivity and a nuancing that places him ahead of his times, or at least ahead of those who counted him as their guru. "This divine grace - even sanctifying grace - does not change our bodies or deep freeze their glandular process. Therefore the holy person may still feel the sex urge whether married or unmarried and at improper times as well as proper."[248]

If Taylor's followers carefully read him, they would have been released from some unnecessary guilt feelings. He wrote, "Sex in itself has a strong pleasurable appeal; no normal person feels repugnance from it naturally."[249] For we who are married, the line between giving and getting is so difficult to define, that the following from Taylor is almost impossible to constantly and faithfully realize: "This divine love turns a husband or a wife into an unselfish and spiritually minded partner, who is more concerned about his companion's happiness than his own, and more concerned about everyone's eternal spiritual welfare than about earthly pleasure."[250] We may be tempted to agree with M. Scott Peck that sex is one of God' most fiendish inventions. Hopefully we will not find it so fiendish as to resort to the early Church Father Origin's solution. Look it up!

Taylor's Gender Miscues

If Taylor is ahead of his time in discussing sex, women would probably assess him as behind the times in his theology of gender. In his section on "Woman's supreme role" he claims, "Even when married, a

---

[247] W. T. Purkiser, Richard S. Taylor, and Willard H. Taylor. *God, Man, and Salvation* (Kansas City: Beacon Hill Press of Kansas City, 1977) 276.
[248] Taylor. *Life in the Spirit*, 197.
[249] Ibid., 197.
[250] Ibid., 198.

woman's supreme purpose is not to bear children, or to satisfy sexually either herself or her husband. It is to help her husband be the kind of man he ought to be, and 'get to heaven.'"[251] Such was the case for Taylor's first wife, Amy. Family members and Taylor himself have testified that Amy's life was totally oriented around her husband.

> I was very fortunate in the young woman I married, for none could have been more suited for roughing it in small churches, small salaries, evangelistic work; pulling up stakes and going back to school, pinching pennies, doing without money often, and doing it all cheerfully and efficiently, than my first wife, Amy. Without her sacrificial spirit, her complete oneness with me and absolute commitment to the ministry, and her managerial abilities, I could have never earned four degrees (with a family), and accomplished the writing and other things it has been my privilege to do.[252]

Richard Taylor was a fortunate man, and was correct in expressing his gratitude; no doubt a marriage made in heaven. But he was wrong to impose this role upon women as a universal standard. Such was not the case for many women in the Bible: Deborah, Mary Magdalene, Dorcas, Priscilla, and I am not even sure, for Mary, the mother of Jesus. The nineteenth century Holiness Movement, perhaps more than any other American religious strain, exemplified women who found purpose other than taking care of their husbands: Phoebe Palmer, Frances Willard, Martha Inskip, Hannah Smith, and Elizabeth Cady-Stanton. In Taylor's world, a single woman would not be fulfilled.

Taylor commits a double fault with women. He admonishes women about dress and has little or nothing to say about men. This has caused "holiness" women needless anxiety, pain, and expended energy by focusing on just what a sanctified woman is to wear and how much of it. This has been one of the primary fallacies of the Holiness Movement and provides exhibit A for majoring on minors. Guilt plagued legalism has been the result and Taylor does not provide much help.

---

[251] Ibid., 194.
[252] "Personal Resume," (December, 1984).

Other Miscues, in Particular Eradication

In three other areas I take issue with Taylor, the first two minor, and the third major. The first minor concerns his exuberant description of the apostles as totally changed personalities after Pentecost. After the entrance of Steven and Phillip into a Pentecostal ministry in Acts 6, the conversion of Paul in Acts 7, and the commissioning of Paul and Barnabas in Acts 13, the original twelve (of course Matthew for Judas) are reduced to almost zero sum in the Biblical account. We are left to myth, legend, and scanty historical detail. What we do know is that Peter who preached with such boldness still exhibited his cowardly prejudice. (This may have been sin improperly so-called.) Paul recalled that "Before certain men came from James, we used to eat with the Gentiles. But when they arrived, he began to draw back and separate himself from the Gentiles because he was afraid of those who belonged to the circumcision group. The other Jews joined him in his hypocrisy, so that by their hypocrisy even Barnabas was led astray" (Gal. II: 12-13).

The epicenter for Christianity's centrifugal force would soon shift from Jerusalem to Antioch. Acts 8:1 will forever remain a mystery: "On that day (Steven's stoning) a great persecution broke out against the Church at Jerusalem and all except the apostles were scattered throughout Judea and Samaria." The corporate twelve seemed to have been left behind.

Another minor issue is found in Taylor's exploring love's requirements for treating others. "The Ten Commandments forbid certain actions because these actions are not only unfair but injurious. They hurt others. In some way, they deprive their victims of some God-given right. They are actions which mainly obstruct someone in his pursuit of life, liberty, and happiness."[253] Allowing himself to fall into this Jeffersonian-Deistic-humanistic black hole is almost unpardonable. Better stated, sin is anything that obstructs someone from realizing their God given potential in Jesus Christ. The translators of the authorized King James were wise enough not to allow any word in the original to be translated "happy" or "happiness." (I realize that John Wesley and many others in the Holiness Movement associated holiness with happiness,

---

[253] Ibid., 178.

but I do not have space philosophically or psychologically to explore this half-truth.)

I take major issue with Taylor's insistence on the word "eradication" as the most accurate and representative metaphor for depicting God's transforming transaction within the human personality. His main illustration consists of light being eradicated from a room.[254] It seems that he has mixed metaphors. For Taylor dispel and eradicate mean the same thing; he needed a dictionary. Dispel comes from the Latin *dispellere* meaning to drive asunder leaving the possibility that it may return. Eradicate also comes from Latin, *eradicare*, meaning to root out. If something is rooted out, there is no possibility of it returning. I spent a summer pulling up oak stumps, sectioning the roots, crawling under the stump to cut the tap root, and then prying the stump out. I removed somewhere between fifty and one hundred stumps that summer. Over a half century later, not one of them has grown back. Dispelling darkness is placing something in the darkness that is not there, light. Eradicate means to remove something that is already present.

How Taylor argues for eradication and at the same time argues against materiality, or any kind of substantive representation of inbred sin, to this writer seems a contradiction. This leads me to my second reproof from Richard Taylor; his rebukes were always gentle and nothing other than Christian. As the Director of the D. Min. program at Nazarene Theological Seminary, I had allowed a dissertation that had focused on a substantive definition of sin. The student was not arguing for the biblical or theological truth of his perspective, but only that a particular educational institution had consistently held to this position. Taylor was not quoted in the dissertation, but two of his books were included in the bibliography. Though he did not explicitly say so, I was left with the conclusion that Taylor did not want to be associated with a substantive interpretation of inbred sin. This would have been the case since Taylor is held in high esteem by the particular institution which the dissertation examined. He blamed me for letting the dissertation pass.

But the above technicalities, or one might say, semantics, are not the real problems. My reader is no doubt aware that all metaphors and analogies do not have to be completely consistent in order to be

---

[254] Ibid., 62.

helpful or accurate. And all metaphors hold within them an inherent law of diminishing returns regarding communication. But words do carry ideas and ideas do matter for better or worse. When I was a student at Asbury Theological Seminary, my Harvard Ph. D. professor told the following story: He was particularly allergic to poison oak, and a vine of it grew in his yard. He had tried several remedies to eradicate the poison oak, but it kept returning. Just before he was to perform a wedding for a former student, he contacted it, leaving his face covered with rash as if he had stuck his face in a burning bush. He decided to take violent action, i.e., administer the final, ultimate solution. He dug the poison oak out with a backhoe. He then poured gallons of gas into the hole, lighting it on fire. After the trench was entirely scorched and gutted, he poured several hundred pounds of salt into the hole. He then recovered the hole. After leveling the ground, he hired a concrete company to pour a patio over the place where the poison oak had grown. Is it possible that such a narrative might leave the hearer with a false sense of confidence? After all, our first parents, without original sin and living in the Garden of Eden, fell to sin. The Garden of Eden was not nearly as foolproof or failsafe as my professor's backyard.

Taylor's Treatment of "Sarx"

In 1972, Nazarene Publishing House commissioned W. T. Purkiser, Richard Taylor, and Willard Taylor to write a biblical theology. Because of its deductive method, the authors' endeavor should probably be defined as more a systematic theology than a biblical theology. I do not find evidence that the Bible gave direction to the whole of the project or that inductive study yielded some new insight which would have preempted theological perspectives that were already in place. Proof texting was the primary methodology, if not the only methodology for the 675 pages of text, and the approximate thirty-five hundred verses which were referenced, some multiple times. In other words, the authors used Scripture to support the official dogma (party line) of the Church of the Nazarene.

Out of the thirty-four chapters in the book, Richard Taylor wrote twelve, and it is no surprise that one of Taylor's chapters was "Man in Sin." The essence of sin is self-sovereignty and self-idolatry. Thus, Taylor intends to deny any hint of sin's empirical existence, original or inherent.

"It goes without saying, of course, that sin is not an entity or any kind of substance in the soul, in spite of Paul's persistent personification of it, as if it were an independent agent."[255]

The above self-sovereignty results in the flesh gaining ascendency over the mind and for his proof text Taylor chooses Roman 7. When Paul uses the word "I," according to Taylor, he is not speaking of himself, but the plight of anyone. The text raises several questions, not adequately answered by Taylor or perhaps anyone else. Highly problematic is verse 22, "For in my inner being I delight in God's law; but I see another law at work in the members of my body, waging war against the law of my mind and making me a prisoner of the law of sin at work within my members."[256] The Greek word for delight, *synedoma*, is used only this one time in the New Testament. Arndt and Gingrich translate the phrase "I joyfully agree with the law".[257] My first question: Is this the biblical law or Kant's "starry skies above and the moral law within?" My second question asks why I delight in blueberry pie more than apple pie? It may have something to do with my taste buds, or my mother's ability to make a blueberry pie more appealing than an apple pie. Isn't delighting in the law of God, delighting to do God's law? Is there a higher state of grace than delighting to do God's will? Taylor perceptively asks, "What could be more schizophrenic than the situation as Paul summarizes it?"[258] Taylor then states that "The polarity of sin is stronger than the polarity of reason?"[259] I ask, is delight more associated with affection or reason? Fighting against the mind that delights is the flesh or *sarx*. It seems that if universal sinful man should delight in anything, it would be the flesh. Does Paul mean that he hates the pleasures of the flesh? Or rather that he feels guilty after having submitted to it?

---

[255] W.T. Purkiser, Richard Taylor, and Willard Taylor. *God, Man and Salvation*. (Kansas City: Beacon Hill Press of Kansas City, 1977) 299.

[256] Colleague, friend and New Testament scholar Andy Johnson opines that Paul is speaking of a faithful Jew's normal respect for the law, which ended in disillusionment in that it did not bring spiritual victory as promised in the Old Testament. This was also the interpretation of my colleague, friend, and theologian Albert Truesdale. But again I remind the reader that the Greek word used here for delight is an unusually strong word.

[257] William F. Arndt, and F. Wilbur Gingrich. *A Greek-English Lexicon of the New Testament and Other Early Christian Literature* (Chicago: The University of Chicago Press, 1957) 797.

[258] Taylor. *God, Man and Salvation*, 293.

[259] Ibid.

I am presently reading *The Push*, a memoir by Tommy Caldwell, the most accomplished rock climber in the world, having conquered what was thought to be an impossible "free ascent," the Dawn Wall located in Yosemite National Park. He places his fingers in barely perceivable cracks, and pulls himself up without aide, pick or pulley. The training and discipline required to do this is beyond my imagination; "keeping the body under," the phrase used by Paul in 1 Cor. 9:27 (KJV) has never been surpassed. Caldwell confesses, "Perhaps more than most pursuits, climbing is self-glorifying and self-serving. As we ascend, we risk becoming our own God."[260] Caldwell has conquered the flesh, or what are particular manifestations of the flesh. He has not conquered the flesh which is an extension of his ego. But his confession might lead us to believe that his finitude on the face of a granite wall grants more self-awareness than professions of holiness.

Taylor has gotten the self-sovereignty right, but not necessarily its manifestation. Docetic or not, Gnostic or not, Manichean or not, Platonic or not, Christianity has always had problems as to what to do with the body. Paul in his single state, which he believed superior to marriage, a stance which most clergy adopted early in the life of the church and has continued in Roman Catholicism, and the myriad expressions of monasticism have not helped us.

Strangely, Paul does not identify this law in his members (bodily parts) working against the law of God until the last verse of Chapter 7 which he identifies as *sarx*. (Of course there were no chapters and verses when Paul wrote this.) He then uses the word *sarx* eleven times in the first thirteen verses of Chapter 8. Is the law of the spirit and the law of the flesh as dichotomous as Paul seems to make it, or as we have interpreted it? Or is it a matter of balance which at times is difficult to define in sex, eating, exercise, recreation, etc.? (Of course, Paul understood nothing about testosterone. The single test for differentiating between a man and a woman used by the Olympic Committee is the amount of testosterone in the bloodstream. A man normally possesses four times as much testosterone as a woman.)[261] For the Holiness Movement, the

---

[260] Tommy Caldwell, *The Push: A Climber's Search for the Path* (New York: Penguin Publishing Group) 48.

[261] David Epstein. *The Sports Gene: Inside the Science of Extraordinary Athletic Performance* (New York: Portfolio/Penguin, 2014) 70.

either-or-ness of entire sanctification is predicated on the either-or-ness of the Spirit versus the flesh. The expectation of Spirit-controlled automation over the body can lead to disillusionment. For that reason, we need to follow Paul's confession to the most fleshly church he ever pastored or founded: "I beat my body and make it my slave so that after I have preached to others, I myself will not be qualified for the prize" (I Cor. 9:27). Obviously, Paul thought this rational awareness and choice could only be enabled by the Holy Spirit. (Holiness folk, often living in the Midwest and South, have not been exemplary in diet, a critical issue for the flesh.)

Confusingly, Taylor somehow believed that the body is not a necessary apparatus for psychological and spiritual growth. "Only secondarily and temporally, does he inhabit a fleshly body....the body of flesh and blood we now possess is viewed as an accessory, not necessary for either manness or personhood."[262] I'm not sure that Taylor really believed this in that the uniqueness of Christianity is not found in a belief in immortality, but the resurrection of the body and somehow its personal identity after this earthly life. Taylor's position is in stark contrast to Dallas Willard's argument that the body is essential to spiritual growth and utilizing the means of grace.[263]

Relationships and Moral Freedom

Taylor, in order to guarantee moral freedom, and individual culpability or responsibility, diminishes the power of relationships in determining moral behavior. He writes, "For to overemphasize man as a creature *in* relationships is to lead to a concept of him as a creature of relationships. This is pure determinism."[264] I perceive this to be an overcorrection to relational theology which was popular in the 1970s and an overreaction to any kind of determinism. When Taylor speaks of determinism, he no doubt has in view Skinner's behavioralism or Freud's Oedipus Complex, some unified theory which explains all of life as automatic outcomes which are non-negotiable. In pure determinism the human being's behavior is totally programmed by forces over which

---

[262] Taylor. *God, Man.* 262.

[263] Dallas Willard. *The Spirit of the Disciplines: Understanding How God Changes Lives* (San Francisco: HarperCollins, 1988).

[264] Ibid., 265.

the individual has no control: his genes, his environment, his instincts and urges, anything and everything which impinges on his identity or thinking at any given moment.

Although a Christian worldview combats any kind of ironclad determinism, we all believe in some kind of determinism, especially Christians who express gratitude for parents who nurtured them, neighbors who took them to church, or Godly grandparents who prayed for them. But unfortunately, if someone has been a social worker in the poorest county in America, which I have, or been in some of the world's largest refugee camps, which I have, or led work crews to the inner city, which I have, one begins to suspect that there are sinister forces that are pulling towards Hell rather than Heaven, or at least creating a hell here on earth, not entirely of the individual's own doing. In order to maintain personal responsibility, mea-culpability, one does not have to create the autonomous individual charting his own course. An over emphasis on moral freedom produces pride and lack of empathy and especially loses the humility which states both in word and deed, "There but by the grace of God go I."

My wife had to appear in court the other night for a traffic violation. Upon pleading guilty, paying our fine and leaving, Brenda asked a perceptive question, "Why are all those people poor" (or at least look poor)? Most of them requested a "continuance" because they could not pay their fine or they need further legal help because of the seriousness of their infraction. Does poverty lead to breaking the law or does breaking the law lead to poverty? Probably neither would fall under a definitive and certain prediction, but a correlation cannot be denied. Taylor affirms this when he writes, "Only an infinite God can perceive without error the interwoven lines of responsibility, the multiple vectors of influence, and the shades of motives and intention that comprise the moral fabric of human life. In the scales will be placed endowment and opportunity, deception and innocence, malice and simplicity, pretense and sincerity."[265]

Taylor's Eschatology

---

[265] Ibid., 658.

In defense of Taylor, his eschatology is non-dogmatic and escapes or transcends the present-day enamourment with dates, the anti-Christ, and the contemporizing of symbols found in The Book of the Revelation. He also takes a jab at evangelical folk religion depicting heaven as a family reunion. "Whether family and friendship groupings that have been precious in the Lord on earth will in any measure be resumed as preferred society, we do not know not?"[266] Taylor fails to pursue this inquiry, which begs the question, "What about streams of consciousness throughout eternity for both God and persons? If I make heaven, will I note that someone I dearly love is not there? Does God shut off his omniscience regarding the millions who are suffering in Hell? Evidently, the temporal understanding of consciousness, according to Taylor, will somehow extend into eternity. "Whatever may be the case with God, eternity in relation to man is not incompatible with time in the sense of consciousness or succession of events; finite creatures could scarcely exist in meaningful activity without these modes."[267]

Meaningful activity in this life is what makes Heaven so difficult to comprehend. My air-conditioned bedroom is much more enjoyable because I have born the heat of the day. Is there no heat of the day, sweat of the brow in Heaven? Will no one in Heaven ever know the joy of finding the lost coin after sweeping and searching diligently? Will I know the fulfillment of reaching the mountain top because my legs have ached and my lungs have sucked air when I climbed it? In a sense, we cannot imagine if we think carefully of a world better than the one we live in. So Leibnitz may have been right, that this is the best of all possible worlds. (But this insight simply suggests my provincialism, because I do not live in a majority world country.) Or is it that our finitude cannot grasp the infinite? In trying to establish a definitive track between this world and the next, Taylor derails. "He creates in us a 'bit of heaven' that becomes our spiritual sensor of invisible realities, generating a honing extinct that keeps pulling us onward....This he does by acclimating us to heavenly joys and occupations."[268] Much, if not most of the world, is without this acclimation, certainly the one billion people who go to bed hungry every night, and the twenty-six thousand children who die of starvation every day.

---

[266] Ibid., 671.

[267] Ibid., 662.

[268] Ibid., 670.

Taylor particularly struggles in trying to define and set up God's Kingdom on earth. The Kingdom of God for Taylor is essentially futuristic with little to no realization on earth. His pessimism for here and now may be correct. The percentage of the world's adherents to Christianity over the last century has remained static at approximately thirty-two percent, while Islam has almost doubled its market share from twelve percent to twenty-two percent. If one accepts Taylor's scheme that reaching Heaven is predicated on a rational individual choice to accept and follow Christ as Savior, Hell is becoming increasingly populated. At the present time, Christian attitudes toward Muslims is doing little to reverse this global phenomenon.

Though Taylor's eschatology is mostly futuristic, he does believe in Kingdom realization here and now. "With divine power it penetrates and infiltrates itself among the Kingdoms of the world."[269] He gives little to no hint as to how this is to be practically accomplished or as to what it would look like. He makes no reference to the social gospel, a faithful attempt by such persons as Washington Gladden, Walter Raushenbusch, and Charles Sheldon who provided snapshots of the Kingdom. I think that I have had glimpses of the Kingdom at Wayne Gordon's Church in North Lawndale, Illinois and Chris Simmons' Cornerstone ministries in Dallas, Texas, not to speak of a village in India, a *ger* in Mongolia, and a brush-arbor church in Malawi.

A "Psychology" of Holiness

The strength of Taylor's *Understanding Ourselves: Acquiring a Christian Mind: Biblical Studies in the Psychology of Holiness* is his challenge for the Christian to be informed and to think clearly. He has brought to the forefront an issue that has become even more critical since he wrote, "We tend, most of us, to allow our minds to go with the tide, carried along with the world's agenda....we are bombarded daily with logical fallacies, many of them diabolically designed to deceive."[270] Taylor wrote this before tweets, blogs, Facebook, Snap chat, Instagram, and all of the lies and uninformed opinions that daily besiege us. Critical

---

[269] Ibid., 623.

[270] Richard S. Taylor. *Understanding Ourselves: Acquiring a Christian Mind: Biblical Studies in the Psychology of Holiness* (Salem, OH: Schmul Publishing Company, 1997) 36-37.

and informed thinking is rushing towards extinction. Taylor is overly optimistic by predicting, "When we once awaken to the greatness of the mind, and what it means to love God with the mind, we will never again be content with mental mediocrity."[271] Alas, the Christian community majors in mental mediocrity and has adopted a partisan conservativism controlled by Fox News and the Republican party. Fox News might not be any more wrong than CNN or NPR, but to think dialectally or to articulate both sides of an issue, is beyond the average Evangelical and in particular individuals who designate themselves as "holiness." Taylor was more correct as he "shuddered to think of what he had heard in some Sunday School classes."

Why he began his "psychology of holiness" with a discussion of "duty" is indefensible. Taylor is particularly off course when he declares, "Self-understanding begins with knowing our duty to God" and "to think of our relationship to God in terms of duty quickly uncovers the real self."[272] I suggest that "duty" often camouflages the real self, eventuating into nationalism, ethnocentrism and the legalism of self-righteousness. Douglas MacArthur was a case in point. No one ever exemplified "duty, honor and country" more than MacArthur, and no one was ever more intent upon glorifying himself. (He probably outdid Napoleon.) All of life was a stage entrance for MacArthur: dressing the right way, showing up at the right time, and claiming credit when he should have directed the spotlight on others who were equally, if not more worthy. Not that MacArthur wasn't brave, conscientious and a thorough tactician. The image of the corn cob pipe, aviator glasses, slouched hat, leather jacket, walking ashore in the Philippines were guarantees for a front page photo op. It was said of MacArthur that he never flitted an eyelid without thinking about it. No one ever wedded image and duty so successfully as did MacArthur. The irony is that the general's lifestyle may not have differed that much from a holiness lifestyle. Obviously why he performed his duty, to feed and bolster his gargantuan ego, differs greatly from what should motivate one's duty to God.

In the above sense, Taylor is correct to argue that inbred sin is sub-volitional. This seems to undercut Wesley's primary definition of sin as a "voluntary transgression of a known law." Taylor's psychological

---

[271] Ibid., 35.
[272] Ibid., 19.

model bypasses both faculty psychology and ego psychology. The former was popularized by Jonathan Edwards, Francis Wayland, and a host of other mental-moral philosophers of the eighteenth and nineteenth centuries. They, almost without exception, divided the mental faculties into intellect-affections-will. The affections consisted of the desires and values which defined or drove a person - the elements of one's character. This particular model had a lot to say for it because its exponents believed that an individual could not and would not act outside of, or other than, their character. The only way that character could be what it ought to be, thus act correctly, was by supernatural conversion. This understanding of character raised the question as to how converted a person could be, a question popularized mainly by Samuel Hopkins, but also touted by many mystics such as Madame Guyon, Meister Eckhart, and Catherine Adorna. At the heart of disinterested benevolence is the question, "Can a person act towards another individual in such a manner, that there is no explicit or implicit, covert or overt concern for the return of that interest or deed on his or her self? Disinterested benevolence is the essence of love, love being the primary definition of holiness for both Wesley and Wynkoop. One is left with the question: "Is it more important to know about love or about sin?" Or more accurately, in the holiness scheme, where should the emphasis be?

In the twentieth century, faculty psychology was replaced with ego or depth psychology popularized by Freud, Jung, and Erikson, who produced legions of followers all with their slightly or radically revised versions. Freud's psychoanalysis postulated that each individual is composed of a superego, ego and an id with the ego acting as a referee or regulator between the super ego (the moral law) and the id (the pleasure principle, mainly sexual).

Jung added his version dividing consciousness (immediate awareness or knowledge), pre-consciousness (that which can be recalled only after some reflection) and unconsciousness (those elements of life that are so subterranean that they manifest themselves in dreams, neurosis, psychosis, etc.) Many of the symbols are universal, verifying for Jung a "collective unconscious" which unites to some extent, all human kind. Translating psychology into theology, always difficult, one might find the cross or the Star of Bethlehem within the collective unconscious.

Erik Erikson added his developmental model, an epigenetic and chronological progression throughout the entirety of a person's life. Each of the eight stages are defined by a tension which has to be negotiated, for example trust versus mistrust, intimacy versus isolation, and generativity versus despair. None of these stages are perfectly negotiated or conquered and I find them helpful in understanding unhealed crevices in my life. (We will return to this model in chapter 9.)

Taylor shows no evidence of having read seminal thinkers in psychology, who were never completely right and sometimes straight out wrong. Taylor has conducted his own model of the human personality which for the unregenerate person consists of happiness-freedom-self-pleasing. Unwittingly, he has bought into Freud's pleasure principle, the id, by defining freedom for the unregenerate as the avoidance of "pain, crippling disease, hunger, loneliness and bondage," and the pursuit of buying what we want, going where we will and living as we please.[273]

And if this be the case, undoubtedly a person is in bondage. Taylor understands that true freedom can only come through discipline, but does not give credit to the many who know little of that kind of bondage, and have given themselves to the mastery of an instrument, a sport, and overcoming the overall slovenly habits of both mind and body. They often seem to be freer than the entirely sanctified. According to Taylor, the regenerated but unsanctified person changes only one part of the equation, a transition from freedom to obedience. The unsanctified are still preoccupied with their own happiness, "In this painful process God shows the new Christian that happiness is still more important to him than God's glory, and self-pleasing is still the governing motive of his life."[274] According to Taylor, this particular situation leads to misery, which might suggest that if one is not going to be a sanctified Christian, it might be better not to be a Christian at all. This position was suggested by C.S. Lewis in *Mere Christianity*.

> The Christian Way is different: harder, and easier. Christ says 'Give me All. I don't want so much of your time and so much of your money and so much of your work: I want you. I have not come to torment your natural self, but to kill it. No half-measures are any good. I don't want to cut off a

---

[273] Ibid., 89.

[274] Ibid., 93.

branch here and a branch there, I want to have the whole tree down. I don't want to drill the tooth, or crown it, or stop it, but to have it out. Hand over the whole natural self, all the desires which you think innocent as well as the ones you think wicked - the whole outfit. I will give you a new self instead. In fact, I will give you Myself; my own will shall become yours."....He never talked vague, idealistic gas. When He said, 'Be perfect' he meant it. He meant that we should go in for the full treatment. It is hard; but the sort of compromise we are all hankering after is harder - in fact, it is impossible.[275]

The Taylor-sanctification model consists of holiness-obedience-Christ-pleasing. Taylor is correct by declaring, "When the battle of the wills is settled, something wonderful happens. When we abandon our freedom and self-rights for total obedience, we discover that we are now free-er than ever before."[276] But I'm not as sanguine as he when he asserts, "When our fundamental interbeing has been so restructured that Christ-pleasing is now the governing motive of life, we discover that pleasing Christ is pleasing self, and what a delightful, comfortable, secure way of pleasing self it proves to be."[277] This description does not fit Christ in the garden, and neither does it fit the prayer we pray partaking in Wesley's Covenant Service.

Christ has many services to be done; some are easy, others more difficult; some bring honor, others bring reproach; some are suitable to our natural inclinations and temporal interests, others are contrary to both. In some we may please Christ and please ourselves; but there are others in which we cannot please Christ except by denying ourselves. Yet the power to do this is assuredly given us in Christ. We can do all things in him who strengtheneth us.[278]

Even more troubling is the assumption that the model of not pleasing self belongs only to Christians. I showed to one of my classes a film of a Buddhist ministering to AIDs victims. It put me to shame.

---

[275] C. S. Lewis. *Mere Christianity* (New York: HarperCollins Publishers, 1980) 195-197.

[276] Ibid., 96.

[277] Ibid., 96-97.

[278] John Wesley and Charles Wesley, *John and Charles Wesley: Selected Prayers, Hymns, Journal Notes, Sermons, Letters and Treatises*, ed. Richard J. Payne and Frank Whaling. (Mahwah, NJ: Paulist Press, 1981) 386-387.

At times, Taylor is naive that the kind of God-pleasing which he depicts is automatic or *de facto* for the entirely sanctified. I respond that we will have to pull ourselves away from the television, computer, I phone; the list is almost endless. And though not familiar with Erikson and others who enable us to know ourselves (psychology can be an exacting prophet), Taylor astutely writes, "The mind is needed to come to a mature understanding to the tricks our own mind can play on us, so the mind sits in judgment on itself."[279] He further states, "When our self-esteem is so bound up with a protected ego that we cannot admit fallibility, than we are still sick spiritually and need a deeper dip into the sanctifying Grace of God."[280] I say "Amen" but at the same time, Taylor's insight begs the question, "Is there any work of grace that moves us beyond the need of defending our ego?" One might answer that no ego can stand the whole load of truth dumped on it at one time. This is a maturing process that, unfortunately, many sanctified people have bypassed on their way to heaven.

For one half century, Richard Taylor was the most influential person within the conservative American Holiness Movement. In all probability, he furnished course texts and supplemental reading for "holiness schools," such as Kentucky Mountain Institute, God's Bible School, and Hobe Sound more than any other person. But he also serves as a proverb for those of us who continue to write longer than we should. His denominational publishing house began to shun him, and he had to turn to smaller niche printers such as Schmul Publishing Company. A book which was published posthumously, *A Return to Christian Culture*, possibly should have been titled "Conformed to Western Ideas of Christian Culture." While correctly noting the vacuous content of contemporary media, entertainment and art, he evidenced being caught in a time warp, contoured by his age and acculturation to the people and places that were now shaping him as much as he had influenced them. He condemned the guitar as normally a product of lazy creativity, and people who take up the offering in 'hiking clothes." He opined that the Christian home could be the most attractive spot on the block, and somehow argued for an absolute aesthetic in arranging the pictures and furniture in a house. Incredulously, he related, "One morning when I was trying to pray, it suddenly dawned on me that the chair didn't belong

---

[279] Taylor. *Understanding*, 103.
[280] Ibid., 105.

there; it needed to change places with the chair in the opposite corner. So my devotions were punctuated by some quick furniture moving. I tell you, it was easier to pray afterward. I was adjusting the room to the 'laws of God.'"[281]

Unfortunately, much of Taylor's thinking became outdated, his metaphors antiquated and his frames of reference unfamiliar to the generations who followed him, and have been unable to find the same solace and certitude in a framework which gave him abundant confidence. Few individuals such as C. S. Lewis, Reinhold Niebuhr, and Leslie Newbegin are able to write timeless material. Richard Taylor, like myself, was not in the class of these theological and literary geniuses. Today, he is only read by those persons who are already converted to his theological persuasion, which leaves the possibility of converting anyone to the position of entire sanctification as almost nil. The person whom he most adamantly condemned would champion the new holiness paradigm, proved herself a more capable writer than Taylor, and it is she whom we next examine.

I'm sure Richard Taylor went to Heaven. If Heaven wasn't ready when he got there, it soon would be. Just a little rearranging of the furniture.

---

[281] Richard S. Taylor. *A Return to Christian Culture or Why Avoid the Cult of the Slob?* (Salem, OH: Schmul Publishing Company, 2004) 45.

Chapter 4:
Mildred Wynkoop

Background

Mildred Wynkoop possessed and exhibited self-awareness. Events, relationships, religion, and temperament, found their confluence in her *A Theology of Love*. First, she was a woman in a man's world. For some quarter of a century she traveled as "co-evangelist" with her husband, Ralph Wynkoop, on the camp meeting and revival circuit of the Church of the Nazarene. Although being a better preacher than Ralph, particularly in content, she was something less than "co." In spite of being part of the Holiness Movement which had been birthed by both men and women in the pulpit, she was acutely aware that fundamentalism and its diminishing role for women was engulfing her denomination, the Church of the Nazarene. Fundamentalism's rigid biblical literalism, dispensational millennialism, and silencing of women, painted her into a corner which she resented. Her resentment was not subdued by attending Northern Baptist Seminary in Chicago for a Ph.D., the school representing the antithesis of the far more conservative institutions of the Southern Baptist Church, such as Southwestern Baptist Theological Seminary in Fort Worth, Texas, and Southern Baptist Seminary in Louisville, Kentucky. In 1984, she reflected on her life in the Church of the Nazarene: "But during the 20's, the 30's, another stream of preaching distinctly a strongly-flavored fundamentalism, harsh, judgmental, unyielding, divisive.... With it came emphasis on so-called modesty – always directed to women. The danger women were to men, began to be preached, and I felt strangely alienated and withdrew."[282]

---

[282] Nazarene Archives, Wynkoop Collection "My Life," February 16, 1984, File 1427-2.

Mildred did not need fundamentalism to cause her to "withdraw." She was a first-generation American, her father having been born in Norway and her mother in Switzerland. Her mother Mary Dupertius moved to the U. S. at age six, her family first settling in Kansas, but ultimately making their home in the Seattle, Washington area. Her father's boyhood odyssey was far more adventuresome. Oliver Bong as a teenager went to sea, jumping ship off the coast of San Francisco, and traveling by land to Seattle. Oliver Bong and Mary Dupertius were married in December of 1904, and Mildred, the first of six children, was born September 9, 1905. The couple Anglicized their name to Bangs, but Mildred's father always spoke with a Scandinavian accent.

Oliver was industrious, securing financial stability for his family by building houses, and with the proceeds bought a dairy farm where Mildred grew up.[283] The Bangs joined the noisy band-playing, amen and hallelujah-shouting Salvation Army, not exactly akin to Oliver's quietist Quaker heritage. But it was there that both Mary and Oliver were converted to Christ. The family sought middle ground in the Seattle First Church of the Nazarene, the denomination Mildred would serve for the rest of her life. But this religious landing hardly provided an environment that Mildred's temperament so desperately craved. As a small girl she had been so timid and shy that she had to be home-schooled for her first year of formal education. The shouting and aisle-running Nazarenes were an increasing embarrassment to the maturing, petite, soft-spoken woman, a model of decorum and modesty.

Oddly, as a student at Northwest Nazarene College, Nampa, Idaho, she found herself on the camp meeting circuit during the summer representing the College. This experience, where she met her soon-to-be-evangelist-called husband, should have prepared if not motivated her for the revivalistic enterprise that seemed to suit her husband's disposition more than hers. Ralph Wynkoop was anything but a flame-breathing, dart-throwing, hell-threatening preacher, and neither of them were stereotypical Nazarene evangelists. In fact, they experienced difficulty in keeping a full schedule. Mildred's discomfort was especially heightened

---

[283] Brief biographies can be found in Johan Tredoux, *Mildred Bangs Wynkoop: Her Life and Thought* (Kansas City: Foundry Publishing, 2017) and Stan Ingersol, "The Woman Behind the Words: Mildred Wynkoop and Authentic Faith," Nazarene Archives, Wynkoop Collection, article undated.

when touring churches of southern Nazarenedom. She sized up other evangelists on the trail: "They relied on audience response to keep their rhetoric flowing, and the exhortation to shout and say 'Amen' began to turn bitter. Our sanctification was questioned when we didn't supply the noisy background which was wanted." Wynkoop confessed, "A new wrinkle appeared. Some very sincere men and women felt impelled to bring down the glory by yelling in church. I simply curled up inside and almost died of rebellion and shame."[284]

Mildred's brother helped widen the chasm that both of them experienced in the Church of the Nazarene. Carl, who taught at Olivet Nazarene College while completing his Ph.D. at the University of Chicago, found his labors at Olivet analogous to a square peg in a round hole. He increasingly felt out of place and took credentials with the Methodist Church, spending almost his entire teaching career at Saint Paul's School of Theology in Kansas City. Very bright and something of a curmudgeon, Carl became the world's foremost authority on James Arminius. In his last years, he came full circle by writing the first and, to this date, only comprehensive biography on Phineas Bresee. But his sentiments were not so congenial when he wrote his sister in March of 1958. "Olivet is becoming intolerable. We are now in one of the most inane 'revival meetings' I have ever seen. Ross Emrick, (Bob's brother,) is a good boy, but he can't preach, and the whole appeal is on the basis of platitudes and emotions. How a church can maintain Christian life without a Biblical basis is beyond me. We get great crowds of seekers— freshmen and sophomores—and each one is good for coming again for at least four meetings, maybe eight. I wonder what it means to them? Their response is not a response to the Bible and its message, for the Bible has scarcely been read or mentioned this week."[285]

Disillusionment with Normative Holiness Preaching and Her Termination at Western Evangelical Seminary

The above communication only deepened Mildred's dissatisfaction and disillusionment with altar call Nazarene worship,

---

[284] Nazarene Archives, Wynkoop Collection, "My Life," February 16, 1984, File 1427-2.

[285] Nazarene Archives, Wynkoop Collection, Letter, Carl to Mildred, March 19, 1958.

especially regarding entire sanctification. Throughout her childhood and even early adulthood, she repeatedly went to the altar, some forty times according to her. Even though she sometimes testified that she had been entirely sanctified, her spiritual thirst was not quenched. The systemization and codification of the doctrine and in particular, the methodology of receiving the "blessing," had not worked. In a moment of spiritual defeat and disgust, she tore the page out of her Bible which recorded all of her altar trips.

> I tried to look a piety I couldn't feel. I shouted when it seemed the right thing to do. I prayed loud when the preacher said we ought. And rather suddenly, the whole unsavory farce broke around my head, leaving me a full-fledged skeptic, cold-blooded and adrift. The divine formula upon which I had pinned my faith, didn't work.[286]

According to her biographer, Johan Tredoux, "This conflict broke her health. She was tubercular, and had to be left in California while her husband took a new church in Oregon. "Here she was 29 years old, the product of a Nazarene home, two Nazarene colleges, a part of H. Orton Wiley's circle, and a Nazarene pastor's wife, yet she felt she needed to get as far away from an evangelical church as she could."[287] Her faith was restored by attending an Episcopal Church. The church's communion services were like a "life-belt thrown to her." She later recalled, "The utter frankness and the complete absence of any stereotyped expressions helped to freshen the truth to me. It was not salvation, but the beginning of my road back to God."[288]

All of Wynkoop's theological journey, both intellectual and emotional, came to a focal point during a five-year teaching stint at Western Evangelical Seminary, Portland, Oregon, where she had earlier received her Master of Divinity degree. In 1959 under duress, she resigned from her professorship, or some might say, she was fired. When this author asked her brother, Carl, why his sister was fired, he exclaimed, "Heresy!" One would hardly use the word *heresy* concerning Mildred Wynkoop in any normative sense of the word. But none the less, she deviated from the theological consensus that had brought Western

---

[286] Tredoux, 28.

[287] Ibid., 39.

[288] Nazarene Archives, Wynkoop Collection, Mildred Wynkoop: "What Holiness Means to Me," File 2227-14.

Evangelical Seminary into existence, though the consensus was by no means embroidered with a clear circumference.

Western Evangelical Seminary was originally named Western Evangelical School of Religion, by a group of Evangelical United Brethren who adhered to a conservative theology, with one of its main tenets, entire sanctification, as an instantaneous second work of grace.[289] Its leadership brought on board several other holiness denominations, mainly Free Methodist, Wesleyan, and the Northwest Yearly Meeting of Friends. This conglomerate chose as its first President a District Superintendent with the Evangelical United Brethren, Paul Petticord. Petticord had been on the original preaching staff for a newly formed Evangelistic association called Youth for Christ. Other evangelists included Billy Graham, Harold Ockenga, and Oswald Smith. The founding Dean was Delbert Rose, a conservative holiness exponent, advocating two-step entire sanctification until his dying day at 99 years of age.

Fairly early on, it became clear that the Seminary constituency consisted of two groups, though there were people who felt compatible with either. One group espousing traditional language of the American Holiness Movement, gravitated around Multnomah County Holiness Camp Meeting, and the other, not so rigidly defined, was more comfortable attending the official Evangelical Church of North America (which the former EUB's named themselves) Camp Meeting at Jennings Lodge, a location immediately south of Portland, and the ultimate location of the Seminary.

At first, Wynkoop thought she was temporarily replacing Eldon Fuhrman, a conservative holiness advocate while he finished his doctorate. This belief, at least for her, was confirmed by the fact that during her first year as a theology professor, there was no official installation service. When President Paul Petticord did offer a public installation, he explained he had to go slowly because the professor, was a woman, Wynkoop refused his offer. In spite of her refusal, she was retained as a professor, signing a yearly contract and quickly becoming the most popular teacher on campus.

---

[289] Glen Williamson. *Born for Such a Day: The Amazing Story of Western Evangelical Seminary* (Portland, OR: LaSabre Press, 1974).

In Wynkoop's first semester, November 3, 1955, she preached a message in chapel under the title, "An Existential Interpretation of the Doctrine of Holiness." Why she used the word existential is not clear other than to add a sophisticated nuance to her sermon. She did not use the word existential in the normative sense of existentialism as advocated by Camus, Sartre, Heidegger, and a broad array of thinkers who have given their own interpretation to this amorphous and slippery term.[290] By the word "existential" Wynkoop meant practical, experiential, or every-day holiness. "But the danger we face is in offering a belief in the doctrine of holiness that does not issue in a full and satisfactory expression of that faith in daily living situations."[291]

By using the word "existential" Wynkoop had unnecessarily invited criticism. Plus, nowhere in her presentation did she reference traditional holiness language such as second blessing, baptism of the Holy Spirit, or cleansing from inbred sin. From that moment until leaving five years later, the radical holiness movement hounded and criticized her. Petticord found himself in the middle of a tug of war, and according to Wynkoop, became her antagonist, and jealous of her popularity. As the conservative Holiness Movement became more opposed to Wynkoop, the students became fonder of her. On February 16, 1958, she wrote John Riley, President of Northwest Nazarene College, "It is this label 'radical' which brings me into the picture inadvertently…fairly or otherwise the Seminary position on holiness has been interpreted as being that of a very radical brand….I came in simply as a holiness teacher and without being too aware of the dilemma, I steered down a middle course which I now find out is tending to heal a great rift which is running through the holiness group in the Northwest."[292] Wynkoop may have been too optimistic at this point. Most enlightening was a letter written by Vic Walter on May 19, 1959, a graduate of WES who sized up the situation for her.

---

[290] Webster defines the term as a philosophy postulating the "individual as a self-determining agent responsible for his or her choices." *Webster's Encyclopedia, Unabridged Dictionary of the English Language* (San Diego: Thunder Bay Press, 1996) 678.

[291] Mildred Wynkoop, "An Existential Interpretation of the Doctrine of Holiness," a message presented in Chapel Service, Western Evangelical Seminary, Portland, Oregon, November 3, 1955, 1.

[292] Nazarene Archives, Wynkoop Collection, Letter, Mildred Wynkoop to John Riley, February 16, 1958.

Without meaning to seem unduly unkind to Dr. Petticord, it seems to me that two things are occurring…First, he is not willing to cut down un-Christian opposition to his staff and risk temporary setback in the conference for long-term gain, and secondly, he is experiencing the forces which he himself created and stirred up (Perhaps created is too strong a term here.) and unleashed on the proverbially wicked East in order to start his school. Now that WES was showing promise of becoming a soundly academic school as well as a soundly spiritual one and thus, beginning to really carry a weight of witness in the Church world, these very same forces which were used to build the school, are turning on the school. The idea of (names four people as representing the radical holiness position) a holy committee on thought control fills me with righteous indignation…[293]

By the time of the Walter letter, Mildred had already resigned with a gracious letter to Paul Petticord, January 14, 1959. The informal communication to her mother enables us to understand Wynkoop's emotions and thoughts at this juncture in her life. "I was only going to be teaching for the first two quarters, they are really making life miserable for the President. I have never been in such an atmosphere. They say no one can boot a teacher out like that, especially the one they like best."[294] A week later, she again wrote to her mother.

At the spring banquet, the seniors had written a wonderful tribute to me and all of them had signed it. They called me up to the front and read the whole thing and then I thought they would never stop cheering. It was embarrassing and yet it was wonderful. I was told that two-thirds of the student body have signed a statement of request that I not be left off the teaching staff. The faculty is begging me to not consider anything else but to stay. The people on the outside are making life miserable for the president who has taken a dislike to me. I am told by those who are in position to know that the only trouble is that I am a woman, and he is desperately jealous of a woman who has a following.[295]

---

[293] Nazarene Archives, Wynkoop Collection, Letter, Vic Walter to Mildred Wynkoop, May 19, 1959.
[294] Nazarene Archives, Wynkoop Collection, Letter, Mildred Wynkoop to Dear Mother, May 19, 1959.
[295] Nazarene Archives, Wynkoop Collection, Letter, Mildred Wynkoop to Dear Mother, May 23, 1959.

Whether Wynkoop correctly interpreted Petticord or not, is up to the reader and those who have some personal knowledge of his legend. By the time I came to WES in 1983, he was gone, having died of a heart attack in 1975. Petticord was a great man, but as all great men, flawed. He saved face by allowing the students to collect $5,000 for Mildred to become a roving teacher for the Oriental Missionary Society (one of the missionary organizations supported by WES, the other World Gospel Mission) in Southeast Asia. After a year in that role, she became a theology professor at Nazarene Bible College in Japan. What is important about the WES episode is not to assign guilt to one party or the other; all college and graduate school presidents are at times put in a situation where the only choice is the lesser of two evils. What is important is that between 1955 and 1959, Mildred Wynkoop's holiness theology was hammered out on the forge of controversy. She had seen the good and ugly side of entire sanctification proponents. But this would not be the last time that her thought and character would be refined by the fires of theological disagreement. This would come later during her last teaching stint as Theologian in Residence at Nazarene Theological Seminary.

A Theology of Love

Mildred Wynkoop's book *A Theology of Love* is subjectively and experientially driven. This does not mean that she approaches John Wesley and the American Holiness Movement without careful scholarship, sustained inquiry, and the attempt to extract herself from personal history in order to provide objective analysis. What it does mean is that she (as she fully admits) felt a need to analyze and provide answers to the spiritual disjunctions and contradictions that she had observed in her own life and the lives of others. Neither was she unaware that her perceptions lay between herself and the objects of her interpretation. She was fully cognizant that none of us are free to think as we ought, only as we perceive. She quoted John Wesley's sermon "Catholic Spirit:" "If it be, give me thy hand. I do not mean be of my opinion, you need not. I do not expect or desire it, neither do I mean 'I will be of your opinion.' I cannot; It does not depend on my choice; I can no more think than I can see or hear, as I will. Keep you your opinion, I mine; and that as steadily as ever."[296]

---

[296] Mildred Wynkoop. *A Theology of Love* (Kansas City: Beacon Hill Press of Kansas

Yet, no one ever worked harder at changing opinion than John Wesley. Wynkoop was true to her spiritual hero. The title of her magnum opus, *A Theology of Love: The Dynamic of Wesleyanism*, is not misleading; she used the word Wesley or its cognates, Wesleyan or Wesleyanism, some 772 times. She was not unaware that she interpreted Scripture through a Wesleyan lens, and may have been aware but not willing to admit that Wesley suffered from critical contradictions in his own life, which shaped his thinking and writing. To put it in another way, several of the problems which Wynkoop addresses in the American holiness culture in which she was nurtured, as we have already argued, were created by Wesley himself. The failures of Wesley to match personal experience with his expressed theology of "Christian perfection," she seemed unwilling to investigate.

Some have labeled Mildred Wynkoop a "process" theologian. That she was not, not in the sense of Schubert Ogden and John Cobb, Jr. Nowhere in her writings can one find a growing, maturing, developing, changing God. God is perfection; always has been and always will be. The only sense in which Mildred can be labeled "process" is her understanding of the work of God in the souls of individuals. Spirituality is a maturing process, from the first dawning of prevenient grace to post-mortem glorification and probably beyond. As we have already explored, conservative holiness folk questioned her theological integrity because of her emphasis on the process of entire sanctification, to which she perceived the American Holiness Movement had not given sufficient attention and had wrongly interpreted Wesley. Others countered that her over-correction eliminated holiness as a second work of grace, and did away with much of the *ordo solutis* as defined by Wesley or the subsequent Holiness Movement. To the contrary, "secondness" was important to Wynkoop, but not in a manner that would satisfy all holiness exponents. She made some straight-forward non-hedging statements such as the following: "Wesleyan theology asserts (1) that sanctification is a this life experience (2) that it is a relationship to God, logically distinct from and morally a quite different dimension than justification (3) that it follows regeneration (4) that it is crisis-oriented as well as life-oriented (5) and in a proper sense it can be called a 'second crisis.'"[297]

City, 2015) 60.
[297] Wynkoop. *A Theology*, 339.

As a major contributor to holiness thought and life, Wynkoop is deserving of sustained effort to understand her for any serious scholar of the American Holiness Movement in the twentieth century. Notwithstanding her tendency to gloss over Wesley's contradictions, Wynkoop herself gave sustained and honest inquiry to both him and the American Holiness Movement. The following I propose is a linguistic exploration of both her contributions and what I believe to be her misunderstandings or contradictions.

The Credibility Gap

First on Wynkoop's agenda was the "credibility gap," the disconnect between the testimony of holiness exponents and what they had experienced or exhibited in everyday life. To put it simply, she observed a disconnect between walk and talk.

> The absolutes of theology may satisfy the mind; but the imperfection of the human self seems to deny all that the perfection of Christian doctrine affirms. We seem to proceed from a different world of thought when preaching doctrine than when we preach "practical" sermons. The practical sermon "pulls the stinger" out of a doctrinal presentation. This has created a vast and disturbing dualism between idea and life, between profession and practice. Such a dualism fosters either bewildered dishonesty (in interest of loyalty) or abject discouragement.[298]

Though Wynkoop does not exactly ask the question, she certainly implies it: Are holiness people less judgmental, less contentious, more loving, more prayerful, more engaged with their neighbor, and carry a deeper burden for the 26,000 children who daily die of starvation, a child every six seconds on planet earth, than other religious brands? These questions could be broached infinitum and cultivate either spiritual pride or honest confession. Wynkoop reminds us that holiness is not primarily refraining from something, but doing something. Unfortunately, the negative aspects of holiness, separation from the world, have been emphasized to the peril of the positive, such as Charles Wesley's "A Charge to Keep." If the Holiness Movement lost a generation, or is losing the millenials, may the cause not be in part, that we have not presented a worth-while purpose for which to live and die. In a seminal book,

---

[298] Ibid., 45.

actually better than its title, *Why Conservative Churches are Growing*, Dean Kelly argued that persons attend churches because they find a worthwhile cause beyond themselves, and are given tasks compatible with their gifts and aptitudes in which they find fulfillment.[299]

If anything, Wesleyan holiness theology promotes a religion of action. Wesley did not systematize theology, he applied theology. Wynkoop described Wesley's social involvement, a social involvement that stretches credulity, but is more or less accurate:

> Wesley put his hand in many matters, not always considered quite proper for a clergyman…. In 1748, He founded a school for boys at Kingswood, Bristol, and wrote textbooks. He published 233 original works on a variety of subjects. He completed a Christian library. He wrote a four volume History of England. He wrote a book of birds, beasts, and insects. He wrote a medical book. He set up a free medical dispensary. He adapted an electrical machine for healing, and cured more than one thousand people. He set up spinning and knitting shops for the poor. He received 40,000 pounds for his books but gave it all away.[300]

And we thought all of the above had to wait for William Booth's Salvation Army, Walter Rauchenbush's liberal social gospel or Russell Conwell's "institutional church." "Herein is the risk," says Wynkoop, "not only that this theology (holiness) may slip into the hazards to the right and to the left, but also that the abiding vitality of the Spirit of God may thrust men out into new and unconventional dimensions of Christian outreach and that the forms which structure the organization and language may not be flexible enough to accommodate its own life."[301]

Entire Sanctification as an Abstraction

The second serious problem which Wynkoop disects is entire sanctification as a reductionistic abstraction. She does not exactly frame the problem as such, but her indictment runs throughout *A Theology of Love*. According to Wynkoop, populist holiness theology has abstracted

---

[299] Dean Kelly. *Why Conservative Churches Are Growing* (New York: Harper and Row, 1972).

[300] Wynkoop, *A Theology*, 66-67. Quoted from Cyril J. Squire, *A Lithograph of Wesley.*

[301] Wynkoop, *A Theology*, 50.

the second work of grace from the order of salvation, thereby reducing other equally or even more important divine human interactions as incidental or subordinated to the experience of entire sanctification. Thus, holiness as a distinct instantaneous second work of grace became the shibboleth, the litmus test, the ticket for entrance into and continued inclusion in an exclusive group who labeled themselves "holiness." This exclusiveness is very similar to "speaking in tongues," as a sign *qua non* for being labeled a bonafide Pentecostal. Both of these groups, first cousins, antagonists and "better" than the other, adopted "holier than thou" attitudes, each claiming to have a corner on truth.

> In the course of the years since Wesley, one pair of terms, *holiness* and *sanctification*, has gone through a strange metamorphosis. It has changed from its rich connotation, in Scripture and in Wesley, to a very limited meaning, and made to bear the full responsibility for most of the biblical and existential meaning of full salvation....
>
> Perhaps the more serious reductionism is to limit even that one pair of terms to one aspect of the total, biblical meaning, namely, to a second work of grace....
>
> The most serious effect of this progressive narrowing of concept is that the anemic "abstract" connotation of the once vibrant, dramatic, dynamic word reacted back onto itself and became the sole meaning of every occasion of the word in Scripture. There are those who hold that no scripture which does not use the word *sanctification* or *holiness* is considered to be a holiness passage. And worse, the voice of the Word is by this silenced....
>
> *Sanctification* cannot stand alone in theology. It cannot be lifted up out of the complex of theological doctrines to be separated from them. The interlocking relationships of all Christian doctrines are integral to the life and meaning of every other one. To lift faith, love, cleansing, justification, sanctification, crisis, or process (et al.) out of the complex is "abstracting" it, and the doctrine is then called "abstract."[302]

Abstraction was at the heart of the early sectarianism that "came out" under the holiness banner. Timothy Smith, as a Nazarene, and who understood himself as a holiness exponent, noted the outburst of "fanaticism that sickened the average churchman and at the same time forced the holiness leaders on toward stronger independent

---

[302] Wynkoop, *A Theology*, 306-307.

organizations."[303] The Southern Methodist Bishops in 1894 clearly identified the reductionist distillation of the Gospel as "holiness associations, holiness meetings, holiness preachers, holiness evangelists and holiness property....We do not question the sincerity and zeal of these brethren; we desire the Church to profit by their earnest preaching and godly example; but we deplore their teaching and methods insofar as they claim a monopoly on the experience, practice, and advocacy of holiness, and separate themselves from the body of ministers and disciples."[304]

It may have been for the above reason, as well as others, such as the unity of the Bride of Christ, that the Methodist Episcopal Church Bishops rejected an 1881 request by holiness exponents John Miley, Daniel Steele, and Asbury Lowery for a national convention promoting holiness. The Bishops responded, 'It is our solemn conviction that the whole subject of personal experience...can be maintained and enforced in connection within the established uses of the Church."[305] Indeed, "holiness" had become a specialty at the expense of vital orthodoxy, ignoring or giving little attention to such doctrines as the Trinity, the Atonement, and the ongoing Intercession of Christ. The important doctrine of justification by faith withered. Wynkoop adroitly summarizes, "When the interrelatedness of justification and sanctification is severed, and justification is slipped under sanctification as a sort of poor basement apartment under the luxurious, upper-floor living quarters, or it is made to mark the difference between first and second-class Christians, something essential is lost in the meaning of each of these terms."[306] Abstracting entire sanctification from the totality of God's interactions with individuals would be like "taking the physical heart out of a man and expecting to find in that heart all that man is. The heart is not the man, and the man does not survive long without that fantastically intriguing muscle connected to him so vitally. The man has a heart; the heart is not the man."[307]

---

[303] Timothy L. Smith. *Called Unto Holiness-The Story of the Nazarenes: The Formative Years* (Kansas City: Nazarene Publishing House, 1962) 53.

[304] Ibid., 41.

[305] Timothy Smith, "The Theology and Practices of Methodism, 1887–1919," in *The History of American Methodism* Vol. II, ed. Emory Bucke (Nashville: Abingdon, 1958) 620.

[306] Wynkoop, *A Theology*, 308.

[307] Ibid., 307.

Obscuring Justification by Faith

The abstract expression of and testimony to entire sanctification often obscured a vital Wesleyan truth, often missed by the Holiness Movement, that justification is sanctification begun. In a sense, the holy process has begun in a person's life with prevenient grace even before the intentional "drawing nigh to God," as a cognizant, volitional step. This is the inner light, according to Quakers, which is the gift of God to every person. The emphasis on justification by faith (as well as other creedal emphases) places Wesley squarely in the Reformation as a centrist. The full scope of plumbing both the Western and Eastern Church Fathers, which provided the critical building blocks for Wesley constructing his theology, was lost on much of the Holiness Movement. This is not to say that Wesley did not make what he thought were improvements or the renuancing of concepts that would ensure that his theology did not fall into the errors of predestination, antinomianism, imputation at the expense of impartation, and the needless dichotomy between faith and works. Of the foremost Reformation truth "justification by faith" (really the truth that was the turning point in his life) Wesley wrote, "So then that 'whosoever believeth on him shall be saved' is, and must be, the foundation of all our preaching; that is, must be preached first....but salvation by faith strikes at the root, and all (errors) fall at once where this is established. It was this doctrine which our Church justly calls a strong rock and foundation of the Christian religion."[308]

In this writer's perception, if we are going to emphasize a work of "grace," it should be justification by faith, the difference between life and death, Heaven and Hell, light and darkness. It is the most critical fork in the road which needs to be carefully defined, clarified, and proclaimed to all. Wesley had such a high view of the "new birth" that those who had experienced this miracle of grace, "'walk after the Spirit,' both in their hearts and lives. They are taught of Him to love God and their neighbour, with a love which is as 'a well of water, springing up into everlasting life.' And by Him they are led into every holy desire, into every divine and

---

[308] John Wesley, "Salvation by Faith," *Wesley's Standard Sermons* Vol. I, ed. Edward Sugden (Grand Rapids: Francis Asbury Press, 1955) 49-50. Note that this sermon was first preached June 11, 1738, after Wesley's Aldersgate experience on May 24. Though he may have later doubted the certainty of the experience, he never deviated from the doctrine.

heavenly temper, till every thought which arises in their heart is holiness unto the Lord."[309] In most holiness teaching, this experience of grace was reserved for "entire sanctification," as differentiated from justification by faith.

Entire Sanctification as False Security

Wesley and Wynkoop discouraged any kind of arrival theology which professes infallibility, standing in a state of grace devoid of constant and continual dependence on the Holy Spirit. Above all, they stressed a salvific understanding of incessant relying on the atonement and the perennial intercession of Christ. Christ's work was not finished on earth; it continues in Heaven. Wynkoop quotes Wesley as does everyone in the relational progressive camp, but no less true: "Does not talking of a justified or sanctified *state*, tend to mislead men? Almost naturally leading them to trust in what was done at one moment? By saying, 'Whereas we are every hour and every moment pleasing or displeasing to God according to our works: according to the whole of our inward tempers and our outward behavior.'"[310]

That Wesleyan holiness people believed that there was a state of grace achievable, which precluded backsliding, or made possible sinless perfection, was never a claim of the American Holiness Movement, properly so called. But two problems arise, the perception of those who evaluate the holiness position from the outside and those insiders who have somehow concluded that entire sanctification is akin to eternal security. As a layperson told me, then in his seventies, "I went to the altar twice (in college) and I haven't been back since." The first misperception was exemplified in Harold Lindsell's book, *The Holy Spirit in the Latter Days*.[311] The Calvinistic Lindsell was a clear and informed thinker, but made a mistake interpreting A. M. Hills as teaching a state of grace whereby the recipient of said grace "cannot sin." In a review of this book which I wrote in 1983, I admitted that Hills was often overly zealous in his language such as "dead to the solicitation of evil." But in the Hills work to which Lindsell referred, Hills has included a chapter "How to

---

[309] Wesley. *Works,* Vol. V, 89.

[310] Wynkoop, *A Theology,* 204.

[311] Harold Lindsell. *The Holy Spirit in the Latter Days* (Nashville: Thomas Nelson, 1983).

Keep the Blessing" where he wrote, "There are thirty volumes on the desk before me on the subject of sanctification, and not one of all the authors pretends to teach that there is any state of grace attainable in this life from which a child of God may not fall."[312]

J. A. Wood, more perceptive than most nineteenth-century holiness writers, wrote, "If by sinless perfection be meant infallibility or a state in which the soul cannot sin, we answer, No. We believe in no such perfection in this life and further, we know no one who teaches such a thing. Although it has been asserted over and over thousands of times by the opposers of Christian perfection."[313] The Holiness Movement should have taken more responsibility for this assertion and could have done more to correct it. It is not uncommon for someone to say to a person in the Church of the Nazarene or some other holiness denomination, "Don't you people teach sinless perfection?"

Unfortunately, the accusations of the "opposers" have not been entirely baseless and without merit. After preaching in countless holiness camp meetings and revivals across the spectrum of holiness denominations, I somehow received the informal and unwritten code that ninety percent of the people present needed no spiritual help while ten percent did. Wynkoop perceptively responded to this particular self-righteous position of which holiness exponents have been guilty. "Those who hold this view cannot account for the vicious and base temptations in the Christian which assails him, nor the need for the constant discipline and spiritual nourishment of the whole person which is demanded for good and faithful Christian living. There are many who feel it is a disloyalty to a theological commitment to ask forgiveness of God or man because by doing so, it seems to deny the power of the Holy Spirit to make sin virtually impossible — at least so long as one is 'sanctified.'"[314]

---

[312] A. M. Hills. *Holiness and Power* (Cincinnati: Revivalist Office, 1897) 60.

[313] J. A. Wood. *Perfect Love* (South Pasadena, CA: published by the author, 1891) 44.

[314] Wynkoop, *A Theology*, 223.

Altar Theology

The above is closely tied to what may be the primary and most practical problem for holiness folk: the seeking of an experience rather than God; the seeking of an "it" rather than a person, the seeking of an attribute of God rather than God himself. This particular pursuit has entailed endless quibbles and endless introspection as to what the experience consists of and how to go about finding it. Wynkoop writes, "Holiness in God is not one attribute among others. He does not have holiness. Holiness is not a quality which stands against justice or love. God is holy. Holiness is the nature of God in which all elements of his being exist in perfect balance and relation."[315]

Wynkoop undercuts "altar theology," (I think rightly so) by stating, "It is not the task of the preacher moreover to tell anyone where and when the inner cleansing is to occur. In the zeal for counting results, there has 'grown up' a pattern methodology that is pressed with so much urgency as to dangerously obscure the real issues."[316] The real issue is all of God in possession of all of the person. After one discovers that this has not happened, or the contents of the actual package do not match what was actually promised, disillusionment and despair set in. I have been on the platform of a camp meeting, often observing what I perceived as the manipulative altar call from a clever and very oratorical evangelist, watching the persons who came forward, praying at the top of their voices at the same time, two or three deep across an altar that was fifty feet long. I concluded that the scene was as ritualistic as a Roman Catholic mass. Both salvation and sanctification had to be obtained in a certain way, and outside of that way, God could not and would not work. If individuals did not conform to the traditional methodology in the assessment of the insiders, the seekers would probably come up short.

Overdependence on the Concept of Morality

While arguing for a biblical Hebraic relational understanding of love as the ultimate Christian ethic, Wynkoop, from my perception, makes an egregious error. In order to close the "credibility gap," she used the word "moral" (or its cognates morality, moralistic, or moralism) 703

---

[315] Ibid., 359.
[316] Ibid., 379.

times in her book, *A Theology of Love*. (She uses the word righteousness 89 times; thus, I suggest that her error is more of degree than an absolute either-or.) Moral, though a New Testament concept, is not a New Testament word. No Greek word in the New Testament should be translated by the word moral. Of the eleven definitions given in Webster's unabridged dictionary, six of them use the word conduct: "Pertaining to or concerned with the principles or rules of right conduct with the distinction between right and wrong."[317] Wynkoop wrote: "Holiness is moral to the core – love to God and man. These are qualities of the self in relation to the person of God and man.[318] She has given a religious content to a term culturally formed and sociologically defined, and has proven to be a battle ground surrounded by various disciplines, among them anthropology, sociology, psychology, theology, and neurological science. C. S. Lewis in *Mere Christianity* argued for universal laws of conduct and thus, there must be a universal ruler or creator of those laws that bind humanity together, attributing moral dignity to Homo sapiens as differentiated from other species of life. These absolutes, according to Lewis, are the retained image of God in all individuals.

Freud reversed Lewis's argument in his *Civilization and Its Discontents*.[319] We should not do unto others, because we are afraid they will do the same to us. In other words, morality is a communal contract for survival. We are not going to stop and argue the truth of either of these propositions, only to quote what I have written elsewhere: "In a world of nuclear threat, our Christian nation with its messianic pretentions, operates not so much by the maxim of Jesus, 'do unto others as you would have them do unto you,' but by 'be careful what you do unto others because they might do the same unto you.'"[320] To put it another way, morality is necessary for survival as explained by Jacques Ellul.

> In reality, the good which morality affirms is a good determined by necessity. It is not a good within the scope of liberty and the free gift. In spite of all his pretentions —intellectual, spiritual, and moral — man is remarkably

---

[317] Webster's, 1, 249.

[318] Wynkoop, *A Theology*, 175.

[319] Sigmund Freud. *Civilization and Its Discontents* (London: Penguin, 2002).

[320] Darius Salter. *God Cannot Do Without America: Matthew Simpson and the Apotheosis of Protestant Nationalism* (Wilmore, Kentucky: First Fruits Press, 2017) 657.

predetermined. When he calls such and such an act good, when he develops this or that ethical system, he is in no sense taking a stride into the absolute, nor bursting out suddenly into the domain of freedom. He continues to be conditioned by his heredity, by his biological life, by his environment, by his education, by his human relationships.[321]

In defense of Wynkoop, she is consistently clear that moral righteousness necessitates grace, and a relationship to God can be dissipated by moralisms, rules, legalism, platitudes, etc. Taking aim at the Holiness Movement and on target Wynkoop states,

> *Moralism* has been tried and found wanting. Hebrew moralism is the classic example. It is easier to keep law than to be right. But keeping the law without being right ends up in the self-righteousness that is both repulsive to the onlooker and spiritually disappointing to the law keeper. When the dynamic of holiness theology wanes, its ideals tend to be translated into a moralism that isolates people from the life in which they need most to be immersed. Moralism ends in spiritual bankruptcy.[322]

At other times, the above clarity between New Testament righteousness and morality does not exist, or does not have a distinct demarcation for Wynkoop. "It has been observed that the exhortations of the New Testament are not centered around the word holiness or sanctification but around the moral responsibility men have to God in the presence of the provision for and the gift of sanctification.... Not 'Lord justify me' but 'have mercy on me' is the Christian prayer. Similarly, not 'Sanctify me' but 'Make me a fit place for thy dwelling' is the proper Christian petition."[323] I ask: wouldn't this indwelling make me a fit place? Does God dwell anywhere that is not a fit place? At this point, Wynkoop has constructed a straw man, in that I have never heard anyone pray, "Justify me." But she was correct, if she reminded us that "self-justification" was a spiritual stance vehemently condemned by Jesus (Luke 11:15, 18:9-11).

---

[321] Jacques Ellul. *To Will and to Do* (Philadelphia: The United Church Press, 1969) 63.

[322] Wynkoop, *A Theology*, 377.

[323] Ibid., 374.

Wynkoop goes on to write, "If the contexts are carefully noted around the words cognate with holiness, two emphases seem to stand out clearly. One is the centrality of Christ and the call to responsible discipleship, and the other has to do with moral rectitude."[324] One page later, "Rather holiness is a positive quality. It is radiant moral health – *perfect integrity* (italics hers.) It is the very life of God, expressing itself in all relationships."[325] The word integrity comes from integer, a whole number; in other words, the essence of integrity is wholeness. Who has perfect wholeness? What one of us does not need the defense mechanisms of compartmentalization, sublimation, rationalization, and compensation, to shore up our fragile and wounded egos? Perfect integrity would be in perfect congruence between what I am and what I claim to be. Or if we borrow Marshall McLuhan's language, the medium (the self) would be in exact agreement with my message (who I claim to be). McLuhan postulated that only in Jesus Christ do we find perfect agreement between the medium and the message. Specifically McLuhan stated, "In Jesus Christ there is no distance or separation between the medium and the message. It's the one case where we can say medium and message are in complete union."[326]

The Pelagian Accusation

Taylor accused Wynkoop of being Pelagian; and she may have exhibited tendencies, but not for the reasons he stated. Taylor indicted Wynkoop for erasing original sin and thus preempting the need for entire sanctification, the removal of original sin. Her definition of original sin is not as concrete and analogical as Taylor and much of the Holiness Movement would prefer. She wrote: "Men find themselves locked by their own love into an orbit about a center. Sin is love locked into a false center, the self."[327] And further, "The epitome of pride and carnal arrogance is to raise one's own miserable self to the pretention of being a god."[328] Wynkoop believed that original sin was better described

---

[324] Ibid.

[325] Ibid., 360.

[326] David A. King, "McLuhan's Still Current Theory Deeply Rooted in Catholicism," *The Georgia Bulletin*, (October 24, 2013). http://georgiabulletin.org/column// david-a-king/commentary/2013/10/mcluhans-still-current-media-theory-deeply-rooted-in-catholism/

[327] Wynkoop, *A Theology*, 165.

[328] Ibid., 166.

as an orientation, a false frame of reference, rather than a taint or disease inherited from the first Adam. Taylor assesses that Wynkoop effectively adopted Charles Finney's doctrine of sin which ruled out an inherited disease of nature which was below the will and consciousness.[329]

Mark Olson picked up on the Pelagian tendency, arguing that Wynkoop, in attempting to close the credibility gap, overcorrected. "By driving a sharp wedge between substantive and relational concepts of human nature, sin, holiness, and perfection and other related doctrines Wynkoop necessarily departed from John Wesley."[330] While admitting that Wynkoop shows no evidence of reading from Charles Finney, Olson argues that Wynkoop's theology is more in keeping with Finney than with Wesley. Possibly neither Richard Taylor nor Mark Olson have considered that the real culprits are Nathaniel Taylor, Horace Bushnell, and dozens of other nineteenth-century "new divinity" exponents.[331] Plus, the thousands of American pastors who have stood in the pulpit with a theologically vacuous, humanistic positive-thinking Gospel. As E. Brooks Holifield argued, Sigmund Freud, Carl Rogers, and a slew of others, misdirected Americans to pursuing self-actualization instead of salvation.[332]

To Saran Wrap any person and put a single label on the package, is almost always misleading and unfair. Pelagius has not received his just due. He lived in a time (350-425?) when both society, (Roman) and the Church (Constantinian) were the most corrupt in the history of human kind. Pelagius became a fearless preacher of righteousness. He did not believe that the will was absolutely free. Individuals could act rightly only by the grace of God. According to his biographer, John Ferguson, Pelagius anathematized those who denied the necessity of the assistance of God's grace in every single action. In other words, grace

---

[329] Taylor, "Why the Holiness Movement Died," *God's Revivalist and Bible Advocate*, March 1999, 25.

[330] Mark Olson, "Strange Bedfellows: A Reappraisal of Mildred Wynkoop's *A Theology of Love*," *Wesleyan Theological Journal* , Vol. 42, No. 2, Fall 2010, 196-217.

[331] Ibid., 217. Olson does state that "Yet, not withstanding all her quotations of Wesley and her claims to wear his mantle, her theology differs from his in very significant ways, leading to a Wesleyan theology that is more in agreement with the core principles of New Divinity Calvinism, which Charles Finney represents."

[332] E. Brooks Holifield. *A History of Pastoral Care in America: From Salvation to Self-Realization* (Nashville: Abingdon Press, 1983).

meant "the initial endowment together with what Augustine called cooperating grace. What he could not accept was prevenient grace in Augustine's sense, an irresistible power independent of the will which forced the will."[333]

Of course, Pelagianism denotes negativity while Augustinianism carries a positive connotation. This assessment should be questioned by Wesleyans since the latter touted concupiscence as an inherent, unavoidable and non-remedial condition of human nature while in a temporal state, and Augustine is the father of double predestination as much or more than any other person, though he did not take it to its logical conclusion (double predestination) as did John Calvin and Theodore Beza. Ferguson correctly notes that Wesley defends Pelagius and concludes, "If a heretic is one who emphasizes one truth to the exclusion of others, it would at any rate appear that he was no more a heretic than Augustine,"[334] who believed in predestination, in the physical inheritance of the original taint through man's sexual nature and the damnation of unbaptized infants.

I suggest that Olson overcorrects Wynkoop's overcorrection. He believes that Wynkoop's system agrees with Finney's concerning the freedom of the will, as an inherent attribute of human nature, not a gift of prevenient grace as in Wesley. To the contrary, Wynkoop quotes Wesley, "No man living is entirely destitute of what is vulgarly called *Natural Conscience*. But this conscience is not natural. It is more commonly called preventing grace."[335] She further states, "This poured out love Wesley called prevenient grace or preventing grace. All men are preserved savable. No man can save himself. He can claim no merit

---

[333] John Ferguson. *Pelagius: A Historical and Theological Study* (Cambridge: W. Heffer and Sons, 1956) 174.

[334] Ibid., 183, 184. What Wesley actually said about Pelagius is: "I verily believe, the real heresy of Pelagius was neither more nor less than this: The holding that Christians may, by the grace of God, (not without it, that I take to be a mere slander.) 'go on to perfection,' or, in other words, 'fulfill the law of Christ.' When Augustine's passions were heated, his word is not worth a rush. And here is the secret: St. Augustine was angry at Pelagius: Hence he slandered and abused him, (as his manner was,) without either fear or shame. And St. Augustine was then in the Christian world, what Aristotle was afterwards: There needed no other proof of any assertion, than *Ipse dixit*: "St. Augustine said it." John Wesley. *The Works of John Wesley*, Third Edition, vol. 6 (London: Wesleyan Methodist Book Room, 1872), 328-329.

[335] Wynkoop. *A Theology*, 105.

or credit for *any* good he ever does. Before he exercised his ability, this prevenient grace had been given him and the power to use it is also a gift of God."[336] She is even more clear at this point in her foundations of *Wesleyan Arminian Theology*. "Man is totally corrupt and helpless in himself. Grace is back of every good or ability in man. Not even the Christian, no matter how established he may be, possesses goodness in himself."[337]

Nonetheless, Olson wrongly states, "What Wynkoop is opposing is the perspective that faith is a gift of divine grace an impartation from God to the person. Instead, faith is an inherent natural attribute of 'relational beings.'"[338] Nowhere can I find in Wynkoop that faith is other than a gift of divine grace. She quoted the Wesleyan hymn, "Free Grace" and she certainly would not have missed its import:

'Tis not by works that we have done;
  'Twas grace alone His heart inclined;
'Twas grace that gave His only son
  To taste of death for all mankind.

For every man He tasted death;
  And hence we in His sight appear,
Not lifting up our eyes beneath,
  But publishing His mercy here.

By grace we draw our every breath;
  By grace we live, and move, and are;
By grace we 'scape the second death;
  By grace we now Thy grace declare.

From the first feeble thought of good
  To when the perfect grace is given;
'Tis all of grace: by grace renew'd
  From hell we pass through earth to heaven.[339]

Thus, both Taylor and Olson incorrectly accuse Wynkoop of being Pelagian. (Even Pelagius was not as Pelagian as Pelagianism.) But if there be such a thing as Pelagianism with an overemphasis on morality,

---

[336] Ibid., 162.

[337] Mildred Wynkoop. *Foundations of Wesleyan Arminian Theology* (Kansas City: Beacon Hill Press of Kansas City, 1967) 69.

[338] Olson, 201.

[339] Wynkoop, *A Theology of Love*, 99.

Taylor and Olson were correct, but not for reasons they perceived. It is at this point and not the elimination of grace that Wynkoop was akin to Finney and Bushnell. I cannot argue that Wynkoop does not undercut herself by claiming that moral integrity is the goal of redemption: "God deals with men as responsible persons and every step God requires of man from the first stirrings of conviction to the last responsible act in life is in the interest of moral integrity."[340] This certainly contradicts the Westminster catechism in that the chief purpose of human kind is "to glorify God and enjoy him forever." As Ellul argues, the life and teachings of Jesus were a rebuke to a religion of morality and substitution of one system of morality for another is a "subversion of Christianity." He wrote,

> Love obeys no morality and gives birth to no morality. None of the great categories of revealed truth is relative to morality or can give birth to it; freedom, truth, light. Word, and holiness don't belong at all to the order of morality. What they evoke is a mode of *being*, a model of life that is very free, that involves constant risks, that is constantly renewed. The Christian life is contrary to morality because it is not repetitive. No fixed duty has to be done no matter what course life may take. Morality always interdicts this mode of being. It is an obstacle to it and implicitly condemns it, just as Jesus is inevitably condemned by moral people.[341]

Wynkoop was against almost everything that Finney represented and practiced. She would not have agreed with his "moral suasion," his pragmatism, his methodology for revival, and in particular, his scared-into-heaven preaching. The problem is more subtle than Taylor detected. At least seven times, Wynkoop disclaimed Pelagianism, either for herself or for Wesley.[342] She may have protested too loudly, but I do not think she incorrectly explicated the Pelagian heresy in describing Wesley's middle way between Augustine and Pelagius. The truth is, we don't need Pelagius to be Pelagian. Meritocracy is difficult to escape; impressing God is tough business. And its temptation is difficult to detect, much less always overcome. The primal temptation was the showdown in the wilderness, "If you are the son of God, prove yourself." Do we ever get beyond proving ourselves? A perceptive friend of mine editing one of my books, at my mention of Pelagianism, noted in the margin, "Aren't

---

[340] Ibid., 187.

[341] Jacques Ellul. *The Subversion of Christianity*. (Grand Rapids: William B. Eerdman Publishing Company, 1984) 71.

[342] Ibid., 97, 161, 184, 192, 215, 232, 238.

we all?" Is it possible to detach our morality from our security in God? I constantly live within the temptation to list what I do which defines me as a Christian.

The Limitations of Wynkoop's Wesleyan Ethic

Allow me to again remind my reader that Wynkoop is searching for a Wesleyan ethic. But her failure to reference Bonhoeffer, Barth, Reinhold Niebuhr, and other contemporary ethicists leaves her moral ethics grounded in the eighteenth rather than the twentieth century. Richard Hays, in *The Moral Vision of the New Testament*, reviews four ethicists and their use of Scripture including: Reinhold Niebuhr (Christian realism which is overly pessimistic), Karl Barth (obedience to Christ but overly optimistic about individual interpretation and application), John Howard Yoder (Christocentric and biblically-based, but unrealistic for the Church at large, depending on isolated and ingrown groups), and Schüssler Fiorenza (historically sophisticated exegesis but skewed reading of text).[343]

More important than referencing ethicists, is Hays grounding his moral vision in the meta-narrative of Jesus. He contrasts Jesus' teaching with that of the Pharisees. "Woe to you, teachers of the law and Pharisees, you hypocrites! You give a tenth of your spices, mint, and dill and cumin, but you have neglected the more important matters of the law, justice, mercy and faithfulness" (Matthew 23:23). Jesus' ethical methodology included outlandish stories that "shock us into thought by positing unexpected analogies – analogies that could not be discerned within conventional categories of knowledge."[344] These stories overturn our conventional way of thinking. "To 'understand' these parables is to be changed by them, to have our vision of the world reshaped by them. To 'understand' them is to enter the process of reflecting about how our lives ought to change in response to the gospel – a gospel that unsettles what we 'know' about responsibility and ethics."[345]

---

[343] Richard B. Hays. *The Moral Vision of the New Testament: A Contemporary Introduction to New Testament Ethics* (San Francisco: HarperSanFrancisco, 1996) 215-290.
[344] Ibid., 300.
[345] Ibid., 301.

Dennis Kinlaw referred to Jesus as the "supreme third-grade teacher." I would take that a step further and assess Jesus as the superb graduate school professor, whose classes I would have avoided. And if his course had been required, and titled something like "But I say unto you," I would have seated myself in a corner desk and never raised my hand. But that is just it, there is no place to hide for any of us. As a religious person, it is impossible for me to enter into dialogue with Jesus without painting myself into a corner, because he always uses "gotcha" pedagogy. I am the priest who passes by on the other side; I am the elder brother; I am the rich man; I am the unforgiving debtor.

Even if reading holiness through a Wesleyan lens, I do not understand how Wynkoop can claim a biblical ethic with so little reference to the Sermon on the Mount, which is viewing holiness on a high-definition, 4-D 70" television screen. Jesus is the incarnation of the Great Reversal: God sacrifices himself for humankind, even for those who hate him. Jesus' teachings leave all of us fallen short of the perfect law of God and the Sermon on the Mount; we are to return good for evil. Jesus promised that the Holy Spirit would "teach you all things, and will remind you of everything" (John 14: 26). The prompting of the Holy Spirit does not eliminate careful study and reflection, but the Holy Spirit is the only possibility for these "impossible" sayings of Christ to become a reality.

American morality pursues happiness which is defined by the greatest welfare of the whole, the smooth operation and material prosperity of society. But of course, what defines a society as good and beneficial is as slippery as trying to catch a fish bare-handed. Morality is much different than piety, the latter focused upon God, often beyond reason and human concepts of "fairness" (a word not found in Scripture). Over and over again, I read the Old Testament with a condemning frown, or at least a questioning mind, as God kills every man, woman, boy, and girl in the five cities of Judea (Joshua 10). Or women who are stolen from a local Canaannite tribe, in order to repopulate the tribe of Benjamin (Judges 21). My seven-year-old grandson recently asked me, "Papa, why is the Bible so tragic?"

And we Arminians must at some point confess that the reason we condemn double pre-destination, is that it does not meet our standards of fairness, or does not define love by a reasonable, moral content. American theology has essentially destroyed the inscrutable sovereignty of God with a reasonable, humanistic morality. I am not sure that most evangelicals understand that God is excellent because he is God; they understand him via preachers who fill American pulpits, and tout culturally informed presuppositions, with what Christian Smith refers to as a "moralistic therapeutic deism."[346] I would not put this as strongly as Joseph Haroutunian in his seminal work, *Piety versus Moralism*, as he indicted Samuel Hopkins, but his argument needs to be seriously considered:

> The attitude of man towards such a deity must necessarily be different from his attitude to his fellow-creatures, as different as God is from man. To regard the eternal and almighty Sovereign of the worlds with that "friendly affection," which one may extend to a schoolmate or a fellow-citizen, amounts to nothing less than damnable presumption. The God of Calvinism stands in a category infinitely superior to that of any and every created thing; therefore, to define holiness as "love to God and our neighbor, including ourselves" is blasphemy.[347]

Though I am not a Calvinist, I have to confess that the American pulpit has for the most part dismissed a sovereign God.

Wynkoop certainly did not commit blasphemy by her emphasis on morality as defining our relationship to God by sorting through our relationship to people to which there is a truth, but a truth greatly reduced. If not careful, we have romanticized holiness as interpreted by emotive sentiment and the redemptive plot line of the musical *Les Miserables*, "To love another is to see the face of God." Jonathan Edwards would not permit himself to lose sight of the fact that, to be authentically religious, and to be moral, are two different things. Morality is natural and genuine, spirituality is supernatural. Or to put it another way with the help of Haroutunian, "God's love for His creatures is subsumed under his love for His own glory. In creating the world God had 'respect to the creature's happiness,' only in so far as true happiness consists in the worship and service of God in seeking the glory of God, which is the

---

[346] See Christian Smith and Melinda Denton in *Soul Searching: The Religious and Spiritual Lives of American Teenagers* (New York: Oxford University, 2005) 118-171.

[347] Joseph Haroutunian. *Piety versus Moralism: The Passing of the New England Theology* (New York: Henry Holt and Company, 1932) 85.

proper exercise of true virtue."[348] The American Church is not prone to meditate on Isaiah 55: "For my thoughts are not your thoughts, neither are your ways my ways, declares the Lord. As the heavens are higher than the earth so are my ways higher than your ways and my thoughts higher than your thoughts" (Isaiah 55:8-9). The word "moral" does not allow sufficient separation between heaven and earth, the otherness of God and the finitude of human existence. Ironically, Wynkoop fell into the very pit she was trying to avoid, moralism, which easily became legalism, a disease with which the Holiness Movement became infected.

Wynkoop and Current Moral Development Theory

With such an intense and paramount emphasis on morality, Wynkoop partially bought into moral development theory as taught by Lawrence Kohlberg and touted by Donald Joy. While I admit to favorable parallels between the order of salvation from a soteriological perspective and ethical maturity from a pedagogical perspective, there are at the same time major departures. Kohlberg assumes that knowing what to do in a given situation ensures the power to do. He believes that religion of any kind has no bearing on a person's ability to act justly; thus, we can forget about God. Ethical development for Kohlberg is at least partially socio-economically driven, in that "middle class and popular children progress farther and faster than do lower-class children and social isolates."[349]

Kohlberg's stage 6, the highest level of moral development, depicts an individual who is autonomous, oblivious to what the group thinks, and transcends receiving affection or esteem from one's peers. As Doug Sholl states, "Those at the highest level of moral maturity are 'characterized by a major thrust toward autonomous moral principles which have validity and application apart from authority of the groups or persons who hold them and apart from the individual's identification with these persons or groups.'"[350] Unfortunately, stage 6 post-conventional ethical thinking and action is reserved for only a few moral supermen

---

[348] Ibid., 75.

[349] Lawrence Kohlberg, "A Developmental Approach for Moral Education," *The Humanist*, ed. Paul Kurtz (Buffalo: Hoffman Printing Company, 1972) 14.

[350] Doug Sholl, "The Contributions of Lawrence Kohlberg to Religious and Moral Education," *Religious Education*, ed. Randolph Miller (New York: The Religious Education Association, 1971) 366.

(Kohlberg did not include women) such as Socrates, Jesus, Martin Luther King, Jr. and Nelson Mandela.

Donald Joy buys into the lock-step theory of Kohlberg when he writes, "Note that Christian Holiness therefore, seen as an advanced response to God's grace, by which a transgression is made from the letter of the law to the spirit of the law, from response to external demand to response to a sermon written on the heart, is developmentally unlikely to occur before age 23, and more likely if it occurs at all in the early 30s."[351] Is Joy claiming that God's promise "I will put my law in their hearts and I will write them in their minds," (Hebrews 10:16b) (The same concept is expressed in Jeremiah 31:33, and Ezekiel 36:27), would be unlikely if not impossible for a 20-year-old Christian? By using Kohlberg to tout a Wesleyan spiritual formation which eliminates reification, codification, and the "rigormortis of legalism," Joy buys into a developmental system, which emphasizes "growth, developmental, and personal response to issues in the *respondent's own time and sequence* as of ultimate importance."[352] While I readily admit that persons in the Holiness Movement have been given bad advice about when and how to seek entire sanctification, in contrast to Joy's assertion, it would seem that the sovereignty and wisdom of God are of *ultimate importance*. The aphorism "timing is everything" needs to be changed to "God's timing is everything."

Wynkoop questioned developmental moral thinking by stating, "But since it is religious relationship, it can become a genuine reality at any stage in the development of human life. Love is possible in any and all stages of life, but there are changes in love continuing through life that cannot be implanted whole anywhere."[353] Wynkoop showed little evidence of having read Lawrence Kohlberg, but instead relied on the interpretations of Donald Joy and Catherine Stonehouse (coincidently both of them Free Methodists and professors at Asbury Theological Seminary). Thus, Wynkoop was ambushed, resulting in observing that, "Jesus was born as a human being and He had to progress through physical growth with all the stages involved in that....This does not

[351] Donald Joy, "Human Development and Christian Holiness," *The Asbury Seminarian* Vol. 31, (1976) 23.

[352] Ibid., 25.

[353] Mildred Bangs Wynkoop, "Wesleyan Theology and Christian Development," *The Asbury Seminarian*, Vol. 31, (1976) 39.

mean that badness, or humanness, had to be beaten out of him, but that He needed to go through all of the stages all men must go through to come to maturity."[354] It seems to me that when Jesus as a twelve year old said to his anxious worried-sick parents who had been searching for him some forty-eight hours, "Don't you know I must be about my Father's business?" he must have skipped a stage or two. While it is true that God normally does not make instantaneous saints, it is equally untrue that, "'Full sanctification' does not leap over the developmental levels, transporting a person into the highest level without the trouble of taking every step in between."[355] Wynkoop was hood-winked by a humanistic moral development theory that she did not fully understand.

Not Further Back or Deeper Down

The above brief foray into moral development theory provides a transition for examining Wynkoop's most egregious theological error. Both Richard Taylor and Mark Olson picked up on this significant and incorrect departure from Wesley. Olson writes, "Wynkoop believes that the substantive perspective understands holiness to make a *sub-volitional transformation*. But this is wrong says Wynkoop, since holiness is relational, and relationship must involve volition. Salvation cannot mean an alteration in the sub-volitional nature, because this is not a relational change but an ontological one."[356] Taylor wrote, "For just as holiness may be a conscious relationship of obedience and love – hence thoroughly moral at all times, so our doctrine of sin, implied Dr. Wynkoop, must correspond. That only could be sin which was fully responsible at the moral moment. She expressly repudiated any underlying sinfulness of birth nature, deeper down and further back than the conscious willing."[357]

When Wynkoop declares that original sin is not "further back or deeper down," than rational responsibility, she simplifies the complexity of sin and limits the power of transforming grace. Wynkoop argued it was wrong to believe in an "original sin that was further back and deeper down than the person and beyond the place where language

---

[354] Ibid., 38.

[355] Ibid., 40.

[356] Olson, 199-200.

[357] Taylor, Why The Holiness Movement Died, 25.

can go or thought conceive."[358] By attempting to escape a substantive definition of sin by keeping entire sanctification on a rational level, Wynkoop has erred. She has claimed an epistemology that does not exist, knowledge and understanding which go to the deepest levels of my moral problems. Non-understanding does not remove a given issue from moral responsibility. I'm not sure that all Nazi guards at Dachau or Auschwitz understood the immorality of their role. But none of us would fail to call them immoral just because nationalism and ethno-centricity had formed their consciences beyond their comprehension. Wynkoop amplifies her position.

> If God acts toward man apart from his thinking and choice; if salvation is "applied," to man by a supernatural alteration of his mind, body, psyche, "deeper down" than his conscious life, where he cannot be held responsible; if man can expect a "psychological mutation" so that he no longer needs to feel the full force of temptation, then - though God is a personal Being and man is a person - "personal relationship" is a fiction, biblical salvation is a myth.[359]

Her statement deserves linguistic analysis:

A. "Apart from thinking and choice." God not only provides prevenient grace beyond thinking and choice, he appears to people, speaks to people, and even transforms people beyond thinking and choice. God is doing that today, in particular among Jews and Muslims. A wife who lost her Jewish husband to a cerebral hemorrhage related that six months before his death, God began to speak to him and angels appeared to him, and "We both became Christians." Was Paul actively and consciously seeking Christ when he was struck down on the Damascus Road by a blinding light and captivating voice?

B. "Salvation is applied to him by a supernatural alteration of his mind." Can any person have the mind that was in Christ (Philippians 2) without the transformation of the Holy Spirit? While Wynkoop has claimed a Hebraic understanding of persons, she has touted a mind-soul dualism foreign to Scripture.

---

[358] Wynkoop, *A Theology of Love*, 171.
[359] Ibid., 176.

C. "Deeper down than the conscious life." People do all kinds of evil, acts that are deeper down than their conscious life, rape, murder, theft, etc., driven by urges, passions, and tempers, beyond their understanding and possibly beyond psychoanalysis.

D. "Psychological mutation so that he no longer needs to feel the full force of temptation." I do not know what Wynkoop meant by mutation. So again, we turn to Webster: "A sudden departure from the parent type in one or more heritable characteristics, caused by a change in a gene or chromosome."[360] Genetic expert Thad Polk writes, "Studies have shown that certain people are innately more susceptible to addiction than to others." And "So there may actually be a scientific basis to the idea of an addictive personality - that is, of a person who is at risk of getting hooked on any kind of addictive substance or behavior."[361] So Christianity is now facing a new question: Can God's grace effect genetic transformation? Is there grace sufficient to enable "sudden departures" from habits and behavioral patterns that have possibly been passed down through generations, or behavior caused by some traumatic event that took place in the life of a fetus, the infant before conscious memory or even a small child? Listen to the story of medical researcher Samuel K. Biser:

DNA is not immune from life. Life is reflected onto it.

For example, childhood mistreatment and early trauma change the genes in the front of the brain— throughout the lifespan—and into the next generation of infants as well. This is a long tail of co nsequences.

I believe this is what happened to me and my genes, because of a massacre that almost killed my Dad. He grew up in a small town, Felshtin, in the breadbasket of Russia, called the Ukraine. It was like Kansas in the U.S. On February 18, 1939, a gang of

---

[360] Webster, 1269.

[361] Thad A. Polk. "The Addictive Brain," *The Great Courses* (Chantilly, VA: The Great Courses, 2015) 26-29.

armed assassins on horseback, called the Cossacks, rode their horses into town and slaughtered about 600 Jews. That included many of my father's family and friends. It was murder-time in the countryside.

The shock of that trauma was blasted onto my father's genes — and later onto mine. His mother made him lay motionless in a ditch for a whole day —covered in snow, to hide him from madmen with swords.

My Dad told me he remembered seeing a young orphan, who had been befriended, loved, and taken in by his Jewish neighbors—point out a Jew hiding in a ditch, like my Dad.

The orphan shouted to the horsemen, *"Here's a Jew over here you missed. Kill him."* So they did.

After the killings, the Cossacks turned the pigs loose into the streets to eat dead Jewish bodies.[362]

E. "Though God is a personal being and man is a person – personal relationship is a fiction, biblical salvation is a myth." That's exactly what Freud thought, and because of personal experience, academic knowledge and theological conviction, I refuse to be in his camp.

Summarizing, we note that Wynkoop cut herself off from her Wesleyan-Holiness tradition at two points, or even more critically from both Wesley and Edwards. They would have disagreed with her emphasis on morality and her neglect of the sub-volitional. Both eighteenth century theologians believed that there was an involuntary act of sin which was sub-volitional, but not beyond the grace of God. Note the similarity of language between the two. Edwards: "A very malicious man may be unable to exert acts to an enemy or to desire his prosperity: yea, some may be so under the power of a vile disposition, that they may be unable to love those who are most worthy of their esteem and affection."[363] Wesley: "Yea, sometimes it may even border upon distraction making

---

[362] Samuel K. Biser. *Genetic Miracles: For People with an Inherited Disease - Who Need a Miracle to Stay on Earth* (Waynesboro, Virginia: Samuel Biser Press, Incorporated, 2016) 43.

[363] George Marsden. *Jonathan Edwards: A Life* (New Haven: Yale University Press, 2003) 442.

the man 'drunken though not with wine,' suspending the exercise of the memory, of the understanding, of all the natural faculties....such as the freedom of his will; free only to evil; free to 'drink in iniquity like water;' to wander farther and farther from the living God, and do more 'despite to the Spirit of grace!'"[364]

Overreaction to "Emotionalism"

Wynkoop derails at another juncture, which is understandable given her negative experience in the contrived emotionalism of Nazarene camp meetings. Both Edwards and Wesley defended physical manisfestations, transrational behavior, each recognizing the "danger of enthusiasm." Neither of them discounted swooning, prostration, shouting, running, leaping, etc., recognizing that all of it could be counterfeited by Satan or human ingenuity. Had Wynkoop understood that such exercises often, if not always, are dictated by one's temperament, she may not have so strongly reacted to her heritage. Wesley was an excellent guide in discerning the authentic presence of God recorded on January 31, 1739.

> About three in the morning, as we were continuing instant in prayer, the power of God came mightily upon us, insomuch that many cried out for exceeding joy, and many fell to the ground. As soon as we were recovered from shock and amazement at the presence of his majesty, we broke out with one voice, "We praise thee, O God; we acknowledge thee to be the Lord."[365]

Of course whatever happened on the British side was amplified ten-fold on the American side. One only has to read the journal of Benjamin Abbott to know that he was extraordinarily attuned and susceptible to the operations of the Holy Spirit, if not a spiritual lunatic. In fact, for the uninitiated, to be in his presence was down-right dangerous.

> Witnesses said that, when Abbott preached, there was weeping, melting, falling, screaming, screeching, rolling, shaking, and thumping. The effects were so overwhelming

---

[364] Wesley, *Works*, "The Spirit of Bondage and Adoption," Vol. V, 103-104.

[365] Quoted in Ann Taves. *Fits, Trances, & Visions: Experiencing Religion and Explaining Experience from Wesley to James* (Princeton: Princeton University Press, 1999) 72.

that many leaped out of the window and piled up at the door trying to escape. When one young man for hours "lay so dead a state, and continued so long that his flesh grew cold, and his blood was stagnated to his elbows," Abbott himself became alarmed. "I concluded to go home, and nor proceed one step farther, for killing people would not answer."[366]

To the misperception of many, the National Camp Meeting Association for the Promotion of Holiness, the *classicus locus* of the American Holiness Movement, exhibited none of the above phenomena. Under the sane and yet intensely spiritual guidance of John Inskip, William McDonald, as well as others, the presence of God was no less palpable, than the above Methodist gatherings, in their annual gatherings which sometimes numbered in the tens of thousands. One attendee at the 1868 Manheim Pennsylvania Camp Meeting left the following narrative:

The writer left the stand in the midst of the scene, and went up along the left-hand outside aisle. Such a sight he had never seen before. Thousands were in the attitude of prayer. An awful presence seemed to rest upon the multitude. There were suppressed sobs, and praises, too.

There were those who insisted that at one time they heard a strange sound, as of a rushing mighty wind, and yet as if subdued and held in check over that prayerful congregation. The writer went to his tent, far back from the circle, but God was everywhere. It was an awful season. Souls were wrestling with God, who was unrolling to many the long, long list of their sins. Unfaithful church members were looking and shuddering over the dreadful past. The people were face to face with God.[367]

Even the New Testament Church struggled with the tension between "quenching the Spirit" and doing all things "decently and in order." Such was the discerning genius of Edwards and Wesley, who as men of religion were desirous that neither they nor their followers miss the "mysterium-tremendum" of God, which according to Rudolph Otto, appears as a "strange and mighty propulsion towards an ideal good, known only to religion and in its nature, fundamentally non-rational..."[368]

---

[366] John Firth. *The Experience and Gospel Labors of the Reverend Benjamin Abbott* (Philadelphia: D. & S. Neall, 1825) 89.

[367] Darius Salter. *American Evangelism: Its Theology and Practice* (Grand Rapids: Baker Books, 1996) 99.

[368] Rudolph Otto. *The Idea of the Holy* (New York: Oxford University Press, 1923)

Otto argued that the experiences of the *tremendum mysterium* show "that above and beyond our rational being lies hidden the ultimate and highest part of our nature, which can find no satisfaction in the mere allaying of the needs of our sensuous, psychical, or intellectual impulses and cravings."[369] Whatever happens in the subterranean recesses of our being, Edwards, Wesley and Wynkoop believed that religious experience, whether it be positive or negative, can only be evaluated in the light of rational, Christian character.

Mildred Wynkoop wrote *A Theology of Love* almost one-half century ago. In the light of present-day theories on neurological science, damaged emotions, genetic inheritance, post-traumatic stress, habit formation, virtue practice, addictive behavior, and thousands of psychological-sociological studies, I wonder if she would still disavow God's transforming grace, going "further back and deeper down" than cognitive processing and rational intentionality. If so, she would be misinterpreting Wesley who had much to say about tempers and dispositions that might not be fully comprehended, but are not outside of moral responsibility and not beyond the transforming grace of God. While Wynkoop has made a valuable contribution to Wesleyan Holiness scholarship (and she was a scholar), she also overreacted to some issues that needed to be addressed. Not ironically, much of her correcting was subjectively driven by events in her psyche of which she was not unaware, but not fully conscious of the sublimation motivating her. All of us have means of coping, some more healthy than others. Mildred Wynkoop's theological paradigm was at least partially constructed by a father who spoke with an accent, a shy disposition, firing at Western Evangelical Seminary, embarrassment at the crude behavior of Nazarenes, courageous forays into a man's world and above all, disappointment in both the formula and methodology so narrowly defined for her to become a "holy" person. It is hard for me to imagine anyone who would have been more a misfit as an evangelist on the Nazarene camp meeting trail. Her gifts and calling lay in other areas, and we can be grateful that she found and employed them.

When Ken Grider received Rob Staples' "Current Wesleyan Debate" paper, 1979, he emphatically said, "This day will forever be a

---

36.
[369] Ibid., 36.

watershed moment in the history of the Church of the Nazarene. Ken was fearful that many of the younger budding theologians of the Church of the Nazarene shared the theological sentiments expressed in Staples' paper."[370] Grider did not exaggerate the impact of Staples' thesis. Staples and Wynkoop were first cousins, if not fraternal twins. Yes, there was much guilt by association, as I will argue in the following chapter. But those who aligned themselves against Staples and Wynkoop were correct; the relational paradigm which they promoted was very different than the holiness formula which until that time, had defined the Church of the Nazarene. Both of them would survive the "Ordeal by Fire" and champion the cause which would become the new paradigm for a right relationship to a holy God.

Wynkoop wrote to Stephen Nease, President of the Seminary, on March 6, 1979, "When such persons as you, and Rob Staples and Alec Deasley, as well as the seminary, should be imprisoned in a web of suspicion, false and cloudy charges, fear and distrust, I find myself aroused to action. Of such situations have been made cruel inquisitions (McCarthyism) destroyed reputations, and the tragic set-back of the Church through history." She then wrote, "Now to be under a cloud of heresy, at least by innuendo, is a grief too deep for words, but accepted without rancor. That too was in my covenant with God, made some 40 years ago."[371] NTS Professor Paul Orjala is reported to have said while Mildred was speaking in the NTS chapel, "There is the most dangerous person in the Church of the Nazarene."[372] Sadly, her life had come full circle in an unfortunate way. The theological battle in which she found herself at Western Evangelical Seminary at the beginning of her career was not nearly as intense as the exchange of fire at Nazarene Theological Seminary where she was "Theologian in Residence" at the end of her career. This time she was not so much a target as she was caught in the crossfire. This battle we will attempt to analyze in the next chapter.

---

[370] Email, Steve McCormick to Darius Salter, January 16, 2019.

[371] Nazarene Archives, Nease Collection, Letter, Mildred Wynkoop to Stephen Nease, May 6, 1979.

[372] Rob L. Staples, "My Ordeal by Fire: The Record of a Crisis I Faced as Professor of Theology at Nazarene Theological Seminary," courtesy of Steve McCormick, 15.

A Glorious Serendipity

In the day of multiple services at First Church of the Nazarene in Kansas City, I sat in my car at the back door of my church, waiting for my wife to emerge. (It seems like a full third of my life has been given to this activity, a perception created by my exaggerated importance of time). Situated about 25 feet from the door, I watched an event evolve that could not have been constructed at the most inspirational height of my imagination. Richard Taylor and Mildred Wynkoop walking alone, were converging for a cataclysmic encounter, both of them exactly timed to reach the door at the same moment. Taylor, still living in the Northwest, was visiting Kansas City, while Wynkoop was showing up for worship at her home church. I was witnessing something which in all likelihood had never happened before and would never happen again. The condemner would meet the condemned, the accuser the accused, the orthodox the heretic, the male the female, and the insider the outsider. Richard Taylor had claimed that Wynkoop's *A Theology of Love* had been more responsible for the death of the Holiness Movement than any other single person, writing, or event.[373]

By this time, Wynkoop was almost bent double, having been crippled by osteoporosis, and Taylor still maintained his tall and regal posture. He opened the door, warmly smiled, and with a nod of his head acknowledged Mildred's presence. She looked up with a smile and offered gratitude for his gentlemanly gesture. They walked in together. I did not perceive an awkwardness on either of their parts. Neither of them exuded or possessed any malice that would have precluded them from Heaven. The door which Taylor opened for Wynkoop on that Sunday morning was a symbol for Heaven's Gate that is wide enough for diverse, theological opinions. Perhaps while I am writing this, both of them are standing at the Throne laughing about their one-time theological quibbles, all of which lose their antagonism in the ocean of God's grace. Both Taylor and Wynkoop exhibited an element of Christian character which is so sadly lacking in 21st century American culture. Disagreement does not have to descend to disrespect; neither does disagreement necessitate negating or denigrating someone else's dignity.

---

[373] Taylor. "Why the Holiness Movement Died," 25.

Chapter 5:
A Troubled Denomination

The Quanstrom Thesis

In 2000, a life-long Nazarene completed a Ph.D. dissertation at Saint Louis University, an institution of high academic reputation. Mark Quanstrom titled his investigation, *A Century of Holiness Theology: The Doctrine of Entire Sanctification in the Church of the Nazarene: From Extravagant Hope to Limited Expectation.* A Jesuit school seemed a strange place to complete a dissertation on Wesleyan Holiness theology, but nonetheless, Quanstrom wrote a carefully nuanced examination of the evolvement or devolvement of the Nazarene Church's distinguishing theological commitment throughout the twentieth century. When the Church of the Nazarene published the dissertation in 2004, it gave Quanstrom's work a new title: *A Century of Holiness Theology: The Doctrine of Entire Sanctification in the Church of the Nazarene, 1905-2004.* Obviously, what was most significant about this change was "from extravagant hope to limited expectation," Quanstrom's thesis for the dissertation, was left out. Thus, on the copyright page, the work is credited to dual authorship: Mark R. Quanstrom and Beacon Hill Press of Kansas City. This and other changes were made in the dissertation, which we will examine.

Quanstrom placed the beginnings of the Church of the Nazarene within an age of "optimism." For all American Christians, the twentieth century was to be the "Christian Century." In fact, one could argue that the entire Holiness Movement was rooted in a utopian view of life. (This was not Quanstrom's scope of inquiry, though he did quote Edward Bellamy's *Looking Backward*, written in 1888.) Utopian optimism was one of Timothy Smith's salient themes in his often referenced *Revivalism and Social Reform.*

> Indeed the whole stream of nineteenth-century romanticism was a fitting context for the optimism which ruled in Phoebe Palmer's parlors as Americans sought "immediate entire sanctification by faith." A similar mood lay back of New Harmony, the Oneida Community, and the Washingtonian movement, as well as Brook Farm. The merging of the romantic spirit with the boundless hopefulness of the postwar years in no wise lessened the receptiveness of multitudes awakened by a generation of revivals to the confident promise, "If we walk in the light as He is in the light, we have fellowship one with another, and the blood of Jesus Christ God's son cleanseth us from all sin."[374]

Quanstrom clearly stated in his hypothesis that this optimism would fade and along with it, a lack of confidence that God could and would enable purity in a sin cursed world. "In short, by the end of the century, entire sanctification would not be taught so much as an instantaneous change in the heart of the believer appropriated by consecration and faith, but rather more as an unremarkable event and a process of growth, if taught at all."[375]

The Church of the Nazarene began with a theology which equated entire sanctification with the baptism of the Holy Spirit. This equation was popularized by Aaron Merit Hills, who might be called the first systematic theologian in the Church of the Nazarene. Hills had attended Oberlin College, where the streams of Charles Finney's Palagianism still fully flowed. Finney, unlike Wesley, believed that man was morally free, a freedom that did not need God's grace to rightly respond to truth. Hills did not teach Finney's "moral suasion" theory of propagating the gospel, but like Finney did equate entire sanctification with the baptism of the Holy Spirit. Finney would later have plenty of support from Methodists Daniel Steele, J. A. Wood, and Asbury Lowery. The Church of the Nazarene placed Lowery's *Possibilities of Grace* on its "ministerial course of study," where it remained for 45 years. The book

---

[374] Timothy L. Smith. *Revivalism and Social Reform* (Nashville: Abingdon Press, 1957) 143.

[375] Mark Quanstrom. *A Century of Holiness Theology: The Doctrine of Entire Sanctification in the Church of the Nazarene: From Extravagant Hope to Limited Expectation* (Unpublished Ph.D. dissertation, St. Louis University, 2000) 14. All Quanstrom quotes will be from the dissertation unless otherwise noted.

carried a rather belligerent tone, what one might describe as a "holiness or hell theology." Lowery wrote,

> No doubt the Churches are today largely under condemnation growing out of this very delinquency (of seeking entire sanctification), while many Christians, who have shut their eyes and flung off conscious obligation, have really vitiated their title to heaven. They are living in willful disobedience, and, therefore, under guilt. If such is the alarming condition of those who disregard holiness, what shall we say of those who antagonize it...? Can such persons have any living hope of heaven? What is the difference between the rejection of pardon and the rejection of sanctification?[376]

Lowery failed to recognize that the acceptance of pardon was the acceptance of sanctification, what Wesley referred to as "initial sanctification." These cracks in the foundation detected by later and more serious theological engineers, would be at least partial cause for the collapse of the holiness edifice. Part of the crumbling was also due to extravagant claims made by holiness writers such as Lowery, in particular freedom from temptation: "The baptism of fire and the Holy Ghost makes the heart proof against the incursions and havoc of temptation."[377] Lowery, with his faulty logic and simplistic psychology, did not realize that if a temptation does not penetrate a person's consciousness, it is by definition no longer a temptation. J. A. Wood claimed that entire sanctification would make Christian work "natural and easy."[378] Even the theologically astute Daniel Steele, a professor at Boston University, wrote concerning the entirely sanctified person, "He who is on so intimate terms with our ever-blessed God will enjoy the *highest possible degree of happiness*...bliss will be supreme and eternal. The vicissitudes of life, from health to sickness, from riches to poverty, from applause to abuse, may ripple the surface of this profound happiness, but they cannot disturb its immeasurable depths."[379]

An entirely sanctified Kansas farmer suffering crop failure, or a Pittsburg steel worker on twelve-hour shifts and hardly able to feed his family, may have experienced some disturbing doubts as he sang a Haldor Lillenas song, "Glorious Freedom" written in 1917.

---

[376] Ibid., 39.

[377] Ibid., 45.

[378] Ibid., 47.

[379] Ibid., 47.

Freedom from all the carnal affections; Freedom from envy, hatred and strife; Freedom from vain and worldly ambitions; Freedom from all that saddened my life! Freedom from fear with all of its torments; Freedom from care with all of its pain; Freedom in Christ, my blessed Redeemer, He who has rent my fetters in twain![380]

As the conflict between modernism and fundamentalism drew lines in the sand, the Church of the Nazarene, as did other conservative denominations, developed a fortress mentality. Even though the founder Phineas Bresee had been a Methodist, most Nazarene leadership was not versed in Wesleyan nuances and with little first-hand knowledge of Wesley's writings, absorbed the tenets of fundamentalism, particularly the inerrancy of the Bible and the pre-millennial return of Christ. The 1928 General Assembly of the Church of the Nazarene adopted the following: "We believe in the *plenary* inspiration of the Holy Scriptures by which we understand the sixty-six books of the Old and New Testaments given by divine inspiration, inerrantly revealing the will of God concerning us in all things necessary to salvation, so whatever is not contained therein, is not to be enjoined as an Article of Faith."[381] Note that the Article did not claim that the Scriptures are inerrant in regard to verbal inspiration, scientific data, or historical fact. But most Nazarenes would have made these assumptions and thus, the very use of the word "inerrant" would have been satisfactory.

More importantly, the 1928 General Assembly authorized H. Orton Wiley to write a systematic theology which would eventuate into three volumes written over a period of twenty years. Wiley was much more versed in Wesley than had been Hills, especially in the doctrine of prevenient grace. But he was closer to Hills than Wesley, in that he claimed entire sanctification was, "wrought by the baptism of the Holy Spirit."[382] Wiley stressed entire sanctification as an instantaneous work, and although he did not use the term eradication, still emphasized cleansing and purity. He used some exaggerated language such as "perfect humility, perfect meekness, perfect self-denial and perfect resignation."

---

[380] Haldor Lillenas."Glorious Freedom," *Sing to the Lord* (Kansas City: Lillenas Publishing Company, 1993) 4.

[381] Quanstrom, 56.

[382] H. Orton Wiley. *Christian Theology*, Vol. II (Kansas City: Beacon Hill Press of Kansas City, 1969) 467.

However, unlike Hills and contemporary holiness evangelists, Wiley was more cautious in qualifying what entire sanctification would or would not do for the Christian.

> It is true that this redeemed and perfected spirit, dwells in a body which is a member of a sinful race, but his spirit may be lifted from darkness to light, while his body remains the same "muddy vesture of decay" that it was before this spirit was redeemed. Consequently it is still beclouded with weakness, in that the soul is under the influence of material things, and will be until the creature itself shall have put on incorruption and immortality.[383]

The Founding of Nazarene Theological Seminary

By the time that the 1948 General Assembly rolled around, the Church of the Nazarene had been through two world wars, a depression, and now existed in a "Cold War" with the threat of an all-out nuclear showdown with the Soviet Union, enough to make Christians hope for the "rapture." However, the Church of the Nazarene was not counting on immediate bail out and would proceed as if God would provide enough time to complete the building of a seminary, an action which had been taken by the 1944 General Assembly. A seminary was the *sine qua non* that the denomination had come of age, and needed an educated ministry to deal with an increasingly complex society. Nazarene Theological Seminary which opened its doors in 1945 was charged with the denomination's paramount doctrine: "Finally the primary purpose of the institution shall be to conserve, maintain, advocate and promulgate the great Bible doctrine of 'Entire Sanctification' as a second distinct work of divine grace wrought in the heart of the believer subsequent regeneration."[384]

For the most part, the Seminary represented the popular theology of the denomination, that the baptism of the Holy Spirit was the essence of entire sanctification. This view was emphasized by two of the seminary's early theologians, Kenneth Grider and Richard Taylor. Grider claimed that even though equating the Baptism of the

---

[383] Ibid, 500.

[384] Harold Raser. *More Preachers and Better Preachers: The First Fifty Years of Nazarene Theological Seminary* (Kansas City: Nazarene Publishing House, 1995) 28.

Holy Spirit with instantaneous entire sanctification was not taught by Wesley. "We in the Holiness Movement may properly call ourselves Wesleyans, even though we agree with the early fathers, East and West, that entire sanctification is wrought by the baptism with the Holy Spirit in disagreement with Wesley."[385]

Taylor was particularly vocal in emphasizing that the baptism of the Holy Spirit equaled entire sanctification and further, that the disciples were entirely sanctified on the day of Pentecost. For Taylor the changes in the disciples were self-evident:

> There were marvelous qualities which characterized them immediately and fully: the bursting forth of spiritual vitality, the pushing back of the horizons, the sudden spiritual understanding and insight, the deliverance from the paralyzing fears and tensions, the perfect unity of spirit and fellowship, the clear-eyed, pure-hearted, undivided allegiance to Jesus Christ, the calm courage in public identification, the buoyancy of spirit in facing peril and loss, the disregard of all selfish consideration. There was no exception in respect to anyone recorded in the Book of the Acts who genuinely and definitely experienced this Spirit-baptism....Such changes constituted the great miracle of Pentecost![386]

Developing Divergences

At the same time Taylor was emphasizing that entire sanctification would instantaneously solve the principle of inbred sin, a subtle shift was taking place. Some Nazarene leaders began to note that too much confidence was being placed on an instantaneous experience to the neglect of spiritual disciplines necessary to grow in or beyond entire sanctification. One such person was D. Shelly Corlett, the second president of NTS, who emphasized that the life of holiness was far more important than the terminology of a formula. Corlett, though he did not use the term "arrival theology," explicated clearly the need to get beyond any kind of static spiritual satisfaction.

---

[385] J. Kenneth Grider. *A Wesleyan Holiness Theology* (Kansas City: Beacon Hill Press of Kansas City, 1994) 373.

[386] Richard Taylor. *Life in the Spirit* (Kansas City: Beacon Hill Press of Kansas City, 1966) 81.

In this discipline or conquest there is the overcoming of prejudices, attitudes and mannerisms which may hinder the full and symmetrical manifestation of holiness in the life... There is also the conquest of one's natural dispositions. The naturally impetuous person must develop patience; the timid, hesitant, backward person must overcome these hindrances by the help of God; the natural critic or cynic must overcome that tendency and cultivate a charitable attitude toward others.[387]

To put it another way, a person had a whole lot of spiritual spade work to do after being entirely sanctified.

On the original faculty of NTS was Stephen S. White, a University of Chicago Ph.D. In order to distinguish Nazarene theology or real holiness theology from a Keswickian theory of suppression, White insisted on the word "eradication." He emphasized that "the eradication of the carnal mind, the old man, or inbred sin is meant when it is held that entire sanctification frees from sin."[388] Hugh Benner, the first president of NTS, said "Amen!", claiming that eradication was more biblical and Wesleyan than some "palatable phraseology currently in use."[389] Even though White stressed the radical nature of entire sanctification, he did raise an issue that may have not yet been suggested, or sufficiently addressed.

Entire sanctification does not regiment us. It does not make us all to be equally congenial. There will still be more natural fear in some than in others; and women will, as a rule, be more subject to modesty than men. There is the probability that one who has had years in sin before getting saved and sanctified will have more memories to battle with as he lives his Christian life than he who was saved and sanctified early in life.[390]

By reading the above, one would assume that White had taken some psychology course which caused him to believe that there may be an unconscious level within human existence filled with memories, wounds, habits, desires and other accumulated history that entire sanctification does not reach, much less remedy. Increasingly, Nazarenes

---

[387] Quanstrom, 118.

[388] Ibid., 121.

[389] Ibid., 122.

[390] Ibid., 124.

were reading books clarifying what sanctification would not do, rather than what it did do. There was a collective disillusionment settling over the Church of the Nazarene, an admission that some holiness exponents may have claimed more for the crossing of Jordan than entrance into Canaan warranted. "Beulah Land" was filled with rough terrain and unruly enemies difficult to subdue, and if the Book of Judges is reliable history, impossible to exterminate.

In 1960, the Church of the Nazarene added to its ministerial reading list William Deal's *Problems of the Spirit Filled Life*. Deal emphasized constitutional make-up; personality traits and temperaments, causing responses to particular circumstances to seem like carnality, but were due more to psychological factors. Deal charged that the Holiness Movement had erred in its insistence on uniformity in experience and conduct. "There are some persons whose constitutional makeup is of a high tension-nervous type. Such persons are generally very sensitive, easily impressed, highly imaginative, and emotionally balanced so delicately that they have difficulty remaining poised."[391]

Another book added to the ministerial course of study in 1964 was *The Spirit of Holiness* written by Everett Lewis Cattell, former missionary to India, president of Malone College, Canton, Ohio, and a leader in the Ohio Yearly Meeting of Friends (which became the Evangelical Friends-Eastern Region in the 1970s). If it is possible to look, act and talk like a holiness person, Everett Cattell was exhibit A. He communicated wisdom and serenity in both word and deed. Moderate in all things, he thought before he spoke, every word measured and accompanied with appropriate emphasis and emotion. Thus, his brief book is packed with practical advice as to how to live a sanctified life, not expecting too much or too little of oneself. For Cattell, one could live in the reality of honesty and humility while at the same time giving testimony to the transforming and sanctifying grace of Christ. True to his Quaker heritage, Cattell not only emphasized instantaneous entire sanctification by the Holy Spirit, but also constant guidance by the Holy Spirit for ethical direction.

The lustful look condemned by Jesus is not necessarily so. The fact of attraction, appreciation and pleasure regarding a woman's beauty is not sin or carnal in itself. But it is extremely easy to cross the line where this legitimate exercise

---

[391] Ibid., 135.

of God-given impulse becomes an occasion for self to slip out into independence again, and for the look to become carnal. Probably when one becomes aware of his look taking on aspects of improper desire he is crossing over and must exercise discipline. But this question of crossing the line, in this as in so many other areas which we have set forth, leaves us utterly dependent upon the still small voice of the Holy Spirit for its answer.[392]

He also stressed the necessity of ongoing confession and forgiveness in order to keep one's relationship to God and others without offense.

First of all, let us recognize our condition as sinful. It must not be covered up by reference to the wonder of our original crisis experience of surrender and cleansing or sanctification. Too many have thus accumulated a lot of unforgiven sin by assuming that since they had such a glorious experience back there, and carnality was eradicated, that surely nothing now can be wrong. Whatever eradication means — or crucifixion, or putting to death the old man — it is not a chunk of something *material* that is done away. Rather, it is a wrong *relationship* between us and God that is destroyed. But just because it is a relationship, an immaterial rather than a material something, it can as quickly be reinstated as destroyed. The cure, then, is fresh repentance and forgiveness and cleansing as we put the relationship right again. And happy is the one who has learned to make this adjustment instantly and quickly.[393]

Unfortunately, the above moderation was not true of many holiness writers, several which the Church of the Nazarene recommended for its ministerial course of study. Kenneth Grider took issue with J.A. Wood's claim that, "the sanctified soul is never without comfort" or "without peace." Grider disagreed with his contemporary Donald Metz who, in his *Studies in Biblical Holiness*, claimed that for the sanctified, "a consistent personality is displayed in all relationships," and that there would be "an absence of any spiritual conflicts." He was especially critical of James O. McClurkan, the founder of the southern wing of the Church of the Nazarene (though none of his writings were required reading) who claimed that "the sanctified heart is absolutely cleansed of

---

[392] Everett Cattell. *The Spirit of Holiness* (Grand Rapids: William B. Eerdmans Publishing Company, 1963) 50.
[393] Ibid, 40.

all....race prejudice. Holiness deepens and sweetens and broadens the nature until every man of all and every section and nationality and color or condition is loved as a brother." Grider countered that, "since racial, educational, cultural and other prejudices are learned environmentally, they are not aspects of adamic sin and are not necessarily routed in entire sanctification."[394]

In 1965, the Christian Holiness Association under the leadership of Leo Cox, Wilber Dayton and others, founded the Wesleyan Theological Society as an "academic commission" of the organization.[395] Obviously, the theological professors of the Church of the Nazarene's colleges and seminary would attend the Society's yearly meeting.[396] John Wesley's theology, which before this time had lurked in the background of the Church of the Nazarene, was now brought to the forefront. The Christian Holiness Association had unwittingly brought a "Trojan horse" into the camp. Papers presented at the Society (which we discussed in Chapter 2) highlighted exegetical problems, historical contradictions, and glaring discrepancies between what John Wesley taught and the American Holiness Movement assumed that he taught, or had not really cared as to what he taught.

The Wesley Connection

Though we have already scrutinized Wesley, we still need to ask, "Why should the Church of the Nazarene bother with John Wesley at all?" The reason for fascination with John Wesley's teachings on holiness is not easy to clarify and lends itself to speculation. Like an orphan child, the Church of the Nazarene began a search for its theological parent. (Keep in mind that Phineas Bresee had found himself without appointment in the Methodist Episcopal Church because of his association with a Los Angeles mission. The mission fired him, which initiated his founding the Church of the Nazarene in 1895.) By the 1960s,

---

[394] J. Kenneth Grider. A Wesleyan Holiness Theology (Kansas City: Beacon Hill Press, 1994) 463-467.

[395] John G. Merritt. "Fellowship in Ferment: A History of the Wesleyan Theological Society, 1965-84." Wesleyan Theological Journal, Vol. XXI, No. 12 (Spring/Fall, 1986).

[396] Ibid, 193. During the first twenty years of the Society, Nazarenes made by far the most contributions to the WTS Journal, 57, as opposed to the next highest made by the Wesleyan Church, 38.

the isolationist period was over, and the Church of the Nazarene craving a wider acceptance, would merge into mainstream evangelicalism.[397] Throughout the nineteenth century the Holiness Movement welcomed Quakers, Presbyterians, Congregationalists, and even Baptists.

Phoebe Palmer, the mother of the Holiness Movement, was a Methodist. The founders of the National Camp Meeting Association for the Promotion of Holiness, were almost exclusively Methodists: John Inskip, William McDonald, John Searles, William Osborn, and Alfred Cookman as well as others, almost all of them personal friends of Phineas Bresee. Most of the Church of the Nazarene had been founded, formulated and populated by associations which were members of the National Camp Meeting Association. If that was not enough, throughout the 70s, when the seminary was in its heyday, several of the faculty, Kenneth Grider, Paul Bassett, Albert Truesdale and Richard Taylor had done Ph.D.s at Methodist institutions: Drew, Emory, Duke and Boston University. William Greathouse, having done academic work at Vanderbilt, president of the Seminary, 1968-1976, at the height of the Seminary's numerical success, was a serious scholar of the writings of John Wesley.

These scholars pointed out discrepancies between the traditional teachings of the Church of the Nazarene and what Wesley actually taught on such issues as prevenient grace, sanctification begun at justification, the will is not absolutely free, no sinless perfection; and that according to Wesley, many individuals are sanctified only a short time before death. Wesley's teaching on the "witness of the spirit" was particularly confusing, and varied greatly from Phoebe Palmer's altar theology. Statements in Wesley led some to believe that entire sanctification was immediately available to all Christians, and other statements implied that the experience of holiness should be taught to only those mature enough to receive it. John made the attainment of Christian perfection more possible than did his brother Charles. As Stephen Gunter writes, "Charles employed the scriptural metaphors almost exclusively to describe the ideal experience. The practical result of this was that the

---

[397] The Church of the Nazarene joined the Christian Holiness Association in 1969, the National Association of Evangelicals in 1984, the World Methodist Council in 1999 and the Global Wesleyan Alliance in 2011. Email from Stan Ingersol July 20, 2018.

experience described by Charles was rather abstract to the average convert."[398]

Wesley's claim that he did not teach sinless perfection muddied the waters for Holiness exponents who thought they could live above sin in this life. As Mark Quanstrom quaintly, if not facetiously concludes, "The 'plain account' of the distinct doctrine of the Church of the Nazarene, which asserted the instantaneous eradication of the sinful nature by a second work of grace, was becoming anything but a 'plain account.'"[399]

Formal and Official Responses

As the Academy within the Church of the Nazarene pushed for a less mechanistic and formulaic interpretation of entire sanctification, a motion came to the 1985 General Assembly to remove the word "eradication" from the Church's Article of Faith on original sin. The Article of Faith stated, "We further believe that original sin continues to exist within the life of the regenerate until eradicated by the baptism of the Holy Spirit."[400] Lyle Pointer, then pastor of San Jose California First Church of the Nazarene, motioned for the following replacement statement: "Original sin continues to exist with the new life, until the heart is cleansed with the fullness of the Holy Spirit."[401] The motion failed, and the Church, for the time being, retained its "eradication" and "baptism with the Holy Spirit" language. Quanstrom assesses that, "When the majority of the delegates defeated Pointer's amendment and voted to add the new article of faith (the difference between sin and infirmity) to the old article instead of replacing it, they were representing a movement within the Church of the Nazarene trying to understand entire sanctification in a way that, according to those who proposed the change, would eventually mean its permanent irrelevancy."[402]

When Mildred Wynkoop's *Theology of Love* came out in 1973, the official publication of NTS, *The Tower*, reviewed it as a work that was equal in importance to those of Harald Lindstrom, H. Orton Wiley,

---

[398] Gunter, 293.

[399] Quanstrom, 150.

[400] Ibid., 151.

[401] Ibid., 155.

[402] Ibid., 156.

and Timothy Smith. The official graduate school of the Church of the Nazarene had knowingly or unwittingly endorsed a book that sharply differed from the denomination's stance on the doctrine of entire sanctification. Wynkoop's insistence that John Wesley did not equate the baptism of the Holy Spirit with entire sanctification was supported by other conservative holiness scholars, namely Leo Cox at Marion College (now Indiana Wesleyan University) and George Allen Turner at Asbury Theological Seminary. The denomination found itself in a bind. Was it going to be a child of John Wesley or was it going to adhere to A. M. Hills and H. Orton Wiley?

The tension mounted at Nazarene Theological Seminary, and further fuel was placed on the fire by Rob Staples, who was as I have already suggested, a kissing cousin if not a fraternal twin of Mildred Wynkoop, at least theologically. Staples, as did Wynkoop, emphasized a relational understanding of entire sanctification, citing Martin Buber's "I - thou" theology. In the meantime, the Nazarene General Superintendents, believing that Wiley's *Christian Theology*, first published in 1941 was becoming outdated, commissioned H. Ray Dunning, a professor at Trevecca Nazarene College who had done his doctoral work at Vanderbilt University to write a new systematic theology. Not all of the Superintendents were confident that Dunning, a Wesleyan scholar, would stay true to the Articles of Faith. Thus, an editorial board was appointed to supervise Dunning's work. Nonetheless, Dunning received a vote of confidence from Melvin (Bud) Lunn, head of the Nazarene Publishing House, a powerful voice within the denomination. "I believe he has the intellectual and spiritual maturity to produce a work that will be irenic. I predict, however, that there will be some interesting discussions along the way since there are varying points of view on the advisory committee."[403]

The Battle Line Is Drawn

"Interesting discussion" was a vast understatement. Forces were rushing headlong to an intersection without stoplights or stop signs, or to use another common metaphor, theological matters within the Church of the Nazarene were about to "hit the fan." In March of

---

[403] Quanstrom, 173.

1979, Rob Staples presented to the NTS Breakfast Club, "The Current Wesleyan Debate on the Baptism of the Holy Spirit."

Staples began by dropping a bombshell:

> While having much to say about entire sanctification, and also much to say about the work of the Holy Spirit in the total process of salvation all the way from prevenient grace and conviction of sin to final glorification, Wesley said very little about the "baptism with the Holy Spirit." When Wesley did speak of the Pentecostal experience, he referred to it as "receiving" the Holy Spirit. "Baptism language" was practically non-existent. At times he does use the expression "fullness of the Spirit," but he is not consistent in his application of the term and perhaps never used it with doctrinal precision, even when the important matter of chronology is taken into consideration. In his sermon "The First Fruits of the Spirit," preached in 1745, the expression "filled with the Holy Ghost" is used to describe the justified believer who has not yet been cleansed from inward sin. And in 1758, Wesley says that Paul's experience of being "filled with the Holy Ghost" was a part of the apostle's conversion. On the other hand, in 1771 he can use the term "fullness of the Spirit" as an equivalent of Christian perfection. But even in cases such as the latter he does not relate this "fullness of the Spirit" to what happened at Pentecost. Usually Pentecost is described as the "receiving" of the Spirit in what, in Wesley's mind, constituted the "conversion" or the justification and regeneration of the disciples. The evidence for this is abundant and unequivocal.[404]

Because word quickly got out that Staples did not support the traditional American Holiness position, which made entire sanctification synonymous with Baptism with the Holy Spirit, Staples' road to his first four-year contract with NTS would prove to be rocky. For the regularly scheduled meeting September 24-25, 1979, the NTS Board of Administration was unable to come to a decision for the four-year contracts of either Staples or Charles Isbel. Thus, another meeting of the Board of Trustees was conducted February 20, 1980. (Doubts about the four-year contracts were probably not the only reason for the special meeting, but Staples believed that Stephen Nease, President of NTS, was unsettled by the theological rumblings concerning entire sanctification.) Staples wrote to Millard Reed, board member and pastor of Nashville First Church, that he found the whole process demoralizing, both to him

---

[404] Rob Staples. "The Current Wesleyan Debate on the Baptism of the Holy Spirit" (Unpublished paper presented to Nazarene Theological Seminary Breakfast Club, 1979) 3.

and the faculty. Believing that the Seminary Board had no constitutional authority to judge his loyalty to the Church and its doctrine, the Board had "now usurped and then undercut the administration (the faculty and curriculum committee) at a very critical point."[405]

The Charles Isbel Debacle

After much discussion and confusion, as possibly no one on the Seminary Board had read "The Current Wesleyan Debate" paper, (except Paul Cunningham) and probably would have not understood many of its intricacies if they had, the board voted to grant Staples a four-year contract, but that would not be the case for Charles Isbel. It just so happened at the very time the board was meeting, *A Thief in the Night*, a rapture movie was being shown on a Christian station in the Kansas City area. *The Kansas City Times* desired to know what local theologians thought about the movie. The newspaper reached Charles Isbel, a bright young graduate of Brandeis University, professor of Old Testament at NTS. Isbel was not all that concerned with winning friends and influencing people and certainly not committed to representing the collective mind of the Nazarene constituency.

The conversation was set up to go a particular way by the reporter, or one might say that Isbel was baited. The reporter recalled that earlier in the month, mainline "liberal" churches had gathered in New York to discuss the new electronic church phenomenon. At that meeting, David Osborne, director of newspaper services for the National Council of Churches, stated that, "Problems with the TV preachers were more of a rehash of the age old conflict between liberal Christian theology and fundamentalism than anything else."[406] Isbel responded, "I guess I'm one of those liberals who according to the views of those who made the movie would be cast into hell." Isbel further stated, "I have room in my heart for Christian people who believe that way, but I don't think it's really fair to draw lines and say that if you don't believe the Scriptures literally, then what you get is eternal damnation."[407]

---

[405] Letter, Rob Staples to Millard Reed, October 19, 1979, included in Rob Staples' "My Ordeal by Fire."

[406] Ibid.

[407] Steve Nicely, "TV Church May Set the Stage for Religious Conflict" *The Kansas City Times* (Tuesday, February 19, 1980).

Isbel had identified himself as a liberal who did not take the Bible literally. The NTS Board inquisition that had been focused on Staples now directed its attention to Isbel. Seminary President Stephen Nease called Isbel and asked for clarification and what he (Nease) should say if his newspaper response came up in the NTS Board meeting the next day. Instead of clarification, there was a testy exchange between Isbel and Nease. Isbel blurted out, "Would you like to have my resignation?" To which Nease responded, "That would make my job easier."[408] Possibly, both of these men later regretted their impulsive communication. But the die had been cast and Isbel knowing that his contract would not be renewed, resigned.

Had Isbel been a "scapegoat" in possibly the most turbulent time in the seminary's history? Coincidentally, he had been a favorite student of Staples at Bethany Nazarene College and they had remained close friends as colleagues on the NTS faculty. Had Isbel taken the fall for Staples? (As of this writing, for the entire seventy year history of NTS, Isbel is the only person to lose his job for his theological opinions.) No doubt, out of mixed emotions of guilt feelings and genuine concern for the welfare of his friend, Staples stated to his class the day after he was granted a four-year contract, and the board adjourned:

> Concerning this former student of mine who is now my colleague, I wish to go on record as having the utmost faith in his integrity, a deep respect for his knowledge and skills, and eternal appreciation for his friendship in a period of strain for both of us, a sincere fervent hope for nothing but the best for him in the future, and an intention to keep in touch with him wherever his steps may lead.[409]

The following is the statement read by Staples (one of the most eloquent wordsmiths I've ever heard) to his Wesley's Theology class on February 21, 1980, the day after he was granted a four-year contract by the Board of Trustees:

> I am sometimes amazed when I reflect that during my 26 years of full time ministry, the most excruciating pain I have felt, the most intense suffering I have endured, the most devastating anguish I have known, have been inflicted upon

---

[408] Staples, "My Ordeal," 10.
[409] Ibid. NP.

me by the Church which I love, to which I have given my life, and which I will continue to serve…

But I still believe in the Church—when she dares to be what she is. I still have hope that windows may be opened and fresh breezes will blow, that we will rediscover our real Wesleyan-Holiness heritage, that we can find our real identity not as a provincial religious group fearfully driving herself defensively into a doctrinal cul-de-sac or fencing herself into a theological ghetto, drawing the robes of self-righteousness about her while a needy world passes by hardly giving her a glance. I have hope that we will <u>decide to be what we are</u> a vital part of the "one holy catholic church." I continue to hope that we will be mature enough as a denomination to be willing to re-examine presuppositions, to allow a true spirit of inquiry to exist, and not be afraid to really be what we are.[410]

The Gag Order

Some nine months before Staples would be eligible for a vote on tenure, the Church of the Nazarene hosted a Theology Conference in Overland Park, Kansas, December, 1982. Eugene Stowe, a General Superintendent and former President of NTS, read a paper, "Higher Education and Our Holiness Heritage." He traced the doctrine of entire sanctification back to Francis Asbury and John Wesley. Pulling himself up to the full sovereignty of his office, he declared before the one hundred Nazarene leaders and scholars from across the United States: "We must continue to preach and teach that Pentecost was the occasion of the entire sanctification of the one hundred twenty disciples in the Upper Room. The cleansing and empowerment of these believers by the firey baptism with the Holy Spirit on that day, is undeniable, scriptural evidence that there is a second definite work of grace. This truth is non-negotiable. *Any discussion of Spirit baptism which questions this position cannot be tolerated.*"[411] (italics mine.)

Stowe had thrown a five-gallon can of gasoline on a fire already getting out of control. Of course, his gag order had an opposite intended effect; the next two or three hours were spent discussing the exact issue on which he had attempted to put a quietus. Stowe further stated,

---

[410] Ibid, NP.

[411] Eugene Stowe, "Higher Education and Our Holiness Heritage," (Nazarene Archives, December 1982) 17.

"No amount of contemporary social pressure from a predominantly hedonistic society enamored with situation ethics should induce us to compromise the guidelines and standards of our general and special rules."[412] Did Stowe believe that hedonism was undermining the overworked and underpaid professors throughout the Church of the Nazarene's educational institutions? He may have been the only dissenting voice when the Board of General Superintendents pronounced Staples as Nazarene orthodox, only a brief time later. But unlike the U.S. Supreme Court, the Board of General Superintendents did not record the minority vote, at least for public perusal.

The Continuing Staples Conflict

As Staples approached the September 1983 tenure vote, the same issues that had been prevalent in 1980 resurfaced. The Special Advisory Committee met on September 26, 1983, and it was this committee that would recommend Rob Staples for tenure. It was composed of four members from the Board of Trustees and four faculty members, plus the Chair, Seminary President Terrell Sanders. One of the Board members was Paul Cunningham, by this time Chairman of the Trustee Board and possibly the only Board of Trustee member who had read Staples' "Current Debate" paper. When the committee interviewed Staples, Cunningham asked Staples if his view prevailed how would he explain entire sanctification to "Fred the Plumber?" In spite of Cunningham's inquisition, it was he who recommended Staples for tenure to the Faculty and Curriculum Committee. It was also the Special Advisory Committee which requested that the Board of General Superintendents interpret the denomination's understanding of the relationship between the baptism of the Holy Spirit and entire sanctification.

On Monday, September 26, Staples effectively defended his position on entire sanctification before the Committee on Faculty and Curriculum. This committee was chaired by Paul Cunningham who found himself in an adversarial role with Wes Tracy who championed Staples' cause. Staples was granted tenure and interpreted the final outcome: "Cunningham, a creative chairman, found a way to compromise, namely by putting before the Committee the action taken earlier in the smaller committee to grant tenure to Staples and send the notorious paper (The

---

[412] Ibid. 18.

Current Debate) to the Board of General Superintendents for a ruling — thus separating the question of my tenure from the larger theological issue of Spirit baptism."[413] Since Staples' paper accompanied the request for the General Superintendents to clarify the relationship between Holy Spirit baptism and entire sanctification, Cunningham was forcing the Board of General Superintendents to rule on Staples' interpretation of entire sanctification.

The Board of Trustees' decision was something of an oxymoron, a probationary tenure. If the General Superintendents decided that Staples was not holiness orthodox, the tenure grant would be overruled, since the time of tenure would not begin until the new contract year, July 1, 1984.[414] Staples added a sixteen page addendum to the original paper and forwarded them both to the General Superintendents, November 21, 1983.

Staples contended that there had never been unity of thought within the Church of the Nazarene concerning entire sanctification. He relied on his New Testament colleague, Alex Deasley, who had argued that the bifurcation of thought which emerged in Wesley's lifetime chiefly, as between himself and Fletcher, has continued from that day to this.[415] Deasley argued, "Even within that fork of Wesleyan thought, which has equated entire sanctification with the Baptism of the Holy Spirit, there have been both uneasiness and disagreement in the handling of the evidence in Acts."[416] Staples furthermore claimed the disciples were sanctified on the day of Pentecost, but they also became born again as New Testament Christians on that day. This was not the normative understanding of most holiness exponents, who interpreted the disciples as being "saved" before the day of Pentecost and entered entire sanctification as a distinct second work of grace on the day of Pentecost. Fortunately for Staples, the Board of General Superintendents ruled in his favor March 2, 1984.

---

[413] Staples, "My Ordeal," 20.

[414] According to my friend and former colleague William Miller, "tenure" has less meaning in a confessional than a non-confessional school. A heresy trial and dismissal are always possibilities. "Bill" spent thirty-one years teaching and administrating in Nazarene schools in higher education and also eight years as Director, Institutional Evaluation and Accreditation for the Association of Theological Schools.

[415] Staples, "Current Debate," 40.

[416] Ibid.

Dear Doctor Cunningham:

This letter is in response to your letter written in October, 1983, to Dr. Orville Jenkins conveying the request of the Board of Trustees of Nazarene Theological Seminary that the Board of General Superintendents interpret the <u>Manual</u> statement regarding entire sanctification, particularly as it impinges on the current discussion in the holiness community with respect to the relationship of Pentecost and the baptism with the Holy Spirit to entire sanctification.

As you requested, Dr. Rob Staples sent copies of his paper to each member of our Board, to which he appended a rather detailed clarification of his personal position on sensitive issues, in particular his view of the relationship of Pentecost to the entire sanctification of the apostles. It is the consensus of the Board that Dr. Staples' view is in accord with our interpretation of Article X.

After thoughtful consideration and discussion of these issues, the Board of General Superintendents voted to communicate to the Board of Trustees of Nazarene Theological Seminary, through you as a chairman, the action:

The Board of General Superintendents rules that Article X of the Nazarene "Articles of Faith" is an adequate articulation of the biblical doctrine of entire sanctification as understood by historic Methodism and the modern holiness movement, recognizing as it does "various terms representing its different phases, such as 'Christian perfection,' 'perfect love,' 'heart purity,' 'the baptism with the Holy Spirit,' 'the fullness of the blessing' and 'Christian holiness.'"

We reaffirm the historic position of the Church of the Nazarene that the apostles, previously converted, were entirely sanctified by the baptism with the Holy Spirit on the Day of Pentecost and remain for us models of Christian holiness. Faithfully yours,

William M. Greathouse, Secretary
Board of General Superintendents[417]

What is odd about the ruling of the General Superintendents is that they affirmed both Staples' position and the present Article X statement of faith. The two are in disagreement, if not diametrically opposed. At that time Article V on "Sin, Original and Personal" used the word "eradication," which was changed to "fully cleansed" in 2001. Article X

---
[417] Letter from William Greathouse to Paul Cunningham, March 2, 1984, included in "My Ordeal."

on entire sanctification used "wrought by the baptism of the Holy Spirit." Since Staples was not in agreement with either of these formulations, we can only conclude that the General Superintendents desired to include both a Wesleyan and nineteenth century position on Christian holiness. It also must be said that Staples had made an exegetical and historical argument which was so cogent and comprehensive that he was difficult to refute. Being from Kentucky, (I am married to a Kentuckian) Staples was as shrewd as any Kentucky politician. He had grounded entire sanctification in Christology for a denomination already attempting to escape the clutches of neo-Pentecostalism. The following was crucial to his argument:

> If holiness is described as Christ likeness, that is a self-defining term. At least it is as self-defining as any term can possibly be. Its meaning is quite clear. The figure of the flesh-and-blood Jesus in the New Testament is very concrete, not merely as an abstraction, not a nebulous term lacking in content. But if we shift away from this to pneumatological terms (Spirit-filled or Spirit-baptized) we have introduced terms which are not self-defining in content. There are many "spirits" in the world, and it is necessary to define the content of the Holy Spirit.[418]

The Resulting Wound

In spite of vindication, Staples was severely wounded; the controversy exacted an enormous physical and emotional toll. He had believed that Cunningham not only desired to get rid of him, but to do "a clean sweep, cleansing the Church of its most dangerous elements."[419] On March 8, 1984, Staples wrote Cunningham:

> For the past four or five years, while this issue has been discussed, I have been the recipient of some distasteful treatment, consisting of a violation of General Rule II-5, which prohibits the "spreading of surmises injurious to the good name of others." Much of this (but not all of it) has come from members of the Board of Trustees. I do not question the motive of anyone. I am sure that each person meant well and, on the basis of a limited knowledge of the issues involved, did what he believed to be in the best interest of the Church. But,

---

[418] Staples, "Current Wesleyan Debate," 26-27.
[419] Staples, "My Ordeal," 22.

unfortunately, the practical result is the same as if the motive had been evil. When surmises are spread, one's good name is injured, regardless of the motive. But I can do no less than forgive, since Christ has forgiven me so much.[420]

On April 18, 1984, Cunningham wrote Staples, attempting to placate his adversary.

In your particular case I have never had any malice against you, nor have any members of the Board of Trustees of which I am aware. In fact, you would perhaps be interested to know I was the one who made the motion that you be granted tenure. I have appreciation for you and your teaching ministry. I am at the same time, of course, concerned that the teaching of our doctrinal distinctive not be enmeshed in a climate of confusion and division, but rather that the position of our church be clearly taught by our Nazarene educators.[421]

Cunningham further wrote:

I sincerely regret any emotional pain that you and your family have experienced during this time but assume all involved understand that any time we take a controversial position we may become the subject of close scrutiny and some misunderstanding. Nonetheless, each of us must pursue the course that maintains our authenticity as disciples and our integrity as students of the Word.[422]

But Cunningham was not going to allow his attempts at reconciliation to pass without arguing for his position that the baptism of the Holy Spirit is synonymous with entire sanctification. After quoting Purkiser, Wiley, and Charles Carter, he stated, "It is difficult for me to understand how our pastors in the making, and the constituents to whom they will ultimately minister can accept our distinct doctrine of entire sanctification when it is preached on a multiple choice basis."[423] Staples' response to the "Fred the Plumber" question particularly rankled Cunningham. Cunningham claimed that he was not attempting to "cultivate simplicity and understanding at the expense of truth.

---

[420] Rob Staples letter to Paul Cunningham, March 8, 1984. Included in "My Ordeal."

[421] Paul Cunningham letter to Rob Staples, April 27, 1984, included in "My Ordeal."

[422] Ibid.

[423] Ibid.

Rather it was an attempt to underscore the need to communicate the truth of the Gospel in such a matter as would be comprehensible to the spiritually unenlightened."[424] But Cunningham was doing exactly what he said he was not doing: he was making entire sanctification palatable for rapid strain free consumption. He probably did not realize that he was propagating Phoebe Palmer's "The Shorter Way." In other words, the receiving of the Holy Spirit at regeneration, and the filling or baptism of the Holy Spirit in Acts 2 as entire sanctification, as interpreted by most holiness folk at the turn of the century had been a neat, preachable, and logical equation. But God is not always logical (at least from my perspective, or maybe God doesn't have a Western mind) and sound exegesis may lead to complexity instead of clarity. Holiness theology had developed into a neat, pragmatic altar call. It was this pragmatism or reductionism that Staples condemned.

> At its core, this remark betrays a philosophy of pure pragmatism — one of the least Christian of all motivations. Truth is not to be defined as "what works best." This remark (Fred the Plumber) ignores the obvious historical fact John Wesley was very successful in presenting his message to the coal miners of Bristol (who had less education than today's plumbers!) without the use of Spirit-baptism language. Let us therefore insist that our doctrine be determined by the careful exegesis of the Word of God, and not by a pragmatic interest in what sells easiest to anybody — plumber or potentate![425]

The exchange between Staples and Cunningham represented a watershed in the educational institutions of the Church of the Nazarene. Paul Cunningham, pastor of College Church in Olathe, Kansas, and for all practical intents and purposes founder of Mid-America Nazarene University, represented with that community a conservative nineteenth century interpretation of holiness. Staples represented a holiness paradigm that allowed for diverse interpretations. The aftermath of this particular showdown ensured that no Nazarene professor would ever be fired for his interpretation of entire sanctification.

---

[424] Letter from Paul Cunningham to Rob Staples, April 13, 1984, included in "My Ordeal."
[425] Rob Staples, "My Ordeal," 51.

Reverberations Throughout The Denominations and Quanstrom's Conclusions

The theological imbroglio now shifted from the Seminary to the denomination. When Ray Dunning's *Grace, Faith and Holiness* was released in 1988 as supposedly the official systematic theology of the denomination, Richard Taylor, now retired from the Seminary, cried "foul." He did not see much holiness in Dunning's work, at least holiness as historically defined by the Church of the Nazarene. Taylor wrote John L. Knight, Chair of the Board of General Superintendents (who until 2016 was the only General Superintendent with an earned Ph. D. to have ever been elected): "To endorse a textbook which in any significant point departs from the *Manual* or shifts the center of gravity from traditional mainline Wesleyanism to a new or aberrant center would be impermissible as an act and disastrous in its consequences, not the least of which to officially render our creedal Statement a dead letter."[426] The decision? Dunning's work would not serve as the official theology of the Church of the Nazarene, but would serve as a "representative theology."

Abetting this verdict was a respected author and leader in the Church of the Nazarene, W. T. Purkiser. In a letter written to Knight, Purkiser argued, "I doubt seriously that anyone can do now what H. Orton Wiley did 45 years ago. Our church is getting more and more pluralistic all the time, and we are able to tolerate different points of view on nonessential matters."[427] For Richard Taylor and many other Nazarenes, switching an easily understood formulaic paradigm for a not-so-easily understood relational paradigm was not a "nonessential matter." And, had anyone of Purkiser's stature ever used the word "pluralistic" to describe the Church of the Nazarene? Its traditional holiness paradigm was fraying around the edges. Dunning desired to uproot the Church of the Nazarene from its nineteenth century holiness soil. "This perversion always takes place when some historically conditioned formulation of the Christian faith is crystallized and held onto as the final statement as in the case of fundamentalism's fixation with the 17th century Protestant orthodoxy, or any theologian of the holiness movement sanctifying the 19th century formulations."[428]

---

[426] Quanstrom, 179.

[427] Ibid., 180.

[428] Ray Dunning, *Grace, Faith and Holiness* (Kansas City: Beacon Hill Press of Kansas

Quanstrom's Conclusions

Now is the time to ask, is a Ph.D. candidate going to be objective and honest, working under a doctoral committee and defending his thesis before that committee? Or, is he going to be more objective and honest working within the confines of a denomination which has nurtured and trained him, and no doubt contributed to his ability to do a terminal degree? On one hand, there has been a certain gratification for the academicians in a Jesuit institution to enable one of their students to shred the central doctrine of a small Protestant denomination. On the other hand, it takes a certain amount of courage (some would say disrespect) with an overused cliché, "to bite the hand that has fed you." Whatever the case, the Church of the Nazarene did not publish Quanstrom's critical conclusions, as I will demonstrate via footnotes below.

Throughout the 1990s, the battle lines between a traditional understanding of entire sanctification represented by Richard Taylor, Kenneth Grider, and Donald Metz, and relational understandings represented by Dunning, Wynkoop, Staples and an increasing number of professors and students both at the Seminary and Nazarene undergraduate schools, sharpened and intensified. In 1999, the Board of General Superintendents attempted some damage control by sending a mission statement to every pastor within the denomination. The Superintendents opted for the traditional paradigm: "Then in the divine act of entire sanctification, also called the baptism with the Holy Spirit, He cleanses us from original sin and indwells us with his holy presence."[429] Quanstrom assessed, "In light of the continual evolving (or devolving, depending on one's point of view) definitions throughout the denomination's history, however, and in light of almost three decades of divergent explications of the doctrine, it is difficult to imagine that the mere assertion of a formulation of the doctrine would bring resolution to the problem of a lack of theological definition of entire sanctification."[430]

In the above encyclical, the Superintendents also declared, "We believe that human nature, and ultimately society, can be radically and

---

City, 1988) 37.
[429] Quanstrom, 199.
[430] Ibid. NPH left out.

permanently changed by the grace of God. We have an irrepressible confidence in this message of hope, which flows from the heart of our Holy God."[431] Quanstrom appraises, "Early in the century, Nazarenes had believed that the grace of entire sanctification would so transform human nature that a person would be almost angelic in their dispositions and their behaviors. This personal transformation would have the inevitable effect of transforming the world."[432] Quanstrom continued: "As the century wore on, the radical optimism which was reflective of an optimistic American culture at large, gradually faded. An apologist for the traditional articulation of the doctrine of entire sanctification adjusted definitions in the light of this new theological realism."[433]

According to Quanstrom, the traditionalists such as Taylor and Purkiser, even though they insisted on eradication of sin by the baptism of the Holy Spirit, increasingly stressed what entire sanctification would not do by elaborating on infirmities that could only be eliminated by growth in grace beyond entire sanctification, if conquered at all. Seemingly, both groups, the traditionalists and the revisionists, had "effectively emasculated the promise of entire sanctification, at least as it had been understood at the beginning of the century."[434] Quanstrom concludes that these changes, "challenge the mission of the denomination which at one time anyway, understood its sole reason for being to consist in the proclamation of the possibility of freedom from sin resulting in a gloriously transformed human nature."[435]

The Editorial Board for Beacon Hill Press of Kansas City did not deem it prudent to make public Quanstrom's conclusion and ending question: "The Church of the Nazarene at the beginning of the 21st Century is thus confronted with a theological identity crisis, with no clear resolution."[436] Quanstrom left the matter open: "Can there be a theologically realistic formulation of the doctrine of entire sanctification that preserves the promise of the grace consistent with the problem of man? If not, the Church of the Nazarene must reconcile itself to being

---

[431] Ibid.

[432] Ibid. NPH left out.

[433] Ibid., 200. NPH left out.

[434] Ibid., 201. NPH kept.

[435] Ibid. NPH left out.

[436] Ibid. NPH left out.

a denomination without clear theological definition concerning its cardinal doctrine."[437]

Both Quanstrom and the NPH version concluded: "It is evident that the Church of the Nazarene is not ignoring this lack of theological precision concerning the doctrine of entire sanctification....The Church of the Nazarene still affirms the possibility of human nature being radically and permanently changed by the grace of God."[438] Both Quanstrom and NPH also claimed that Nazarenes with great zeal (NPH stated "authentically and with great zeal") sing "Holiness Unto the Lord is Our Watchword and Song."[439] One wonders if after his careful analysis and many negative conclusions, if Quanstrom really believes "Holiness unto the Lord" is still the "watchword and song" of the Church of the Nazarene. Keith Drury, and Richard Taylor, if he were still living, would lament "Holiness unto the Lord" is no longer the watchword and song of the Church of the Nazarene. (This author agrees with Taylor.)

William Kirkemo's Analysis and the Present Status of the Doctrine of Entire Sanctification

In 2008, William Kirkemo completed a D. Min. dissertation at Asbury Theological Seminary titled, *Substantialist and Relational Understandings of Entire Sanctification among Church of the Nazarene Clergy.* He discovered two variables important for our study. First, "The average age of those favoring a Wesleyan/Holiness understanding on the Holiness/Relational Index was over forty-five, while the average of those favoring a Wesleyan/Relational understanding was under forty-five."[440] This resulted in a correlation between the age and the type of holiness language which a pastor used. Older pastors used traditional language such as "entire sanctification" or "second blessing" while younger pastors used more relational terms such as consecration, full surrender and discipleship.

---

[437] Ibid, 202. NPH left out.

[438] Mark Quanstrom, *A Century of Holiness Theology* (Kansas City: Beacon Hill Press, 2004) 180-181.

[439] Ibid., 180.

[440] William Kirkemo. *Substantialist and Relational Understandings of Entire Sanctification Among Church of the Nazarene Clergy.* (Unpublished D. Min. dissertation, Asbury Theological Seminary, 2008) 121.

Second, pastors of smaller churches, under fifty, used traditional language for Wesleyan-Holiness, while pastors of larger churches, above fifty, bypassed the traditional language of the Holiness Movement. Of course, cause and effect are difficult if not impossible to establish. Pastors who use conservative holiness language may be conservative in other ways such as strictures on dancing, theatre attending, drinking wine, etc. This stance creates a high threshold for outsiders to cross over. By taking the higher road, or one might say the straight and narrow, these pastors believe, that by being faithful to "truth," their church was not an option for individuals looking for cheap grace. A few of the pastors believed there was a direct correlation between their low attendance and "strong preaching of entire sanctification." But Kirkemo observed that the "attendance decline may rather be the result of using language and metaphors that are confusing to the current ontological perspective, shared by much of the North American culture."[441] Muted Nazarene identity is often an attempt to lower the threshhold and widen the door for newcomers.

Overall, Kirkemo was more positive than Quanstrom about the current state of holiness emphasis within the American Church of the Nazarene: "With so many voices claiming otherwise, I was surprised that an overwhelming majority of Nazarene clergy reported a high commitment to, and personal experience of entire sanctification. In particular, I was surprised that 93 percent of the clergy understood that God has cleansed the stain of original sin from their lives."[442]

Kirkemo did a random sampling of 385 pastors, 191 pastors returning the completed questionnaire. Although an almost 50 percent response is very high, one has to wonder about the over 50 percent who did not reply. No doubt, some pastors would not take the time to fill out any kind of questionnaire. However, some may have had a negative response to Kirkemo's stated purpose in his cover letter. "I am conducting a national survey of Church of the Nazarene pastor's theology of entire sanctification."[443]

---

[441] Ibid., 122.

[442] Ibid., 108.

[443] Ibid., 128.

Kirkemo interviewed three pastors who were graduates of NTS. Two of them expressed admiration for the camaraderie exemplified by the NTS faculty in spite of underlying theological turmoil. A third pastor expressed an insight worth quoting in full:

> This group of theologians succeeded in holding divergent understandings of entire sanctification while they taught with congeniality in the same institution yet they "failed, because they didn't hash it out among themselves; they could of, they should have." The goal, he believes, should not have been "he's right and she's wrong," but instead, "Here is our position for the denomination, and here are the varying ways of expressing it." Expressed in another way, they did not develop, out of their divergent understandings of entire sanctification, a conjunctive theology that would be faithful to both the Wesleyan-Holiness and Wesleyan-Relational trajectories."[444]

The Nature of Academic Institutions

Much of the above has been about how professional academic institutions interact with their sponsoring denominations, and in particular how professors maintain both credibility and integrity within a confessional institution. I suppose that every denomination has its Richard Taylor believing himself to be the theological watchdog for its seminary, if not the whole denomination. Taylor referred to Nazarene faculty who did not propagate entire sanctification, as he interpreted it, as "lackadaisical."[445] To William Greathouse, then a General Superintendent, he wrote "Bill, we had better make up our minds to be consistent, which may mean cleaning house. For years, gentle little jokes have been made of my ability to 'smell heresy' even where it wasn't, but I smiled at the jokes and tried to keep still, knowing all along that the reality was no joke. Our problem is that at a very deep level our denomination by and large lacks theological savvy or else we choose to look the other way."[446]

Did Taylor believe that firing dozens of Nazarene professors because they could not pronounce "shibbolith" correctly before a board of inquisition was in the spirit of Wesleyan holiness? Did he really

---

[444] Ibid., 118.

[445] Richard Taylor. "Why the Holiness Movement Died," *God's Revivalist and Bible Advocate* (March 1999) 25.

[446] Letter, Taylor to William Greathouse, March 7, 1987, Nazarene Archives.

believe that those professors who did not agree with him were listless and without energy? Taylor's real enemies, if there were such, were the energetic, probing professors who were still attempting to clarify Wesleyan holiness. Taylor further showed his naivete in that he was calling for the broadest thinker, most catholic, ecumenical, and one might say, most respected person in the Church of the Nazarene to provincialize the thinking and teaching of Nazarene higher education professionals. It had been Greathouse who had encouraged Staples to write the paper, "The Current Wesleyan Debate."[447]

Even more ironic, is that William Greathouse's last book, *Wholeness in Christ: Toward a Biblical Theology of Holiness*, was to be something of an ex cathedra pronouncement on entire sanctification from the most respected Wesleyan thinker within the Church of the Nazarene. Greathouse did not tie together the baptism of the Holy Spirit on the Day of Pentecost with entire sanctification. Greathouse asked of those who received the Holy Spirit on the Day of Pentecost, "Were they *entirely* sanctified?" He answered by way of Wesley: "The great company added to the Church that day received the Spirit just as believers receive him today in justification, which is the beginning of sanctification."[448]

Obtaining a Ph.D. from a credible institution requires uprooting one's family, moving to some high-rent district such as Boston, Chicago, or northern New Jersey, subsisting on bread and water, two years of course work, a reading knowledge of two foreign languages, rigorous comprehensive exams (in my case two seven hour exams, and two three and one-half hour exams) writing a three to five hundred page book with one thousand to two thousand footnotes and defending it before very intimidating intellectuals. As an older colleague of mine said, "Anybody would be glad to quit hitting themselves in the head with a hammer." Unless you are neurotic, which most Ph.D.s are.

Upon employment by one's denominational school to teach, s/he may have to teach for three or four years, while teaching at least one new course per semester. Most of these courses, especially in small liberal arts schools, will have nothing to do with the narrowly-defined

---

[447] Staples, "My Ordeal," 5.

[448] William Greathouse. *Wholeness in Christ: Toward a Biblical Theology of Holiness* (Kansas City: Beacon Hill Press of Kansas City, 1998), 70.

parameters in which she did her academic work. S/he is fighting for survival.

Then the decision has to be made as to what one is going to teach in said academic course. What textbook is she going to use? Something that was written one hundred years ago? The answer is yes and no. Yes, if it was written by Luther, Calvin, or Wesley. No, if it's a holiness preacher or academician who wrote a century ago. So let's find some Wesleyan-Holiness authors that have written in the area of hermeneutics, evangelism, preaching, systematic theology, Old Testament, New Testament, etc. They hardly exist. The reformed theology publishers Baker, Zondervan, Eerdmans, Fortress, Westminister/ Knox as well as many others, have cornered the market. The Francis Asbury Press was founded in 1983, and shortly thereafter sold to Zondervan. When Zondervan was bought out by Harper Collins in 1988, Zondervan did not deem the Francis Asbury imprint as profitable and gave it back to the Francis Asbury Society. (When I asked the chief academic editor at Zondervan if he knew that the Harpers were a staunch Methodist family, he did not.) In other words, possibly seventy-five percent of the textbooks used in Wesleyan Holiness institutions are written from the perspective of the reformed tradition. For that reason, Mildred Wynkoop in her WTS Presidential Address challenged the scholars who sat before her to "write, write, write."[449] With inflated course loads at small financially-strapped institutions, writing is very difficult.

Then what is one going to teach when s/he is standing before a group of students? Mouth the platitudes that s/he received twenty years ago while in undergraduate school? Probably not. "Truth" has to be stated in fresh, relevant, contemporary, entertaining, attention-grabbing ways. C.S. Lewis quipped that in Hell, it is perpetually three-o-clock in the afternoon. Much class time feels the same. "Let me see if I can challenge you, provoke you, enable you to think beyond what you learned in Sunday school, or simply keep you awake." All of this pushing the envelope cannot be done without changing the envelope. But changing the envelope cannot be done without changing the content of the envelope. And none of us want to find ourselves in the situation of the erudite Professor Charles Norton, who because of his age wore

---

[449] Mildred Bangs Wynkoop. "John Wesley - Mentor or Guru?" *Wesleyan Theological Journal*, Vol. X (Spring 1975) 13.

out his welcome at Harvard. "In the old man's last years, flight from his undeniably sententious lectures via fire escape was apparently not unknown to dapper youth."[450]

Add to the above, that there is always some buzz-word, catch-word, some leading edge idea, some new thinker to explore, the latest paradigm on the theological market: relational theology, process theology, open-ended theology, spiritual formation, church growth, the missional church, the emergent church, none of which can entirely be avoided. (I heard another new one the other day, "Constructive Theology.") Most interpretation that professors dish out will be forgotten by their students, but some of it will be retained. The retainment causes a slight, if not major, shift in perspective. Simply by being on the cutting edge of say "form criticism" both professors and students are subtly affected. Richard Taylor made at least one observation which was exactly right as I heard him say: "These subtle differences lead to major divergences down the road."

A professor in a Nazarene undergraduate school participated in the "Jesus Seminar" and was fired. One of the leading voices in that seminar was John Crossan, who wrote, "*The Historical Jesus: The Life of a Mediterranean Jewish Peasant*."[451] That one book, scholarship at its most profound and comprehensive level, helped me understand what Jesus was about more than any other book I have read. Ironically, Crossan does not believe in the Deity of Christ or any position close to it.

Thus, the Church of the Nazarene, just as do all conservative denominations, found itself in conflict with the scholars it had hired to preserve and protect its theological tradition. In order to preserve one has to know what one is preserving. This pursuit demands entering closets and pantries that those of a more conservative bent would prefer to remain shut. Or even worse, to crawl under the house and find out that the joists are rotten or not made of the best materialsupporting the edifice. The Church of the Nazarene is certainly not a house of cards, but

---

[450] James Turner. "Secularization and Sacralization: Speculations on some Religious Origins of the Secular Humanities Curriculum, 1850-1900" in the *Secularization of the Academy*, eds. George M. Marsden and Bradley J. Longfield (New York: Oxford University Press, 1992) 87.

[451] John Dominic Crossan. *The Historical Jesus: The Life of a Mediterranean Jewish Peasant* (San Francisco: HarperCollins, 1991).

as all organizations, it has not been, nor is it now, the perfect structure. But it is only through this process of looking back in order to go forward that corrections and repairs can be made so that the organization can continue to be relevant to a world desperately needing the message of heart holiness.

Chapter 6:
Wilmore and Henry Clay Morrison

Henry Clay Morrison

No doubt many Kentuckians would claim that God stood somewhere around present-day Lexington when he created the earth. Bucolic pastures, rolling hills, manicured horse farms, shaded lanes canopied with the boughs of maple, elm, ash trees, and thoroughbreds grazing in the distance lend credence to the argument. Some Kentuckians may even believe basketball is God's favorite game, even if they aren't convinced that a mint julep is His drink of choice. Those of a more religious bent point out that Kentucky has been favored by visitations from God perhaps more than any other American state. In 1800, James McGready instituted the camp meeting at "Rogues Harbor" in Logan County, noted for its blatant sinfulness, and witnessed scores of remarkable conversions. Barton Stone picked up on the methodology, and observed even more spectacular results at the site of a Presbyterian church located in rural Bourbon County just outside of Paris, Kentucky. (The small log church is still there.) Choosing an area suggesting Kentucky's favorite whiskey, in proximity to a pretentious town named after Europe's citadel for infidelity, seems to be just the sort of humor in which God revels. Indeed, Kentucky seemed to be anything but fertile ground for religion. Stone recorded concerning the prostrations, barking, jerking, and whatever did happen at Cane Ridge in August of 1801, "So low had religion sunk and such carelessness universally had prevailed, that I thought that nothing common could have arrested the attention of the world; therefore, these uncommon agitations were sent for this purpose."[452]

---

[452] Quoted in Ellen Elsinger. *Citizens of Zion: The Social Origins of Camp Meeting Revivalism* (Knoxville: The University of Tennessee Press, 1999) 221.

If culture has anything to do with human development, it was no surprise that Henry Clay could hold the U. S. Senate with its packed galleries spell bound for hours, as he championed the cause of the Union. But religion seemed to hold little sway for the bourbon-drinking, card-playing, dueling, and feuding Kentucky Senator, and to this day, he is the State's most esteemed citizen and favorite son. When John Quincy Adams and Henry Clay found themselves on assignment together in Belgium, 1814, negotiating the "Treaty of Ghent," the Kentuckian came in at 5:00 a.m. after a night of drinking and card playing, as Adams was rising for his morning practice of Bible reading and prayer.

Kentuckians are quick to forgive and may be even quicker to forget. When a pious Methodist couple bore a son, March 10, 1857, they named him Henry Clay. Three weeks later, his mother, Emily, attended a "Quarterly" meeting and consecrated her son to God. Upon returning home, she picked up the child and while walking back and forth across the room, weeping, laughing and praising God exclaimed, "Today while I was at church, I gave my little Henry Clay to God to preach the gospel, and I believe that he accepted the gift. And when I am dead and gone, this baby boy grown into manhood will preach Jesus."[453] "Dead and gone" were all too prescient in that the mother, Emily, died when the son was two years old. Henry's father, whom the son could remember seeing only once, died a brief time later as a mule trader in the area of Vicksburg, Mississippi. At a young age, Henry and his slightly older sister lived with their paternal grandparents on a farm just outside of Glasgow, Kentucky. Though the family was Baptist, the thirteen-year-old boy was converted in a revival at the Boyle Creek Methodist Church.

Henry Clay Morrison more than fulfilled his mother's consecrated vision for her son. By the early 1900s, he may have well been the most spell-binding preacher in America. As a young man, he was dangerously handsome, daring to adopt the attire of an Edwardian cut-away tailed coat which he always wore whether to a picnic, camp meeting, or Annual Conference. If there be any such thing as a born leader, Morrison's charismatic personality and steel-trap memory, creative imagination, sonorous voice, and confidence in his own opinions, made him the center of attention wherever he happened to be. For the first four decades of the

---

[453] Percival A. Wesche. *The Life, Theology and Influence of Henry Clay Morrison* (unpublished Ph.D. dissertation, University of Oklahoma, 1954) 4.

twentieth century, he was the most popular and commanding preacher on the holiness camp meeting circuit. When he took a congregation down into hell to look around, and admonished his hearers to tuck their arms in, so they would not be singed with any cinders, his auditors heeded his warnings, literally pulling their elbows to their ribs.

In that our virtues and strengths can easily become our vices and weaknesses, Morrison was at times given to pride, impatience, and sharpness of speech. Paired with John Church at a camp meeting, Morrison gave in to the temptation to out preach his co-evangelist, which he easily did. Around midnight, Church observed his tent flap being raised, and a figure crawling in and for several minutes weeping at his feet. Such fallibility and humility further endeared Morrison to thousands of his admirers. William Jennings Bryan regarded Morrison as America's greatest pulpit orator. In 1910, Morrison became president of Asbury College, Wilmore, Kentucky, twenty years after its founding by John Wesley Hughes. His biographer Percival Wesche wrote, "As Morrison walked across the campus, his long white hair and his Prince Albert coat gave him the appearance of a prophet–preacher from another generation."[454] As Dennis Kinlaw remembered, "When Morrison entered a room, he did not need to take control, he simply was in control."[455] In short, Morrison was larger than life and would have been successful at anything, actor, politician, or business man.

Morrison was a consistent, convinced preacher of "second blessing" holiness, as defined and shaped by the American Holiness tradition. He equated the baptism of the Holy Spirit with entire sanctification, which he believed himself to have experienced. While pastoring in Highlands, Kentucky, 1886-1887, (just below Cincinnati, now Ft. Thomas) Morrison, under the influence of the theologian Thomas N. Ralston, pastors W. S. Grimstead, and Horace Cockrill, sought the "second blessing," and received it in dramatic fashion. J. N. Young was holding revival services at Highlands Methodist Episcopal Church and visited Morrison's room to recommend cancelling the protracted meetings because of the sparse response, to which Morrison responded,

---

[454] Ibid., 169.

[455] Kenneth Cain Kinghorn. *The Story of Asbury Theological Seminary* (Lexington, KY: Emeth Press, 2010) 42.

"Why, Doctor," said I, "the power of God is all over this hill." Throwing up my hands, I said, "The power of God is in this room; I feel it now." Instantly, the Spirit fell on me and I fell backward on a divan, as helpless as a dead man. I was conscious of the mighty hand of God dealing with me. Dr. Young leaped up, caught me in his arms, and called me again and again, but I was powerless to answer.

Just as I came to myself and recovered the use of my limbs, a round ball of liquid fire seemed to strike me in the face, dissolve, and enter into me. I leaped up and shouted aloud, "Glory to God!" Dr. Young, who still had me in his arms, threw me back on the divan and said, "Morrison, what do you mean. You frightened me. I thought you were dying. Why did you act that way?" "I did not do anything, Doctor," said I, "the Lord did it." I arose and walked the floor, feeling as light as a feather.[456]

Champion for Holiness Fundamentalism

During the last decade of the nineteenth century, Morrison was increasingly alarmed by the inroads made by liberalism in the American Protestant Church and particularly his own denomination, the Methodist Episcopal Church South. In 1888 he founded a periodical, *The Old Methodist*, and changed the name of the weekly magazine to *The Pentecostal Herald* in 1897. This periodical would become the most widely circulated, independent voice within American Methodism, with a subscription which grew to 50,000 in 1942. Morrison summarized, "During the first fifty years, more than sixty million copies of this paper have gone out to be read by millions of people...more than two millions religious books have been sown through the nation and around the world, and more than a million Bibles and testaments from the Pentecostal Publishing Company."[457] In his periodical Morrison fought evolution, promoted prohibition, condemned Methodist heresy, and propagated what he thought to be non-negotiable doctrines of the Church which included the virgin birth, the deity of Christ, substitutionary atonement, the ultimate authority of Scripture, and the Church's preparation for the second coming of Christ. Above all, the publication would accent the doctrine of entire sanctification, keeping the Wesleyan Holiness flame

---

[456] Wesche, 58.
[457] Ibid., 92.

from being extinguished. "No church paper was defending the doctrine of sanctification as preached by the fathers and founders of the church, but there was mis-representation, unbelief, and ridicule abounding everywhere. This was the situation when I located to evangelize and publish a full-salvation paper. The opposition was intense and in many instances very bitter."[458] Beyond this purpose, Morrison was going to take on not only Methodism but all that he thought wrong in the American Protestant Church.

In an exacting analysis of Morrison's preaching and writing, Ronald Smith argues that the founder of Asbury Theological Seminary bought into fundamentalist dispensationalism, which included a belief in the pre-millennial return of Christ. Smith states, "From 1898 throughout the remainder of his life, Henry Clay Morrison developed a polemic that was, in his opinion, the logical doctrinal response of one in a mainline Methodist Evangelical tradition as it sought to combat what Morrison deemed to be the corrosive influence of modernity. The two most corrosive factors of the modern era, Morrison would contend, were the diminishing impact its views had with respect to the authority of scripture, and the centrality of conversion."[459]

Morrison was not the first prominent Methodist to adopt pre-millennialism. Others were William Blackstone, William Godbey, and William Nast. However, they were headed into a strong headwind of both British and American Methodism which had been solidly post-millennial throughout the nineteenth century. Kenneth O. Brown lists 24 Methodist theologians and biblical exegetes with their works, all who were post-millennial.[460] These included Richard Watson, Adam Clark, Thomas Ralston, William B. Coke, and Minor Raymond. As post-millennialism became associated with modernist evolution, and pre-millennialism identified with conservative theology, vituperation and name calling broke out in American Methodism. Milton Terry of

---

[458] Henry Clay Morrison. *Some Chapters of My Life Story* (Louisville: Pentecostal Publishing Company, 1941) 142.

[459] Ronald E. Smith. *"Old Path Methodism" in a Modern World: Henry Clay Morrison's Campaign for the Evangelical Option in the Modern Period* (unpublished Ph.D. dissertation, Madison, NJ: Drew University, 2005) 317.

[460] Kenneth O. Brown. *Leadership in the National Holiness Association with Special Reference to Eschatology, 1867-1919* (Unpublished Ph.D. dissertation, Drew University, 1988) 228-230.

Garrett Biblical Institute referred to Methodist evangelist L. W. Munhall as a "vociferous and pessimistic cur...a self-centered, inane, mechanical, illiterate, and mad evangelist."[461] The early leaders of the National Camp Meeting Association correctly believed that rigid eschatology would dilute the main purpose of the Association, second blessing holiness. Third NHA president Charles Fowler sorrowed when one holiness exponent referred to the eschatological views of another as a "damnable heresy."[462]

As American evangelicalism became increasingly caught up in the dispensationalism of John Nelson Darby and C. I. Schofield, entire sanctification became associated with readying one's self for the "rapture," with all of its almost countless interpretations. Brown argues that the Holiness Movement after the death of Fowler would become almost, if not completely, pre-millennial. Morrison, as much or more than any other individual, would lead the way.

Modernism was an attempt to reconcile evolution and various developing theories about the formation and age of the earth with the biblical narrative. Obviously, there were tensions between Genesis 1-2 and Darwin's evolution, and Morrison sided with A. J. Gordon, Bob Jones, Sr., William Jennings Bryan and other well-known fundamentalists. Morrison and Bryan were mutual admirers, the latter invited by Morrison to speak at Asbury College. Smith suggests that Morrison's work "builds on the rigorous doctrinal discussions of fundamentalists and adds the additional theological component of Christian perfection to articulate a theology of progress which he understood to be one of the dominant motifs of the age. In doing so, he created a pragmatic and theological confluence between belief and practice that had a significant influence in the main stream of Methodism."[463]

Morrison's Dispensationalism

Even more surprising was Morrison buying into an agenda that had totally escaped the American Holiness Movement for the entire nineteenth century. Smith states, "Morrison's dispensation belief

---

[461] Ibid., 280.

[462] Ibid., 278.

[463] Ibid., 318.

corresponded directly to the work of C. I. Scofield. Scofield divided history into periods of successive divine dispensations which when rightly interpreted, revealed God's comprehensive, 'pattern for the ages,' a method of interpretation that then became the dominant theme for unifying Bible study. There were seven dispensations, the last being the Millennium when God would set up a visible kingdom on earth."[464] But this view left Morrison with a theological dilemma. For the most part, dispensationalists increasingly embraced rapture theology, a snatching of the Church from an apostate world. And while Morrison, as most camp meeting evangelists, increasingly preached on the "Second Coming" accompanied by the "signs of the times," he held on to the same utopian vision that had been espoused by Matthew Simpson and the post-millennial views of Methodist theologians Thomas Ralston and John Miley. Morrison wanted to believe that the Christian perfecting of individuals would in turn perfect the world, or at least American society.

Give a nation a faithful ministry in its pulpits, men who feel the call and awe of God upon them; men who will be true to His word, declare His truth regardless of consequences, who will faithfully instruct men in righteousness and warn them against sin; men who will rebuke wickedness among the rich as well as the poor, who making the word of the Lord the sword of the Spirit, will strike mightily against the sins of the people and warn them of judgment to come meanwhile, with tender and loving heart, calling them to repentance and pointing them to the Lamb of God who taketh away the sin of the world. Such a nation can but be blessed. There will be power in the churches; the fires of devotion will glow upon millions of family altars; there will be order and happiness in the home; the schools will be centers of spiritual and intellectual development; there will be honesty in commerce, justice in the courts, civic righteousness will prevail, moral standards will be high, social life will be pure, the fear of God will pervade the earth, the love of Christ will reign and rule in the hearts of men, the Bible will become the revered and honored book, and the kingdom of heaven will be set up in the hearts of the people; and our crucified and risen Lord "shall see of the travail of His soul, and shall be satisfied."[465]

From one perspective, pre-millennialism was a win-win situation for Morrison's camp meeting evangelism. The sanctifying of individuals would lead to the perfecting of the moral order and societal transformation. But the revolutionary revival which never came called for Christ to return and set up his millennial kingdom on earth. Morrison

---

[464] Ibid., 324.
[465] Quoted in Smith, 341.

was correct in observing the evangelistic harvest when he proclaimed the "second coming" as a camp meeting evangelist. He failed to detect the irony of preparation for greeting the bridegroom, motivated by fear. Those of us who spent our childhood and teenage years during the 50s and 60s have vivid memories of "left behind" anxiety. If one fast forwards from Morrison to Billy Graham, there was a parallel between Graham's communistic warnings, red nuclear threats and doomsday warnings of Christ's return.

Morrison's Apocalypticism and Contemporary Events

Morrison was astute enough to not set or predict apocalyptic dates as did those who found chronological correlation between contemporary events and biblical symbolism, in particular, those images found in the Book of the Revelation. However, he did repeatedly reference developments unfolding in Israel and interpreted Russia as the arch-enemy of Christianity. Neither did he name the "anti-Christ" nor the "beast." But over the long span of his writing and preaching, world events presented him with satanic villains such as Kaiser Wilhelm, Hitler, and Stalin. "The Kaiser is not the final Man of Sin spoken of in the Scriptures who shall almost entirely dominate and rule the world in the closing day of the dispensation, but he is the forerunner of the coming son of Satan....no one human individual in all the world has brought such suffering and ruin to all the world as the German Kaiser."[466] (Did he forget about Genghis Khan?) Morrison hypothesized, "If Germany had been saturated with evangelical Bible truth, had the pure gospel of a free and full salvation, been faithfully preached throughout the nation, the present war with its heartless cruelties would have been a moral impossibility."[467]

For Morrison, the Kaiser's defeat would be the completion of the sixth dispensation; the covenant of grace in and through Christ to both Jews and Gentiles until Christ's second coming, which made no sense even without being able to predict World War II and the slaughtering of six million Jews. Even more questionable was Morrison's rhetoric spewed

---

[466] Henry Clay Morrison. *The World War in Prophecy: The Downfall of the Kaiser and the End of the Dispensation* (Louisville: The Pentecostal Publishing Company, 1917) 55.
[467] Ibid., 45-46.

out against straw men, unidentified other than "pacifists." (Henry Ford and Rufus Jones?)

> We have no enemies half so dangerous, and who hate us with so deep and bitter a hatred, as those political demagogues, newspaper copperheads, and disguised spies, who would rejoice to see our transports go down at sea, and our armies cut to pieces on the French frontier. They are but seeking to bind the hands of the administration at Washington; to prevent our race of men from enlisting to defend the honor of the flag. They would sink the ships that carry food to the suffering women and children in Belgium. They would deposit explosives in great passenger vessels and send them down in mid-ocean with all on board, without any compunction of conscience. They endorse and gloat over the brutality and outrages of the German Kaiser. Like the unfortunate Jews who cried out on the sad hill of Calvary, "His blood be on us and on our children," they are willing and glad to share their part of responsibility for this horrible crime of the ages.[468]

For the most part, Morrison does not make wild and prophetical assertions and conscientiously stands on biblical authority, attempting to be no more specific than Scripture. Most outlandish are his attempts to provide sociological, political, and cultural analysis. The following excerpt is exemplary of Morrison moving beyond his areas of expertise, and unwittingly prescribing eugenics, the extermination of the "unfit."

> Scientific physicians will tell you that sin has so polluted the physical life, so shattered the nervous system, and sown broadcast disease of every kind, that millions of people are unfit to wed and produce children. Immorality is making such inroads upon society that state legislatures are passing laws to prevent the marriage of those persons whose physical condition is such that their offspring must necessarily be fearfully diseased; and the most learned and thoughtful men are telling us that something radical must be done, and done soon, or the world will be crowded with hospitals and lunatic asylums; that the fearful and increasing number of suicides will multiply, and finally the human race will become extinct.[469]

The following prediction has not yet happened, and raises the question as to whether Morrison would have supported a third party,

---

[468] Ibid., 72-73.

[469] Henry Clay Morrison. *The Second Coming of Christ* (Louisville: The Pentecostal Publishing Company, 1914) 26.

such as the Prohibition ticket. He also could have had in mind Eugene Debs and the Socialist ticket, which he would not have supported, or Theodore Roosevelt's 1912 Progressive Party.

> While the Republican Party has held the reins of government most of the time, the Democratic Party has been a powerful influence in the balancing of justice. Each great party has been a checkmate on the other, so that, on the whole, we have had most excellent government. Unfortunately, at the present, there are indications of disruption and the breaking up of the old parties at a time when there is much unrest and dissatisfaction among large groups of our people. The disintegration of either, or both, of the old parties would give opportunity for the organization of a strong radical party, under the leadership of a very dangerous class of men with convictions and objectives quite out of harmony with those principles that have dominated and guided our American life and civilization.[470]

When Morrison attempted economic analysis and solutions for the Great Depression, he was most bewildering and one might even say, amusing.

> Suppose some friendly genie at the setting of the sun could wave a magic wand over the nation that would destroy every gasoline propelled vehicle of travel, or road and farm machinery; suppose this same genie at the rising of the sun could wave this same magic wand over the nation and bring into existence fifty millions of good strong horses, what a transformation that would be! One splendid result — the people would stay at home for awhile and get acquainted with each other. At once harness makers would be compelled to employ two millions of men to make harness for these horses; those building and keeping roads in order would need to employ a million men to take the place of road machinery; the wagon, buggy and carriage factories would call for three or four millions of men to build vehicles.
>
> These fifty millions of horses would eat a hundred millions of bushels of corn in less than a month; within one week, after they appeared on the scene, wheat would shoot up to $1.50 and $2.00 per bushel. All farm products — corn, wheat, oats, hay — and everything that grows upon the farm would be valuable; the millions of the capitalists would begin

[470] Henry Clay Morrison. *Is the World Growing Better or Is the World Growing Worse?* (Louisville: The Pentecostal Publishing Company, 1932) 49-50.

to flow back to farm populations, the town bank would be prosperous, the thrifty farmers would flock to the stores to supply their needs, the factories would be compelled to put on a full force of laborers and work day and night to supply the demands of prosperous people.[471]

What one is to make of the above is perplexing. It is easy to condemn the myopia of someone who wrote over a century ago. In order to sell books or newspapers, sensationalism is always a temptation. Morrison was not beyond tabloid titillation, and as I wrote about Matthew Simpson, who edited *The Western Christian Advocate*, 1848-1852, "He recognized that in order to maintain readership, he needed a steady stream of societal news. He attempted a balance between solemnity and sell-ability, titillating sensationalism and quotidian mundaneness."[472] There wasn't much mundaneness about Henry Clay Morrison, and if a bit of exaggeration was needed for readership or descriptions of trends that went without documentation, so be it. Amazement was more important than substantiation as exemplified by the following: "This lad at seventeen will attend dances where the participants dance in the nude, and think such conduct is proper. He has no faith in, or reverence for women, whether they are married or single. He is an evolutionist."[473] And the following: "The physicians tell us that the slaughter of the unborn is widespread, and newspapers reveal the fact that infanticide among our civilized people is quite common. Meanwhile the fondness of poodle dogs grow into a shocking fashion. It is reported that babies can be bought in some of our great cities for $2.00 a piece, while poodle dogs are eagerly sought in the market at prices ranging from $100 and upward."[474]

As today, though "Christians" would not delve into the evil described, there is some kind of vicarious fulfillment in reading or hearing about it. We need to be aware of evil and its subtlety, but one wonders if such graphic imagery and descriptions are needed.

Henry Clay Morrison was at his best as a preacher of righteousness and the necessity and possibility of a holy life via the baptism of the Holy

---

[471] Ibid., 45-46.
[472] Salter. *God Cannot Do Without America*, 215.
[473] Morrison. *Is the World Growing Better?* 138-139.
[474] Morrison. *The Second Coming.* 43-44.

Spirit and the cleansing blood of Christ. No one ever exemplified greater or better sanctified imagination. As he took his camp meeting crowd into heaven, he gave them a tour, allowing them to observe who was there. As a tour host, he alerted his visitors to a regal figure coming in the distance. His observers asked, "Is this the archangel Gabriel?" "No!" was the quick reply. "Is it Mary, the mother of Jesus?" Another wrong guess. "Well, who is it then?" The host replied, "It's Mary Magdalene, from whom Jesus cast out seven demons!" This was Wesley's radical optimism of grace, which Morrison excelled in proclaiming.

But if one is preaching camp meeting after camp meeting, and Morrison was at Indian Springs, Georgia, summer after summer, the preacher has to come up with new material, some of it inferior. Before gatherings of thousands within the Holiness Movement, no preacher was considered more capable than Morrison, and thus, there is the temptation to think more highly of oneself than one ought to think. The cult of personality was as prevalent for camp meeting preachers as it is today for televangelists. Thus for persons without television or radio, much less internet, Morrison was the single most important authority for thousands of Americans who found the two weeks of camp meeting the singular high point of each year. These individuals without media other than a newspaper and a religious periodical looked to a religious luminary for not only spiritual direction but for political expertise and economic advice. Morrison at times could be amazingly prescient as the following depicts modernity, the rise of Wal-Mart, and other behemoths that have sucked the life out of small town America.

> Here is a city of eighteen thousand people; it is a prosperous little center of trade and traffic. It cannot escape the hungry eyes of the vultures of predatory wealth. One of five different combinations of chain stores is set up in this city. The managers of these stores buy in such vast quantities, and often goods of an inferior quality, that they can undersell the local merchants; and the people pour into them. The home merchants who pay the taxes, build the schools, support the churches and make the little city a prosperous and comfortable place to live, are driven out of business; the churches and all of the institutions of the town suffer. The money received by the chain stores week by week, is shipped away to some great city, and never comes back; so far as the people who earned and

spent it are concerned, it is out of circulation forever; had just as well been dumped into the river....[475]

Challenging Harry Emerson Fosdick

Morrison's individualistic salvation model offered no solution for systemic evil, which he graphically described, but did not believe that a working covenant with God would usher in the Millennium as did his post-millennial ancestors. Morrison's constituency was much different than the thousands who gathered at the cavernous Riverside Church in northern Manhattan each Sunday to hear Harry Emerson Fosdick. Fosdick was anything but orthodox in that he did not believe in the virgin birth, a substitutionary atonement, the Deity of Christ, the inerrancy of Scripture, the bodily resurrection, and the miraculous nature of healings performed by Christ. Fosdick was a very intelligent, slippery eel, and Morrison mistakenly attempted to catch him in a societal system and cultural setting which was far different than the ethos in which the camp meeting preacher operated. Fosdick was a complicated person in a complicated context. He operated within a venue that Morrison only read about and thus offered little to no remedy. Church historian H. Shelton Smith places Fosdick within a Christocentric, liberal tradition and further writes that he was "assailed as fiercely by the radicals on his left as the radicals on his right. Both parties wanted him to cut loose from his historic moorings but for different reasons: The fundamentalists because he was too liberal; the radicals, because he was too conservative."[476] Smith claimed that Fosdick's sermon "Shall the Fundamentalists Win?" ignited the "hottest controversy that ever raged about any sermon in American history."[477]

To explain the trajectory of a life by identifying only a few influences or events, is an oversimplification. For our purposes, the following distillation will have to suffice. Fosdick was born into a middle-class, Buffalo, New York home that was deeply pious, but with high cultural aspirations. His biographer gives us a glimpse into this

---

[475] Morrison. *Is the World Growing Better?* 65-65.

[476] H. Shelton Smith, Robert T. Handy, Lefferts A. Loetcher. *American Christianity: A Historical Interpretation with Representative Documents,* Vol. II (New York: Charles Scribner's Sons, 1963) 295.

[477] Ibid., 295.

rare combination. "Typical of the home's atmosphere are the scenes of the father, accompanying himself at the piano as he sang hymns in Latin, of the father and mother playing piano and flute duets, and of the father seated on the floor, preparing charts to illustrate a Chautauqua lecture, or the development of the alphabet, or the mother sat at the table preparing a Chautauqua lecture on Madame de Stael."[478] Needless to say, this kind of intellectual stimulation was quite different from the daily chores young Henry Clay carried out on the Kentucky farm.

No one was surprised that the precocious, bookish Harry was chosen to deliver the high school senior commencement oration, and graduated summa cum laude from both Colgate University and Union Theological Seminary. Again his biographer writes, "Fosdick possessed a quick supple mind, and near photographic memory; an ability to absorb the ideas of others and meld those ideas with his own. It was a mind admirably suited to his future role as interpreter and mediator and apologist."[479] It was a mind that would produce some thirty books and preach hundreds of carefully reasoned sermons heard by millions, both in person and on radio.

In 1901, twenty-three-year-old old Fosdick enrolled at Union Theological Seminary, New York City, and was not prepared for witnessing first-hand the poverty and degradation that was unsurpassed by any other place in America. The underside of New York was a shock for a young man who had been nurtured by Christian ideals and Victorian values. Fosdick was not able to navigate an environment he described as a hotbed of "knavery, debauchery, and bestiality."[480] The theological

---

[478] Robert Miller. *Harry Emerson Fosdick: Preacher, Pastor, Prophet* (New York: Oxford University Press, 1985) 14.For an excellent treatment of Madame de Stael, see Nell Irvin Painter. *The History of White People* (New York: W. W.Norton and Company, 2010) 91-103. Painter writes, "Reaching across time and space, her work has inspired women writers as various as George Sand, George Eliot, Harriet Beecher Stowe, and Willa Cather. De Stael also furnished a template for the American transcendentalist Margaret Fuller, the brainiest in her company of elevated spirits. All of that was yet to come but in her own time de Stael also built the crucial conveyor belt between German thinkers of all kinds and a vast audience of lay readers in France, Britain, and the United States who lacked direct access to writing in German. She publicized the genius of Goethe, the naturalist religion of transcendentalism, and the way of categorizing Europeans as members of several different races." 91.

[479] Ibid., 35.

[480] Ibid., 47.

platitudes on which he had been raised were kicked back in his face, and he may have been even physically threatened. He was faced with problems which he would address in both word and deed for the rest of his life. His hero Walter Rauschenbusch, who lived and worked in "Hell's kitchen," left a lifelong impression on the young seminary student and pastor.

For reasons we are unable to trace here, both of Fosdick's parents suffered a nervous breakdown and Harry would experience the same. During his first year at Union he dropped out, and spent four months in a mental sanitarium. He later recalled, "You not only feel sick but you feel humiliated. If you had diabetes, you would be ill, but it would not be compounded with humiliation, that you would be ashamed of yourself."[481] This experience intensified his empathy for others living in the overwhelming pressure of an increasingly urbanized and industrialized society. According to his biographer, the practical result of his helplessness was a dependence on prayer, and communicating the same to his parishioners. He would also devote much of his ministry to counseling and staying abreast of the latest developments in psychology. Though he was already headed toward ministry, his breakdown was the ultimate event that sealed the deal. "Until then I had intended to teach about religion, rather than to preach the Gospel, but henceforth, I wanted to get at people, real people, with their distracting, anxious, devastating problems."[482] It was little surprise that Fosdick's sermons resembled counseling sessions, existential preaching addressing both personal and societal problems.

Fosdick and Morrison lived on two different planets, and in that Fosdick possibly more than any other person incarnated modernism, the holiness preacher used him for theological target practice. Of course if you want to crucify someone, find the most disagreeable statements possible and take them out of context. In *The Follies of Fosdick*, Morrison mainly took issue with Fosdick's book *As I See Religion*. Fosdick stated, "All theology tentatively phrases in current thought and language the best that, up to date, thinkers on religion have achieved; and the most hopeful thing about any system of theology is that it will not last."[483]

---

[481] Ibid., 48.

[482] Ibid., 49.

[483] Harry Emerson Fosdick. *As I See Religion* (New York: Harper & Brothers, 1931)

Fosdick was wrong in saying that the most hopeful thing about theology is that it would not last. That is the least hopeful thing about it. Morrison was equally wrong by saying that "Evidently Dr. Fosdick does not believe that we have yet found an infallible foundation upon which to build a system of divine truth."[484] Fosdick was not addressing Christ as our foundation, which he certainly believed would last, but the fallible and incomplete theology about Christ as to doctrine. Fosdick argued, "As for doctrine, that is always important. Let a physician get his doctrine about scarlet fever right or he will bungle his task. So in religion, we want the best churches and the truest thinking we can get."[485]

Morrison attacked the following from Fosdick: "Often with feverous militancy, always with deadly earnestness, they had made up their minds that religion must be saved. Such an attitude is a sure sign of senility; it has uniformly preceded those historic faiths that have grown old and passed away."[486] In retort, Morrison reminded his readers that, "There is quite a number of serious people that will not agree that the historic faiths have grown old and passed away. No doubt, they have passed away in the mind of Dr. Fosdick."[487] Could Fosdick have been referencing the medieval tyranny of the church, the misguided crusades, and salvation via merit? Morrison lampooned Fosdick's argument that, "While the early Christians battled stoutly for the things they believed, their major stress was not somehow to save their faith, anxiously defend it, and see it through. Their faith saved them, defended them, and saw them through. It carried them. It was to them health, peace, joy, and moral power."[488] From this author's perspective, would not this have been true of the disciples rejoicing that they were worthy to suffer in his name and Paul and Silas singing in prison? Morrison suggested that Fosdick read the eleventh Chapter of Hebrews. Morrison and Fosdick would have found common ground admiring the heroes of the faith, Fosdick no less appreciative than Morrison.

5.

[484] H. C. Morrison. *The Follies of Fosdick* (Louisville: Pentecostal Publishing Company, 1936) 11.

[485] Fosdick, *As I See*, 6.

[486] Morrison, *Follies*, 21.

[487] Ibid.

[488] Ibid., 23.

Morrison was more correct when bracketing the following, "Moreover, when the modern mind hears the creeds upon which many of the churches still insist, with all the corollaries brought out by controversy, and urged as indispensables of religious truth – old cosmologies, doctrines of biblical infallibility, miracles like virgin birth or physical resurrection–the reaction is not simply incredulity, although incredulity is undoubtedly emphatic – but wonder as to what such things have to do with religion."[489] Fosdick was not saying that he did not believe in the virgin birth (which he did not), he was arguing that orthodoxy as stated in the Apostle's Creed, is incredulous to the normative, natural person. Though I do not agree with Fosdick, he did not believe that such creedal affirmations were necessary for a relationship with God. But he did believe that a personal relationship with God was not only possible, but necessary.

In *As I See Religion*, Fosdick argued that "Phenomena such as conversion, transformation of character, and integration of personality through prayer can be studied objectively; and while some may think it possible to explain them on non-religious grounds, no one thinks it possible to explain them away."[490] He further wrote, "Squirm and twist as we will, we cannot be rid of this experiential fact which, of old, theologians praised as the sovereignty of God, and which a poet like Francis Thompson calls the Hound of Heaven."[491] The heart of the argument in Fosdick's book *As I See Religion* was against an American faith, which was cheap, sentimental, and egocentric. No one ever more accurately placed their finger on the central problem of American Christianity than the following:

> The ultimate answer to the new attack, however, does not lie in the realm of intellectual discourse. The attack will continue until we popularly achieve a type of religion which does not come within its line of fire. Our real trouble is egocentric religion, which does egregiously fool its devotees. A comfortable modernism which, eliminating harsh and obsolete orthodoxies and making a few mental adjustments to scientific world-views contents itself with a sentimentalized God and a roseate optimism will, if it continues, encourage the worst opinions of religion as a pacifying fantasy. Such

---

[489] Ibid., 27.

[490] Fosdick, *As I See*, 17.

[491] Ibid., 25.

a lush gospel will claim its devotees, but minds with any sinew in them turn away. Modern Christianity has grown soft, sentimental, saccharine. It has taken on pink flesh and lost strong bone. It has become too much flute and too little trumpet. It has fallen from the stimulating altitudes of austerity and rigor, where high religion customarily has walked. Its preachers have become too commonly religious crooners. In consequence it is called a mere wish-fulfilment because it acts that way. "No completely healthy intelligent person," says one of our psychologists, "who has not suffered some misfortune can ever be truly religious." That is not so much intellectual judgment as peevishness, but the writer could easily claim that he had much to be peevish about.[492]

And Fosdick was possibly the pulpit's most astute critic of the scientific paradigm to which he was attempting to adjust the Christian faith. There was the ever leering temptation of a materialistic determinism undermining the possibilities of grace.

Important as the service of science has been, the persistent pressing of the question, "Is it scientific?" into every realm has depleted our living; and our hard-headed factual thinking, with its hard-headed and often hard-hearted factual results in a highly mechanized and commercialized civilization, is proving to be starvation diet.[493]

Fosdick accurately analyzed modernism. In a sermon strangely and intriguingly titled, "A Fundamentalist Sermon," he stated concerning Hell and pre-destination: "The old theological forms in which our forefathers endeavored to put such facts, I take to be as dead as Sennacherib, but I call your attention to the sobering truth that in comparison with the candor and fearlessness with which the old time Christianity faced these facts, our superficial modernism with its sing-song from Coue, that every day, in every way, we are getting better and better, sounds soft and lush and sentimental."[494] But in all likelihood, Morrison had not read this sermon as he had perused little of one of the most prodigious preachers to ever stand in an American pulpit. What did Morrison accomplish by attacking Fosdick? How many of his camp

[492] Ibid., 116-117.

[493] Ibid., 132-33.

[494] Harry Emerson Fosdick, "A Fundamentalist Sermon," in 20 Centuries of Great Preaching Vol. IX, editors: Clyde E. Fant and William M. Pinson (Waco, TX: Word Books, 1971) 46.

meeting attendees and *Pentecostal Herald* readers had ever heard of Fosdick? I dare say that none of the early holiness leaders such as John Inskip, William McDonald, and Charles Fowler ever defined themselves by tearing down someone else. Morrison as much or more than any other person changed the agenda of the American Holiness Movement.

If one is to gain followers, it is best to have an enemy. The confluence of evolution, biblical criticism, modernism and secularism, provided the perfect opportunity for circling the wagons. No less than the Stewart brothers, Lyman and Milton, who published *The Fundamentals*, Morrison had discovered the paradigm that would work for the College of which he was President and the Seminary which he founded. Wilmore, Kentucky, was a long way, not just in miles from the city that would become known as Gotham. It was the old archtypical contrast between the pristine pure country and the colossal wicked demons that haunted from the underground sewers of a metropolis. In fact, for Morrison, it was unlikely that one could even live in such a city and be Christian. On December 13, 1922, in an open letter to Fosdick, Morrison wrote in his *Pentecostal Herald*, "It is generally understood that the country is not looking to wealthy, fashionable, city churches for either the great saving truths of the gospel, or the demonstration of those truths, and sanctification of heart and holiness of living. Fashionable congregations know little of the depth of Christian experience, of self-denial and cross-bearing; of forsaking self and following Jesus."[495] Morrison did not realize that his polemic may have been almost as sociologically as theologically scripted.

Julian C. McPheeters

Julian C. McPheeters, born in 1889, had been raised on a farm and knew the value of hard work. And like Morrison, he experienced entire sanctification: "In that one swift second I took this step of faith, my soul was flooded with glory divine."[496] Also like Morrison, McPheeters requested his Conference appoint him as a full-time evangelist, which it did. At the age of twenty-seven, McPheeters met Morrison and by 1932, he was on the board of Asbury Theological Seminary. At the age of 41,

---

[495] H. C. Morrison, "Letter to Fosdick," *Pentecostal Herald* (December 13, 1922) 8.
[496] Kinghorn, 109.

McPheeters became pastor of a new and large Glide Memorial Methodist Episcopal Church in San Francisco. Four years later, Morrison entrusted McPheeters with the editorship of the *Pentecostal Herald*, upon the founder's death. Thus, McPheeters became editor of the magazine for twenty-seven years. When Morrison died in 1942, McPheeters became President of Asbury Theological Seminary, and for the next six years also served as pastor of Glide Memorial Church. McPheeters was in the mold of Morrison: a great camp meeting preacher, a charismatic personality, a mind that memorized reams of Scripture, with boundless energy, the ability to develop relationships with wealthy people, and above all, the explicit teaching and preaching of entire sanctification as a definite second work of grace.

But though McPheeters was a champion of Christian orthodoxy, he was more irenic than Morrison. He did not have to fight the same battles againt modernism as did Morrison. World War II had dispelled any illusion that the twentieth century was the Christian century, and the realism of the Neibuhr brothers became, if not the reigning theology, a definitive challenge to liberalism's pallid and sentimental assumptions. As the Holiness Movement had known all along, sin could not be simply explained away as psychological maladjustment and hereditary misfortune. Thus, with official Methodist seminaries still holding on to the last vestiges of personalism, modernism, and other here today and gone tomorrow theologies, Asbury Theological Seminary, founded by Morrison in 1923, was primed for students who wanted to serve Methodism equipped with an evangelical, if not fundamentalist, theology.

The Claude Thompson Explosion

Everything was smooth sailing, until a theological typhoon smashed into Wilmore, its origins remaining mysterious to this day. In 1947, Asbury College graduate and Drew University Ph.D. Claude Thompson (who had also done post doctoral work at Oxford and Edinburgh) became Theology Professor at Asbury Seminary, his life-long dream. Asbury Seminary historian Kenneth Kinghorn calls Thompson "an evangelical, Wesleyan Christian, a man of much prayer who daily read from his Greek New Testament, and was in full accord with A. T. S.'s doctrinal beliefs."[497] But Thompson was not a fundamentalist, believing in Scriptural inerrancy tied to a verbal dictation theory of the Bible, and neither was he a dispensationalist. What made the vitriolic attack on Thompson's theology even more ironic is that his 823 page dissertation, a positive assessment of *The Witness of American Methodism to the Historical Doctrine of Christian Perfection*, (four volumes) is the most extensive treatment ever given to the subject.

Even though Thompson seemed to be everything that a Wesleyan Holiness seminary would desire in and of a professor, complaints began to leak from his classes. The complaints were not specific, but in that Thompson had studied under Edwin Lewis who some thought taught a cosmic dualism, both Kinghorn and Scott Kisker suggest guilt by association. After interviewing Thompson, McPheeters assured key denominational leaders Free Methodist Leslie Marston and Wesleyan Methodist Stephen Paine that Thompson was orthodox. But McPheeters' claim that Thompson was one of his best professors was little more than a thumb in the dyke. To the dismay of most of the students and a majority of the trustees, nine Asbury employees including six professors led by Harold Kuhn, threatened to resign unless Thompson was fired. Ironically, Kuhn was a Quaker, a denomination that has excelled in the peaceful settlement of disputes and unfortunately has circled the globe with an amorphous theology best described as latitudinarianism. "Gossip, half-truths, misinformation, and falsehoods" continued to

---

[497] Ibid., 62. Maxie Dunham recalled, "At Candler School of Theology my favorite professor was Claude Thompson." Kinghorn, 190. Beth Ury, now 94, stated of Thompson, "He was the most gentle, loving person." Conversation with author, November 1, 2018. Albert Truesdale, who had Thompson as a professor, when the latter was in his last days dying of cancer, writes, "During my first year at Emory, I enrolled in a directed study course in Christology to be conducted by Dr. Claude Thompson. He was bed-fast and in the late stages of terminal cancer. So once a week I sat by his bedside as we discussed the reading he had assigned. Dr. Thompson was gracious, and keenly engaged in the topic. Thomas J. Altizer had only recently left Emory. There were still 'death of God' proponents on the faculty. Dr. Thompson was a haven of orthodoxy for a Nazarene Ph.D. student trying to navigate Emory University. Altizer and company had not altered Claude Thompson's orthodoxy. He taught from his bedside as though God and the Christian faith were still in charge and ready to shepherd me. I particularly remember Dr. Thompson's funeral service in the Candler School of Theology Chapel. We sang the great hymns of Christian hope and victory. As Mrs. Thompson walked out of the chapel she had the glow of the resurrection on her face." Email to this author from Albert Truesdale, Ph.D. on October 25, 2018.

wash over the Seminary, and the "nine defying the Board of Trustees continued to call for Thompson's dismissal and charged McPheeters with tolerating modernism at the Seminary."[498] When Kuhn protested by handing in his resignation, McPheeters responded:

> In fact Harold, you and I both know that Thompson and Bob and Dean Turkington and Reynolds are not modernists. They may not teach as you teach and they may not please you altogether, and they may not please me altogether, but to say they are modernists is to make a statement that cannot be supported by actual evidence....If you cannot be happy [at Asbury] and cannot co-operate, then the only thing to do is to resign, but I had seriously hoped that you would find it in your heart to do the big Christian thing and help us work that situation out.[499]

McPheeters' pleading defense of Thompson did no good. Even Board Member "Fighting Bob Shuler," the California champion of fundamentalism, defended Thompson by saying "Christian men should be no less honorable than a worldly court of justice. No court made up of infidels would punish a man without evidence of his guilt. We cannot resolve an emergency by acting dishonorably."[500] Shuler's son, Bob Shuler, Jr., on the faculty of ATS, was a best friend of Thompson.[501]

Apparently the "nine" did not think they were dishonorable, and the imbroglio continued to rage. McPheeters could not put out the conflagration consuming the campus and beyond. Thompson courageously decided that the only way out for both him and the Seminary was to resign. With no rancor, but with a wound he carried for the rest of his life, he communicated, "May God bless all of you and continue to prosper this Institution, which I have more loved than any other school."[502] Upon Thompson's resignation, two of the "nine" rushed into the Board Meeting, sticking their fingers in McPheeters' face, and demanding to be

---

[498] Ibid., 178.

[499] Scott Kisker, "The Claude Thompson Controversy at Asbury Theological Seminary: Holiness Theology in Transition," *Wesleyan Theological Journal*, Vol. 33, No 2 (Fall 1998) 242.

[500] Kinghorn, 179.

[501] Donald Dayton brought this to my attention. I think Dayton is correct interpreting that the controversy mainly revolved around a fundamentalist hermeneutic of inerrancy. Email April 4, 2019.

[502] Ibid.

exonerated less they be held responsible for Thompson's ouster.[503] When the denouncing party continued to maintain that Asbury Theological Seminary was contaminated by modernism, trustee John Paul stood and denounced, "I am ashamed of you. As to modernism being rampant at the Seminary, there is just as much chance for modernism to be fostered, protected, and defended in Asbury Theological Seminary, as there is for *The Pentecostal Herald* to build and operate a distillery in Louisville."[504]

When Edwin Lewis caught wind of the events which had unfolded concerning one of his prized students, he saw to it that Asbury lost its accreditation with both the Methodist Church and the American Association of Theological Schools. In spite of these penalties, McPheeters continued to lead the school through rapid growth throughout the fifties. When told that he would have to resign for the school to regain accreditation, McPheeters immediately did so. In accepting the Presidency, Frank Stanger wrote, "The story of our loss of accreditation and the struggle of its restoration will long remain a familiar one in our history....but no story can be unhappy if its ending is happy."[505] That was not true. A holiness school had exhibited before the world attitudes, actions, stances, which to say the least were unChristian. Scott Kisker writes, "In the case of Asbury, Calvinism-friendly holiness bodies won the day, indicating a change in the character of holiness and its relationship to the broader, Christian world. The important alliance of the Seminary was not Methodist, but a less defining, Reformed-influenced grouping called 'evangelicalism.'"[506] I would change Kisker's "evangelicalism" to "fundamentalism," or at least a neo-fundamentalism, as represented by Carl Henry, Harold Ockenga, and the N.A.E. The fundamentalist birds of Morrison's screeds against modernism had unfortunately come home to roost. They always do.

Frank Stanger and A Change in Emphasis

When Frank Stanger was inaugurated into the Presidency of Asbury Theological Seminary in 1962, after having served three years as McPheeters' assistant, the School made a subtle shift in theological

---

[503] Ibid.
[504] Kinghorn, 181.
[505] Ibid., 209.
[506] Kisker, 247.

emphasis. Stanger certainly believed in holiness, and testified to a second definite spiritual experience when he was a sophomore in high school.[507] But Stanger had not been a charismatic preacher as had Morrison and McPheeters. Entire sanctification as a second work of grace for those two had been centrist and explicit. For Stanger, the holiness agenda would be allowed to wander through the halls of the Seminary as it pleased, with each professor interpreting its place in the Wesleyan ordo solutis. For the first two presidents of Asbury, the nineteenth century Holiness Movement took precedence over Methodism, and lived within the tension between the two. In the Stanger administration, that tension was almost completely dissolved. Stanger was a capable administrator, enabling the Seminary to regain accreditation and credibility as a sound and evangelical option for conservative Methodists and smaller holiness denominations, in particular, Wesleyan Methodists and Free Methodists. McPheeters prophesied that Stanger's inaugural would be a "soundboard for heralding the name and message of Asbury Theological Seminary, to multiple thousands of people....It will be the Seminary's single one opportunity to declare her single solid stand on the great fundamentals of the evangelical faith, and likewise, her distinctive position and mission for spreading scriptural holiness throughout the world."[508]

In his Inaugural Address, Stanger stated, "Asbury Theological Seminary was raised up to defend the Wesleyan doctrine of Christian Perfection. At the time of its founding that was about the only Wesleyan doctrine under serious fire. But since then almost the whole range of evangelical doctrines has come under fire. Therefore, I want Asbury to enlarge its commission. Certainly it is not to neglect its original purpose but to add to it the defense of evangelical truth in its entirety."[509] Stanger was correct in arguing for a full, orbed theological education, but his challenge ran the risk of the Wesleyan doctrine of Christian perfection, as it had been taught by Morrison and other holiness specialists, melding into generic evangelicalism. The question remained, how far could Asbury enlarge the periphery without weakening the center?

---

[507] Kinghorn, 215.

[508] Ibid.

[509] Frank Bateman Stanger, "The Inaugural Address of Dr. Frank Bateman Stanger," *The Herald* (October 17, 1962) 18. Stanger quoted someone else for this statement, but did not reveal his source.

Having himself experienced miraculous physical healing, Stanger made healing a cornerstone of his teaching and preaching. He also took interest in the liturgical renewal movement taking place in Methodism, and wrote for *The Herald* in 1976, "I am making a spiritually-impassioned appeal for either the discovery or rediscovery of a sense of reverence of corporate worship in evangelical churches."[510] Upon this announcement, Stanger formed a chapel committee to plan "six formal chapel services with printed orders of worship, with liturgy and sacred music sung by the Seminary Singers."[511] Whatever the value of moving towards a formal worship paradigm, the Seminary was departing from the camp meeting altar call and spontaneity by which Morrison and McPheeters had been shaped, and in turn fashioned the two Asburys. The holiness vine rooted in the nineteenth century was withering.

There was another paradigm shift. Throughout the first half of the nineteenth century, the most important publicity for both of the Asbury institutions was not carried out by official development or publicity departments, but by a coterie of evangelists who worked out of Wilmore, that is, called Wilmore their home. Among them were Tony Anderson, C. I. Armstrong, H. M. Cochenour, Howard Callis, and Maurice Stevens, and others who preached as their specialty "entire sanctification," enabling both Asbury institutions to keep Wesleyan holiness in the foreground. Also, many of the professors were out preaching. Strange, even for a conservative, evangelical school, the Asbury institutions for decades did not hold Monday classes, so that the professors and evangelists "could close out" on Sunday night, not having to travel on the Sabbath, and could be in classes on Tuesday morning.

The Founding of Wesley Biblical Seminary

The evolving pluralistic interpretations of the two-step formula taught by the American Holiness Movement became increasingly disconcerting to the holiness element at the Seminary, in particular Ivan Howard, Wilber Dayton, Delbert Rose, and William Arnett. Howard and Rose left for Jackson, Mississippi, and founded Wesley Biblical Seminary, with Ivan Howard as its founding President and Delbert Rose as its first Dean. Wilber Dayton, who had already left Asbury to become

---

[510] Kinghorn, 31.
[511] Ibid.

President of Houghton College, joined the faculty in 1975. Howard was a unique individual, not graduating from high school until he was 34 years old and completing a Ph.D. at the University of Iowa when he was 64 years old. Unfortunately, he died of a sudden heart attack only two years into his Presidency, at which time Eldon Fuhrman became President.[512] Fuhrman had been Professor of Theology at Western Evangelical Seminary, Portland, Oregon.

Wesley Biblical Seminary was begun by the Association of Independent Methodist Churches and supported by the Congregational Methodist Church and the Methodist Protestant Church, all headquartered in Mississippi. However, many of its students came from conservative holiness denominations located in the North, such as the Evangelical Church of North America, the Evangelical Methodist Church, the Wesleyan Church, and the Churches of Christ in Christian Union. Also, students of conservative holiness schools such as Kentucky Mountain Bible College, God's Bible School, and Circleville Bible College (now Ohio Christian University) chose Wesley Biblical Seminary as a graduate school because it openly taught the core traditional Wesleyan-holiness paradigm. Over the years, these students sat under very capable professors such as John Oswalt, William Ury, William Arnold, Gary Cockerill, Wilber Dayton, Leon Chambers, Matt Friedeman and Sandra Richter. Following Eldon Fuhrman, WBS had effective Presidents: Harold Spann for 11 years and Ron Smith for 13 years. Both faculty and administration were committed to the American Holiness Movement's interpretation of entire sanctification, and most of the faculty was steeped in John Wesley. In 2008, WBS boasted the largest enrollment in its history, 148 students.

After surviving for forty years, WBS faced a governance and organizational crisis in 2013, and almost went out of business. After enrolling almost 150 students in 2008, that number dropped to 25 in 2013, with approximately a 40 count total enrollment. In 2013, WBS graduated 38 students but in 2014-15, only five students each year.[513] In 2013, WBS inaugurated John Neihof, Jr. as its seventh President. Neihof,

---

[512] Martha M. Howard. "A First-hand View of the First Ten Years of Wesley Biblical Seminary and of Its Founding President," (July 1994) unpublished and furnished by Wesley Biblical Seminary, Jackson, Mississippi.

[513] Retrieved from SIR_2018_WesleyMS.pdf. Strategic Information Report Wesley Biblical Seminary, 2017-18.

having been raised in the conservative holiness movement and with a Ph.D. in Communications from the University of Kentucky, has brought renewed energy and vision to the school. As of this writing, (October 2018) WBS has 120 students (total head count) with sixty percent of them being non-Caucasian. WBS continues to take advantage of its location in Mississippi, leading the Association of Theological Schools with a high percentage of African American students.[514]

Timothy Tennent and Asbury Theological Seminary

In 2009, the Asbury Theological Seminary hired Timothy Tennent as its eighth President. Tennent, with his Methodist background, is seemingly committed to entire sanctification, though he did his Master of Divinity at Gordon Conwell Seminary. Asbury Theological Seminary has continued to prosper, aided by a 60 million dollar gift from Ralph Beeson, founder of the Liberty National Life Insurance Company. Though Wesleyan in orientation, and still furnishing more pastors than any other seminary for the United Methodist Church, the belief in "second blessing holiness" as a litmus test for holding a professorial position on the faculty has long vanished. Some perceive that Tennent, having not been raised in the Holiness Movement, does not bring with him negative baggage and is conscientiously attempting to return the Seminary to its historical commitments. (As John Oswalt told this author, "It is those who have been raised in the Holiness tradition who have problems with entire sanctification; those who have been raised on the outside, when presented with the possibility of heart holiness, more readily accept it"). Others interpret what was once the citadel of Wesleyan scholarship committed to protecting and propagating the doctrine of holiness of heart and life, as having broadened its scope and lost its focus.

Tennent is probably the most scholarly individual to ever fill the presidential chair of Asbury Theological Seminary. His over five hundred page *Invitation to World Missions* is a gold standard text for a course in Missiology. In the book, Tennent does not mention the Holiness Movement but rather gives a full orbed treatment of Pentecostalism. Tennent writes

---

[514] My gratitude to John Neihof, Jr., for filling in the details of this brief sketch. Sadly, Neihof died suddenly of a massive heart attack on March 8, 2019, a great loss for WBS and all of us who counted him as a friend.

In contrast (to the Enlightenment), Pentecostalism emerged among uneducated peoples who were the least influenced by the Enlightenment worldview. Furthermore, their personal experience with the Holy Spirit gave them reason to believe that the same Holy Spirit who acted supernaturally in the lives and witness of the apostles is active today in similar ways. The result of this conviction has been the emergence of a global Pentecostal pneumatology that *anticipated* God's ongoing intervention in the world through miraculous healings, prophetic guidance to the church, demonic deliverance from evil, and an empowered witness to the world. In short, the Holy Spirit continues to usher in the first fruits of the New Creation into the fallen world. Many of the future realities of the kingdom are now fully available to all believers through the person and work of the Holy Spirit.

....The Pentecostal sense of the immediacy of God's presence and power has struck a responsive chord in Christians everywhere and has helped to stimulate fresh evangelistic and missional activity. It is also a wonderful reminder of how crucial it is that the noetic principle in theology (reflection, reason, propositional statements, etc.) always must be balanced by the *ontic* principle (immediacy of God's presence, personal experience with God, etc.) If either of these tendencies is allowed to run unchecked, the church falls into error.[515]

In a blog, "Conversion through faith in Jesus Christ: Why I am a Methodist and an Evangelical," Tennent states:

As a relational term, entire sanctification means that your whole life, your body, and your spirit, have been re-oriented. Entire sanctification means that our entire heart has been re-oriented towards the joyful company of the Triune God .

To be sanctified is to receive a gift from God which changes our hearts and reorients our relationship with the Triune God and with others, giving us the capacity to love God and neighbor in new and profound ways.[516]

This statement is representative Wesley, but makes no reference to "instantaneous" or "secondness," which captures the real uniqueness of Wesley. Tennent's summation while being theologically sound, would

---

[515] Timothy Tennent. *Invitation to World Missions* (Grand Rapids: Kregel, 2010) 425-426.

[516] Timothy Tennent, posted in blog: "Conversion through faith in Jesus Christ: Why I am a Methodist and an Evangelical."

come up short for holiness conservatives. It is safe to say, that Tennent's hiring in 2009 rather than the 1970s when this author was a student indicates a more inclusive Wesleyan matrix for a new generation of students looking for a clearly pronounced Evangelicaism, rather than a trumpet call to holiness immediately attainable. Tennent did not bring to Asbury's campus an amorphous John Wesley; a Wesley less tethered to the Holiness Movement was waiting for him when he got there.

Chapter 7:
Dennis Kinlaw, The Francis Asbury Society and the Pentecostal/Holiness Showdown

The Birth, and Development of Dennis Kinlaw

Dennis Franklin Kinlaw was born to Wade and Sally Kinlaw, June 26, 1922, in Lumberton, North Carolina. Although the father was an attorney, he secured the job of postmaster in Lumberton. As Dennis recalled, lawyers and doctors were starving during the Depression, and because his dad was one of few Republicans in a Democratic county, he secured the appointment in the post office. Dennis always claimed that in any direction from Lumberton, one passed through a swamp: Black, Green, Bear, and Horseneck.

Genuine revival came to the Lumberton Methodist Episcopal Church, and Dennis would later recall that the services were held by a Nazarene evangelist. Because of the spiritual renewal, Wade Kinlaw met for prayer with two or three men each morning at the courthouse. One of these men had been a patient at Dix Hill in Raleigh, North Carolina, which carried the negative connotation as a "lunatic asylum." This particular man made his living driving a fruit truck. When Wade Kinlaw and the fruit truck owner heard that Billy Sunday was scheduled to preach in Boone, North Carolina, (a full day's drive away) they made the trip. After listening to Sunday the truck owner suggested, "I need to buy a load of fruit in Florida, and why don't you go with me?" Kinlaw consented, though Dennis would later comment, "My dad believed in working six days a week."

The two of them spent the night at Indian Springs, Georgia, and discovered that a camp meeting was in progress. Upon sitting spellbound, listening to Henry Clay Morrison, Wade Kinlaw said to the truck owner,

"You go on down to Florida and get your fruit, and pick me up on the way back." Kinlaw determined he would bring his family to the camp the next summer. Dennis later reflected, "They took my sister, but they did not take me, and when she returned I knew something wonderful had happened to her, and I was determined to go the next summer." Dennis recalled his life changing night as a thirteen-year-old at Indian Springs Camp Meeting.

> A joy flooded my inner being, a joy of a deeper magnitude and of a different essence than anything I had ever known before....It was the sense of a Presence, an Other, who had come to me. All of the bits of glory of that moment seemed to be the natural accompaniments that came with the holy Presence. It was not just that I felt that he had now entered into me and that I now possessed him. Rather, he had welcomed me into himself. I did not have to reach out to touch him. He was in me, and I was in him.[517]

Of course, one did not fall under the spell of Henry Clay Morrison without attending Asbury College, and there Dennis met Elsie Blake, whom according to him, he chased for the rest of his life. For fifty-nine years he was married to a woman who had discovered Asbury College listed in an almanac; it showed up early in the alphabet, and she liked the name. As a forty-three year old, Dennis finished a Ph.D. at Brandeis University in Mediterranean Studies. He descended back on Wilmore in 1964 to become Professor of Old Testament at Asbury Theological Seminary. John Oswalt, a student at ATS, (because Dennis had told him that is where he needed to attend seminary) said to Frank Stanger, "He could expect all of his brightest students going into Old Testament. When he asked me why I said such a thing, I answered it was because Dennis Kinlaw was teaching Old Testament. In the upshot, I was proven quite correct. In that short five years, some twenty-five people went on for further study in Old Testament, and several of them have made important contributions to the field, something that gave Dennis considerable pleasure."[518]

A little known chapter in Kinlaw's life was a key to his development and his utter dependence on God. When he was a senior

---

[517] Cricket Albertson, "A Pivotal Impact," *The High Calling* (July –August, 2017) 6.

[518] John N. Oswalt, "In Memory of Dr. Dennis F. Kinlaw," *The High Calling* (July – August, 2017) 11.

in high school, he was given a role in a Christmas program at his home Methodist church. His assignment was to carry a lit candle down the aisle, place the candle in a candelabra, recite an 8-line poem, after which he would take his place in the choir. As he came down the aisle, the candle began to shake, and by the time he stepped on the platform his hand was so uncontrollably wavering, both he and the congregation were fearful he was going to burn down the church. After he somehow placed the candle in the candelabra, he started on his poem, but could only remember the second line, and after muttering through that, attempted to go back to the first line which escaped him. So our future famed preacher and college president embarrassingly fled the church. Dennis would later take an aptitude test and discover that he was in the bottom 10 percent of the general population in manual dexterity, and close to the bottom one-third in public speaking. In other words, he wasn't cut out for much of anything.

Fast-forward to his freshman year in Seminary when as a 21-year-old, he informed the love of his life, Elsie Blake, that they could not get married because he had no money, plus he owned only one brown tweed suit, and her dad would expect a formal wedding. During that year, 1943, his mother and dad died four months apart, and in November, he had just returned from his mother's funeral. He was physically and emotionally spent, and weeks behind in his studies.

In the meantime, an evangelist had cancelled a revival date at First Friends Church, Portsmouth, Virginia, pastored by Roy Clark. Clark contacted his daughter Lucy (a senior at Asbury College who would later be one of my most gracious parishioners in Canton, Ohio,) to see if she knew anyone who would preach the planned two-week revival. During her devotional time, Dennis Kinlaw came to mind. When she approached him with the proposition, he responded with a fairly definitive "no" based on the rationale that he had just returned from his mother's funeral, was emotionally drained, behind in his seminary assignments, plus it was a two-week revival and he was to speak twice a day. He did not tell her that he had only six sermons and he had preached only one revival in his life which had been an exercise in futility. Lucy responded, "Well, pray about it."

I am not sure that the desired revivalist did much praying, but he did speak to his closest friend, who surprisingly said, "Dennis, I think you ought to do that." Well, certainly the seminary Dean whose sovereign job was to keep students from missing classes would discourage such an enterprise. But when the fledgling student shared with Dean Larabee his "can't find anyone else" opportunity, the Dean responded, "Dennis, I think you ought to do it." Thus, the invited evangelist responded to Lucy Clark with a qualified "yes," with the request that Lucy's dad would preach in the morning, and Dennis would speak in the evening.

Kinlaw found himself on a twenty-four hour train ride to Portsmouth, Virginia, better known in World War II as Norfolk, the U. S. Navy's largest base within the continental United States. Roy Clark warmly greeted him on the train platform, and informed the evangelist that he was to speak that night. Somehow the communication that the pastor preach the morning services had not been transmitted, plus the evangelist was to speak on a daily radio program. (Later, Roy Clark would host one of the most popular radio broadcasts in Portland, Oregon.) This meant that the six-sermon preacher would speak over 40 times in a two-week span.

The twenty-one-year-old evangelist had two of the most productive weeks of his life. In only one service was there a barren altar, and no one was more surprised than the preacher! On the last night, a beautiful young lady, dressed as if she were from a wealthy family, sat on the front pew beside her uniformed Chief Petty Officer husband. He glared and she stared with a blank puzzled look, the preacher avoiding eye contact throughout his sermon. When he gave his invitation, the debutante looked in the face of the plain-dressed Quaker lady who had invited her with a "What I am supposed to do?" She fell across the altar followed by her husband. He cried out, "I am backslidden, headed for hell, and I need forgiveness." Of course the Christ whom the husband and wife came to meet was more than ready to meet them.

But what happened to Dennis during those two weeks was as, if not more important than what happened in the church. First, he observed a pastoral couple "team," hungry for God and for their people to know God. He experienced a church that was a genuine body of Christ, a church that was a corporate witness to the love of Christ, "genuine brothers and sisters in the Lord." One night an attender presented him a silver Hamilton pocket watch with the advice, "With what you are doing, you ought to be able to keep time." One afternoon, a lay person took him shopping for black dress shoes. Another afternoon, a church member had him fitted for an expensive dark blue suit. On the last Friday night, the youth group gave him a shower, six pairs of underwear, six pairs of socks and pajamas. The couple with whom he was staying must have been examining the contents of his suitcase. Dennis was the recipient of "Quaker relief at its best." And to his stunned amazement, at the end of the last service, the church handed him a check for $300.00. Dennis rhetorically asked his congregation, the Yearly Meeting of Evangelical Friends, Eastern Region, "Do you know much $300 was in 1943?" He was immediately on the phone with Elsie proclaiming, "We can get married," and a month later, they walked the aisle in Loudenville, New York.

When Dennis returned to Wilmore, word had gotten out that he was an evangelist, and "God dropped me into evangelism for the next three years." That experience as a twenty-one-year-old evangelist in a Quaker church throughout the long decades of being the most popular preacher within the American Holiness Movement, served as a lingering reminder that it was not him, but the Holy Spirit dwelling within, and he never lost the tremble in his hand, almost like Jacob who would forever limp (another one of his favorite texts). He was heard to confess, "Sometimes I preach better than I am capable."[519]

Kinlaw and the Holiness Paradigm Shift

In 1968, Dennis Kinlaw became president of Asbury College (this author's first year there as a student). For many of us, Dennis Kinlaw had the most capacious mind, the most charismatic personality, the most gracious and appealing platform style, and was the greatest preacher of anyone we had ever known or heard. He was a Renaissance man, an eclectic reader, not simply consuming vast amounts of material from the early Church Fathers, biblical scholarship, Church history, current Protestant and Catholic theology, and just about any other intellectual

---

[519] The author heard this presentation in person at the Yearly Meeting of the Evangelical Friends – Eastern Region, Canton, Ohio, August, 1980. The recording was graciously furnished by Amy Yuncker, Malone University Archivist.

discipline, but had the ability to translate what he had read for a graduate school class or camp meeting crowd. More amazingly, he combined an insatiable appetite for both knowledge and people. He loved conversation, and would make his conversant believe that he or she was the most important person in his frame of reference. This passion for people was evident beyond one on one conversation. It was communicated from the pulpit. Combine profound insights into Scripture, a rich southern accent, a trademark chuckle, innate gifts for communication, an ability to paint a panoramic biblical perspective, to glean from a text of Scripture what others could not, imaginative narrative style for a post-modern age, symbol and metaphor which grabbed attention, and you have, by consensus, the most respected and eagerly listened to speaker within the Holiness Movement for a half-century, 1960-2010.

Parodoxically, Dennis appealed to both holiness conservatives and holiness liberals. He rarely used the traditional language of second blessing, or instantaneous crisis, much less eradication, or the death of self. Old Testament professor David Thompson argued that Kinlaw represented a paradigm shift such as that described by Thomas Kuhn in his *The Structures of Scientific Revolutions*. In a conversation Thompson had with Kinlaw about his message on Exodus 3: 1-15, 20:1, "The Spirit Calls Us to Advance," Dennis admitted that his sermon had been in "broad strokes," typical of his ministry "developed over years of calculated attempts to communicate the call to Christian holiness effectively to the widest audience possible." Thompson amplified:

> But those listening carefully for the holiness or Wesleyan movement's pet phrases to be repeated went away disappointed, for the flag words were conspicuous by their absence in this great holiness preacher. Nothing Dr. Kinlaw said could not have been said at a Keswick convention, a Southern Baptist conference or a Roman Catholic renewal convocation.[520]

Kinlaw accomplished the above shift in several ways. First was his all encompassing picture of God's holiness. Of course this emphasis was enabled by his Ph.D. in Mediterranean Studies, being conversant in Hebrew as well as other Semitic languages. But even more importantly, he was a lifelong student of Scripture. If as G. K. Chesterson claimed,

---

[520] David L. Thompson, "Kuhn, Kohlberg, and Kinlaw: Reflections for Over-serious Theologians," *Wesleyan Theological Journal* Vol. 19, No. 1 (Spring 1984) 19.

the most important thing about a person is his concept of God, and if the most important thing about preaching is getting God right, Kinlaw excelled. He quoted William Temple who insisted that, "If our concept of God is wrong, the more religious we get, the more dangerous we get to ourselves and others."[521] Kinlaw's life was consumed with attempting to communicate the biblical God, and allowing this same God to communicate to him. After listening to Dennis preach at Asbury Theological Seminary, my brother-in-law Greg Adkins exited Estes Chapel confessing, "He makes me want more of God."

This God which Kinlaw found in Scripture was so gracious, loving, and all-pursuing (prevenient grace), that the preacher made his listeners long to be in God's grasp. His grandson asked him, "If a person is honest and thinks straight and works at it – does his homework – isn't it possible for that person to find God without revelation?" The grandfather responded, "The question isn't whether you can find God; the question is can you escape him!"[522] This was the God of Francis Asbury, his favorite historical person. The following was typical of Kinlaw's ability to weave together theology and history, "Now, when Jonathan Edwards got up in the morning he thought 'out of the goodness of God, it may be today that I'll meet someone somewhere who is one of the elect.' But when Francis Asbury got up in the morning he thought, 'Every person I meet today is intended by God in his love to be in the elect, and I am responsible for witnessing to him.'"[523]

Second was Kinlaw's ability to see what others could not see, the supreme task of the preacher. We often think of imagination as seeing what is not there. But possibly even more important is the ability to see what is there. One is reminded of Annie Dillard's comment: "The secret of seeing, then, is the pearl of great price. If I thought he could teach me to find it and keep it forever, I would stagger barefoot across a hundred deserts after any lunatic at all."[524] Dennis was not a lunatic, but he nonetheless, commanded a great host of followers who longed to see.

---

[521] Dennis Kinlaw. *Let's Start with Jesus: A New Way of Doing Theology* (Grand Rapids: Zondevan, 2005) 16.

[522] John Oswalt, "Maintaining the Witness: An Interview with Dr. Kinlaw," *The High Calling* (September - October, 2013) 13.

[523] Ibid., 11.

[524] Annie Dillard. *Pilgrim at Tinkercreek* (New York: Harper & Row, 1974) 33.

His profound insight into Genesis 3 is intriguing. He commented on God's replacing fig leaves with animal skins. "The thrust of the text seems to be that it was God's merciful act to give each one better protection from the other, than they themselves could provide."[525] The key to all relationships is the Trinity, the self-giving of the persons of the Trinity, who do not need to protect themselves from one another, but freely give themselves to one another. Almost all of Kinlaw's thought was informed by Trinitarian theology; whether explicit or implicit, it was always there. At the heart of Trinitarian theology is self-giving: "Normally, shepherds keep sheep so that they can eat them or wear the wool, or sell them so someone else can eat or wear them. Now Jesus tells us about a shepherd who keeps sheep, not so that he can eat or wear or sell them, but so that the sheep can actually eat and wear him."[526] Christianity is the world's only religion in which the God does not demand a sacrifice from his subjects, but sacrifices himself. "But Jesus pictures a new kind of Deity: one who demands sacrifice from himself before sacrifice is accepted from his worshippers. The altar is not the one in the Temple, but the one outside the Holy City on Golgotha – the Cross. And the sacrifice on that altar is not a sheep or a human, the sacrifice is God himself, in Christ."[527]

Listening to Kinlaw, even for the most seasoned preachers, was akin to the experience of the two Native Americans, who were sending smoke signals to one another in the New Mexico desert, early in the morning, July 16, 1945. Suddenly, they saw the most enormous, billowing plume that they had ever observed, erupt in the distance. One Indian signaled to the other, "Sure wish I had said that!" As John Oswalt confessed, "All of my original thoughts come from C. S. Lewis and Dennis Kinlaw."[528] Many of the rest of us could say the same. Someone asked Kinlaw what was the most profound theological thought that he had ever had, and he quickly responded, "God wants to have the same fellowship with me that the persons of the Trinity have with one another." Wish I had said that.

Third, Dennis loved symbolism which attracted him to the "Inklings," in particular Charles Williams and Dorothy Sayers. He

---

[525] Kinlaw. *Let's Start*, 118.
[526] Ibid., 86.
[527] Ibid., 87.
[528] In a conversation between this author and John Oswalt on June 31, 2018.

excelled in metonyms, tropes and metaphors, symbols representing our relationship with God. The one that he found most prevalent and powerful in Scripture is family, and in particular, marriage. He was fond of saying that the Bible begins with a marriage (Adam and Eve), there is a marriage in the middle of it (Cana), and at the end, the Bridegroom returns for his Bride. In commenting on Isaiah 62:4, Hephzibah means "My delight is in her" and Beulah means "married."[529] Thus, the promised land is a married land. "Intriguingly, the human social institution we call marriage was in Yahweh's mind, before the creation of the world, and was devised as a divine pedagogical tool to teach human creatures what human history is all about."[530] No one ever depicted human sexuality in more sacred language than did Kinlaw, and at times, making the old-timers blush. In speaking of circumcision, "This mark which indicated that a man was in covenant relationship with Yahweh was placed on the most private part of the body." Kinlaw further emphasized, "Human sexuality is a far more sacred thing for God's followers and a far more significant thing in God's eyes, than most of us have dreamed....His claim on the world seems to have implications for his claim on human sexuality as well. God's purpose for coming to us in Jesus is to restore sanctity to those holy things that humanity has corrupted, sexuality among them."[531]

And if the Bible depicts holiness primarily in relational terms, sin is understood as a breaking of relationships. For that reason, God constantly reminded Israel of her adultery, fornication, and unfaithfulness. For Dennis, the ultimate expression representing our love for God was found in a husband's love for his wife, as commanded in Ephesians 5:22: "Husbands love your wives as Christ loved the church and gave himself for it." Given Kinlaw's penchant for metaphor and expertise in the Old Testament, it is not surprising he would turn his attention to Charles Williams' interpretation of the "Song of Songs." This relationship or romance as depicted by Solomon is not simply for the purpose of pointing to something beyond the physical, in order to allegorize the erotic, but to say that creation is good, sex is God's gift, thus enjoy it. For Williams, faithful, married love "is good in itself. It does not need to be spiritualized to have human worth. It should be enjoyed for what

---

[529] Kinlaw, *Let's Start*, 58.
[530] Ibid., 62.
[531] Ibid., 63.

it is in itself. Yet, it cannot but speak of more."[532] Paradoxically, erotic love is good in itself, but points beyond itself. A wholesome transparent relationship with one's spouse should remind us of what our relationship can be with God. And our relationship with God should, of all places, be reflected in our marriage. Kinlaw writes, "God gave his gifts for our joy because he loves us. To enjoy them less, even for spiritual reasons, is no tribute to him. To rejoice in their goodness does not displease him. To let them replace or obscure him, is the ultimate deprivation for us and the supreme offense to him."[533]

If sin, for Kinlaw, is primarily a broken relationship with God and others, it is more of a deprivation than a depravation. It is not something deposited in our being or genetically transmitted to us by Adam or even Satan, but in Luther's expression, love "curved in on itself." Kinlaw quotes Robert Jansen, "In order to account for....native depravity of the heart of man, there is not the least need of supposing any evil quality... wrought into the nature of man by any positive cause... either from God or the creature. All that is needed is for the supernatural presence of the Spirit not to be given."[534]

The Biblical Preacher

Behind everything Kinlaw preached or wrote was exegesis in the original languages. The Hebrew word for turn is *panah*, and its root is *panim*, meaning face. Thus, sin is to turn one's face from God. If we go to the New Testament, we find that the Greek word for unrighteousness, *adikia*, is derived from *a*, a privation, and *dik*, translated right, just as we use the words atypical, apolitical, asexual, etc. For Kinlaw, the best explanation for the plight of humanity is not found in the breaking of the Sinai code in the wilderness, but the breaking of a relationship in the garden. Adam and Eve treat each other as objects, instead of as persons, means instead of ends, just as they can now put and keep God in the third person. Instead of the Thou, which God is and ever should be, the loving 'I am,' has now become for them the threatening 'He who is.'"[535]

---

[532] Dennis Kinlaw, "Charles Williams' Concept of Imagery Applied to the Song of Songs," *Wesleyan Theological Journal*, Vol. 16, No. 1 (Spring 1981) 91.

[533] Ibid.

[534] Kinlaw, *Let's Start*, 120.

[535] Ibid., 118.

In that Kinlaw skirted a substantival view of sin, one can almost hear echoes of Mildred Wynkoop, though he demonstrated no evidence of having read Wynkoop. Why did he receive such little criticism from the conservative element of the Holiness Movement and she so much? For one thing, Dennis was an astute politician in the good sense of the term. He utilized whatever language he thought appropriate for his audience. But the answer is far more profound than that. No one in his generation preached biblical holiness more accurately, more carefully, and more intriguingly than Dennis Kinlaw. His sermons were labyrinths of biblical truth, like following a guide in uncharted territory, when all of a sudden, one sees the Taj Mahal, Petra, or something far more miniscule, but just as important. Dennis found hidden gems only available to a keen mind, an insatiable hunger for truth, and a willingness for sustained inquiry. Biblical study was Kinlaw's golf game, his recreation, his delight no less than an avid fisherman catching a ten pound bass. Whatever part of his Wesleyan heritage he fulfilled, and there were several aspects, nothing was more apparent than his identity as a "Bible moth."

Kinlaw could fold himself around a biblical text, and squeeze all the juice from it. Such was his exposition of the "Mind of Christ," based on Philippians 2. "Let this same mind be in you as was in Christ Jesus." To our surprise, it's not the sinner who knows he does not have the mind of Christ, but the Christian. "We have to become Christian before we find out how deep the sin is in us. I never felt as guilty before I was converted, as I have felt a million times since."[536] Why do we need the mind of Christ? "The crux of our sin problem is also the center of our soul's potential. The essence of sin is self-interest and our sinful state is estrangement from God."[537] Kinlaw further claimed, "There's nothing defective with our conversion experience, but conversion only starts us on the path of further insight into the real nature of our relationship with God."[538] As the relationship grows we become more sensitive to who we are: self-aggrandizing, self-sufficient, self-promoting, and self-defending creatures. "Self-interest is the supreme characteristic of a sinful person" and in particular, pastors. Pastors "quail or strut according to their standing in the Annual Conference; status and position are at the

---

[536] Dennis F. Kinlaw. *How Every Christian Can Have the Mind of Christ* (Nappanee, IN: Evangel Publishing House, 1998) 17.
[537] Ibid., 26.
[538] Ibid., 95.

forefront." Kinlaw perceptively observed, "I don't think I have ever heard a minister say, 'I have the appointment of my life, there are dozens of people in that community, and I have an opportunity to reach them.'"[539]

In the Philippians 2 passage, Kinlaw gave particular attention to "that each of you look not to only your own interests, but to the interests of others" (2:4). Kinlaw noted that the word "only" does not appear in the Greek. The King James scholars added the word "only" because they did not believe a person could be completely freed from their own interests. But Kinlaw did. The Holy Spirit can free us from ourselves, and enable us to be for others. One of the ways this can happen is through our intercession for others. As he constantly did, Kinlaw turned to an intriguing word play in the original language. Intercession comes from the Hebrew word *paga*, "to meet." And thus an intercessor is a person who comes to other persons to meet. "The picture is rather clear: On one hand, you've got a world in its sin and its need. On the other hand, you've got a God who has within himself everything that is necessary to redeem that world. So God is looking for somebody who can bring the redeemer God and sinful world together."[540]

The above was particularly apparent in Abraham's intercession for Sodom which ultimately saved the family of Lot. (Abraham was Kinlaw's favorite biblical character.) In the Genesis 18 narrative, Kinlaw noted that God stood before Abraham and not vice versa. God was going to stay put until a redeemable number could be found. The early scribes emended Genesis 18:22 to "But Abraham remained standing before the Lord" which the King James reads. The original Hebrew reads, "And Yahweh remained standing before Abraham." Of course, for the monotheistic Jews, it was improper for a king to stand before a subject. A correct interpretation is that God is the initiator of our intercession, pleading for us to bring our burden. As he often did, Kinlaw applied the text to himself: "The sovereign God stands in the shadow of my conscience saying, 'Kinlaw, there really is a lost world out there. Don't you care enough to stand with me in prayer so that perhaps it can escape judgment?'"[541]

---

[539] Ibid, 102.

[540] Ibid., 114.

[541] Dennis F. Kinlaw. *Preaching in the Spirit* (Grand Rapids: Zondervan, 1985) 43.

Kinlaw and The Christian Holiness Association

In April of 1985, Kinlaw spoke to a CHA Seminar with the title, "Preaching Holiness and the Hope of the World." In recalling a conversation with a seeker seeking a clean heart he confessed, "If I had hammered her with our doctrinal language, she would have thought that I was speaking Nepalese or Chinese." In regard to the CHA and the Holiness Movement he frankly admitted, "I don't know that we have much of a future, but the truth has." He followed with, "People are hungry for purity of heart. If we ditch the message, God is going to raise someone else up." More revealing were his answers to a couple of questions at the end of the session. One pastor told how he had preached on entire sanctification but had not given a specific altar call. About ten days later one of his parishioners came into the experience of heart holiness. The pastor asked if he had been correct in not calling for an immediate response. Kinlaw responded with the historical reminder that Wesley never gave an altar call. "We push new converts prematurely. They mute their witness because they do not come clean. They testify, because that is what is expected, but oscillate because they do not come clean or are not crystal clear." Wesley himself was hesitant to testify to entire sanctification, but Kinlaw did believe that our spiritual Father had experienced holiness of heart and life. He also observed that for Wesley, "There was not a quick formula and unlike him, we push people before they authentically experience the fullness of God's grace."[542]

During his presentation Kinlaw spoke of hidden agendas that sabotage Kingdom enterprises, which our forefathers would have referred to as "carnality." When an attendee asked him what he meant by hidden agendas, he answered with a story, as Jesus often did. He had known Albert Orsburn, who was a London Divisional Commander for the Salvation Army. His ministry was so successful and his Division grew so rapidly, that his superior officers demanded that the Division be divided in two. Orsburn resisted, and as he protested, he found himself slipping spiritually. He argued with the higher ups, and he later confessed, "Unwittingly, I had begun to fight, not for the Kingdom, but for my

---

[542] Dennis F. Kinlaw, CHA Seminar, preaching on "Holiness and the Hope for the 21st Century," DVD, April 1985. In this author's possession, and also available on cassette in the CHA files, Asbury Theological Seminary Archives.

position in the Kingdom, and the Spirit was grieved." Unfortunately, as Orsburn confessed, "When the Spirit grieves, the Spirit leaves."

Orsburn ended up in the hospital after an automobile accident, and heard Gospel singing in an adjacent room. "As I heard them sing of the glories of God, my heart began to yearn again to have that kind of intimacy with God. I wept my heart out in repentance. God forgave me, and the Spirit came and filled my heart afresh. This experience resulted in Orsburn writing a hymn, which is still retained in *The Songbook* of the Salvation Army, "All My Work is for the Master." One verse reads: "Savior, if my feet have faltered on the pathway of the Cross,/ If my purposes have altered or my gold be mixed with dross,/ O forbid me not Thy service, keep me yet in Thy employ,/Pass me through a sterner cleansing if I may but give Thee joy!"[543]

One of the characteristics that endeared Dennis Kinlaw to so many others was the "sterner cleansing" which he was willing to embrace and confess, whether in private conversation or public proclamation. His transparency and honesty authenticated heart holiness. He never preached with a Messiah complex. One of his favorite sayings was, "I'm either where you've been, where you are, or where you ought to be, and you are either where I've been, where I am or where I ought to be." Dennis never preached as if he had arrived; he always placed himself under the text. Before it spoke to others, the text first spoke to him.

Founding of the Francis Asbury Society

Dennis rightly believed that the days of the Christian Holiness Association were waning. The Convention had become a gathering place for denominational executives to network, to communicate with like-minded people, and at best, to hear holiness preaching from Earl Wilson, Wingrove Taylor, Thomas Hermiz, James Earl Massey, Paul Rader, and a long list of other Wesleyan exponents. Dennis was not about to start an organization named after himself, such as the Dennis Kinlaw Evangelistic Association. Thus, in 1982, he and Harold Burgess founded the Francis Asbury Society in Wilmore, Kentucky. The Society gave itself to publishing holiness books, holding retreats, supporting a coterie of evangelists, a preaching institute, and a symposium for

---

[543] Kinlaw. *The Mind of Christ*, 73.

theological dialogue. "Titus Women" teams by 2013 had spoken at some 30 different retreats and gatherings for women. The Francis Asbury Society today hosts a "Come to the Fire" Conference annually under the capable leadership of Beth Coppedge, Linda Boyette, Stephanie Hogan, Erin Hill, and others. They are active in producing discipleship materials relevant for either women in the home, or in the corporate world.

In 2010, the Francis Asbury Society moved into a magnificent 10,843 square feet building that rivals any ski lodge in Aspen, Colorado. The stated purpose of the Association was and is the "Retrieval, interpretation, and promotion of a message: the God-given message of a clean heart, unbroken communion with God, and the indwelling power and presence of the Holy Spirit."[544] As the executive director in 2013, Ron Smith determined that the Society would be "theologically engaged. The universal message of redeeming and sanctifying grace needed to be expanded to an international audience."[545] Smith calculated that by 2013, the Society had placed publications in "150 countries and distributed millions of books that emphasized some facet of our biblical Wesleyan theology."[546] When John Oswalt asked Kinlaw in 2013 concerning the Society, what he wished he would have done differently, he responded with a fearful regret: "We perpetually shift from the ideology that formed the Institution to using the Institution for personal things. We see ourselves in the Institution, not in the truth for which it stands. I think we have suffered from some of that. That is what concerns me most."[547]

Whether the F.A.S. can continue momentum after the passing of Dr. Kinlaw, who died April 10, 2017, remains to be seen. Constructing a 2.5 million dollar building was mostly due to his ability to attract donors. The Christian Holiness Association never owned a headquarters building in its 136 year existence. Did F.A.S redirect resources from C.H.A. and contribute to the latter's demise? I doubt it. But the founding of the FAS did send an implicit message that the bureaucratic structure of the C.H.A.

---

[544] J. Paul Vincent, "A Kind of Answer: Leadership in the Kingdom," *The High Calling* (September/October, 2013) 5.

[545] Ibid., 19.

[546] Ron E. Smith, "A Vision for Ministry: Where the Rubber Meets the Road," *The High Calling* (September/October 2013) 8.

[547] John N. Oswalt, "Maintaining the Witness: An Interview with Dr. Kinlaw," *The High Calling* (September/October 2013) 13.

organizational support rather than individual involvement was no longer workable. For the most part, the Francis Asbury Society has received its leadership and finances as well as other kinds of support from the Asbury College and Asbury Theological Seminary constellation. Whether in the years and decades ahead it can move beyond this provincialism into ministries similar to London's Tyndale House or the Billy Graham Cove Conference Center, just outside of Asheville, North Carolina, is a critical question.

President of Asbury College and God to the Rescue

In 1967, Asbury College found itself in a severe administrative crisis. In December, 1967, the Board of Trustees fired its President, Karl Wilson, after only sixteen months in office. Only an immoral act leads to such a swift exit and Wilson was anything but immoral. No one ever questioned his integrity; the perfectionism of personality and the perfectionism of theology found frictionless agreement in Karl Wilson. That may have been part of his problem. When it came to questionable irregularities which are a part of all institutional legacies, Wilson had no ability to look the other way. He would not gently step around the lumps in the carpet. Some say he wanted to open financial books from the past; others say he was inept; others claim that the school's stance on holiness was at stake. Whatever, Karl Wilson, for several months after his ouster, barred himself in the Presidential house, refusing to leave, while the local newspapers had a field day and one student scrolled in chalk "Holiness or Hell" across a campus sidewalk.

Karl Wilson was inaugurated on Tuesday, March 28, 1967, and terminated on December 28, 1967. What could a man have done over a nine-month period that so roiled his employers? Those who elected him knew him as a fellow board member, and as the eleven-year pastor of Dueber Avenue Methodist Church in Canton, Ohio. For one-half century this church had sent a steady stream of students to Asbury, perhaps more than any other church in the College's history. Asbury historian Joseph Thacker gave little analysis of the matter other than Wilson had walked into an accrediting self-study, but Thacker was unspecific about any notations calling for rectifications or improvements in the Institution. He writes, "This was the most detailed and thorough study of the College, and involved faculty, staff, and members of the Board of

Trustees. Tensions were created in several areas. Among these were concerns about faculty salaries and ranking, and censorship of certain college publications. Ultimately, the accumulation of problems resulted in divisions among faculty, students, board members, and alumni."[548] Obviously, running a college was much different than pastoring a church. And though Wilson certainly did not collapse into a catatonic state, he may have been indecisive while attempting to reconcile conflicting power brokers on a college campus.

Add the above to the general unrest and anti-authoritarianism that were afflicting U. S. colleges and Asbury wasn't much different than any other U. S. school when Dennis Kinlaw took the administrative reins as President in the summer of 1968. It was during that summer I first heard Kinlaw's name while attending Brown City Camp Meeting in Brown City, Michigan, where Jimmy Lentz was preaching. When Lentz heard I was to attend Asbury that fall, he confidently declared, "You will like him; he is a prince of a guy." That was not the only time I would hear that exact appellation of Kinlaw.

Karl Wilson's departure solved nothing other than making the way for Kinlaw to assume the Presidency. Conflict over long hair for men, mini-skirts for ladies, and a general unrest that belied the school's holiness tradition, continued to envelop the campus. So just why God chose to walk into Hughes Auditorium on February 3, 1970, is a matter of speculation. There have been many questions asked as to why God visited Asbury College, but nobody on campus ultimately doubted that He did visit. Eight days of one continuous worship service, with students confessing sins, being reconciled to fellow students, making first-time commitments to Christ, moving beyond the religious heritage handed down to them by their parents, and seeking to be entirely sanctified. All classes were cancelled during those eight days; there was an almost unbroken retinue of students standing at the pulpit of the 1,500 seat Hughes Auditorium, praising God for new-found victory. When one's entire life has been given to attending one-hour worship services while looking at his watch and wondering when this thing is going to be over, one could sit for hours when it seemed that only minutes had passed. Steve Seamands said it best, "It seemed as if God suspended time and

---

[548] Joseph A. Thacker, Jr. *Asbury College: Vision and Miracle* (Nappanee, IN: Evangel Press, 1990) 210-211.

space."[549] When a Chicago newspaper reporter called Kinlaw and asked if the "Revival" was simply something that a few people got together and worked up, the President answered, "Well, there are always people in Wilmore trying to do that but haven't succeeded. It seems that Jesus walked into Hughes Auditorium on Tuesday morning, and hasn't left yet."

Back to the reasons. Asbury had experienced similar awakenings in 1935 and 1950, but nothing like the magnitude of 1970. Custer Reynolds, Dean of the College, devoted the Tuesday, February 3rd Chapel service to student testimonies, not a normative practice for most schools, even Christian colleges. As the "extended chapel" headed into the late afternoon hours, and classes had been pre-empted, Reynolds called Kinlaw, who was preaching in Banff, Canada, informing the President, "We've got a problem." "Oh yeah, what is it?" "Chapel that started this morning is still going on." Kinlaw immediately responded, "Don't stop it!" Other Christian college presidents may have dissimilarly responded. Kinlaw recalled, "I never felt the presence of God more powerfully than when I stood in that phone booth."

In those days, Asbury had no intercollegiate athletics. Thus, it did not need to call Centre College or Union College to call off a basketball game. Students on campus were praying for a revival, and some even prophesying a "spiritual awakening." Asbury had been birthed by people who believed in revival, promoted revival, and conducted revivals, both in the local church and on the camp meeting trail. Revival was as much or more an activity for the Wesleyan Holiness tradition within America, as any other religious strain. But to believe that God was favoring one theological tradition over another, is sectarian pride and exceptionalism at its worst. All reasons for God's visitation on February 3rd, 1970, are assumed under God's wisdom and timing. Our student body was defined and divided by cliquishness and clannishness as much as any other school in America. Though we did not have fraternities and sororities, being an insider or outsider was defined by where one sat in the college cafeteria, and with whom one hung out or about how many of one's ancestors had attended Asbury. Student elections and politics consumed Asbury, and the student newspaper attempted to keep competing factions intensified

---

[549] Retrieved from the DVD, "When God Comes" produced by Asbury College.

to a fervent pitch. Kinlaw simply concluded about the revival, "We needed it more than anyone else."

The pre-eminent mood of God's visitation was a spirit of love that consumed the student body. The animosities in these jealousies, contentions, and unforgiveness melted away, far more quickly than the snow on the ground.

Almost wherever the story was told, and it was feebly told by students who could hardly put two sentences together, what happened at Asbury was almost exactly duplicated. On that Sunday night, two Asbury students showed up at Olivet Nazarene College, Kankakee, Illinois, informing the pastor, Don Irwin, an Asbury College graduate, that God had sent them to tell about the revival. Dressed in jeans with the rest of their attire and mein equally unimpressive, the two were not relying on image for gaining access to the Sunday night worship service. The Church was kicking off revival services that night with Paul Cunningham serving as the evangelist. With the Asburians sitting in Irwin's study, the pastor looked at the evangelist and the evangelist looked back at the pastor, not knowing what to do with these intruders. Irwin decided to give them two minutes, and the heavenly visitors did not even take that. They stood up and exclaimed little more than "God is Great, God is Good." Immediately following their "proclamation," a quartet stood up to sing, and about the second verse, one vocalist peeled off, weeping his way to the altar. At 10:30 that night, there were more people in the church than there had been at 7:30. (Both John Bowling, who was a member of the quartet, and Don Irwin, told me this story.)

John T. Seamands estimated that, "approximately two thousand witness teams had gone out on missions from Asbury College and Seminary. Each team ministered to several churches, sometimes as many as 15 – 25 in a single trip."[550] Henry James estimated that by the summer of 1970, at least 130 colleges, seminaries, and Bible schools, had been touched by the revival outreach and witnesses continued to go to other schools and churches.[551] James wrote:

---

[550] John T. Seamands, "Churches Come Alive," in *One Divine Moment: The Asbury Revival*, ed. Robert E. Coleman (Old Tappan, NJ: Fleming H. Revell Company, 1970) 81.

[551] Henry James, "Campus Demonstrations," in *One Divine Moment*, 55.

Other stories of revival could be told of Houghton (N. Y.), Wheaton (Ill.), Oral Roberts (Okla.), Trevecca (Tenn.), John Wesley (N.C.), Berea (Ky.), Marion (Ind.), Huntington (Ind.), George Carver (Ga.), Canadian Bible (Sask.), Seattle Pacific (Wash.), Fort Wayne (Ind.), St. Paul (Minn.), Central Wesleyan (S.C.), Taylor (Ind.), Eastern Mennonite (Va.), Spring Arbor (Mich.), Canadian Nazarene (Manitoba), Union University (Tenn.), Oklahoma Baptist, Roberts Wesleyan (N.Y.), Weyland Baptist (Tex.), Sue Bennett (Ky.), Grace (Ind.), George Fox (Ore.), Fuller Seminary (Calif.), to mention only a few.[552]

By the above list, it was apparent that God was not booking himself only on Wesleyan-Arminian campuses. One story from my own trekking will suffice. During spring break of that March, it was my privilege to spend several days at Southwestern Baptist Theological Seminary in Fort Worth, Texas. I was in classes where every one of the 85 students in the classroom was on his or her knees, and the professor was prostrate on the floor behind his desk. One senior stood up and confessed. "I have cheated my way through high school and college and seminary, and I want to know how I can make that right." Jack Gray, who along with Roy Fish had initiated the invitation to the three of us (The other two students were Dave Perry and Parks Davis.) wrote, "In the Southwestern Baptist Seminary revival (which seems to be representative,) the variety of decisions made, numbers of people involved, and the spontaneous way in which they responded without anyone having preached or given specific instructions, clearly magnified that the Sovereign Lord was demanding and receiving private audience with individuals."[553]

One of these "private audiences," took place with a Southwestern student pastor on the Sunday morning I was in Fort Worth. As Roy Fish chauffeured me to the church, he said, "I want to tell you some things about the pastor. He is very capable, and as far as I know, has nothing but A's on his transcript." Of course the same thing took place on that Sunday morning as had happened at other churches. Two-thirds of the church came forward, pastor confessing to his people, and people confessing to God and their pastor. And, like other places several exclaimed, "We

---

[552] Ibid., 65.

[553] L. Jack Gray, "Revival in Our Nation: An Interpretation," in *One Divine Moment*, 115.

have never seen anything like this! Nothing like this has ever happened here."

During lunch the pastor requested, "I would like to spend some time with you this afternoon." After dropping his family off at the parsonage, the two of us went to the guest room where I was staying on the Seminary campus. We sat down on beds facing one another. He openly confessed his sins and his failures in the pastorate. "I have been reading this book on the baptism of the Holy Spirit and this author says, 'If you have everything else and you don't have it (I would say 'him,') get it! It makes all the difference.'" This 22-year-old United Methodist novice shared with the slightly older Southern Baptist pastor how he could be filled with the Holy Spirit. When God pours out his Spirit, He gives little to no sectarian preference; in fact, it is not even on his check list.

Kinlaw emphasized that the leaders in revival have often been the "young." Claiming that many of America's most important educational institutions were rooted in revival, he stated, "When the Spirit of God touches a man's heart and renews it, there is an accompanying effect upon the mind, the quickening of the spirit affects the intellect as well as the soul."[554] Kinlaw's profound effect upon so many of us was implanted by his demonstrated and articulated conviction that a person could be both spiritual and educated. I'm not sure that anyone ever made a more appealing and inviting bridge between the spiritual world and intellectual world than did he. Outside of this conviction, he would never have been able to profoundly summarize what began on that snow-covered campus February 3, 1970: "Give me one divine moment when God acts, and I say that moment is far superior than all the human efforts of man throughout the centuries."[555]

Frank Bartleman

In the summer of 1907, Frank Bartleman showed up in Wilmore, Kentucky, to participate in a camp meeting dedicated to intercessory prayer. He was accompanied by S. B. Shaw, a leader in the Holiness Movement. Shaw served as the president of the Michigan Holiness Association, wrote several holiness works, and was an authority on

---

[554] Dennis Kinlaw, "Campus Roots for Revival," *One Divine Moment*, 108.
[555] Cover page, *One Divine Moment,* no number.

revivals, especially the Welsh Revival.[556] More importantly, who was Frank Bartleman? Even though William J. Seymour was the leader and face of Azusa Street, Bartleman was the spiritual force behind the revival. Bartleman had several connections with the Holiness Movement: he worked with the Salvation Army, he pastored a Wesleyan Methodist Church and worked with the same Los Angeles Peniel Mission with which Pheneas Bresee was associated. When he requested that Bresee give him a Nazarene church to pastor, Bresee responded that there was "none available."[557] Living on faith for his financial existence, and tirelessly conducting itinerant evangelism, he experienced intense encounters with God. In July of 1905, when in prayer with Edward Boehmer, he testified,

> Then suddenly, without premonition, the Lord Jesus himself revealed himself to us. He seemed to stand directly between us, so close we could have reached out our hand and touched Him. But we did not dare to move. I could not even look. In fact I seemed all spirit. His presence seemed more real, if possible, than if I could have seen and touched Him naturally. I forgot I had eyes or ears. My spirit recognized Him. A Heaven of divine love filled and thrilled my soul. Burning fire went through me. In fact, my whole being seemed to flow down before Him, like wax before the fire. I lost all consciousness of time or space, being conscious only of His wonderful presence. I worshipped at His feet. It seemed a veritable "moment of transfiguration." I was lost in the pure Spirit.[558]

Bartleman gave himself to intercessory prayer, of which the following is typical:

> The Spirit of prayer came more and more heavily upon us. In Pasadena, before moving to Los Angeles, I would lie on my bed in the daytime and roll and groan under the burden. At night I could scarcely sleep for the spirit of prayer. I fasted much, not caring for food while burdened. At one time I was in soul travail for nearly twenty-four hours without intermission.

---

[556] See Charles Edwin Jones. *A Guide to the Study of the Holiness Movement* (Metuchen, NJ: The Scarecrow Press, 1947) 61, 256, 741.

[557] Frank Bartleman. *Azusa Street: The Roots of Modern-day Pentecost* (Plainfield, NJ: Logos International, 1980) iv.

[558] Ibid., 17.

It nearly used me up. Prayer literally consumed me. I would groan all night in my sleep.[559]

During Azusa Street's halcyon days, 1906 – 1909, Bartleman often corresponded with Evan Roberts, leader of the Welsh Revival. In fact, Roberts may have been more responsible for the Azusa Street Pentecost than any other person living outside of the United States. Bartleman recalled, "This was the third letter I had received from Wales, from Evan Roberts, and I feel their prayers had much to do with our final victory in California."[560] What Roberts was to the Welsh Revival, Bartleman was to the Azusa Street Revival, making him one of the most important Christian leaders in America during the first two decades of the twentieth century. Even though Bartleman preached seven times in Wilmore, he felt somewhat less than welcome, recalling that, "The camp was pretty well divided. Many of the saints were hungry for more of God. Conditions proved very detrimental to this." Bartleman concluded, "The holiness manifested I felt was of a rather acrid nature. It was not a 'Pentecostal camp.'"[561] (Acrid carries the connotation of extremely or sharpfully stinging or bitter; exceedingly caustic.)[562] Whether Bartleman's assessment carried a measure of truth, or he was simply culturally or temperamentally out of place, is up to the reader. He had just come from God's Bible School in Cincinnati, but made no such disparaging remarks about Martin Wells Knapp or his colleagues.

The Toronto Blessing in Wilmore

History is terribly repetitive, but not necessarily monotonous or boring. Almost ninety years after Bartleman visited Wilmore, Randy Clark showed up in the epicenter of the Holiness Movement, representing the latest spiritual upheaval on the North American continent, the "Toronto Blessing." Denny Strickland, Steve Seamands, Bob Neff, and others, attempted to celebrate the 25th anniversary of the Asbury College Revival by hosting a "Light the Fire" Conference at the Wilmore United Methodist Church with Clark as the main speaker. Strickland was the leader of a Friday night Vineyard Fellowship meeting

---

[559] Ibid., 19.
[560] Ibid., 35.
[561] Ibid., 108.
[562] Webster, Unabridged, 18.

in Nicholasville, Kentucky; Seamands, Professor at Asbury Theological Seminary, is the son of Wesleyan Holiness bluebloods on both sides of his family; and Neff was a history professor at Asbury College who had been miraculously healed from cancer. All three of these gentlemen, as well as others, were hungry for a deeper work of grace in their lives and in the communities which they represented. Clark had served as the preacher for the Toronto Blessing during the first year of its existence. The four-day event, February 20 – 23, 1995, would prove to be the most divisive, disruptive, and controversial incident to ever take place in Wilmore: a church split, people fired, and lingering, bitter antagonism.

A complete analysis of the "Toronto Blessing" is beyond the scope and purpose of our investigation, but limited reflection is in order. The term "Toronto Blessing" refers to a "spiritual renewal," which began at the Toronto Airport Christian Fellowship, in January, 1994, exhibiting strange phenomena, such as uncontrollable laughter, roaring like a lion, violent jerking of the body, and much prostration on the floor, termed being "slain in the Spirit." Of course those familiar with early Methodist awakenings both in Great Britain and the United States would know that none of this was new. More far-fetched were the three hundred or so who claimed to have received gold or silver fillings in their teeth.

One of the most judicious treatments of the Toronto Blessing was given by James Beverley, a professor of Theology and Ethics at Ontario Theological Seminary, in Toronto, Canada. Among the positive aspects at the Toronto Blessing are the minimal emphasis on money, non-legalistic teaching, the desire to be biblical, the understanding that the Church needs to be revived and the vital relationship between revival and evangelism. The negatives include weak preaching, a reductionistic view of the Holy Spirit at the expense of Christology, its anti-intellectual spirit, and a faulty understanding of "signs and wonders." Beverley argues that being slain in the spirit and laughter are of a different nature than New Testament miracles such as the blind seeing, the deaf hearing, and the dead being raised. "None of the manifestations associated with the Toronto Blessing are inherently miraculous. Each one of them can be imitated by most people. An actor could be hired to attend an evening meeting and imitate all the manifestations, and no one would be able to distinguish that person from others under the 'real' manifestations."[563]

---

[563] James A. Beverley. *Holy Laughter & The Toronto Blessing: An Investigative Report*

B. J. Oropeza, Professor of Biblical and Religious Studies at Azusa Pacific University, gives a more critical appraisal of the events at the Toronto Airport. He observes that though the Revival has entertained visitors from around the world, the church has had little influence on Toronto itself. The church running between 250 and 350 has failed to grow. Rodney Howard Brown, the South African champion of "holy laughter," can at times seem manipulative as he shouts, "Fill!...Let it bubble out your belly....laugh like this....Ah ha hah, ah ha ha ha ha.... Wooooo! Wooohoooo!"[564] Oropeza argues that assembly-line slaying in the Spirit, church members sequentially falling down when the preacher lays hands on or blows on them, "discredits God's sovereignty. This has more to do with mimicking, suggestion, and peer pressure than with God's Spirit."[565] But, Oropeza confesses that lives have been changed by these physical manifestations.

> Many positive changes are reported in the lives of those who experience Holy Laughter. Terry Virgo of New Frontiers writes, "Marriages have been restored in our church, the recalcitrant have been humbled, and the timid have begun witnessing boldly. Half-hearted attenders have become zealots for God." Paul and Mona Johnian claim that Holy Laughter "is more than an emotional outburst or a charismatic fad. It has been accompanied by forgiveness, emotional healing, a desire to witness and the healing of relationships."[566]

Oropeza's overall critique of holy laughter is that it is an in-house Christian phenomenon with little impact on the lost. Those who claim the gift of healing fail to go to the places it is most needed: hospitals, mental institutions, the slums and skid row. Similar to the Holiness Movement, the Toronto Blessing has failed to break down racial, cultural and socio-economic barriers. "While someone is experiencing holy laughter for the umpteenth time at a Vineyard Church, another gang member in south-central L. A. who never heard a clear presentation of the Gospel, is being gunned down." Oropeza concludes:

> Revival? Until the church once again takes the driver's seat and makes the social-political impacts it did through

---

(Grand Rapids: Zondervan Publishing House, 1995) 158.

[564] B. J. Oropeza. *A Time To Laugh* (Peabody, MA: Hendrickson Publishers, 1995) 44.

[565] Ibid., 117.

[566] Ibid., 91.

people like Edwards and Finney—until the church once again produces evangelists like Wesley, reformers like Luther, artists like Bach, scientists like Mendel, inventors like Bell, thinkers like Pascal, and writers like Bunyan—don't make me laugh![567]

Margaret Poloma did a sociological critique on the "Toronto Blessing" by sending out questionnaires to participants of which 918 responded. When asked what they were feeling when they left the renewal center, "the overwhelming choices were love of God (89 %), peace (89%), love (85%), joy (83%), gratitude (82%), happy (81%), and satisfaction (79%).[568] Most important is that 81% received a new sense of their sinful condition, 91% came to know the Father's love in a new way, and 89% were more in love with Jesus than ever before.[569] Many testified to physical/mental healing and in particular, love for their spouse. The following can be described as nothing less than a total Holy Spirit makeover.

> I cannot describe the wonder. . . .The party started and gets better daily. Instant delivery from drugs, depression, and sexual sin; a transformation so radical that friends, colleagues, and scores of my high school students started making inquiries about what happened to so change me. Healing of sleeplessness (which had led me to an addiction for illegally-obtained sleeping tablets); even a change to my life-style, driving attitudes, work, language (gutter, marine-type tongue); deliverance from high anxiety and stress for which I was well known. The profound sense of total forgiveness, cleansing, and reconciliation with God. And now, a love for the Lord so deep that sometimes it literally aches; a passion for the souls of my school students and others who don't know Christ; a sense of praise and worship that has me singing songs of adoration as I wake up in the morning![570]

The bottom line for Poloma is:

> In sum our findings suggest a relationship between being blessed and being able to bless others. The focus of the TACF renewal on knowing the depth of the Father's love appears to be

---

[567] Ibid., 190.

[568] Margaret M. Poloma, "Inspecting the Fruit of the 'Toronto Blessing,'" *Pneuma: The Journal of the Society for Pentecostal Studies*, Volume 20, No. 1 (Spring 1998) 54.

[569] Ibid., 59.

[570] Ibid., 58.

bearing good fruit — fruit going beyond individual restoration to bless the larger community. At the heart of this process is what has been called *spiritual healing*, a recognition of one's sinful condition and the experience of divine forgiveness.[571]

The Schism

Back to Wilmore. The 1,400 seat sanctuary of the United Methodist Church was packed out each night, people arriving ahead of time. The individuals coming forward were so numerous that the laying on of hands had to be moved to the basement. Half of the attendees were from Wilmore, and the other half, out-of-town. Jeff James, a Wilmore native, the son of Henry James, a forever employee of Asbury College, observed his ten-year-old son Aaron slain in the Spirit, lying on his back after two sixteen-year-old twin sisters had prayed for him. After Aaron came to consciousness, his father asked him why he was laughing while lying on the floor. "That was God tickling me," came the answer. Aaron further stated, "Jesus came and held me and told me that he was going to heal me." Jeff claims that his son was healed from asthma.

Chip Wood, whose ancestors go all the way back to Jacob Young, one of Asbury's most faithful itinerants, oversaw the post-service ministry time that normally lasted until about 1:00 a.m. As the son of Paul Wood, who taught at both Western Evangelical Seminary and Asbury Theological Seminary, Chip grew up in Wilmore. Hundreds came forward, were slain in the Spirit, received holy laughter, and spoke in tongues. Chip, who was given leadership because he was then serving as the pastor of the Wilmore Vineyard Church, testifies: "We were very careful not to predetermine what would happen to a seeker and not suggest a particular response. When this happened, the person was dismissed from the ministry team."[572]

Jeff Calhoun was raised as a United Methodist in Madisonville, Kentucky. The 32-year-old guitarist, having played for the Lexington, Kentucky Philharmonic Orchestra, was asked to participate with the worship team throughout the week. He confessed to being aloof to what was going on in the first couple of services. Wood approached Calhoun

---

[571] Ibid., 69.

[572] Phone conversations with Chip Wood, January 25 and 26, 2019.

the third night and apologetically said, "I think God wants me to pray for you." Calhoun recalls, "I felt a tangible weight on me, and though I did not want to fall as did the others around me, I sunk down to the floor. While I was lying there, I saw a narrow vase covered with dust, filled with grim and soot, like it had been forgotten in a garage." Jeff remembers lying on his back with his mouth open, and God pouring cleansing hot water into him. God said, "As you are opening yourself to me, you need to open yourself to others." Jeff confessed that until that time, he had been closing himself off to family and friends. He testifies that since that encounter in Wilmore, "God has led me into authentic relationships and has allowed me to be accountable to and honest with others."[573]

Mark Nysewander, former classmate of mine at Asbury and then serving as Executive Director of the Francis Asbury Society, was persistently requested by Dennis Kinlaw, President and founder of the Society, not to attend the meetings. In fact, Kinlaw tried to stop the intrusion of the Toronto movement and it was not under the auspices of the United Methodist Church. His efforts were in vain. Nysewander attended the services not as a participant, but as an observer sitting in the balcony. Two months later, Mark was forced to resign. Before leaving, he wrote a two-page single-spaced position paper, explaining his theological perspective. My assessment is that Mark was not guilty of holiness heterodoxy, but that he was not sufficiently against the Charismatic Movement. Mark wrote:

> My intention is to fulfill the purpose of FAS to spread scriptural holiness across the land. However, I am committed to doing that from a post-charismatic position. By that I believe we ought to be open to what the Spirit has said through the charismatic and Pentecostal movements that would fit into our work and even advance what we are about. The whole reformation in worship, gifts, and missions seems to blend with who we are as holiness people. I do not believe the Spirit quit speaking to the church at the end of the last century. I find many significant frontiers of revelation have been discovered in this century that will be a blessing to our holiness message. Also, these newer movements in the church

---

[573] Phone conversation with Jeff Calhoun, January 26, 2019.

need to be constantly reminded of the holiness truth out of which they were birthed.[574]

On May 4, 1995, Harold Burgess, Chairman of the F.A.S. Board, wrote a letter requesting Mark to "step down" based on action taken by the Executive Committee, April 27, 1995, which read:

> In view of the confusion which has come to exist about the Society's identity, we are asking Mark Nysewander to step down from the position of Executive Director, effective immediately. Further, we ask Mark to consider his future involvement with the Society in any other position to be contingent upon distancing himself from the charismatic movement.[575]

During and after the week of the Toronto Blessing visitation, vitriolic attacks were made by Asbury Seminary professors in their classrooms. (Some of them have since admitted that they were not totally accurate, confessing that some may have received help from the Toronto visit.) Even though Seminary President Maxie Dunham and Asbury College President David Gyertson favored the events at the United Methodist Church, at least verbally, fearing political disruption, they refused permission for Randy Clark or his associates to speak in Chapel.

In order to defuse some of the palpable antagonisms engulfing the Wilmore community, Asbury Seminary Provost, Robert Mulholland, arranged for two seminary faculty members, John Oswalt and Stephen Seamands, to present their perspectives to the Seminary faculty on what had taken place in Wilmore just a few weeks before. Mulholland assumed that each professor would render disparate interpretations; Mulholland's assumption was correct. By mostly utilizing John Wigger's *Taking Heaven by Storm,* Seamands traced similar kinds of phenomenology in early American Methodism. He also noted Henry Clay Morrison's "Ball of Fire" experience. Seamands confessed that during the four days of the "Toronto Blessing" in Wilmore, there had been both genuine "manifestations of the Spirit" and "manifestations of the flesh." He recalls,

---

[574] Mark Nysewander, "Statement of Personal Beliefs."

[575] "Francis Asbury Society Executive Committee Meeting Minutes," April 27, 1995, Recorder, Al Coppedge.

I went on to stress that these manifestations of the Spirit are not to be sought or elevated in importance. And they must be "tested" particularly in terms of the fruit they bear in a person's life. If they bear good fruit (in terms of increased desire for Christ, growth in Christlikeness, the fruit of the Spirit, hunger for God's word, love for God and others, etc), then they should in fact be seen as the work of the Holy Spirit. If not they should be attributed to the work of the flesh, mere human emotionalism, autosuggestion, etc.[576]

Oswalt may well be the world's foremost authority on the book of Isaiah. He has written the approximately 1,500 page *The Book of Isaiah,* for *The New International Commentary on the Old Testament,* and the over 700 page commentary on Isaiah for the *NIV Application Commentary: From Biblical Text to Contemporary Life.* John is the only "holiness" person listed as a consultant for Eugene Peterson's "The Message." No one is more respected as a "Bible study speaker" on the holiness camp meeting circuit. Oswalt's book *Called to be Holy: A Biblical Perspective* is a judicious and balanced treatment of God's requirement and provision for holiness in both the Old and New Testament. Oswalt helpfully states, "Christianity is not primarily a moral code to which we agree. Christianity is not primarily a set of ethical standards to which we adhere. Christianity is a life that has been crucified in Christ and is continually resurrected by his resurrection power in us."[577] Staying true to both Scripture and Wesley, Oswalt argues that sanctification is more than an individualistic, personal experience. "One who is in a relationship with God is expected to be holy and that holiness is manifested in transformed social ethics. The goal of redemption is transformed character, and unless that goal is achieved, mere deliverance from a sense of condemnation is misshapen at best and abortive at worst, as it was for the whole generation lost in the wilderness."[578]

Standing before the Asbury faculty, Oswalt gave a finely nuanced, historically documented and theologically buttressed argument as to why the "Light the Fire Conference" was wrong for Wilmore. The conference, as differentiated from the Holiness Movement, put little to no emphasis

---

[576] Email sent to this author by Stephen Seamands, March 4, 2019.

[577] John N. Oswalt. *Called to Be Holy: A Biblical Perspective* (Anderson, IN: Francis Asbury Press, 1999) 109.

[578] Ibid., 34.

on confession and repentance and thus, the ethical dimension and reality of sin were missing. The conference represented faulty theology such as "words of power, intergenerational curses and the need to bind the devil." Oswalt stated, "In the pagan world view where act and result are inseparable, such manipulation is perfectly natural. But in a world of transcendence where God is not this world and cannot be manipulated through words and behaviors in this world, this quest is futile."[579]

What most troubled Oswalt was the notion that miracles could be performed at any time, at any place, by anybody. "Scripture does not support this kind of ubiquitousness. Nowhere does the Bible lead us to expect that miraculous acts are to be done by all believers all the time, or that these acts may be performed at our discretion because we know the appropriate rituals."[580] He then cut a sharp division between religion as rationally understood and transrationally received. The following from Oswalt is indicative of the "Toronto Blessing" tumbling into an academic community: "He does not come to us in a mystical experience. He has come to us as unique nonrepeatable events, and persons in time and space. And the meaning of this is interpreted to us in divinely inspired, rationally and logically related words."[581]

I ask how does, "rationally and logically" work in third world countries? Majority-world countries work within the supernatural, while technologically-enhanced countries work within the natural. How does rational and logical describe the dreams and visions narrated by Nick Ripken in *The Insanity of God*, which we will discuss later? Is Oswalt's world view more informed by John Locke and the Enlightenment than the world view of an individual living in Africa or South America? The following from the Old Testament professor did not leave much room for the presence of the Divine during the four night Toronto Blessing visitation in Wilmore: "The encounter of the individual will with that of God was effectively short-circuited through the creation of an atmosphere of mass hysteria and crowd pressure."[582] In short, it was a "magical" conception related to recent developments in neopaganism that manipulate sources of power.

---

[579] "A revised copy of a paper presented to a forum of the faculty of Asbury Theological Seminary in April 1995," by John N. Oswalt, 7. Courtesy of Oswalt to this author.
[580] Ibid.
[581] Ibid., 8.
[582] Ibid., 10.

I question John's interpretation as to why J. C. McPheeters removed the word "Pentecostal" from the masthead of the *Pentecostal Herald*. "They (Morrison and McPheeters) disassociated themselves from the emotional excesses which some had connected, rightly or wrongly, with the camp meeting. This did not mean they gave up the camp meeting, but it did mean they became increasingly skeptical of any emphasis upon unbridled emotionalism."[583] My interpretation is that they, as well as other holiness groups, did not want to be associated with *glossalalia*, the gift of tongues. Of course, the word excessive is a relative term, and what is excessive to some worshippers is not excessive to others. At various places in this book, regarding British Methodism and American Methodism, and in particular, the camp meeting methodology, I have referenced phenomenology that would have been excessive to most Congregationalists and Episcopalians. Under Asbury's preaching, there was "convulsive shaking," and "jumping and shouting at a strange rate." A. Thomas Walcot observed that early Methodist meetings were "attended with all of that confusion, violence, distortion of the body, voice, and gestures that characterized such a boiling hot religion."[584]

When Oswalt uses the word rational, I presume he is differentiating from irrationality. I prefer the word trans-rationality, phenomena above and beyond my understanding. It is rational to believe that a God that I do not fully comprehend would do something that I do not fully comprehend. Mathias J. Kurschner has argued that, "Charismatic phenomena, convulsions, and other claimed manifestation of the Spirit occurred throughout the life of John Wesley. The attempt to restrict them to the early period of the Methodist movement is misleading and probably the result of personal embarrassment of certain authors with such phenomena."[585] Even if Wesley and Asbury allowed what would be thought by others to be extravagant behavior, or worse yet "enthusiasm," the allowance does not mean that the Methodist leaders at times were not troubled and perplexed as to what their response should be.

Ed Robb, well-known United Methodist evangelist and former Asbury College Board member, wrote a book entitled, *The Spirit Who*

---

[583] Ibid., 4.

[584] Salter, *America's Bishop*, 214.

[585] Mathias J. Kurschner, "The Enthusiasm of The Rev. John Wesley," *Wesleyan Theological Journal*, Vol. 35, No. 2 (Fall 2000) 115.

Will Not Be Tamed, which argues for both openness and caution regarding Pentecostalism in the U.S. and around the world. But the bottom line for Robb is that God is unpredictable, or as I would say, we cannot put God in a box. Robb stated, "Old tradition-bound denominations are giving away to young, vigorous movements emphasizing Scripture and the power of the Holy Spirit."[586] In commenting on the Wilmore event, Robb concluded, "It is often very difficult to discern which Holy Spirit movements are authentic, which ones are manipulated, and which ones are a combination of both. But we must also be open to new things the Holy Spirit is doing."[587]

One of Wilmore's holiness conservatives perceived that Robb was too open and wrote him a letter of disappointment and mild rebuke. For our purposes, we quote from Robb's response:

> I have never spoken in tongues, nor have I ever had a supernatural vision. I am thoroughly Wesleyan in my theology and also in my experience. But, it concerns me that the Holiness Movement is more antagonistic towards the charismatics than almost any group in the church. I believe we should be reaching out and trying to give some solid leadership and stability to a movement that is obviously being used by God to win hundreds of thousands of persons to a saving knowledge of Jesus Christ. I do not see this kind of fruit today in the Holiness movement. In fact, it seems to me that often we have retreated to the periphery of society and the church.[588]

Steve Seamands admitted to this author (we were college classmates) that after the Toronto Blessing visit, he became a "pariah" on campus, and perhaps, "we should have held the event in Lexington."[589] Ron Houp, Jeff James, and others were equally adamant that the event should have been held in Wilmore. Many of the Wilmore younger generation believed the community to be stuck in a spiritual status quo, if not pharisaical pride. The Wilmore United Methodist Church was cut to one half on Sunday morning, 300 to 150; it had been dying for a long

---

[586] Edmund W. Robb. *The Spirit Who Will Not Be Tamed: The Wesleyan Message and The Charismatic Experience* (Anderson, IN: Bristol House Ltd., 1997) 104.

[587] Ibid., 109.

[588] I have obligated myself to not reveal who issued this rebuke and to whom Ed Robb responded.

[589] Conversation with Steve Seamands, August 15, 2018. Steve has recently told me that this Pariah complex vanished within a brief time.

time since the days of Pastor David Seamands (Steve's father) packing it out on Sunday mornings and evenings in the 1970s and 80s. Out of the revival came the Great Commission Fellowship in Wilmore, a church originally running close to 700 on Sunday morning, but now about 350. The official defense of the Wilmore event was written by Steven Beard, who compared many of the Toronto aberrations and physical manifestations to the eighteenth century Wesleyan revivals. Beard lived in Wilmore for twelve years as editor of *Good News Magazine*, the publication of evangelical and conservative United Methodists. Beard wrote:

> Returning to our original inquiry, what then should be a Wesleyan response to extraordinary revival movements such as the "Toronto Blessing"? It would be injudicious to attempt to make ironclad comparisons between what is happening in Toronto and what occurred in England during the Wesleyan revival, except, perhaps, to say that God may work in unusual ways. This is no small factor. After all the manifestations in both cases are peculiar and, simultaneously, the enormous number of people finding salvation and the testimonies of changed lives (the fruit) in both cases are wonderful. Both situations seem to have experienced an extraordinary amount of what might be called the 'manifest' presence of God.[590]

Thus, the Wilmore event was a microcosm of the macrocosmic century-long tension between the Charismatic and Holiness Movements. Both parties acted with integrity, but there were rifts that to this day have never been healed. Should the Toronto Blessing have been invited to Wilmore? No, if the timing is wrong, and it is impossible for one paradigm to yield to another. For instance, I have not referred to John McArthur's and Hank Hanegraaff's critiques of the Toronto Blessing, because whatever the evidence, all of Christian experience is interpreted through their Calvinistic lens, no yielding, bending, or exceptions. But one would hope better of the Holiness Movement, the children of John Wesley, who preached against "bigotry." He wrote: "Shall not God work by whom He will work? No man can do these works unless God is with him; unless God hath sent him for this very thing. But if God hath sent him, will you call him back?"[591] Even more critically, we are followers of One who said, "He that is not against us is for us." So the answer is "yes,"

---

[590] Steve Beard. *Thunderstruck: John Wesley and the "Toronto Blessing"* The entire book was downloaded and sent by Beard to this author, January 22, 2019.
[591] Wesley, *Sermons*, Vol. II, 119.

if God is in the business of bursting old wine skins in order to let new wine flow. Wesley wrote:

> Encourage whomever God is pleased to employ, to give himself wholly up thereto. Speak well of him wheresoever you are; defend his character and his mission. Enlarge, as far as you can, his sphere of action; show him all kindness in word and deed; and cease not to cry to God in his behalf, that he may save both himself and them that hear him.[592]

But such encouragement was not forthcoming. In essence, the rejection of the Toronto Blessing was more of a political than spiritual decision. If the Francis Asbury Society had been swallowed up by the Charismatic Movement, what would have happened to its reason to be? The Society would have been consumed and its identity lost or, at least obscured, by a torrent of Charismatic conventions, seminars, publications, mission outreaches, and the largest churches on the face of the earth. The Francis Asbury Society was founded for the purpose of renewing the Holiness Movement; at the present time, the Charismatic expression of Christianity needs no such resuscitation. Stalemate was the ultimate result of the 1995 Wilmore event. That's not all bad in the light of Paul and Barnabas parting ways (Acts 15), even as both were led by the Holy Spirit and had successful missionary journeys. But they got back together, at least in spirit. That seems to be the only Christian thing to do.

The Wilmore stop held little to no consequence for Randy Clark. He founded Global Awakening, and has preached to crowds approximating 100,000 people in such places as Brazil, Mozambique and India. G. A. emphasizes healing in all of its services, having reported remarkable results such as shorter legs lengthened and the blind seeing. For the approximate $2,500 cost of a trip, any "Christian" can accompany Clark and receive an impartation of a healing gift, and thus become a member of the ministerial team. The routine is rigorous, up early in the morning for a training session from 9:00 a.m. til 1:00 p.m. and then a healing service that evening 6:00 p.m. til 1:00 a.m. Even more impressive is that members are assigned two to a hotel room, and take turns praying for one hour intervals throughout the night.

---

[592] Ibid., 124.

Candy Gunther Brown, a Harvard Ph.D. who teaches at the University of Indiana, Bloomington, and who has accompanied Randy on several trips, notes that he has stayed away from prosperity teaching, and unlike more publicized healers such as Benny Hinn, is accessible to anyone who desires to eat with him at breakfast or lunch. Brown summarizes that Clark "has sought to combine Billy Graham's international network and follow-up through local churches with the supernaturalist approaches of Latin Americans."[593] What troubles Brown is that Clark's ministry does little to address systemic issues such as poverty, joblessness, lack of sanitation, and lack of access to medicine, which are the root causes of many of the physical and emotional distresses for which the ministry teams pray. "After returning home, North American Pentecostals may be even less likely to engage in political or social activism addressing the systemic material causes of global, political, and economic oppression. These Pentecostals may even be confirmed in self-satisfied complacency, since they have done their part by replacing an annual vacation in the Bahamas with a ministry trip to Brazil."[594]

In recent years, Clark has attached himself as a professor to United Theological Seminary, the United Methodist School in Dayton, Ohio. Though the school may not tout him as its most acclaimed luminary, his presence has no doubt served as effective advertisement. Being infused with a renewed economic and spiritual vitality, United has experienced an increase in student numbers, and more importantly, a new sense of purpose and mission while other official United Methodist seminaries are withering. Theological education is anything but abstract at United. By hosting conferences such as "Spirit and Truth," (March 7 - 9, 2019) and "The Methodist School of Supernatural Ministry," (April 3 - 6, 2019). United is making a concentrated effort to combine historic Methodism with contemporary charismatic renewal. It sounds like the best of both worlds.

---

[593] Candy Gunther Brown, "Global Awakenings: Divine Healing Networks and Global Community in North America, Brazil, Mozambique and Beyond," in *Global Pentecostal and Charismatic Healing*, ed. Candy Gunther Brown (New York: Oxford University Press, 2011) 354.
[594] Ibid., 357.

PART II

The following are the five areas, or challenges that Wesleyan Holiness has not been able to navigate, at least satisfactorily, to an urbanite from, let's say, from 1960 to the present. They are not either - or issues; they are on a continuum. They do not eliminate the need for entire sanctification. In fact, in many ways they call for a renewed intensity of holy pursuit, in face of problems that our holiness ancestors never knew existed. I am not suggesting that holiness theology is a simplistic theology for simple people. I am suggesting that holiness theology did not address issues that, if they did not exist for those who attended camp meetings, they did exist for intellectuals, academics, corporate executives and many other species of urbanity. Perhaps the solution would be to build Bible schools and small Christian colleges to serve as a buffer zone, a demilitarized zone between the sacred and profane. This strategy served only to remove the sanctified from the new realities and complexities of life, overwhelming confusion and staggering complications which our faithful holiness leaders (and I in no way want to minimize their faithfulness) could only confront by discerning the aorist tense of a Greek verb.

Thomas Kuhn proposes that progress is not a simple line leading to the truth. "It is more progress away from less adequate conceptions of and interactions with the world."[595] I suggest the same with theology. Even though of the five categories which I discuss in Part II, only one is labeled "The World," the other four "The Self," "The Other, "The Animate," and "The Mind," call for a Christian response to the world which most adequately represents the teachings and actions of Christ. Given a world which is exponentially changing, combined with the fact that one's own identity is constantly changing, Christianity is left

---

[595] Kuhn, xi.

with a daunting task. Part of our task is to identify responses that are inadequate such as enculturation, reification, escapism, dishonesty, and in particular, the willingness to confess failure. Many of us are in bondage to a self-righteousness that is unwilling to learn from other Christians who may be more fully representing the mind of Christ. More often than we think, it may be helpful to listen to someone who is outside of our own tradition. As Molly Worthen says, "The Wesleyan Holiness churches designed their colleges and seminaries as citadels to protect the faithful, not as schools with the confidence to invite all comers and entertain any challenge."[596] Obviously, Worthen has accurately identified response by the Wesleyan Holiness tradition. What is most helpful about Worthen's observation is that she has no hidden agenda, at least that I can identify, to belittle or disrespect the American Holiness Movement.

---

[596] Molly Worthen. *Apostles of Reason: The Crisis of Authority in American Evangelicalism* (New York: Oxford University Press, 2013) 46.

Chapter 8:
The World

Vietnam: A World Falling Apart

My wife lost a brother in the Vietnam War, and I lost a first cousin. For that and other reasons, I watched most of the Ken Burns miniseries, "Vietnam." I learned about the doubts of our highest leaders, Lyndon B. Johnson and his Secretary of Defense, Robert McNamara. (I also watched "The Fog of War" - an interview with Robert McNamara, recalling those events.) I did not realize how much the music of the 60s was stimulated by, or paralleled the events of Vietnam. But most importantly, I was not aware of how much those events consumed and fragmented our society. We were at war at home and abroad. I might just as well have been living on another planet.

Asbury College could not have been more different from Kent State. February 3, 1970, was the beginning of the so called Asbury Revival, an "other-worldly" phenomenon (as I have already inadequately described). Out of miraculous circumstances, events in my life entirely beyond my choice or control, I was present for an event like few people have ever witnessed. From my perspective, it was a genuine outpouring of the Holy Spirit. A spirit of love enveloped our campus, as God melted away the cliquishness, clannishness, and competitiveness which define normal campus life.

I am quite sure that the love experienced at Asbury did not extend to the four students killed at Kent State by National Guardsmen on May 4, 1970. I may have just thought that those students were doing something that they should not have been doing. Kent State, though located in the state immediately north of Kentucky, from my understanding could just as well have been in the Middle East. The worldview of a student at Berkeley, Kent State, or hundreds of other campuses, was decidedly different from the world view of a student at Asbury College. To be sure, the Holiness Movement did not produce Daniel Ellsberg, William Sloane Coffin, Stokesly Carmichael, or Martin Luther King, Jr.[597]

Is this the choice that has to be made: a private, personal, introspective, individualistic pursuit of righteousness as opposed to get your hands dirty, not quite sure if this is the right path, morally-perplexing involvement in the overwhelming cataclysmic crises that are engulfing our planet? A revival at Asbury College is light years removed from a demonstration at Kent State. The genocide crisis, the refugee crisis, global warming crisis and the inequity crisis all seem to be beyond the pale of Wesleyan Holiness theology. What began as urban spirituality in New York City, Phoebe Palmer's parlor, became a rural camp meeting religion, and has never made it back to the public square, other than partisan politics with an agenda created by talk show radio. Holiness churches thrived during the halcyon days of post World War II America, but had nothing to say to a society shattered by Vietnam and Civil Rights. As a Bible college student, 1965-1968, I often heard the prayer, "Bring an honorable end to the War." Only now do I realize that the prayer probably meant, "Whatever happens to the Vietnamese, help America to get out and save face." God must have been deaf or really did not care about preserving America's dignity. I do not think I ever heard anyone pray for the North or South Vietnamese.

In his 1969 Commencement speech at Asbury Theological Seminary, Timothy Smith attempted to articulate a Wesleyan Holiness response to the Beatles, Joan Baez, Bob Dylan, Timothy Leary and Dick Gregory, as they addressed America's disillusion with itself, and in particular, the institutions that defined America's proud cultural ethos: church, academy, and state. Dr. Smith offered a prophetic challenge: "To understand the significance and content of what such flower people are saying does not imply approval of all that they either say and do. But the

---

[597] Donald Dayton refers to Coffin as "one of the greatest men I have ever known. He read Russian literature in the original language. He married the daughter of pianist Arthur Rubinstein, and then the head of the medical staff at Boston General. I will never forget the standing ovation he received after his freshman orientation on Sex Ethics and Control. Imagine lecturing to 1,500 horny young men and getting a standing ovation for telling them to control their urges." Email from Donald Dayton to author April 4, 2019.

questions arising out of their often distorted search for purity, for peace and for love, are welling up everywhere. To these questions the children of the Wesleyan movement, who ought to be God's flower people, have given scant response."[598]

One has to admire the "unknown and unkempt" young man on a street corner in San Francisco, every morning with a loaf of bread he had begged from a nearby bakery. He gave a small piece to each passerby, and he said to each of them, 'I love you.'"[599] Maybe the student was a Nazarene or Free Methodist, but probably not. San Francisco has not been all that friendly to holiness types. But more critical to us, we have not been all that friendly to San Francisco. Isn't that where Harvey Milk was mayor? Sanctified individuals would have probably been picketing against the homosexuals or at least staying away from them while the man on the corner was practicing Christian presence, which is incarnational, non-pragmatic, non-measurable sacramental grace. Christian presence is not an efficiency model, as described by James Hunter, "often re-enforced by a world of hyperkinetic activity, marked by unrelenting interruption and distraction. On the one hand, such conditions foster a technical mastery, that prizes speed and agility, and facility with multiple tasks - for example using email, IM, the cell phone, the iPad, all the while eating lunch, holding a conversation or listening to a lecture. But on the other hand, these very same conditions undermine our capacity for silence, depth of thinking, and focused attention."[600]

Technology – The Failed Answer

The ironic result of the world-wide web is that it localizes us instead of globalizing us. We are not likely to use the computer to find out about refugees from Syria, genocide in South Sudan, starvation in Somaliland, and Muslims who have been run out of Myanmar into Bangladesh. We are more apt to promote ourselves with a "selfie," keep track of the people in our hometown, or possibly read a blog from a specialist in our favorite sport, political party, or whatever. This is a life-devouring activity, which limits reflective thinking about what really

---

[598] Timothy L Smith, "A Wesleyan Response to the New Perfectionism," *The Asbury Seminarian*, 25 (July 1971) 35.
[599] Ibid., 30.
[600] Hunter, 252.

matters. As cyberspace has expanded the possibilities for knowledge it has also intensified attachment to niche thinking and activities. Hardly anyone is arguing that the computer is amplifying America's collective intelligence.

There is no reason to believe that holiness folk are less enamored with Face Booking, niche buying, or obtaining their information from whomever confirms their conviction on whatever issue. The question needs to be asked, how does the fascination (addiction) with electronic "connectedness," carve out space and time which in the past was reserved by confessors of holiness for Scripture reading and prayer? My negative memory bank often in the red because of the Pilgrim Holiness strangeness, was covered and more than balanced by my mother who spent an hour in prayer, praying at the top of her voice each morning. She did not know much about the world, but she covered all she knew about it with prayer. In a chance conversation, a plastic surgeon who attends the same church that I do, and who was also raised in the Pilgrim Holiness Church, recently told me how his farmer father would stand in the field and pray so loudly that the far away neighbors pulled up their windows in order to hear him.

These peculiarities have been mostly erased by the homogenization of electronic sameness that is at odds with the disciplines that have sustained Christianity through the ages: solitude, reflection, community and transcendence over the world's values. The postmodern irony is that in comparison with a Lincoln or a Philips Brooks, whose minds were greater and their world was smaller, our world is greater, and our minds are smaller. To use the language of David Wells, "What is most remarkable about modern people is that they are not in scale with the world they inhabit, informationally, and psychologically. They are dwarfed. And they have been emptied of the metaphysical substance, more precisely it has been sucked out of them. There is nothing to give height or depth or perspective to anything they experience. They know more but they are not necessarily wiser. They believe less but they are not more substantial."[601]

---

[601] David Wells. *No Place for Truth or Whatever Happened to Evangelical Theology?* (Grand Rapids: William B. Eerdmans Publishing Company, 1993) 51-52.

Many cultural observers have warned against the collective dumbing down of discourse and perspective by technology, among them Marshall McLuan, Neil Postman, Gregg Easterbrook, and Sven Birkerts. Birkerts traces the transition from lexicology to photography, the ability to grasp complex ideas, to an ability to read only icons (the golden arches and Target) and to think or listen only in sound bites. In the loss column of the electronic age are a

> fragmented sense of time and a loss of the so-called duration experience, that depth phenomenon we associate with reverie, a reduced attention span and a general impatience with sustained inquiry; a shattered faith in institutions, in the explanatory narratives that formerly gave shape to subjective experience; a divorce from the past, from a vital sense of history as a cumulative or organic process; an estrangement from geographic place and community; and absence of any strong vision of a personal or collective future.[602]

Technology causes us to live in the illusion that we have mastered the world when in a sense, the world has mastered us. Technology offers both a false dependence and false view of progress. I do not have the space to turn this essay into a litany of toxic spills, polluted air, destruction of the ozone layer, and what to do with atomic waste. Gregg Easterbrook argues that for every step forward there is a step backwards. "Solving one problem often creates another: the new problem is noted and fretted about while the original, being solved is forgotten. Call this the 'tyranny of the small picture.' Instead of the big picture we often see the small picture aware only of the lesser negative within the greater positive."[603]

Within a "holiness" rubric, H. Ray Dunning tackled the above over thirty years ago, arguing that the restoration of the image of God includes proper dominion over and reconciliation to the earth.

> It is the loss of the dimension of the <u>Imago</u> which has resulted in the idolatrous attitude towards science and technology, characterizing scientific humanism. This is a mythology that must be repudiated. The Christian understanding is that while such discoveries or inventions are gifts of God, they must be seen as servants rather than

---

[602] Suen Birkerts. *The Gutenberg Elegies: The Fate of Reading in an Electronic Age* (Boston: Faber and Faber, 1994) 27.

[603] Gregg Easterbrook . T*he Progress Paradox: How Life Gets Better While People Feel Worse* (New York: Random House, 2003) 99.

masters. Developing the earth is part of the cultural mandate given man at the creation, but it can only be done in a non-self-destructive way when it is carried out under the lordship of Christ and this in relation to the earth to which the full message of Wesleyan Holiness calls us.[604]

But I doubt that much of Dunning's admonishment filtered down to the average holiness pastor, much less to his/her flock. One wonders how many holiness pastors attain their sermons online spending most of their time in an air-conditioned office staring at a 17" computer screen instead of providing incarnational care for the sheep or sustained inquiry into the word of God.

I do not desire to come across as a Luddite, but truth being told, technology is neither bane nor blessing in facing our real problems. One hardly knows where to start: the transmigration of people, war, genocide, abortion, inequity, poverty, urbanization, persecution, xenophobia, ISIS, greed, misogyny, the sex trade, AIDS, ethnocentricity and nationalism. Most of these issues are dismissed from the average holiness pulpit or any other evangelical pulpit. We have enough problems of our own; dysfunction, depression and despair as we are harnessed to the increasing stresses of modernity. (I have two daughters who are public school counselors, attempting to prevent their students from committing suicide.)

Gaining A Christian World View

But, let's lift up our heads for a few moments. Miriam Adeney pictures a Ugandan woman who has just had her 13th child. The child is born where women have more children than any place in the world "And most of them sick - Malaria, worms, Kawashroder, from not enough food"[605] I have been to Uganda in a van with eleven others, a twelve-hour drive from Entebbe on Lake Victoria all the way to the northern border with South Sudan. "Where these women lived in southwest Uganda there were no roads and therefore no way to take crops to market. The landscape was hilly. As people cut trees for fuel landslides increased.

---

[604] H, Ray Dunning, "Holiness, Technology and Personhood," *Wesleyan Theological Journal*, Vol. 21, nos. 1 and 2, (Spring -Fall, 1986)184.

[605] Miriam Adeney. *Kingdom Without Borders: The Untold Story of Global Christianity* (Downers Grove, IL: InterVarsity Press, 2009) 171.

More arable soil was lost, things seem to be sliding down hill in almost every area of life, yet the region was densely populated."[606]

Two books have pushed me toward Uganda as well as other needy areas of the world. In 2009 Richard Stearns wrote *The Hole in Our Gospel*, a scathing indictment of the American Church for its lassitude, greed and indifference to the majority world. Stearns had worked his way to the pinnacle of American success: CEO of Lennox, the world's largest manufacturer of the finest cutlery, china and silverware. He was the epitome of the "American dream;" vacations, cars, houses and all the rest of the best that American society provides for those who work hard. "It was off to the Wharton School for me, then to corporate America, the American Dream came true — my American Dream. I had majored in microbiology, of all things. I loved the certainty and logic of the sciences, my personal religion of self-reliance resonated well with social Darwinism-survival of the fittest. The strong prevailed! I was succeeding because I was tough, smart and independent. And I had done it, as Frank Sinatra, 'My Way.'"[607]

But gratefully, God interrupted "my way." Stearns became a Christian, not just a nominal Christian; a tithing, Bible study, theology reading Christian. God interrupted again with a call from World Vision to become its next president. (You know, that organization founded by Bob Pierce, who coined the prayer "Break my heart with the things that break the heart of God.") Stearns originally responded to the head hunter, Rob Stevenson, "I don't think so. The way I see it, you seem to be looking for someone who is part CEO, part Mother Theresa, and part Indiana Jones." During the brief conversation, the daunting sacrifice flashed through Richard's mind. "But we live in a two-hundred-year-old stone farmhouse with ten bedrooms on five acres; it's the house of our dreams that we worked years for. You can't expect us to sell it. But what about my brand new company car, the royal-blue Jaguar XK-8; I'd have to give that back."[608]

---

[606] Ibid., 172.

[607] Richard Stearns. *The Hole in Our Gospel: What Does God Expect of Us? The Answer That Changed My Life and Might Just Change the World* (Nashville: Thomas Nelson, Inc., 2009) 77.

[608] Ibid., 34.

The rest is history. Upon taking the World Vision job, Rich found out something that every American needs to discover: almost all poverty is fundamentally the result of a lack of options. "It is not that the poor are lazier, less intelligent, unwilling to make efforts to change their conditions. Rather it is that they are trapped by circumstances beyond their power to change."[609]

What are Americans doing to grant them the power to change? Not much: "American Christians give 2% of their income to the church and 2% of that goes to majority world countries about 5/10,000ths of our income."[610] According to 2005 figures Americans annually spent 705 billion dollars on entertainment and recreation, and five billion dollars on overseas ministries, through 700 national mission agencies including denominational, interdenominational and independent agencies.[611] One thought from the book has continually played through my mind and heart. "Just because you can't do everything doesn't mean you can't do something." And we can all do something, and probably more than we are doing.

A second book which profoundly impacted me, *The Insanity of God*, was written by Gregg Lewis, raised in a holiness home in Wilmore, Kentucky. His father, Ralph Lewis, was for many years a professor of homiletics at Asbury Theological Seminary. Gregg features Nick Ripken, not his real name but a pseudonym, a minister to some of the most dangerous places in the world including Somaliland. There, thousands of men and women sell their last possessions, go without food and water, to buy the narcotic KHAT that relieves their depression for a few hours. Outside of the military headquarters in Mogadishu, "was a mob of several hundred desperate children, bellies bloated by malnutrition, gathered around the walls of the compound. The children were anxiously awaiting what was a frequent, though not daily occurrence. When the carcass of whatever animal had been slaughtered for the leader's supper was heaved over the wall, the starving children descended like locusts, tearing and ripping off chunks of bloody animal hide to chew on and find the little nutritional value it provided."[612] For Nick Ripken and the

---

[609] Ibid., 118.

[610] Ibid., 217.

[611] Ibid., 218.

[612] Nick Ripken with Gregg Lewis. *The Insanity of God: A True Story of Faith Resurrected* (Nashville, BNH Publishing Group, 2013) 42.

people who live there, Somaliland was an "insane and hostile place, a hell in the grip of evil."[613]

Nick Ripken's hellish experiences were not limited to Somaliland, but other parts of Africa as well as Russia and China. Almost all the believers that Ripken met in China (early 1990s) had been imprisoned for their faith. They explained, "Do you know what prison is for us? It is how we get our theological education. Prison in China is for us like the seminary is for training church leaders in your country."[614] He was especially shocked when he witnessed a group of pastors tearing books out of the Bible because they owned no Bible, but would be able to take home a small portion of Scripture. "I could only imagine what joy it would have been for those whose portion of Scripture was the book of Genesis, the Psalms, or the Gospel of John. But I felt bad for the church leader who was handed a smaller portion like Philemon."[615]

For Ripken to survive the tens of thousands of miles to some of the most dangerous places in the world there had to be miraculous intervention. In one Southeast Asian country five men met him of whom he had never heard much less previously met. "At 1:30 in the morning we were praying when the Holy Spirit told us to go to the airport. The Holy Spirit told us we were to go to the first white man who got off the plane. The Holy Spirit told us he was sending the man to answer our questions."[616] God's directions by dreams are quite common in majority world countries.

One Muslim as a soldier had personally killed 100 people, in addition to those he had killed in battle. During one of his dreams he saw so much blood running off his arms, that he thought he was going to go insane, but in another dream he saw a man standing before him clothed in white with scarred hands and scarred feet. "I am Jesus the Messiah and I can get the blood off — if you will just find me and believe in me."[617] After becoming a Christian the new convert smuggled Bibles and even showed the Jesus film. He was captured by Muslim soldiers and beaten almost to death. In six hours of questioning him, Ripken found

---

[613] Ibid., 13.
[614] Ibid., 231.
[615] Ibid., 25.
[616] Ibid., 27.
[617] Ibid., 284.

out about his wife and children. "How do they fit into your ministry.... How do they help you?" The man clasped his scarred hands down on Nick's shoulders and explained "I have given him everything! My body has been broken, I've been jailed, and I've been stoned. I've been beaten, I've been left for dead!" But what the man most feared was that God would ask the same thing of his wife and children. "Jesus is worth it. He is worth my life, my wife's life, and he is worth the lives of my children! I have got to get them involved in what God is doing with me!" Ripken referred to this individual as the "The toughest man I have ever met."[618]

Now is the time to thank God for all the Nick Ripkens of the world, and in particular, the thousands of Wesleyan Holiness missionaries who have encircled the globe over the last century. They have been sent by World Gospel Mission, The Oriental Missionary Society (now One Mission Society) and the many denominations that place themselves under the Wesleyan Holiness canopy. They have labored where there are no Christmas lights, no department stores, no decent roads, no Orkin exterminators, no little league baseball, no McDonalds and often those amenities that we now call necessities, air-conditioning and modern plumbing. But often our efforts have been piece meal white supremacy and condescension with a we know best attitude.

But piece meal efforts bear fruit, and we are not to despise the day of small things. In 1910, the missionary arm of the National Holiness Association sent Cecil Troxel to China. The beginning of the National Holiness Missionary Society (later to become World Gospel Mission) is a story of perseverance and sacrifice. These two men, and the several who followed after, lived in mud houses with dirt floors, slept on brick beds, endured torrential rains, and traveled in ox carts. They cast out demons, witnessed thousands "entirely sanctified," rejoiced with the Chinese in miraculous healings, and were instrumental in the liberation of many wives who were severely oppressed and beaten by their husbands. Li Kung Hsien was pronounced dead and was left in a cold room with a brick on his chest, the presumed corpse awaiting burial. He dreamed he was at Heaven's Gate, and was told by angels he must return to Earth and witness for the Lord which he did for two years.[619] The following

---

[618] Ibid., 247.

[619] W. W. Cary. *Story of the National Holiness Missionary Society* (Chicago: National Holiness Missionary Society, 1940) 259-260.

narrative of demonic deliverance was not all that unusual. A thirty-year-old man was found lying on a brick bed with his hands and feet padlocked. When the missionaries asked for keys and unlocked him, the mother said, "He is ferocious, and will kill you if you loose him." The missionaries proceeded:

> We told him to cry unto Jesus, who would bring him the deliverance he sought. He said the first syllable of the name "Jesus," which is "Yeh" in Chinese, and then started to say the last syllable, "Su," but the moment he came in to "S" of the "Su" be began to hiss and then to make such strange faces that we sensed in a new way Satan's final stand to continue in possession of this struggling individual. His jaws became suddenly locked. We realized that he was trying with all the strength he could muster to open his jaws and say the name "Yeh Su" (Jesus).

Perhaps the greatest miracle occurred in 1914, after Cecil Troxel had been in China for less than four years. A native Chinese said to him, "You are not a foreigner. You are Chinese." When Troxel asked why his interloper perceived him as a native, the man responded, "I have listened to you for one hour. I haven't heard you make one mistake in our language…"[620] Troxel failed to convince the man that he was American born, and raised in America. The missionary concluded, "I had had many a struggle in trying to get the Chinese language. It was a great satisfaction to me to hear one mistake me for a Chinese and accuse me of not being American."[621]

The Success of Pentecostalism

To bring up a very uncomfortable and unsettling point, the efforts of the Holiness Movement have been dwarfed by the cutting edge and wave of evangelical growth in the majority world, Pentecostalism. It does not take a Ph.D. in anthropology to figure out why Pentecostalism has been so successful. It had to make little cultural adaptation from the United States to majority world countries. Pentecostalism wherever, operates within the super-natural, emphasizes the gifts of the Holy Spirit, exercises exuberant physical worship, and is dependent on God for the miniscule details of life. Pentecostalism is indigenous before it arrives.

---

[620] Ibid., 51.
[621] Ibid.

According to Pentecostal scholar Alan Anderson, "Pentecostalism is inherently prone to contextualization: vibrancy, enthusiasm, spontaneity, spirituality for which Pentecostals are so well-known and their willingness to address problems of sickness, poverty, unemployment, loneliness, evil spirits, and sorcery has directly contributed to this growth."[622]

If one gives an invitation for physical healing in an Indian village or an African congregation, expect to stay there for a long time! Everyone will come forward. Even in an African-American worship service in the United States, Pentecostal or not, one is more likely to hear stories of God's miraculous intervention. "God supplied me with groceries, God sent a neighbor over with some laundry detergent, my headache went away, God kept my tire from going flat until I could get home" and so forth. Of course this world view can be easily translated into a health and wealth gospel, which has plagued Pentecostalism. And I am not naïve about other liabilities: the cult of personality, schism because of fragmented theology, false claims to miracles and preachers getting rich at the expense of the gullible.

From the above, one may conclude that Pentecostalism is only successful in marginalized societies. Not so. The loudest tongues speaking session that I ever witnessed was in the largest Methodist church in the world, Seoul, South Korea. It was louder than David Yonggi Cho's church, supposedly the largest church in the world. (The numbers are skewed. They must not remove the deceased from their membership rolls.) I was in a Methodist Church in Belo Horizonte, Brazil, that would have made an Assemblies of God Church in the United States look like the congregation was sedated. As a Brazilian Methodist pastor explained to me, the only two options are Liberation Theology and Pentecostalism. Wesleyan Holiness is not an option because it is not present, at least visibly present. *The International Bulletin of Missionary Research* estimated "that there were 524 million Pentecostal and Charismatic Christians in the world by the year 2000, out of a total 2,000 million Christians."[623] To summarize, Pentecostalism has provided the growing, cutting edge for Christian evangelism around the world for the last half-century.

---

[622] Alan Anderson. *To The Ends of the Earth: Pentecostalism and the Transformation of World Christianity* (New York: Oxford University Press, 2013) 225.
[623] Nole Davies and Martin Conway. *World Christianity in the Twentieth Century* (London: SCM Press, 2008) 76.

The Polarization of the Holiness and Pentecostal Movements

The relationship between the American Holiness Movement and Pentecostalism has been curious. The first person to have analyzed the relationship in a scholarly treatment was Howard Snyder in his 1985 book *The Divided Flame: Wesleyans and the Charismatic Renewal* (He had broached the issue in a previous book, *The Problem of Wineskins: Church Structure in a Technological Age*, 1975.) Snyder traced the Charismatic revival that swept through major universities, the Roman Catholic church, produced the Vineyard Movement, and David Wilkerson's *The Cross and the Switchblade* in the 1960s-70s. Snyder quoted Wesley scholar Albert Outler, who claimed that for Wesley, "No professor of an 'extraordinary gift' tongues (or whatever) is to be rejected out of hand as if he knew what the Spirit should or should not do."[624] Snyder summarized, "The real danger in a negative approach to tongues, is that it may lead to the hyper rationalism of dead orthodoxy. Wesleyans of all people should be open to the working of God in human experience." Howard Snyder quoted David DuPlessis, who spoke at Emory University in the early 1970s: "It amazes me a little to hear contemporary English Methodism talking about the Charismatic renewal in much the same way as an eighteenth-century bishop of London talked about the Wesleys and their enthusiasm."[625] What all Christians need to keep in mind is the astute historical observation of James Dunn. "The inspiration, the concrete manifestations of Spirit in power, in revelation, in word, in service, all are necessary - for without them grace soon becomes status, gift becomes office, ministry becomes bureaucracy, body of Christ becomes institution and koinonia becomes the extension fund."[626]

The irony of the above is that the primitiveness of Pentecostalism has been the Christian brand of choice in the face of modernity. Pentecostalism, more than any other Christian option, is the pure antithesis of secularism. Harvey Cox argued that, Pentecostalism "has succeeded because it has spoken to the spiritual emptiness of our time, reaching beyond the levels of creed and ceremony into the core of human religiousness, into what might be called 'primal spirituality,' that largely

---

[624] Howard Snyder. *The Divided Flame: Wesleyans and the Charismatic Renewal* (Grand Rapids, Francis Asbury Press, 1986) 61.
[625] Ibid., 66.
[626] Ibid., 49.

unpossessed nucleus of the psyche in which the unending struggle for a sense of purpose and significance goes on."[627] Cox cited John Wesley's reference to Montanus (who spoke in tongues) as, "a real Scriptural Christian...one of the best men then upon the earth." According to Wesley, miraculous endowments had disappeared because "'dry, formal, orthodox men' did not have such gifts and condemned them."[628]

Both Pentecostalism and the Church of the Nazarene put down their roots in the soil of paganism's new frontier, Los Angeles, the home of the nascent movie industry. What exactly Phineas Bresee first thought of the Azusa Street Revival is difficult to say. He was a former Methodist and demanded a certain degree of all things done decently and in order. As the nightly religious intensity attracted increasingly greater crowds throughout the waning months of 1906 and the press gave increasing space to the popularity of the spiritual weirdness at an abandoned Methodist Episcopal church on Azusa Street, Bresee decided he needed to say something. In an editorial in the church's first periodical, *Nazarene Messenger,* December 13, 1905, Bresee wrote of the happenings on Azusa Street:

> Locally it is of small account, insignificant both in numbers and influence. Instead of being the greatest movement of the time, as represented in Los Angeles, at least it is a small moment, it has had, and has now, upon the religious life of the city, about as much influence as a pebble thrown into the sea....The speaking in tongues has been a no thing-a jargon, a senseless jumble, without meaning to those who do the mumbling, or to those who hear. Where in a few instances the speaker or some other one has attempted to interpret it has usually been a poor mess.[629]

Never did a "pebble" have such a ripple effect, and never did a preacher more underestimate the day of small things. But more critically, Bresee had set the anti-tongues agenda for the twentieth-century. Out of all the major holiness denominations, including Wesleyan, Free Methodist and Salvation Army, the Church of the Nazarene has been the

---

[627] Harvey Cox. *Fire From Heaven: The Rise of Pentecostal Spirituality and the Reshaping of Religion in the Twenty-first Century* (New York: Addison Wesley Publishing Company, 1995) 81.

[628] Ibid., 91.

[629] Carl Bangs. *Phineas Bresee: His Life in Methodism, the Holiness Movement, and the Church of the Nazarene* (Kansas City: Beacon Hill Press, 1995) 230.

most stridently against tongues. But to the misunderstanding of some Nazarenes, the Church of the Nazarene has no official stance against tongues speaking, at least in *The Manual*. What it does say, with which many neo-Pentecostals would agree, "To affirm that even a special or any alleged physical evidence or 'prayer language', is evidence of the baptism with the Spirit is contrary to the biblical and historical position of the Church."[630]

Whether tongues speaking would be allowed in the Church of the Nazarene, came to a head in the 1976 General Assembly when the General Superintendents issued an encyclical. "We believe that the religious exercise called 'tongues' which is not a means of communicating truth is a false gift and a dangerous substitute; we do not believe in a so-called prayer language."[631] Again on December 2, 2002, the Superintendents stated, "Where such ('tongues') arises, it is the responsibility of the pastor to explain gently our identity and worship practices and to suggest that those who insist on involvement with neo-Pentecostalism relate to those churches that support such practices."[632]

What was curious about the above stance is that it also condemned being "slain in the spirit, shaking, incessant laughter and other similar phenomenon....However, the phenomena are not a part of our accepted worship experience. This is not who we are, this is not what we do." Thus, there is little wonder as to why the trans-rational behavior that was once typical of Nazarene worship, shouting, running the aisles and being slain in the Spirit has all but ceased. According to holiness historian Charles Edwin Jones, "In 1902 Maude Frederick, future wife of Nazarene General Superintendent, J.B. Chapman, commented favorably on one woman's prostration during a meeting at Sharp Top, Texas: 'One soul was laid out under the power of God. God used her in convicting sinners.'"[633] A resolution from the seventh General Assembly of the Church of the

---

[630] *Church of The Nazarene Manual,* 2013-17, Article 903.10 (Kansas City: Nazarene Publishing House, 2013) 378.

[631] "The Position of the Church of the Nazarene on Speaking in Tongues," *Herald of Holiness* Volume 65 Number 20 (October 15, 1976) 4-5.

[632] Nazarene Archives, *Board of General Superintendents Statement,* December 2, 2002.

[633] Charles Edwin Jones. "Tongues Speaking and the Wesleyan-Holiness Quest for Assurance of Sanctification," *Wesleyan Theological Journal,* Vol. 22, Issue 2, (Fall 1987) 117.

Nazarene, 1928, stated "We as a people are a happy, joyous crowd. We believe in preserving a spirit of liberty and emotional demonstration."[634] The above has caused Edwin Jones to conclude,

> In short, the tongues 'threat' combined with other factors in causing Wesleyan holiness people to shy away from their prior reliance on the authority of Scripture and personal convictions. Conformity to rules of conduct replaced convictions about right conduct. And passivity, leader-centeredness and authoritarianism gradually supplanted spontaneity, heartfelt emotion and Spirit-dependence on worship. Increasingly, the quest for holiness was an individual one, largely unsupported and uninspired by the holiness churches corporately.[635]

To put it another way, Pentecostals adversely shaped holiness worship. We are partially formed by that to which we react. Deciding to not become like Pentecostals robbed holiness worship of much of its eccentricities and spontaneity, those elements that distinguished a holiness church from "never depart from the stated worship order" of other denominations. It was for this reason that Asbury and his cohorts had abandoned Wesley's "Sunday Order of Worship" within ten years of Thomas Coke delivering it to the American Methodists in 1784.

One finds the following descriptions when doing a scan of the Church of the Nazarene's Centennial History, *Our Watchword and Song*. Under Mary Lee Harris' preaching, "The scene beggared all description – such crying and stripping themselves of their ornaments...and arose shouting the praises of God."[636] At the Association of Pentecostal Churches annual meeting, April 1907, with whom the Church of the Nazarene would form the Pentecostal Church of the Nazarene in October, 1907, there were "tears and laughter and shouts and every other manifestation of holy joy."[637] The New England train trip home reported, "We sang, shouted, and prayed in the Holy Ghost, and had a miniature camp meeting. Hallelujah!"[638] At the uniting assembly in

---

[634] Ibid., 124.

[635] Ibid., 123.

[636] Floyd Cunningham, editor. *Our Watchword and Song: The Centennial History of the Church of the Nazarene* (Kansas City: Beacon Hill Press of Kansas City, 2009) 185.

[637] Ibid., 149-150.

[638] Ibid., 150.

Chicago, October 1907, the delegates were so filled with "holy joy, that for many it was impossible to restrain it."[639] The "waving of nearly 1,000 handkerchiefs and the repetition of chorus after chorus, was the scene, the better of which we do not to expect this side of the pearly gates."[640] These scenes would be typical of the Church of the Nazarene for the next fifty years.

The Scholarly Exchange

The standard work arguing for an alignment or at least commonalities between the Holiness Movement and neo-Pentecostalism is Donald Dayton's *Theological Roots of Pentecostalism*, his 1983 dissertation at the University of Chicago.[641] Of course he only drove a further wedge between entrenched holiness leaders and American Pentecostal exponents. According to Dayton, Timothy Smith took upon himself a personal crusade to discredit Dayton's thesis. Dayton may overstate the case, but there may be some truth in his interpretation of Smith's response to the ideas which would provide the underpinning for his dissertation. Smith's anti-Dayton arguments came in a paper which he presented to the Society for Pentecostal Studies in 1975. Dayton states concerning Smith's analysis, "His paper was a point by point refutation of what I had sent him without mentioning me by name. As a lowly graduate-student I was terrified and slid lower in my seat hoping not to be recognized, but when the paper ended Vinson Synan jumped to his feet and asked, 'I take it you don't agree with Don Dayton's thesis,' Smith sniffed 'Don Dayton's thesis? All I've seen is a very elaborate hypothesis!'"[642] Dayton further recounted, "On basis of this interchange, the program committee added me to the list of respondents at Tim's banquet address, later published by the Nazarenes as a definitive critique of Pentecostals as irrational, etc. In my response I opined that Tim's theology was closer to Pentecostalism than Wesleyan, a charge that 'infuriated' Smith."[643]

---

[639] Ibid., 151.

[640] Ibid.

[641] Donald W. Dayton. *Theological Roots of Pentecostalism* (Metuchen, New Jersey: The Scarecrow Press, 1987).

[642] Email from Donald Dayton to the author, April 13, 2018.

[643] Ibid.

Later that evening in his banquet address, Smith argued that "Modern glossolalia, seems to me to depart in significant ways from the biblical experience of joy."[644] Smith argued for a rational religion, an implicit condemnation of irrational tongues. "I think the central theme of the book we call the Bible, both in the Old Testament and the New Testament in its clarity and reasonableness — its intention is that we understand."[645]

Curiously, Melvin Dieter, the quintessential historian for the American Holiness Movement, disagreed with his friend Timothy Smith. "In my view, the basic theological and experiential commitments of both the Pentecostal and holiness movements are rooted historically in the holiness/higher life revival milieu of the nineteenth century...The same mother gave birth to us both."[646] Grant Wacker says of the Holiness Movement and other radical evangelicals, that they had "consistently urged believers to strive for an ever-deeper walk with Christ. And that is precisely what Pentecostals have claimed to have accomplished. The plain truth is that they beat radical evangelicals at their own game and beat them soundly."[647]

From my perspective, the Holiness Movement was on the defensive while Pentecostalism was on the offensive. Whatever tongues meant on the day of Pentecost, they symbolized the universality of the gospel. Nathan Hatch argues that, "Methodism did not suppress the impulses of popular religion, dreams and visions, ecstasy, unrestrained emotional release, preaching by blacks, by women, by anyone who felt the call."[648] Pentecostal historian David Martin assesses that "Pentecostalism is an extension of Methodism and of the evangelical revivals and Awakenings....In Methodism, one sees the ancient territorial

---

[644] Timothy Smith. *Speaking the Truth in Love: Some Honest Questions for Pentecostals* (Kansas City: Beacon Hill Press, 1977) 28, 29.

[645] Ibid., 42.

[646] Dieter, Melvin E., "The Wesleyan Holiness and Pentecostal Movement: Commonalities, Confrontation and Dialogue," *Pneuma: The Journal of the Society for Pentecostal Studies*, vol. 12, number 1, (Spring 1990) 5, 6.

[647] Grant Wacker, "Evangelical Responses to Pentecostalism," *The Journal of Ecclesiastical History*, Vol. 47, No. 3 (July 1996) 527.

[648] Nathan O. Hatch, "The Puzzle of American Methodism," in *Methodism and the Shaping of American Culture*, eds. Nathan O. Hatch and John H. Wigger (Nashville: Kingswood Books, 2001) 28-29.

emplacements of religion begin to dissolve into fraternal associations, so that Wesley could continually claim, 'The world is my parish.'"[649]

More than any other segment of evangelicalism, Pentecostalism has presided over a parish without boundaries. They have stood on and carried out Christ's promise in Acts 1:8: "But you shall receive power after the Holy Spirit has come upon you, and you will be my witnesses in Jerusalem, Judea, Samaria, and unto the uttermost parts of the earth."

What Happens to Holiness Types When They Step onto the World Stage?

As to those who transcend the holiness ghetto, we focus on two persons who have stepped on to the world's stage, both of them from the same Holiness denomination. Even though they were from the same denomination, they could not have been more unalike. One of them exemplified bravery and the other bravado. This denomination was the most rural, agrarian, and its camp meetings the most emotional of any of the denominations which participated in the Christian Holiness Association. The Churches of Christ in Christian Union came into formal existence September 25, 1909. Some dozen churches came out of the Christian Union which had been created by peace Democrats, "Copperheads," during the Civil War. This loose connection of churches, mostly located in southern Ohio but also Illinois, Iowa, Indiana, and Missouri, did not buy into the increasingly popular entire sanctification language being espoused by Ohio camp meetings such as Hollow Rock, and Camp Sychar. According to official historian Kenneth Brown (with whom this author attended school at two different institutions), the Churches of Christ in Christian Union did not leave the Christian Union but were expelled for the doctrine of "second blessing holiness."

The new denomination eventually located its publishing house, headquarters, and college in Circleville, Ohio. Even more important, Circleville became the home for Mount of Praise Camp Meeting, 1918, which would rival in size and influence any large camp meetings in America. Building a tabernacle to seat 5,000 people, the denomination paraded the holiness greats across its platform: T. M. Anderson, John

---

[649] David Martin. *Pentecostalism: The World Their Parish.* (Malden, Massachusetts: Blackwell Publishers, 2002) 7.

Church, Joseph Smith, Bona Fleming, and John L Brasher. Church told of an occasion when the people shouted the praises of God for over an hour.[650] One attendee described the preacher and his effect on the congregation

> The tabernacle was full, as it was in those days of the early Camp. People were drawn by the mighty demonstrations of the Holy Ghost as he worked in the hearts of men, and that night Brother Ferneau was at his best in the hands of God. Always active on his feet, and especially so when in the Spirit, he was preaching on the mighty merits of Divine grace. My gaze was diverted from the platform for just a brief moment, and when I looked back, I could hear the preacher but for a moment I couldn't see him. I traced the sound of the voice and there was the man of God standing on the braces which held up the roof, having climbed up the support pole without having lost a word. He was clinging on with one hand and gesturing with his free arm while he thundered out the truth from his heart.
>
> I stood there in amazement as he preached on, then, finding another point he wished to present, he slid almost effortlessly down from his perch, never missing a word, and continued to bless the people with his message. Needless to say as this was going on, he was being backed by the shouts of the saints and spiritual pandemonium broke loose. Waves of glory swept over the audience, as God's approval of the message and messenger was registered.[651]

John Maxwell

John Maxwell is the world's foremost motivational speaker. He recently wrote, "Today I look back and see more than one hundred books, selling more than 28 million copies in more than 50 languages."[652] But this is not only Maxwell's assessment. In May 2014, Maxwell was recognized as the "Number One Leadership and Management Expert in the World" by *Inc. Magazine*.[653] His speaking venues are diverse: Fortune

---

[650] Kenneth Brown and P. Lewis Brevard. *History of the Churches of Christ in Christian Union* (Circleville, Ohio: Circle Press, Incorporated, 1980) 167.

[651] Ibid.

[652] John Maxwell. *Developing the Leader within You 2.0* (New York: HarperCollins Leadership, 2018) 115.

[653] "Top 50 Leadership and Management Experts" (http://www.inc.com/jeff-haden/the-top-50-leadership-and-management-experts-mon.html) Inc. Magazine.

500 Companies, The United States Military Academy, The National Football League, The National Agents Leadership Conference, and The Symmetry Financial Group.

Maxwell grew up in the Churches of Christ in Christian Union. He attended Circleville Bible College, a school of approximately 250 students where his father was president. The school enforced the normative holiness mores: no movies, no dancing and conservative dress for women. Maxwell was a competitive athlete, a good student, a congenial personality, charismatic according to one of his former classmates, and, perhaps, a bit cocky. As a favorite son, a scion, Maxwell did not rest on his privileged position. He applied himself, although he was a big fish in a small pond.

With a healthy dose of self-confidence and ambition, Maxwell realized spectacular numerical growth in his second church, Lancaster, Ohio, Churches of Christ in Christian Union, during the 1980s. During this time, the Church Growth Movement led by C. Peter Wagner (discipled by Donald A. McGavran) defined the role of a pastor. Maxwell hit the seminar trail along with other church growth luminaries such as John Wimber and Rick Warren. With his homespun humor, abundant quotes, and narrative style, no one did church growth seminars better than John Maxwell. Between 1981 and 1995, Maxwell pastored Skyline Wesleyan Church in Lemon Grove, California, a suburb of San Diego, a place where he also experienced numerical growth from approximately 1,000 to 3,000 Sunday morning attendance. By 1995, Maxwell was receiving so many opportunities to speak, not only from churches but also corporations, that he resigned his church in San Diego and since then has given himself full-time to motivational speaking.

After reviewing five of his books, I make the following observations. It doesn't seem that Maxwell himself writes the books, as he constantly thanks persons by name, who "write his books." Maybe he gives ideas to his authors who in turn write a book that he authorizes. Whatever, or whoever, Maxwell's books are readable, interesting, and inspiring. He quotes from a wide array of authors: statesmen, athletes, and industrialists, such as Leo Durocher, Henry Ford, William James, Andrew Carnegie, Thomas a Kempis, David Brooks, Lou Holtz, Bill Gates, and Wilt Chamberlain. This list could be multiplied many times over. Maxwell loves to drop names: my friend Rick Warren, my friend Bill Hybels, my friend Jim Whitaker, my friend Kevin Myers, and my friend Andy Stanley. John mostly references industrial and corporate types such as Edward Land, Steve Jobs, Ray Kroc, Bill Gates, T. Boone Pickens, and Jim Sinegal. How many of these stories and people that Maxwell actually dug up is difficult to discern. He states, "I'm always on the lookout for books and quotes that inspire me, keep my head up, and encourage the members of my team."[654] Nonetheless, in most of his books, Maxwell thanks his researchers. Whoever they are, they come up with some riveting material.

At several points, I identify with Maxwell and his auditors. When in college, I sold door-to-door books for Southwestern Book Company, perhaps the most difficult job I ever had. Sales school was important; Clement Stone as well as others were inspiring. They shot us out of the door like locusts on a corn field. Several weeks later I was standing at noon in Fairfield, Alabama, 95 degrees and 95 percent humidity. I forgot everything that had been said in sales school. But I kept knocking on doors, putting calluses on my knuckles, for 12 hours per day. I was stubborn, poor, hungry, and wasn't going to be embarrassed by quitting. The pride of competition kept me going. I wanted to be "successful."

Something else I have in common with Maxwell: Whatever we have accomplished has little to do with talent, drive, perseverance, or ambition. We were born in America. I am not a one-armed beggar on the streets of Calcutta; I am not without education, working in a Kyrgyrstan mine. I was in a Malawi, Africa home, the wife a retired school teacher and the husband had retired from two sequential careers, as a school headmaster and a denominational president of some 250 churches. In their 80s, their entire income was $25.00 per month, without electricity and running water. Maxwell is the perfect example of an outlier, as described by Malcolm Gladwell, born at a certain time, within a certain set of circumstances, with innate abilities or interests to take advantage of those circumstances. Maxwell states, "As I look back on my life, I can see that the best leaders I had used their gifts to bring out the best in me. That started with my father. Not only did he use his gifts of encouragement to inspire me and give me confidence, he also used his

---

[654] Ibid., 41.

relational connections to introduce me to influential leaders and equip me for leadership."[655]

What I don't have in common with Maxwell is his gifts and desires. I don't think I would be able to do what Maxwell does. I do not have the charisma, the platform presence, the organizational skills, the creativity, or whatever. But each of us made different vocational decisions. I decided the most important thing I could do vocationally was to preach the Bible. I have done this in an amazing array of circumstances: an Indian village, a Mongolian ger, a Russian house, on the outside of an African school, an apartment complex in Bangladesh, large camp meetings of 1,500 persons, a church that seats 4,500, small camp meetings of 100 or less, and small churches of 30 or less, in a cemetery and a seminary. My influence has not been close to John Maxwell's, at least quantitatively.

But there are two groups of people almost completely left out of Maxwell's target audience. The first would be intellectual types, such as academics, scientists, script writers, novelists, historians, philosophers, mathematicians, and physicists, who are not prone to listen to motivational speakers. Neither are the poor, who live in eastern Kentucky, Calcutta, India; Dacha, Bangladesh; and Omsk, Siberia. The gospel is universal and transcendent. But do not read this as a condemnation of Maxwell. My roles as administrator, professor, and pastor have often skirted the poor and marginalized. As I have argued in another book, seminary professors often teach abstractions because they live abstracted from the real world.[656]

I identify with Maxwell in that both of us have been given the privilege to be what and who we are. Neither one of us, the same age, have the term "retirement" in our vocabulary. Maxwell states, "When you do something and you think to yourself, 'I was born for this,' you are on the right track."[657] I have often quoted Samuel Chadwick, "I would pay to preach rather than get paid not to preach," which I have actually done. What percentage of people would pay to work rather than get paid not to work.

---

[655] Ibid., 159.

[656] Darius Salter. *Deep and Wide* (Charleston, SC: Create Space, 2012).

[657] John Maxwell, 38.

I became acquainted with Michael, as our daughters played on the same softball team. Mike, a heavy smoker, developed both lung and brain cancer. He sufficiently recovered (but later died) to be able to watch his daughter. I asked him when and if he would return to work. "Oh, you never have to work again with this kind of cancer," he responded with gratitude. The joke was on me. It is easy to forget that not everyone, not even close, likes their job.

In the mid 1980s, Maxwell gave a series of lectures on leadership to his staff at Skyline Wesleyan Church in San Diego. The gist of these lectures became the book, *Be All You Can Be: A Challenge to Stretch to Your God-Given Potential*. In it he states, "Seeking holiness rather than happiness is a hard thing to do in the culture in which we live, because so much is geared to happiness – whatever makes you feel good. In a secular society, happiness is the aim in life."[658] I suppose this generic statement which states nothing of a Wesleyan distinctive could have been written by John Piper or J. I. Packer. Ironically, the secularization that Maxwell references is exactly what he has become. His three most recent books make little mention of Christianity. The exception is *Developing the Leader within You 2.0*. Somewhat apologetically he lists eleven scripture verses; not that he himself had gleaned but referenced by David Kadalie. John states, "Since I am a person of faith, I have discovered wisdom from Scripture....if you don't connect with these thoughts or are offended by them, feel free to skip past them."[659]

In 1985, thirty-eight pastors participated in a church growth conference conducted by John Maxwell. Four years later, I reviewed the track record of all thirty-eight pastors. "Thirteen of the pastors moved. Five of them dropped out of ministry completely because of retirement, frustration, or whatever. Of the twenty remaining, twelve realized no numerical growth or even declined. Among the eight pastors whose churches did grow, only one had a decadal growth of over one hundred percent in morning worship attendance, which church growth analysts assess as excellent."[660] I suspect that these statistics would be

---

[658] John Maxwell. *Be All You Can Be: A Challenge to Stretch to Your God-Given Potential* (Nashville: David C. Cook, 2007) 26.

[659] John Maxwell. *Developing the Leader*..... 51-52.

[660] Darius Salter. *What Really Matters in Ministry* (Grand Rapids: Baker Book House, 1990) 61.

the approximate track record of thirty-eight pastors chosen at random, having attended a Maxwell seminar or not.

The problem with seminars is that the participants expect to fix a long-term problem with a quick-fix solution. And the problem with a John Maxwell seminar is that Maxwell's personality is more important than Maxwell's principles. Or to put it another way, the principles did not make Maxwell, Maxwell made the principles, and you can't take Maxwell with you following the seminar. The individuals who attend Maxwell's seminars and read Maxwell's books are often desperate, desperate to make a living, to fulfill their quota, to demonstrate an impressive bottom line. What I even more suspect, is that they are desperate for God.

Maxwell has become increasingly inclusive or pluralistic in terms of a faith paradigm represented in an given seminar. He has become less unique, at least explicitly, concerning the faith paradigm that nurtured him, equipped him, and launched him into "success." Could we say that 99.0 percent of Maxwell's followers never connect him with his holiness ancestry, much less, are introduced to the concept of entire sanctification? James Hunter states, "Change comes through the random aggregation of individual actions and choices in a free market of options. What matters for the Christian in this approach to culture, is in entering into the market place with the new creation of new cultural goods. The direction and purpose and coherence of cultural creation matters less because in the end, it will be the market that determines what succeeds or fails."[661] In this "market populism," Maxwell as well as many churches has been reduced to what their followers want, not what they need. He is a composite of Benjamin Franklin, Russell Conwell, Norman Vincent Peale, and Joel Osteen, all who had or have a problem with distinguishing between the American dream and entire sanctification. In Maxwell's ironed out, flattened, generic communication, there is no place for the intricacies of second blessing holiness.

Alvin York

On December 13, 1887, a one-room log cabin in the hills of Pall Mall, Tennessee, welcomed what would be the third of eleven children born to William and Mary York. They named the child Alvin

---

[661] Hunter, 30.

Cullum York. This son would go down in history as performing the single greatest American military triumph in infantry battle. On April 18, 1918, York, with the help of three other men captured 132 German soldiers and killed 25 others in the forests of Argonne, France. When General Julian Lindsey asked him how he did it, York responded, "Sir, it is not manpower. A higher power than manpower guided, and watched me and told me what to do."[662]

The early years of York's life showed little promise. Almost all of his free time was given to drinking, fighting, hunting, playing cards, and getting into whatever trouble was available to him which included cheating and stealing other persons' animals. Alvin later recalled, "I am a bettin' you, Sodom and Gomorrah might have been bigger places, but they weren't any worse. Killings were a plenty. They used to say, 'They used to shoot fellas just to see them kick.' Knife fights and shootings were common. Gambling and drinking were commoner. And lots of careless girls jest used to drift in. It sure was tough."[663]

York began to notice a beautiful young lady named Gracie, who attended a local Methodist Church. That her father was named Francis Asbury "Frank" Williams gave notice that this was a serious Methodist family. Under the preaching of a Methodist evangelist, York was converted New Year's Day, 1915. Being discipled by pastor Rosier C. Pyle, "In just a few months, Alvin was transformed from a drunkard, brawler, and mal-content, to a leader in the church, a Sunday School teacher, a choir leader, and a respected man in the community."[664] Almost at the same time, a group of people held a revival and also built a church in Pall Mall, a group who seemed to be more pious, more intense, and more committed to God than the Methodists. The intruders were The Churches of Christ in Christian Union. Pastor Pyle resigned from his Methodist charge, and took Alvin with him to the new church. But remember that this denomination still held on to its pacifistic roots.

Thus, when York was drafted, he legitimately applied for exemption as a conscientious objector, but his appeal was denied. When

---

[662] Douglas V. Mastriano. *Alvin York: A New Biography of the Hero of the Argonne* (Lexington: University of Kentucky Press, 2014) No page number. E-book retrieved from Mid-Continent Public Library, Kansas City, MO, unpaginated.
[663] Ibid.
[664] Ibid.

in boot camp at Camp Gordon, Georgia, York continued to struggle as he was faced with the possibility that he would be sent overseas to take another man's life. He recorded in his diary, "I jes went to that old camp and said nothing, I did everything I was told to do. I never once disobeyed an order. I never once raised my voice in complaint." When on leave at home, March 27-31, 1918, he fasted and prayed for 36 hours and according to him, was visited by the presence of God, filled with a peace that passeth all understanding. "I am going to war with a sword of the Lord and of Gideon. …I have received my assurance. I have received it from God himself…that it is right for me to go to war, and that long as I believe in him, not one hair of my head will be harmed."[665] Coupled with this assurance, was the fact that Alvin York was the most accurate shot with a rifle of anyone in the U.S. Army, if not the entire world. York could take off a turkey's head when the bird bobbed up behind a log 150 yards away. Thus, York was amazed when his fellow soldiers could not hit a hill, much less a target on the hill. "Shooting at squirrels is good, but busting a turkey at 150 yards…ho ho. So the Army shooting was tolerably easy for me."[666] But more importantly than being armed with a gun, York was armed with his Bible.

> I carried a Testament with me. I have the Testament I carried with me during all my fighting at home now. I read it everywhere. I read it in the dugouts, in foxholes, and on the front lines. It was my rock to cling to. I didn't do no cursing, no, not even in the front line. I cut all of that out long ago, at the time I was saved.[667]

In October of 1918, York found himself in the 82nd Infantry Division, Company G, 2nd Battalion, 328 Infantry, just outside of Chatel Chehery, France. He was on the front lines of the Meuse-Argonne offensive, the largest and most strategic land invasion of World War I. Immediately, 6 of York's 17 member platoon were killed, and 3 others wounded. Instinctively, York charged, rifle in one hand and pistol in the other, the German machine gun nest, and killed 19 German soldiers. While lying on the ground, York was immediately joined by Private Percy Beardsley; both using their pistols killed 8 more Germans, and there were now 25 enemy dead. The German commander, Paul Volmer,

---

[665] Ibid.

[666] R. G. Humble. *Sergeant Alvin C. York: A Christian Patriot* (Circleville, Ohio: Churches of Christ in Christian Union, 1966) 24.

[667] Ibid., 27.

wanting to save his wounded friend lying near York, Fritz Engress, surrendered the rest of his regiment, 132 men. Upon being reunited with General Lindsey, York's Commander, exclaimed most possibly the most famous words of World War I: "Well, York, I hear you have captured the whole damn German army."[668]

York was given a ticker-tape parade in New York, and after endless dinners and speeches where he was definitively out of his element, couldn't wait to get back to Pall Mall. He said no to countless possibilities for making money from his new found fame. In 1922, a preacher wrote him, "I have noticed in the papers you have refused offers of large sums of money to connect with the entertainment world. I believe you are making a terrible mistake by turning down these opportunities to get big and easy money. You owe it to yourself and to your family to get all the money you can."[669] But York had an aversion to money, publicity, and honors. Whenever he saw a stranger walking, York picked him up. On one occasion his wife Gracie asked, "Are you going to let that man put his muddy feet in your nice, clean car?" "I surely am," replied her husband.[670]

He repeatedly turned down a request to make a movie about his life, but finally yielded to Jesse Laskey, with the rationale "The story of his life would arouse Americans to a patriotic stance against Hitler, promoting the cause of York and like-minded citizens, who refused to sit by and let the Nazis devour Europe."[671] One of the problems with the movie negotiations was that York would often slip off without notice as to when or where. When Laskey trailed the war hero to his hotel room at the Hermitage in Nashville, he found York on his knees beside his bed. When Laskey introduced Gary Cooper to Alvin York, he realized he had introduced the two most non-communicative men in all of his life. "If we would have had Calvin Coolidge there, it would have been 3-ring wake."[672]

---

[668] Mastriano, no page.

[669] Perry John. *Sgt. York: His Life, Legend and Legacy* (Nashville: B. and H, Publishing, 1997) No page number. E-book retrieved online from Mid-Continent Public Library, Kansas City, MO, unpaginated.

[670] Ibid.

[671] Ibid.

[672] Ibid.

Making *Sergeant York* ran into a real problem when Asbury Williams, Gracie's father, would not allow his name to be associated with a movie. "Four rich and successful Hollywood writers found themselves boxed in a corner by a frail old dirt farmer, who had never seen a movie and never would. Eventually, they solved their problem by rewriting the character as a fictional uncle."[673] The production company shot 201,616 feet of film at a cost of $1,399,000. Cooper won the best actor Academy Award, beating Orson Wells for his role in *Citizen Kane*. When accepting the Oscar, Cooper stated, "It wasn't Gary Cooper who won this award. It was Sgt. York. Because to the best of my ability, I tried to be Sgt. York."[674]

The movie is weak at several points. The writers and directors demonstrated no comprehension of the convulsive, revivalistic, and transformative nature of York's conversion. Watching the movie leads one to believe that York's pacifistic convictions were from his personal reading of the Bible. The Churches of Christ in Christian Union is completely bypassed, much less any perfectionistic theology which may have influenced York's obedience to both God and his superior officers. Dilution is the trademark of Hollywood, especially if the movie is a propaganda production for patriotism in the face of Nazi Germany. A simplistic message is the only communication that will work.

York received $134,000 in royalties, spending it all on his Bible School and Agricultural Institute which he founded. One of his biographers was no doubt correct when he claimed that York lived the same way he had for the past twenty years on his bottom-land farm in Pall Mall. "He rose early, dressed in khaki work pants, khaki shirt, necktie, and hat."[675] He defended the equality of a black man who put on a military uniform. "The most of us, colored and white, know and are proud that our country was built up by both races, and belongs to us all. Shoulder to shoulder, we've spilled our blood wherever America was threatened. This be a tie no lie can cut."[676]

Alvin York's last days were not pleasant. He owed $72,000 in back taxes; his son, Woodrow, went AWOL from the army; Alvin, Jr. spent months in the Montgomery, Alabama, penitentiary for selling

---

[673] Ibid.
[674] Ibid.
[675] Ibid.
[676] Ibid.

moonshine.[677] These events, a steady stream of writing and speaking, 275 lbs. of obesity and erratic blood pressure, led to a cerebral hemorrhage February 24, 1954. For the next 10 years, York remained mostly a bed-fast invalid. When he received notice that the government had reduced his tax bill to $24,000, he settled into his sheets with "We sure appreciate everything these fine people have done for us and are doing. You know this is a great country."[678]

York died on September 2, 1964. Eight thousand people attended his funeral in tiny Pall Mall, Tennessee. His net worth at the time of death was $5,000. In 1972, the youngest son, Thomas, as a Fentress County, Tennessee constable, was killed in a shootout with a prisoner. York's wife, Gracie, died at the age of 84, in 1984. The remaining son, George E. York, became a minister in the Church of the Nazarene. George passed away January 17, 2018.

Alvin York spoke at God's Bible School where his son George was a student, and attended its summer camp meeting.[679] He had his picture taken with William Jennings Bryan and Henry Clay Morrison at Asbury College. Thus being a leader in the Churches of Christ in Christian Union and exposed to the leadership of Asbury College and God's Bible School, York would have been indoctrinated with the Wesleyan theology of entire sanctification. As far as we know, he never gave testimony to such an experience. Seemingly, when one steps on the world's stage, testimony to entire sanctification gets left behind. But it does seem that York lived a life of holiness. John Maxwell makes no mention of York in any of his books.

---

[677] Ibid.

[678] Ibid.

[679] Larry D. Smith, "Sergeant Alvin C. York: Christian Hero of World War I," *God's Revivalist and Bible Advocate* (November 2018) 8-9.

Chapter 9:
The Self

Entire Sectarianism and Totalism

The preaching of entire sanctification came together in methodology, theology, and epistemology. Methodist preaching called for instantaneous results which included instantaneous entire sanctification as immediately knowable, a knowledge validated by the "witness of the Spirit," and further fortified by Baconian empiricism and Scottish common sense realism. Spiritual utopianism, industrial progress, technological innovation, and nationalistic celebration all found their confluence in the National Camp Meeting Association for the Promotion of Holiness established in 1867. The country, in particular the North, had survived its greatest crisis, and was liberated to relentlessly pursue both individual and corporate fulfillment. As Lincoln proclaimed, it was a "new birth of freedom."

Is it possible to be too optimistic, and too certain, until assurance becomes pride, knowledge turns into parochialism, love becomes exceptionalism and success turns into contempt? In their self-understanding, the Association founders John Inskip, Alfred Cookman, George Hughes, and William McDonald were pure in their motives to start an effort that would have as its stated purpose the pursuit of holiness. It was a progressive initiative, and although almost totally Methodist in leadership, open to all other sects and theological persuasions. It was John Inskip who had been brought to trial by the Methodist Episcopal Church because he allowed mixed seating in worship between the sexes. These men were not backward in any sense of the word. They were steeped in the social sensitivities and catholic spirit of the Wesleys.

But a cannon became unbolted in the hull of the Methodist ship. After the excitement of thousands gathering for a holiness camp meeting, with its spiritual intensity enhanced by a crowd mentality and its contagious enthusiasm, these same people returned to the quotidian mundaneness of an institutional Methodist Church exhibiting moribund tendencies. The Methodist camp meeting leadership attempted to corral the loose cannon of "comeoutism," but the damage had already been done. As late as 1916, National Camp Meeting president Charles Fowler estimated that ninety-five percent of its membership was Methodist.[680] But the exodus stampede had already started. The issue came to a head in the May 1885 National Holiness Assembly Meeting in Chicago. When a "come outer" attempted a filibuster, he had to be sung down and when that did not work, he was physically removed from the church.[681] Sectarian proliferation is always messy.

As the Holiness Movement entered into the twentieth century, and detached itself from not only the teachings of Wesley but the vision of such urbanites as the Palmers and Inskips, it developed its own esoteric interpretation of Scripture, codified its ethics, specialized in a theology peculiar to its sectarian identity, and adopted a separatism which appealed to persons psychologically needing a religion of "totalism." The following from Erik Erikson is helpful in understanding the Holiness Movement and its demise.

> As a Gestalt, then, wholeness emphasizes a sound, organic, progressive mutuality between diversified functions and parts within an entirety, the boundaries of which are open and fluid. Totality, on the contrary, evokes a Gestalt in which an absolute boundry is emphasized; given a certain arbitrary delineation, nothing that belongs inside must be left outside, nothing that must be outside can be tolerated inside.[682]

An ideology that provided certitude proved to be both a bane and a blessing. Holiness churches for the most part did not enjoy a mutuality and reciprocity with other denominations. Their ethics were arbitrary because of cultic leadership that offered misguided and wrong-headed interpretations of such Scripture passages as Peter's "Your beauty should

---

[680] Kenneth O. Brown. *Inskip, McDonald, Fowler: "Wholly And Forever Thine"* (Hazelton, PA: Holiness Archives, 1999) 110.

[681] Ibid., 107.

[682] Erik Erikson. *Identity: Youth and Crisis* (New York: W.W. Norton & Company, 1968) 81.

not come from the wearing of gold jewelry" (I Peter 3:3). Low and brittle toleration translated into an exclusive sectarianism very unlike the clientele that gathered in Phoebe Palmer's parlor or the urbanites who escaped into the forest temple. Developments in the early twentieth century only intensified the other worldliness of the Holiness Movement and prioritized the building of escape tunnels from society rather than bridges for Christianizing "Godless institutions." The following concerning the Church of the Nazarene characterized most if not all holiness denominations.

> They observed a heightened sense of tragedy following the First World War and associated modernism with German historical criticism and philosophy in general. They feared further upheaval from Bolshevism, atheism, and world revolution. Their piety and pessimism outweighed social concern. Fear colored the whole sphere of sociological change. Many Holiness people, like other Americans, became caught up in the view that there was some plot working against the premises and morals of Christianity. The sources of these fears were foreignism, biblical criticism, modernism, Darwinism, Christian Scientism, evolutionism, atheism, and Communism.[683]

Arbitrary delineations and rigid ethics made re-entry for a young person who left home for a liberal arts education almost impossible. Holiness no longer stood for a glorious attribute of God and the gracious activity of grace in the lives of sinners, but a rundown trodden few, meeting in a clapboard building with a sign, "Holiness Church" over the front door. No problem for the insiders who proof texted their existence with "come out from them and be separate" (II Cor: 6:17). And then, there was the rather unfortunate rendering of *peripotesis*, as a "peculiar" people rather than a "special" people. The context is that of being highly favored, "showing the praises of Him who has called you out of darkness into His marvelous light" (I Peter 2:9). This holiness was often left without a winsomeness, so aptly described by Bishop Stephen Neill, as he stood before the World Council of Churches in 1939:

> Most educated men in the world to-day have some knowledge of the Gospels, and some mental picture of the character of Jesus. They realize, perhaps better than many professing Christians, that the only true criterion of

---

[683] *Our Watchword and Song*, 185.

Christianity is likeness to Christ. The heart of their complaint, though perhaps they would be hard put to frame it in words, is that they do not see in Christianity and in the Church that likeness to Christ which they have a right to expect. Real holiness is impressive and attractive; if the Church has failed to hold the respect of the ordinary man, may the cause not be, in part at least, that the children of the Church have failed to set before the world the challenge of unmistakable holiness after the manner of Christ.[684]

A Rigid Ethical Code

Of course sectarianism normally produces further sectarianism, especially if ethics and theology are grounded in cultic rather than sound biblical interpretation. This has been particularly true of the Holiness Movement. Wallace Thornton has explicated the rationale for a dozen or so denominations that have come out of the mainline holiness denominations over the last half of the twentieth century. Taboos against movies, music, wedding rings, television, dancing, and a catalogue of dress regulations for women have propelled these denominations into existence. Thornton is correct in that John Wesley's rationale for plain dress had more to do with stewardship than biblical literalism. But Thornton does not show that stewardship has been evidenced in the lives of those who do not own a television or women who do not cut their hair. In other words, do individuals who display holiness via odd dress give more and go more? Are they more likely to double tithe, spend time in an inner-city mission, be informed concerning the world's refugee crisis, or even spend time in a refugee camp? If not, one may be tempted to title Thornton's book, *Superficial Righteousness* rather than *Radical Righteousness.*[685]

Separatism for separatism's sake locates these groups on a much different ethical platform than that of John Wesley or John Inskip. The National Camp Meeting Association both infiltrated and invited other denominations, and present-day Pentecostalism has leaped across almost all sectarian boundaries. Not so for ethical stances which cause

---

[684] Quoted in John L. Peters. *Christian Perfection and American Methodism* (Grand Rapids: Francis Asbury Press of Zondervan Publishing House, 1985) 198.

[685] Wallace Thornton. *Radical Righteousness: Personal Ethics and The Development of the Holiness Movement* (Salem, OH: Schmul Publishing Company, 1998).

people to stare rather than hunger and thirst after righteousness. I suspect that many of these "conservative holiness practitioners" home school, which almost automatically precludes their children becoming medical doctors, astrophysicists, actuaries, neuroscientists, and a range of other intellectual endeavors now left for pagan secularists to monopolize. Even more critical is for a child to be instilled with the courage and social skills to combat the world and not exemplify Jesus' observation that the "people of the world are more shrewd in dealing than are the people of the light" (Luke 16:8). To put it another way, what happens in the lunch room or on the play ground is equally as important as to what happens in the classroom.

Entering into this external ethical code makes it impossible to be more concerned about what God thinks than what others think. The uniqueness of whom God has created the individual to be gets lost in an unhealthy mix. Molding likeness to one another rather than likeness to God does not eliminate jealousy, envy and pettiness, not to mention the time and energy given to such conformity. Doing God's will often gets confused with doing the group's will, eliminating the possibility for healthy self differentiation. According to Edwin Friedman, healthy differentiation "includes the capacity to maintain a (relatively) non-anxious presence in the midst of anxious systems, to take maximum responsibility for one's own destiny and emotional being."[686]

Of course, to take the above path often brings group disdain, leading to undeserved guilt. This may be part of the reason for the inability of such conformity groups to hang on to a John Maxwell or other maverick kinds of personalities, who possess the kind of individualistic qualities essential for leadership. The secret to all good leadership is not to copy the leader, but to enable followers to develop their full potential in Jesus Christ. In Friedman's words, "A leader (parent or spiritual) who is simply out to replicate his or her followers, as successful as the outcomes might appear, would be like a god who clones his or her image."[687] The following from David Debord precisely identifies the inherent problem with high conformity religious groups:

---

[686] Edwin Friedman. *Generation to Generation: Family Process in Church and Synagogue* (New York: The Gilford Press, 1985) 27.
[687] Ibid., 233.

In intensely anxious relationship systems, the pseudo-self is more vulnerable to being molded or changed by others. It can sacrifice itself for the sake of group cohesion. When the psuedo-self is dominant in the self-system, the distinction between self-concerns and group concerns is blurred. One's relationship with oneself is less appropriate because the pseudo-self is fused with the relationship system. Self-regard is highly influenced by the regard of others. There is less self-determined thought and behavior.[688]

Grounding ethics in a code dictated by an institution detached from a maturing, personal philosophy and understanding, is psychologically and spiritually unhealthy. Thornton is exactly right in that bourgeoisieism and modernity are problems. But dictating a code of ethics with little understanding of what is at stake often leads to internal conflict and unnecessary guilt. Christian character should have almost nothing to do with a list of written "do nots," but personal convictions instilled and motivated by the expulsive power of a new affection. I challenged my students to name any television show that I have ever watched, (which is difficult to do, and I take more pride in this than I should) because I consider television on the whole as inane, vacuous, and a complete waste of time. I have never purchased a lottery ticket, not because of an institutional prohibition, but because I believe life is a matter of grace, not chance. Any married person who does not wear a wedding ring should read *The Jeweler's Shop* by Pope John Paul II (Karol Jozef Wojtyla). In regard to movies, I think that every American should watch *Schindler's List, Saving Private Ryan*, not to speak of *The Passion of the Christ*. I smile when I think about how much my holiness mother, still with all the legalistic and external indicators that she was a holiness person (hair up and no makeup), enjoyed watching *Driving Miss Daisy*.

One might refer to these "radical" holiness groups as soft monasticism, a legitimate and serious effort to combat the world, what Richard Niebuhr referred to as "Christ against culture." Constantinian corruption has always nipped at the heels of Christianity, the constant dilemma of trying to convert the world without falling over into it. Thomas Merton claimed that the prayer life of Monasticism provided the

---

[688] David Debord. *A Pastoral Theological Reconstruction of Self-Regard, Self-Sacrifice, and Sanctification in the Wesleyan-Holiness Tradition* (unpublished Ph.D.dissertation, The Iliff School of Theology, 1997) 158.

real "capital" of society, and that prayer is a more positive force for good that powerful politics.[689] For this argument to bear merit for conservative holiness groups, one has to rightfully assume that they are interceding for the world in a manner beyond the nostalgic longing for the world-transforming revival that never comes. Robert Putnam would argue that these separatist groups do not effect societal change because they are without "social capital." Putnam states, "The difference is that 'social capital' calls attention to the fact that civic virtue is most powerful when embedded in a dense network of reciprocal social relations. A society of many virtuous but isolated individuals is not necessarily rich in social capital."[690] On the positive side, "Faith communities in which people worship together honorably are the single most important repository of social capital in America."[691] However, this can only be true if a given group is more concerned about crossing boundaries than creating them. Putnam quotes Wade Roof Clark, "Conservative religious energies are channeled in the direction of recovery of faith *within* the religious tradition and of reaffirmation of religious and life-style boundaries within the dominant culture."[692] Legalistic holiness groups are not all that concerned with issues beyond those boundaries.

One year after writing *Radical Righteousness,* Thornton reassessed the conservative Holiness Movement with the question, *Holiness or Hubris?*[693] In this essay, he accused the external standards denominations of the same kind of power plays, leadership quests, and materialistic prestige that are exhibited by other church groups or even secular organizations. The desire for respectability has eroded a desire for heart purity: "By focusing on human leadership, personality, and talents, perpetrators of hubris within the Holiness Movement moved the focus from God to man."[694]

---

[689] See Monica Furlong. *Merton: A Biography* (San Francisco: Harper and Row Publishers, 1980) 105.

[690] Robert Putnam. *Bowling Alone: The Collapse and Revival of American Community* (New York: Simon & Schuster Paperbacks, 2000) 19.

[691] Ibid., 66.

[692] Ibid., 77.

[693] Wallace Thornton. *A Response to Keith Drury's "The Holiness Movement is Dead,"* (Somerset, KY: Self-published, 1999).

[694] Ibid., 15.

Thornton's commentary begs the question that he never asks, thus does not answer, "Does conformity to observable standards of dress and entertainment engender pride or mitigate pride?" Do the Amish have less temptation to pride than Presbyterians? Possibly all of us have discovered that hubris cannot be overcome by a code of conduct. While heart purity guarantees some outward manifestations, right conduct in matters both great and small may simply be a camouflage for much more serious issues. As has been said, legalism is an emphasis on minor laws that can be kept at the expense of major sins to which we are enslaved. Oswald Chambers wrote, "Concern for our personal holiness causes us to focus our eyes on ourselves and we become overly concerned about the way we walk and talk and look out of fear of offending God."[695] And I would add "others," in unhealthy and unnecessary ways. Unfortunately, the attempt to be holy by many holiness conservatives, has been reduced to self-preoccupation which eventuates into a "paint by the numbers" self-righteousness. I have a soft spot in my heart for these folk because they are my heritage. Kenneth Collins analyzes the legalism of these dear people:

> Moreover, with its heightened emphasis on separation from the "other," holiness religion may end up glorifying a particular social and cultural ethos—which is actually the reflection of its own social location. Soon the taboos are trotted out, disciplines are packed with strictures, and legalism continues apace. In this phase, some folk may even begin to conclude that they are "holy" precisely because all the taboos, are kept. In the worst cases, some unfortunates will begin to enjoy, even to relish, the spiritual distance between them and their neighbors, those for whom Christ died.[696]

I visited with Melvin Dieter two months before he died. To the question as to why the holiness movement had died, he immediately answered, "formalism." By formalism he meant legalism, the outward form of religion. He told how his parents, leaders in the Pilgrim Holiness Church, had been condemned by other church members because they purchased a snowsuit for his youngest sister. The snowsuit equated to a

---

[695] Oswald Chambers. *My Utmost for His Highest* (Grand Rapids: Oswald Chambers Publications, 1982) February 21.

[696] Kenneth J. Collins. "Why The Holiness Movement is Dead," *Counterpoint: Dialogue with Drury on the Holiness Movement*, ed. D. Curtis Hale (Salem, OH: Schmul Publishing Company, 2005) 67.

girl wearing "pants." Accordingly to Wesleyan District Superintendent, Daniel LeRoy, a contention broke out between the Emmanuel Holiness Church and the Immanuel Church, both in Colorado, about the number of eyelets in a woman's shoe.[697] Of course it always takes another rule to cover a rule, which is why there are 1,000 pages of rules in the *Mishnah*, the oral law of the Pharisees accumulated between 200 B.C. and 200 A.D., a religion of rules Jesus condemned. David Brooks observes that "the hard part of intellectual life is separating what is true from what will get you liked." This is particularly true of the religious life. In the cultic community, approval comes from conformity. When one steps out of said community, the conformist has to immediately adopt the persona of non-conformity. The transition is physically, psychologically, and spiritually challenging, like the quick change artistry of Superman in a phone booth. In order to accommodate one's immediate surroundings, the past is often blocked out, resulting in the psyche inadequately responding to both the past and the present. Part of this tension is healthy, but much of it is played out in neurotic behavior, needing both spiritual healing and possibly psychotherapy.[698]

Negotiating the Healthy Self for Holiness Types

To say that the present generation has no taste for holiness, or no appreciation for the entire sanctification formula, or are turning to other religious paradigms for spiritual nourishment, does not demonstrate that Millennials, Generation Xers, and Baby Boomers are less spiritually inclined than their ancestors. For whatever reason, they have not found the same meaning in Wesleyan holiness or American holiness, which was preached and promised by their parents or grandparents. As to what gives a person meaning is a question with no completely satisfying answer. Though I am not a determinist, experience and observation have verified for me (a subjective statement), that when one traces either virtuous or deviant behavior, the backward look makes sense. But that is only in hindsight. No one could have predicted that Theodore Roosevelt would have assailed San Juan Hill and paddled himself up the

---

[697] Daniel E. LeRoy. *Rediscovering Our Holiness Heritage: How The Wesleyan Church Can Get Back What We Gave Away* (Kernersville, NC: Old Blue Truck Publishing Company, 2018) 57.

[698] David Brooks. *The Second Mountain: The Quest for a Moral Life* (New York: Random House, 2019) 197.

River of Doubt. His one sibling was Elliott, father of Eleanor, a lady who would retain the family name. According to H. W. Brands, "He loved her (Eleanor's mother, Anna) madly but badly, being addicted to alcohol and becoming addicted to the opiates he ingested for pain following the riding accident which shattered his leg....He squandered what remained of his fortune and got a girl pregnant; she threatened a public scandal and had to be bought off by Theodore and the family....Elliott's end came soon enough. Seized by a fit of delirious tremors, he thrashed about uncontrollably, tried to leap out of a window, sweated and foamed, and finally collapsed in a fatal heart attack."[699]

Maybe the same demons drove both Theodore and Elliott, just in different directions. Eleanor would marry someone who unimaginably became more famous than her uncle: the crippled President, the Great Depression President, the World War II President, and America's longest serving President. My mother said she cried when she heard FDR had died. During the war years, his blood pressure had been as high as 240/130, which is probably the reason he died of a cerebral hemorrhage.[700] Why and how he kept going, only God knows. I hope we both make it to Heaven. I would like to meet him, probably without the cigarette in its holder, firmly gripped between his teeth and certainly without the wheelchair or braces.

As my wife asked, "What does this have to do with entire sanctification?" That's just it. Nothing! Entire sanctification as a second work of grace is a niche theology. The disconnect between our theology and the egos described above is not definable, much less bridgeable. David Brooks stresses that we need to be more concerned about the eulogy self than the resume self. We really would like to be the eulogy self, brave, honest, humble, helpful, etc. But our meritocratic society swallows us up and Brooks confesses, "In the process, you end up slowly turning yourself into something a little less impressive than you had originally hoped. A humiliating gap opens up between your actual self and your desired self."[701]

---

[699] H. W. Brands. *Traitor to His Class: The Privileged Life and Radical Presidency of Franklin Delano Roosevelt* (New York: Anchor Books, 2008) 33-36.

[700] Doris Kearns Goodwin. *No Ordinary Time: Franklin and Eleanor Roosevelt: The Home Front in World War II* (New York: Simon and Schuster, 1994) 545.

[701] David Brooks. *The Road to Character* (New York: Random House, 2016) xiv.

Between 1979 and 1983, I completed a Ph.D. in Psychology and Religion, hopefully giving me the opportunity to teach Pastoral Theology. Along the way I became an Eriksonian disciple, though I never met Erik Erikson, whom *Newsweek* magazine called "America's true intellectual." His Eight Stages of Development, from my perspective, offer a plausible explanation as to how or why a person attains meaning, or why not. For Erikson, none of the stages are perfectly negotiated, and neither are they finally negotiated; the triumphs or defeats of each stage are carried to the next until the end of life. This process Erikson labeled, "Epigenetic Development."

We are not going to travel through all eight stages, but I believe all eight could be applied to the Holiness Movement or to individuals within the Holiness Movement. The first stage is "trust versus mistrust," raising the most basic question in life: can my world be trusted? Is it loving, caring, consistent, coherent, dependable, and present for my most basic physical and psychological needs. Concerning trust, Erikson states,

> All religions have in common the periodical, child-like surrender to a provider, or providers, who dispense earthly fortune as well as spiritual health.... and finally, the insight that individual trust must become a common faith, individual mistrust a commonly formulated evil, while the individual's restoration must become part of the ritual practice of many, and must become a sign of trustworthiness in the community.[702]

I suspect that for many in the Holiness Movement, this stage represented a mixed beginning. I trusted the people in our little Pilgrim Holiness Church. They were the real deal. They were fervently consistent, always in church with the lively rituals of loud singing, loud preaching, and loud praying all at one time while kneeling on a concrete floor. The Baptists and Methodists were "dead." We were alive. But that perception flipped the coin. The world was a bad place. Endure to the end, and if one remained uncontaminated, the "Rapture" would provide rescue. Of course all of this cultivated pride and a critical spirit. And though we were the church of rejects and rejection, there was little opposition from the surrounding community. They hardly knew we were there. Because

---

[702] Erik H. Erikson. *Childhood and Society* (New York: W. W. Norton & Company, Inc., 1978) 250.

of this negativism, any possibility for the church to have a positive impact or reach the community evangelistically was erased.

Especially troublesome was the second stage, "autonomy versus shame." Erikson wrote, "As his environment encourages him to stand on his own two feet, it must protect his meaningless and arbitrary experience of shame and of early doubt."[703] Arbitrary! When my mother was converted, having been a very fashionable dresser at least before marriage, she shed her makeup, took off her wedding band, and took on a hairdo that demanded far more attention than her previous hair style. Of course, there was a complete wardrobe overhaul.

The Holiness Movement in which I was raised was characterized by arbitrariness, banality, conformity, and unfortunately shame - anything but autonomy. When I was in the fifth grade (again allow me to remind you in a public school), each child was responsible for morning devotions. My mom wrote mine out, three pages with small handwriting. I can remember only one or two of the main points: "Jezebel wore makeup and she was going to Hell. Take warning!" A heavy jeremiad for a fifth grader to proclaim. This stage lingered for a long time, and spun many out of the Holiness Movement. At the heart of the problem was a tormenting and irreconcilable dualism. One was called to radical conformity on the inside while trying not to conform to the world on the outside, which resulted in a cultic compliance. This transition was especially difficult for women, many of whom looked for other spiritual options.

I find Erikson's fifth stage particularly relevant: "Identity versus Role Confusion." He stated, "The sense of ego identity then is the accrued confidence that the inner sameness and continuity prepared in the past, are matched by the sameness and continuity of one's meaning for others as evidenced in the tangible promise of 'a career.'"[704] Two parts of the identity issue find resonance in both my academic pursuit and spiritual experience. As I pored through the issues of the *Guide to Christian Perfection, Guide to Holiness*, worked my way through the Thomas Upham corpus, read (I think) every book written by Phoebe Palmer and devoured as much of Wesley as possible, it struck me that the same

---

[703] Ibid., 252.
[704] Ibid., 261.

questions that face holiness exponents today were formulated in the very beginning of the movement: Progressive or instantaneous? Take it by faith or wait for the witness of the Spirit? Wesleyan or American? Sinful or sinless? Expect it now or expect it at death? Proclaim it to everybody or just to those whom the preacher believes to be ready? Preach it often or preach it rarely? Testify to it, or do not testify to it?

And as to the role one was to play in society, two issues arose, one more trivial than the other. First, the trivial. I could never get saved because I could not believe. I could not believe because I was disobedient. I wore shorts in order to play basketball, and I was serious about basketball; six hours a day, seven days a week serious - the only freshman to make varsity (a small high school of 125). Samuel Powell, professor of Philosophy and Religion at Point Loma University, adroitly states, "In its most emaciated form, holiness becomes synonymous with conformity to certain behavioral standards, whose specificity increases in proportion to their banality."[705]

But the role confusion became more serious when I returned to Bible school the summer after selling books door to door. Women had come to the door scantily dressed. I lusted and lied. I did not tell the full truth about the dictionary I was selling. Was I the only one working for The Southwestern Company that knew Webster's Collegiate had 144,000 entries, and my Webster's edition carried only 100,000 entries? I sold with a crew from the University of North Carolina. Their world and the world at Kentucky Mountain Bible Institute were on different planets. I was caught in a severe identity crisis between the two which produced irresolvable guilt and depression. (Erikson's third stage is Initiative versus Guilt.)

Let's return to Erikson's phrase, "the tangible promise of a career." This career was defined as the "call of God," a linear concept that visualized or prophesied a particular place or occupation for the rest of one's life. For some, Burundi, Africa, or Calcutta, India, worked out and for others, it did not. For those that it did not, there needed to be

---

[705] Samuel M. Powell, "A Contribution to a Wesleyan Understanding of Holiness and Community," in *Embodied Holiness: Toward a Corporate Theology of Spiritual Growth*, eds. Samuel M. Powell and Michael Lodahl (Downers Grove, IL: InterVarsity Press, 1999) 167.

theological redefinition or tortured rationalization. The former was far more helpful than the latter.

For me personally, Erikson's seventh stage "Generativity versus Stagnation" presents a much brighter picture, at least as I think about my parents. They gave me the greatest gifts of life: their character, integrity, faithfulness to their task in life, perseverance, a vision that aspired for their children, to something better than what had been given them. Many teachers gave of themselves; those gifts that a child takes for granted and prizes only in retrospect, especially those faculty and staff at Mount Carmel High School and Kentucky Mountain Bible Institute who worked without salary, living by faith (unimaginable), people of prayer, and a passionate pursuit of God. According to Erikson, "Generativity then is primarily the concern in establishing, and in guiding the next generation, although there are individuals who through misfortune, or because of special and genuine gifts in other directions, do not apply this drive to their own offspring."[706] My parents gave me generously of their time. I myself have not suffered any misfortune, neither have I had any specific calling or obligations enabled by extraordinary gifts that have prevented me from spending generous time with my four daughters. This investment has never been a sacrifice because I consider it life's greatest privilege.

The Aspirational Self

Who can blame a mother for wanting her children to do well? No one, at least in the case of James and John, whose mother beseeched Jesus for a cabinet post, upon his ascension to the throne; quite a legitimate desire in a world of brokerage, patronage, and class stratification. We should temper our condemnation by reminding ourselves that for this family, economic security and political status had to be obtained without resume and academic degrees. We no less position ourselves today, working with the illusion or deception that our means for getting ahead are less crass, more righteous, or at least more legitimate than the unvarnished, unveiled advocacy of a mother who wanted to make sure that her "sons of thunder" would not waste their gifts as "hewers of wood and drawers of water."

---

[706] Erikson, 267.

Had the mother of James and John been "entirely sanctified" she would have simply put the matter in God's hands, which seemingly she did, but would not have been so forthright or proactive about the matter. Perhaps she could have been sanctified and deceptive at the same time had she researched Rebecca whose subterfuge obtained the blessing for her youngest son. If James and John's mother had been more surreptitious, her intercession would have not exposed her to the harsh criticism of thousands of Sunday School teachers who contrasted the unbridled and carnal ambitions of an overly ambitious mother with the kingdom of God, which needs neither a secretary of war nor a secretary of state.

To visualize ourselves as anything other than the mother of James and John or any less intentional about the welfare of ourselves and those dearest to us, is to be unwilling to sort through our motives, or completely deny self-seeking inherent to the human condition. And to believe that there is some kind of instantaneous work of grace that erases concern for prospering in a dog eat dog world is to ironically interpret holiness as dishonesty rather than humility. Is there a contradiction between wanting to be a self that matters and true holiness? Does holiness lessen the need for validation or just help me to be a bit more subtle about the matter? Not so subtle are the marriage announcements in the *New York Times* as described by David Brooks, where you can almost feel the force of the SAT scores, "It's Dartmouth marries Berkeley, M.B.A. weds Ph.D., Fulbright hitches with Rhodes, Lazard Freres joins with CBS, and summa cum laude embraces summa cum laude. (You rarely see a summa settling for a magna - the tension in such a marriage would be too great.) The *Times* emphasizes four things about a person - college degrees, graduate degrees, career path, and parents' profession - for these are the markers of upscale Americans today."[707]

These "upscale" Americans Elizabeth Currid-Halkett identified as the "aspirational class," people practicing inconspicuous consumption rather than conspicuous consumption. Since conspicuous consumption is available to most Americans through the democratization of goods by the behemoth Wal-Mart, the aspirational class is identified by yoga, violin lessons, organic foods, breastfeeding, and sending their children

---

[707] David Brooks. *Bobos in Paradise: The New Upper Class and How They Got There* (New York: Simon and Schuster, 2000) 14.

to Harvard. This upper ten percent of society snubs their nose at the crass materialism of the middle class, in that it has discovered superior values, a self-awareness that does not belong to those who barely make the payments for their cell phones, big screen TVs and BMWs. For these educational elite, the self is defined by social capital and consumption which "creates class lines that are more stratifying than conventional goods."[708] This high degree of self-consciousness and self-definition is characterized by "knowledge and a value system acquired through extensive acquisition of knowledge — and an aspiration to achieve a higher cultural and social way of being in a nonchalant worldliness about books, news, events, and so forth."[709] The chasm between holiness folk, often uneducated and overweight, and the wine-sipping, NPR-listening, and *New Yorker* reading, aspirational elite is unbridgeable.

The Christian Self

Robert C. Roberts, psychologist at Wheaton, attempted to define a Christian self: "A *psychology* is necessarily about the self, its health, its formation, and its relationships, but in a Christian psychology the stress will be less on what the self thinks or feels about itself and more on what it thinks and feels about others, God and the neighbor."[710] Roberts does not imply the optimism of cruciform theology, a complete sacrifice of the self for the welfare of others; self-denial is only in degree. Roberts claims "The mature Christian has a clear emotional recognition that the desperate desire to be admired for being outstanding is really a perversion of the desire to be loved."[711] This mature Christianity "liberates us from the spirituality of the jungle by removing from competition the issue of our survival. By ensuring that the stakes are never ultimate, the gospel lightens the competition; it makes possible the playful mood proper to 'sport.'"[712] Robert's interpretation of the self may work on the rational level, but does not seem to work on the emotive level. Why was I so emotionally attached to my children when they were at the plate or shooting a foul shot when the game was on the line? My gut tightened

---

[708] Elizabeth Currid-Halkett. *The Sum of Small Things: A Theory of the Aspirational Class* (Princeton: Princeton University Press, 2017) 69.

[709] Ibid., 56.

[710] Robert C. Roberts. *Taking the Word to Heart: Self and Others in An Age of Therapies* (Grand Rapids: William B. Eerdmans Publishing Company, 1993) 51.

[711] Ibid., 169.

[712] Ibid.

every time they swung the bat. It was sheer torture; yet I think I would give away all of my belongings to return to those days. How can I claim to be a Christian, even a sanctified Christian, with such perverted values?

Roberts' key illustration of transcendence above the barbarian "beak and claw" approach to life is a balloon stomp. The last man standing is the child who keeps his balloon tied to his ankle intact, having obliterated the balloons of all the rest. What raucous fun until the same game was played by a class of mentally handicapped children who seemed to have missed the point of competition. They were holding their own balloon in place, so it could be burst by another child, an analogy for a world free of evil, or possibly a foretaste of heaven. But that's not the world we live in. In a world of tyranny, are we to be grateful for those narcissists who desire to be great, making no apologies for their blatant intent to impose their will and image upon the world?

In *The Freedom of Self-Forgetfulness*, Timothy Keller succinctly and correctly states that, "The essence of gospel-humility is not thinking more of myself or thinking less of myself, it is thinking of myself less."[713] But he makes two major mistakes. He argues that Paul did not care what people thought about him. If that is so, why did he make a major defense of his ministry in II Corinthians 11? "Some may boast according to the flesh. I will boast also....Are they servants of Christ? (I speak as if insane) I more so; in far more labors, in far more imprisonments, beaten times without number, often in danger of death," (18, 23). Our identity cannot not be formed in a vacuum. It is at least partially created by how others respond to us, and it is not without political self-interest, but hopefully our response to others will not be completely utilitarian.

Keller then makes a claim that is psychologically and economically misguided, demonstrating little knowledge of a personality competitively propelled and achievement oriented. He claims that self-forgetfulness equates to an Olympic competitor not caring whether he won the silver or gold metal. (Tony Dungy would not be that saintly.) "Wouldn't you like to be the skater who wins the silver, and yet is thrilled about those three triple jumps that the gold-medal winner did?"[714] What

---

[713] Timothy Keller. *The Freedom of Self-Forgetfulness: The Path to True Christian Joy* (Leyland, England: 10Publishing, 2012) 32.
[714] Ibid., 35.

Keller missed is that this particular person would not be competing in
the Olympics. I doubt it is possible to devote the entirety of one's time to
a sport and have no regard for the economic and psychological return on
one's efforts. Timothy Keller has written some great stuff, but he entirely
blew it on this effort, a great title that failed to deliver. I read this book in
hopes of finding help for transcending my highly-driven self, but came
away disappointed by exaggerated spiritual claims both theologically
and psychologically vacuous.

The Disconnect Between Entire Sanctification and Greatness

Candice Millard describes Winston Churchill who for the
expressed purpose of greatness sailed as a 25-year-old to South Africa
as a journalist in the Boer War, placing himself in danger and risking his
life to escape from prison.[715] In 1940, Churchill was chosen by the King
to be Great Britain's Prime Minister in England's "darkest hour." As his
wife helped him dress for his trip to Buckingham Palace to accept his
appointment, she said "Winston, you have dreamed of this day all your
adult life." He responded "No, from the nursery."[716] As we listen to him
thunder to England's parliament the question of entire sanctification
becomes somewhat irrelevant.

---

[715] Candice Millard. *Hero of the Empire: The Boer War: A Daring Escape and the* Making
of Winston Churchill (New York: Anchor Books, 2016).

[716] According to my British friend and colleague, Thomas A. Noble, the appointment
assumed that Churchill would be supported by the members of Parliament. Neville
Chamberlain, the resigning Prime Minister, forwarded the names of Lord Halifax (the
Foreign Secretary) and Winston Churchill (First Lord of the Admiralty). Since Halifax
knew that because he would continue Chamberlain's appeasement, he would not have
the popular or democratic support of the United Kingdom, he withdrew his name,
leaving only Churchill whom the King did not particularly like. Email to author from
Tom Noble, May 22, 2018. Tom's reference to Halifax as a "fine, Christian gentleman,"
reminds me of Jimmy Carter, the most professing and even authentic Christian we have
ever had in the White House, yet lost the mandate to lead the American people and
thus, the 1980 presidential election to Ronald Reagan. I am also reminded of Francis
Asbury's warning to some rowdies at a camp meeting, that they better take caution,
because some of the brethren present had not been sanctified. Asbury stated of the
unsanctified, "For if you get them angry and the Devil should get in them, they are the
strongest and hardest men to fight and conquer." Darius Salter. *America's Bishop: The
Life of Francis Asbury* (Nappanee, IN: Francis Asbury Press, 2003) 157. I suppose that if
we want someone in office to restore law and order and to beat Hitler, we need to elect
the unsanctified.

We shall go on to the end, we shall fight in France, we shall fight on the seas and oceans, we shall fight with growing confidence and growing strength in the air, we shall defend our island whatever the cost may be, we shall fight on the beaches, we shall fight on the landing grounds, we shall fight in the fields and in the streets; we shall never surrender, and even if which I do not for a moment believe, this island or a large part of it were subjugated and starving, then our empire beyond the seas, armed and guarded by the British Fleet, would carry on the struggle, until, in God's good time, the New World, with all its power and might steps forth to the rescue and the liberation of the old.[717]

Lord Halifax assessed, "He has mobilized the English language to fight a war."[718]

A sense of destiny and the aspiration to greatness rested on Abraham Lincoln, a man who exhibited Christianity, but professed little of it. Lincoln confided to his law partner William Herndon that he felt destined to be a great man and at the same time feared he would come to ruin. Although steeped in Calvinism with a due respect for the sovereignty of God, Lincoln would not accidentally tumble into greatness. He was in full agreement with an article about how to succeed in his home town newspaper, *The Sangamon Journal*: "Push long. Push hard. Push earnestly.... The world is so made – society is so constructed that it's a law of necessity that you must push. That is if you would be something and somebody."[719] Lincoln gave his entire life to becoming somebody. He was always in competition: wrestling, jumping, oaring, straight arming an axe, arguing a case, and running for political offices.

Another man who perceived himself to be destined for greatness was Matthew Simpson, Lincoln's friend and arguably America's most powerful clergyman during the Civil War, and who had the honor of preaching Lincoln's funeral. As a 24-year-old he wrote to his Uncle Matthew "When I reflect upon the course which has been marked out for me by Providence these few years, I think that he either designs me for

---

[717] Retrieved from "https://en.wikisource.org/w/index.php?title=We_shall_fight_on_the_beaches&oldid=6803077

[718] From the movie, "The Darkest Hour."

[719] Quoted in Joshua Shenk. *Lincoln's Melancholy: How Depression Challenged and Fueled His Greatness* (New York: Houghton-Mifflin Company, 2005) 73.

a short life or else one marked with peculiar incidence and an arduous responsible character."[720] As I assess in my biography of Simpson, "The thoughts of death coupled with visions of greatness may sound ironic, but are not unusual. The only thing that would stand in the way of greatness would be death. The ambitious fear death because they have a lot more at stake in life and both Lincoln and Simpson were ambitious."[721]

Phoebe Palmer did her best to "push" Simpson into the experience of entire sanctification. According to Palmer, God was obligated to sanctify Simpson or He was a "liar." Palmer forthrightly stated, "It seems to me that you've come to the point of your religious career where God requires that the question should be met and answered before you proceed further.... I will no longer permit the tempter to hinder you from laying hold upon the promise which makes witness of the blessing of entire sanctification."[722]

Palmer's audacity and effrontery were useless. While Palmer was walking "in heaven's own light, Above the world and sin, With hearts made pure and garments white and Christ enthroned within,"[723] Simpson was dirtying his garments with grease and oil from political and ecclesiastical machinery. While Palmer operated in the world of spiritual elitism, Simpson was fighting in the ecclesiastical trenches, settling church disputes, taking an aggressive stance in the Civil War, and applying political leverage as often as he visited the nation's capital. Not to mention Simpson was complicit in the Sand Creek Massacre, 1864, one of the most atrocious Indian incidents to ever take place on American soil. Unfortunately, it was plotted, planned, and led mostly by Methodists, entirely sanctified or not.[724] In spite of being involved in the first three camps of the National Camp Meeting Association for the Promotion of Holiness, 1867-1869, Simpson, second only to Francis

---

[720] George Crooks. *The Life of Matthew Simpson of the Methodist Episcopal Church* (New York: HarperBrothers, 1890) 35.

[721] Darius Salter. *God Cannot Do without America: Matthew Simpson and the Apotheosis of Protestant Nationalism* (Wilmore, Kentucky: First Fruits Press, 2017) 100.

[722] Library of Congress. Simpson Papers, Letter, Palmer to Simpson, no date, Container 13.

[723] Salter, *God Cannot Do*, 509.

[724] See Gary Leland Roberts, *Massacre at Sand Creek: How Methodists Were Involved in an American Tragedy* (Nashville: Abingdon Press, 2016).

Asbury in his influence on American Methodism, turned his back on the Association and never gave testimony to entire sanctification.

This is the time to ask, is there some kind of disconnect between aspiring to holiness and aspiring to greatness, or more accurately sitting on the throne of a bureaucracy with all of its inherent contradictions and political apparatus. C.S. Lewis lamented,

> I live in the Managerial Age, in a world of "Admin." The greatest evil is not done in those sordid 'dens of crime' that Dickens loved to paint. It is not done even in concentration camps and labour camps. In those we see its final result. But it is conceived and ordered (moved, seconded, carried, and minuted) in clean carpeted, warmed and well-lighted offices, by quiet men with white collars and cut finger nails and smooth-shaven cheeks who do not need to raise their voices. Hence, natural enough my symbol for Hell is something like the bureaucracy of a police state or the office of a thoroughly nasty business concern.[725]

Obviously, the dress code needs to be updated, but either Lewis was being overly cynical, or he was accurate in his assessment that corporations in their ability to exist or one might say compete, participate in the rules of competition as dictated by the surrounding culture. A corporation implies a currency for existence, an exchange rate in order to flourish, command respect, secure a promotion, etc. IBM would recognize and demand much different kinds of expertise than say Fort Hood. But an employee in each institution would be highly aware of what is expected for advancement.

Political Capital and Entire Sanctification

No institutions are more regimented than academic communities with both written and unwritten codes. These codes exist not only for academic ranking, but possibly for moving on to another setting that offers greater prestige and financial return. James Hunter argues, while "one may be able to get as good an education at Bluefield State College in Bluefield, West Virginia, as one would at Harvard, but Harvard, as an institution is at the center and Bluefield State is at the periphery of cultural production. Therefore, someone with a credential from Harvard

---

[725] C. S. Lewis. *The Screwtape Letters and Screwtape Proposes a Toast* (New York: The Macmillan Company, 1961) Preface.

will find many more opportunities than someone from Bluefield State and will more likely end up in a position of greater influence than the other."[726] But even we, who are not smart, rich, or connected enough to attend Harvard and remain at Bluefield State or in this case a Wesleyan Holiness college, will not be oblivious to opportunities for impressing the right people: papers presented, books written, and post doctoral work completed.

With all of the above "proving myself" one might label me as unhealthy, even sinful. Mr. "Sanctified" at a holiness institution often informed visitors to his campus, usually persons of more scholarly achievements than his, that he had written forty books. He and I attended the same church as he was beginning to suffer dementia. He informed me that he had been a person of "influence" in the denomination, not recognizing I was already aware of that. Now as I enter dementia, I am faced with the scary thought that I have been able to repress such boasts because of enlightened self-interest and false humility. I do not want to resemble someone who wears so many Sunday School pins that they bang off my knees. The holiness code that enabled me to appear humble in spite of lurking pride may eventually be broken like a rotten minnow net trying to catch a five-hundred-pound blue marlin.

Is writing this book really worth it? Just so that someone will notice, recognize me as a significant other, invite me into the conversation, and accept me as someone who has something to say? Is it possible to accumulate political capital without an awareness that self-interest is at play? In fact, the economic welfare of my family may be precarious if I do not make tenure. Would a certain amount of angst or a confession of incongruence between cruciform theology and aspirations that promote my well being as opposed to bearing the cross of Christ, be in order? I want my name in the line score, no matter how miniscule it may be. I want to matter to the people that matter. When I was chosen as the speaker for the centennial of the small public school I attended, my hand holding the mic was shaking like I had electrodes attached to the ends of my fingers. There were only 75 people there, a third of them my relatives, but of all people I need to impress, are the folks back home.

---

[726] James Davison Hunter. *To Change the World: The Irony, Tragedy, and Possibility of Christianity in the Late Modern World* (New York: Oxford, 2010) 37.

Strangely I was more nervous in that setting than preaching in seminary chapel or a church setting of some 1,500 people.

Holiness Theology's Lack of Interpersonal Psychology

In her scholarly work on women who professed entire sanctification and at the same time exhibited self-assertion in a man's world, Susie Stanley states, "It is ironic that the doctrine of sanctification promotes a theology of the death of self, yet women wrote autobiographies accentuating the individual self and its achievements. The paradox should be obvious but many refuse to acknowledge it."[727] I would add that many of these women were quite autocratic, and had to be, in order to administratively "succeed." Such autocracy and self assertion demanded compartmentalization and rationalization, ego defenses that had not come under the microscope of modern psychology. Is the microscope powerful enough to detect incongruence between holiness and wholeness? One meaning of moving toward wholeness is the ego's decreasing need for defense mechanisms. Defense mechanisms not only buttress the self, but prevent us from identifying underlying motivations for a particular act. Thus, the self exists by way of falsehoods, and it is doubtful that these falsehoods can ever be fully erased.

I have great respect for the scholarship of Bryan Stone, so much so, that I chose his *Evangelism after Christendom: the Theology and Practice of Christian Witness*, as the primary text for an evangelism course which I taught at Seoul Methodist University. Stone's thesis is that it is not enough to convert people to "Christianity;" we need to bring people into a community of kingdom practices, a church more concerned about quality than quantity. We have settled for a contaminated pragmatism which contemplates production more than it values inherent and intrinsic practices which should define a Christian community. Stone does not mince words: "The argument of this book is that the prevailing model of practical reasoning employed to a great extent by contemporary evangelism is inadequate to the Christian faith, eschatologically bankrupt, morally vacuous and tyrannized by a means - end causality that is ecclesiologically hopeless in so far as it externalizes

---

[727] Susie Stanley. *Holy Boldness: Women Preachers' Autobiographies and the Sanctified Life* (Knoxville: The University of Tennessee Press, 2002) 26.

the means from the end."[728] Thus, the following evaluation from Stone is logical: "Yet one of the distinctive characteristics of an ecclesial politics is that conflict is faced from within a social process of redemptive dialog rather than by building up competing power claims or by abandoning one another to the discipline of an impersonal and fixed moral code."[729]

Do we know where a Wesleyan holiness church exists without competing power claims? I once raised the question, "Would a youth group within the Church of the Nazarene be less cliquish, less exclusive, and more accepting than a given group of the same age at a local public high school?" My observations tell me that name recognition of influential people would be more critical in the former than in the latter. With all due respect, if we waited to invite a person to the church of Stone's description we would not invite anyone at all. Bryan Stone's church is a church in abstraction as defined by academia rather than the local church in the raw. And Stone admits that since "the church follows a poor, naked, and crucified Christ, there is no reason to believe that the Church's faithful witnesses will result in masses of wealthy suburban consumers lining up around the block on a Sunday just to be part of our worn-down storefront church."[730]

The individualistic theology of the Holiness Movement never developed an interpersonal psychology, much less what holiness looks like in a world of corporate greed, not to speak of ecclesiastical greed. I found it amusing that one of our Nazarene colleges would communicate with students on another Nazarene campus, "Just in case you are not happy where you are." Somehow we thought we could be Christian selves without developing Christian organizations and denominations. That God's covenant with us as individuals holds profound implications for organizations has, to my knowledge, received scant inquiry from holiness writers. Scott Peck writes, "But God's covenant with us as individuals has another profound indication for our organizational behavior - one which, to my knowledge, has not received attention elsewhere. It is that God *only* covenants with individuals and *does not* covenant - at least any longer - with organizations."[731] An adequate theology of the self can only

---

[728] Bryan P. Stone. *Evangelism After Christendom: The Theology and Practice of Christian Witness* (Grand Rapids, Brazos Press, 2007) 52.

[729] Ibid., 185.

[730] Ibid., 229.

[731] M. Scott Peck. *A World Waiting to be Born: Civility Rediscovered* (New York: Bantam

be constructed by a theology of its relationship within the communities and institutions in which the self participates.

The further one is promoted to the inside of an organization, or appointed to a higher level of the hierarchy, the more disillusionment sets in. For no organization is this more true than the Church, because its employees, at least in the beginning, are so idealistic. After all, this is the "Church," a "Christian" group of people. But just in case the ecclesiastical aspirant had not already noticed, no organization is more given to power plays, nepotism, lineage, and whom you know rather than what you know. "Good ole boy" networks abound, which may include bullying because of position, intellect, money, and other forms of power.

Administration in churches can be particularly inept especially when a "pink slip" is left under the door rather than having an honest face to face conversation. Religious institutions are particularly fragile and allergic to self-criticism which often places individuals in a bind as whether to address a situation at the risk of losing his job. The church, above and beyond all organizations, has not favored dissent. A person in a secular organization admitted, "The troublemaker is often a creative person but truly creative people don't get ahead....Most bosses don't want to hear the truth. And this is particularly true if it disagrees with what they want to do."[732] I sure hope to meet Roger Williams in Heaven. What a great man!

Pastoring a church can be like walking on egg shells. I remember vowing to myself, I was not going to offend anyone in my new church, after finding myself crossways with so many people in my last pastorate. But it wasn't long before I found myself crossways again. It pains me to recall a former seminary student of mine telling me that he was so depressed that while he was out in his fishing boat, if he had possessed a gun, he would have committed suicide. I asked a former Nazarene General Superintendent how many of the five to eight hundred pastoral transitions made each year within the denomination, took place under duress. About two-thirds," he responded. "What are we doing about that?" I asked. The response was, "Nothing."

Books, 1994) 59.

[732] Robert Jackall. *Moral Mazes: The World of Corporate Managers* (New York: Oxford University Press, 2010) 58.

The Tension Between God - Consciousness and Self - Consciousness

Paradoxically, the theology of Christian perfection has attempted to live within the spiritual tension of God-consciousness and self-consciousness. As realization of the discrepancy of the ideal self and the actual self became more apparent, holiness literature began to address what entire sanctification did not accomplish, as much or more than what was spiritually possible in what Francis Asbury referred to as "this sinful lump of clay." Thus the Holiness Movement was forced into almost countless qualifiers and disclaimers. Possibly more healthful would be a confessional awareness as to the inherent contradictions for those of us who desire to live and proclaim holiness. As Wynkoop wrote, "In Wesleyanism, this same tendency to self-interest in salvation often robs those who professedly 'go on to perfection' of the strength of the Spirit-filled life because the true nature of love has been missed. There remains a controlling interest in the self that can never permit soul health and Christian victory."[733]

The popular and well-known camp meeting preacher and holiness exponent, W. B. Godbey, claimed to have arrived at such victory over carnal ambitions for place and position, "I was born a Methodist — my father was a Methodist preacher, but when the Lord baptized me with the Holy Ghost and fire in 1868, he cremated the Methodist along with the Free Mason, the Odd Fellow, the College President and the candidate for the episcopacy."[734] Godbey did not need the Holy Spirit to negate his possibilities for becoming a Bishop; his eccentricities were sufficient for that exclusion. He was not unaware that he always preached without notes directly from the Greek, and he took all of his book orders without writing them down while standing on a hillside, perhaps ostentatiously so. Indeed, the delicate balance between claims to high levels of spirituality, and a realistic self-awareness, may be the most precarious issue for those of us who live in the Wesleyan holiness camp. I am grateful for those individuals whom God has allowed me to encounter on life's journey who seemed to have been genuinely authentic, sanctified selves.

---

[733] Wynkoop, *A Theology of Love*, 210.

[734] Quoted in Donald Dayton's *Theological Roots of Pentecostalism* (Metuchen, NJ: Scarecrow Press, Incorporated, 1987) 165.

T. Walt Hughes reflected on the life of his father, John Wesley Hughes, the founder and first president of Asbury College. John Wesley Hughes was a staunch exponent of entire sanctification and believed himself to have been made "perfect." The son began to notice contradictions in the father's life (as well as other Wilmore-ites), which he would later refer to as a "dual-personality." The father was especially sensitive to criticism, specifically to those who would attack his integrity and the integrity of the college, which he dearly loved, but ultimately left as a brokenhearted man. The son summarized, "Well, Wesley was as meek as Moses. My father was as incapable of meekness as he was incapable of pride."[735] Perhaps the meek "inherit the earth," but they don't build colleges, at least with the intent that their school will become the greatest college in Kentucky, if not the world. T. Walt Hughes became a Presbyterian. Presbyterianism is easier on the conscience. One who does not make extravagant spiritual claims does not have to live up to extravagant spiritual expectations.

---

[735] T. Walt Hughes. *Wilmore, Kentucky* (Compton, CA: M. and A. Books, 1965) 50.

Chapter 10:
The Other

Ingrained Prejudices

My wife and I sat in the theater waiting for the movie to begin. They came in and sat several rows in front of us. A family of six or seven, overweight, shabbily dressed, loaded down with $75 worth of Juicy Fruit, Milk Duds, popcorn, soda, and perhaps beef jerky. All of my socio-economic prejudices kicked in. Remember, education does not erase prejudices, it only rearranges them. These people were undisciplined. They were spending money they do not have, and they will be chomping on popcorn while Americans storm the beaches of Normandy or some such scene. These people defy rational behavior as I define the rules of life. But who knows, maybe they have not been to a movie in a long time and this is their 25th wedding anniversary.

As for another memory, I am in a church in eastern Kentucky on a cold rainy Sunday morning. Within a two minute span fifty children poured into the sanctuary; the potent combination of dirty clothes, rancid hair, unwashed bodies, absent of negating and artificial deodorant, marshaled olfactory assault. Later I would serve as a social worker in that same eastern Kentucky county (which in the 2010 census was the poorest county in America per capita income) in homes with unclean people, dogs which had been who knows where running wild, coal grates on the side of the wall, clothes washed or unwashed piled up, furniture soaked with urine, rotting food in the crevices, and sweat having seeped through the fabric to the frame for years. Where do I sit down? My wife reminds me that at the end of the day I pulled off my clothes in the small rear entrance to the parsonage (I was also pastoring a three-point United Methodist "charge," three churches.) before coming into the house, showering and putting on fresh clothes.

That small entrance provided an olfactory boundary, a decontamination zone, a socio-economic barrier between me and the "poor," the AFDC families, food stamp users or abusers, poor white trash for which I had little genuine compassion. The state of Kentucky paid me to objectify, classify, and, once in a while, have pity on a class of people hidden under a mountain of governmental regulations. I am reminded of J. D. Vance's description of his Breathitt County, Kentucky, grandfather. "Papaw was many things, but he was never cool. He wore the same old T-shirt every day with a front-pocket big enough to fit a pack of cigarettes. He always smelled of mildew because he washed his clothes but let them dry 'naturally,' meaning packed together in a washing machine."[736]

Olfactory and Hygenic Boundaries

Then there was Donny, the lone black who lived in the community where I grew up. He worked at Clayton Fulcher's fish house. He slept on a dirty mattress in a small cinderblock room attached to the fish house. His clothes looked and smelled like fish. He spent most of his working hours shoveling, sorting, weighing, icing, boxing, and loading fish. Where he bathed or washed his clothes I do not know. I am certain that he was never invited into a home within our town of 1,000 people. I do not believe he ever attended one of our four churches. It would be a safe bet that he was never invited to church. I am quite sure that he never ate in one of the two or three small restaurants.

Most of the above could have been handled, at least obscured if not eliminated, with the right sanitizers, room deodorizers, laundry detergent, body deodorant, and expensive perfume. The appeal of sex and smell are the foremost factors in commercialization for almost any product. Marketing aroma is big business. James K. A. Smith writes "The Company's goal is to harness the sense of smell in order to lure shoppers into stores, keep them there long enough to buy something and associate products with added, often nostalgic, values implied by sense (smell being the sense most closely tied to memory)."[737]

---

[736] J. D. Vance. *Hillbilly Elegy: A Memoir of a Family and Culture in Crisis* (New York: HarperCollins, 2016)103.
[737] James K. A. Smith. *Desiring the Kingdom: Worship, Worldview, and Cultural Formation* (Grand Rapids: Baker Academics, 2009) 95.

Odor was a problem in Jesus' time. There are many olfactory references in Scripture. God was supposed to smell good, thus the constant burning of incense in the tabernacle and later in the temple. Ruth, at the instruction of her mother-in-law, Naomi, was to anoint herself in order to entice Boaz (Ruth 3:3). Two of the gifts presented to Jesus by the Magi were aromatic spices, frankincense and myrrh. The most significant expression of worship and affection found in the New Testament may have been the anointing with perfume of Jesus' feet by a woman of ill repute (Luke 7:38). Mary, the sister of Lazarus and Martha, "carried a pound of very costly perfume of pure nard and anointed the feet of Jesus and wiped his feet with her hair; and the house was filled with the fragrance of the perfume" (John 12:3). Mary Magdalene with others intended to anoint the body of Jesus, but Christ's resurrection preempted their planned act of devotion (Mark 16:1).

All of the above have one thing in common, boundaries: the smell of a latrine in a majority world country, the smell of bodies on a crowded bus, the smell of garlic in an Asian restaurant, the smell of sewage in a densely-populated city. When in Dhaka, Bangladesh, I requested to be taken to the most impoverished area of the city. Everybody was trying to sell something; poverty traded for poverty. A Muslim in full Islamic dress approached and invited me to his apartment. I looked at my guide, a young lady of about 25. I wanted to say "no," but because of some vague Christian sentiment said "yes." Jesus went home with a lot of people no matter what they smelled like. I walked up the six flights of stairs, entered the small apartment, perhaps 600 square feet. We sat down; the Muslim beamed with pride as he introduced me to his wife, son and daughter-in-law. Everything around me was worn, appearing old and dirty, that gray tarnish that covers all of poverty. His son was at the university, as well as another son whom I did not meet. I did not accept anything to eat. I have a weak digestive system. He excused himself when the "call to prayer" sounded. The man seemed to be very grateful that I had accepted his hospitality. My host, a major businessman in the city, was not so approving.

I wonder how I would have fared with Jesus and his disciples. They did not seem to be all that concerned with hygiene, not nearly as preoccupied as were the Pharisees. My mother scrubbed me so much that my immune system was destroyed. Cleanliness was next to godliness. Sanctification did little to curb her neurotic tendencies, exhibited by constantly washing her hands, wiping the door knobs off with alcohol, and meticulously washing and drying every plate, dish, and glass. It seemed like her whole life was given to cleaning, wiping, swiping, reading her Bible and praying, but with little socializing. As one of my brother-in-laws said at her funeral, my mother was not slow - she was thorough, and I add, she was prejudiced against any skin color or culture other than her own. I would like to think it was because of ignorance and provincialism, and a religion that offered no alternative. The first church dignitary that I ever encountered as a ten-year-old was a Pilgrim Holiness district superintendent who drove a black Cadillac. Impressive! I also remember the racist joke that he told from the pulpit. Everybody laughed. Of course, this was sixty years ago, in rigidly segregated North Carolina.

A White Holiness Church

From the very beginning, from Phoebe Palmer to the National Camp Meeting Association and from the Association to the come-out denominations, and from then until now, we have been a white church. There was Amanda Smith, a black holiness preacher. But one African American is a curiosity; three is a crowd which demands ostracism. But in Smith's case, "I wonder what a black, female, holiness preacher would sound like in the pulpit!" And for the Hispanic and African Americans who signed up for entire sanctification, they would have to find it in their own houses of worship. When it comes to segregation, holiness people are no different than Baptists, Presbyterians, or Episcopalians. Pentecostals seemed to do better at inter-racial fellowship with enthusiastic worship, speaking in tongues, and a miracle or two. It must be the fulfillment of God pouring out his Spirit upon all flesh at the same time, at the same place. That's probably the best policy if we want God to show up, because we do not know what color his skin was.

In 1973, The Christian Holiness Association adopted the following: "The world will listen to our pronouncements on racism, poverty, and morality when we demonstrate to them what life can be when Christ's tenets are followed.... Let those who express perfect love reaffirm their belief in the value of every person for whom Christ died, regardless of race or color.... Divest...every...trace of racism...and abandon any…form of racism as light comes to them."[738] Out of the seven annual CHA conventions for which I had logistical responsibility as the Executive Director, with the attendees ranging from 5-900, not one black person was present, except for a special speaker such as Wingrove Taylor or James Earl Massey. The convention consisted of delegates from the full spectrum of the 17 member denominations. The Church of the Nazarene, as probably other holiness denominations, could boast of the inter-racial Lamb's Club in New York City, Tom Nees' Community of Hope Church in Washington, DC and Ron Benefiel's Bresee Institute in Los Angeles. But these were considered experimental outreaches in unusual places rather than a major characteristic systemic to the denomination. Only now do I realize that I attended a holiness high school, a holiness Bible school, a holiness college, and a holiness seminary, without encountering one African-American student. I also preached some 50 holiness camp meetings without one African-American being present in the congregation. I do not believe that these institutions were necesarily racist. Evidently, the Holiness Movement was not a religous option for African-American students.[739]

In 2000, Michael Emerson and Christian Smith released their *Divided by Faith: Evangelical Religion and the Problem of Race in America*.[740] Their case was easy to make, but the book raised so much flack that Emerson with three other authors published *United by Faith: The Multi-racial Congregation as an Answer to the Problem of Race*.[741] Finding congregations that accented diversity was not an easy task.

---

[738] Quoted in Ivan A. Beals' *A Racist Legacy: Will the Church Resolve the Conflict?* (Notre Dame, Indiana: Crossroads Books, 1997) 182.

[739] In 1960, Asbury College, the academic crown jewel of the Holiness Movement, adopted a form of "mild integration;" the emphasis was on "mild." The School would accept "foreign Negroes," but would accept American blacks only if they were preparing for Christian service and married. "These provisions were designed to meet objections to inter-racial dating and to having black students living in the residence halls." Evidently, Asbury College was not an attractive option for American blacks. It was not until seven years later, 1967, that Edward E. Williams of Memphis, enrolled at Asbury College, but stayed for only one academic year. He did return for summer school in 1969. Retrieved from : https://www.asbury.edu/about/history/1960-1969/

[740] Michael O. Emerson and Christian Smith. *Divided by Faith: Evangelical Religion and the Problem of Race in America* (New York: Oxford, 2000).

[741] Curtis Paul DeYoung, Michael O. Emerson, George Yancey, and Karen Chai Kim. *United by Faith: The Multi-racial Congregation as an Answer to the Problem of Race* (New York: Oxford, 2003).

Fitting the description were Mosaic Church in Los Angeles, Riverside in New York City, Saint Pius X Catholic Church in Belmont, Texas, and Park Avenue United Methodist Church in Minneapolis.

The authors traced the beginning of the Pentecostal Movement through William J. Seymour and the Azusa Street Revival. "The gatherings were quite amazing because of their diversity. African American and whites attended in similar numbers. People of Hispanic, Asian American, and Native American backgrounds, as well as from other ethnic groups were often present."[742] There was no reference to the Holiness Movement other than to note Seymour and Charles Parham had at one time ministered in holiness churches, Seymour in the Church of God in Anderson, Indiana, and Parham had served as a holiness evangelist. However, the Pentecostal churches themselves were subject to racial strife and division. The attempt to amend *Divided* to *United* left the authors shaking their heads: "The history of the church in the United States leads one to believe that sustaining multiracial congregations is a near impossibility due to racism. One wonders what happened to the faith that reconciled people in the first century."[743] Not much has changed since W.E.B. Dubois wrote in 1929, "The American Church of Christ is Jim Crowed from top to bottom. No other institution in America is built so thoroughly or absolutely on the color line. Everybody knows this."[744]

As Lisabeth Cohen has argued, race division is largely an economic issue. As tract housing was built in the post World War II economy, suburbs defined by subdivisions often excluded blacks with the rationale that property prices would be driven down. Thus, many churches remained white, salving their consciences with the argument that no blacks lived in the area. But this was far more than a nonchalant arrangement. When the black Myers family in 1957 integrated a Pennsylvania housing development, they were subjected to thrown rocks through the window, cross burnings, and Confederate flag waving. A white homeowner rationalized the vicious violence with his assessment that the black husband and father is "probably a nice guy, but every time I look at him I see two-thousand dollars drop off the value of my

---

[742] Ibid., 57.

[743] Ibid., 61.

[744] Ibid.

house."[745] In 1962, a Newark, New Jersey, Mayor's Commission on Group Relations condemned segregation gate keeping, dubbed "segregurbia" with a thinly veiled indictment of the Church: "[T]he free enterprise lurking in many hearts has provided more moves to all white suburbs than the billion words of love have promoted the spiritual advantages of economic and integrated city living."[746]

As segregated blacks and both poor and gentrified whites stayed behind, the churches in the inner city were more likely integrated than suburban churches. When Harry Emerson Fosdick retired, the same Fosdick condemned by Henry Clay Morrison, he gave much of the rest of his life to inner city problems which included segregation. In the beginning days of Riverside Church, Fosdick stated, "If we exclude Negroes from our churches and practice segregation in the sense that Negroes cannot be members, then we might as well be atheists."[747] By 1980, about twenty-five percent of the congregation was black, while the church sits in a prestigious neighborhood defined by Columbia University and Union Theological Seminary.[748] Robert Putnam noted the October 14, 1990, program of Riverside Church: "Among the entries on the weekly calendar for October 14, 1990, of the Riverside Church in New York City a mainline Protestant congregation, were meetings of the Social Service Training Session, the AIDS Awareness Seminar, the Ecology Task Force, the Chinese Christian Fellowship, Narcotics Anonymous, Riverside Business and Professional Women's Club, Gulf Crisis Study Series, Adult Children of Alcoholics, and Martial Arts Class for Adults and Teens."[749] These multiple doors in an inner city church almost guarantee that it will be multi-racial.

Sadly, Hollywood has done a better job addressing the race issue than has the Church. At least, when we got past D.W. Griffith's *The Birth of a Nation*, there has been *Guess Who's Coming to Dinner*, *The Defiant Ones*, *In the Heat of the Night*, *To Kill a Mockingbird*, *Driving Miss Daisy*, *Loving*, *Mississippi Burning*, *The Ghosts of Mississippi*, and *Mudbound*.

---

[745] Lizabeth Cohen. *A Consumer's Republic* (New York: Random House, 2003) 217.

[746] Ibid., 213.

[747] Miller, 461.

[748] Ibid., 463.

[749] Robert D. Putnam. *Bowling Alone: The Collapse and Revival of American Community* (New York: Simon and Schuster Paperbacks, 2000) 66.

My favorite is *Places in the Heart*, starring Sally Field and Danny Glover. The setting takes place in cotton-growing Waxahachie (pronounced Walksahatchie), Texas during the Depression. The wife (Field), soon to be widowed is married to the town sheriff who breaks away from his Sunday dinner to answer a disturbance call. A thin, small, drunk black boy is waving a pistol and accidentally kills the sheriff. The boy is lynched. The wife has to keep manning the farm for which she hires a black man (Danny Glover). The two of them are remarkably successful until the Ku Klux Klan beats the hired hand almost to death, forcing him to leave the farm fearing for his life. The amusing part is played by John Malkovich, a blind man who drives the Ku Klux Klan off with a pistol, identifying all of them by their voice. The most theological ending to a movie that I have ever seen depicts a tall elderly preacher (he could not have been an actor) reading from 1 Corinthians 13, after which the congregation participates in communion. Passing the bread and wine to one another is Sally Field, her husband, the boy who killed him, the adulterer restored to his wife, Danny Glover, the members of the KKK, and John Malkovich - an accurate picture of the kingdom of God, what the church is supposed to be, but perhaps just wishful thinking. In fact, so farfetched that one of my seminary students did not even get it.

Remarkable Stories of Crossing the Barrier

But we do not have to go to a theatre or rent a DVD to find vivid snapshots of the Kingdom. In his book, *Devotion*, Adam Makos tells the story of two Navy pilots, Tom Hudner and Jesse Brown, who flew clumsy prop Corsairs during the Korean War. Tom was from a patrician family in Fall River, Massachusetts, and Jesse from a tenant farm in Mississippi. Tom was not a Christian, and Jesse was a Bible-reading, praying, non-drinking, non-smoking Christian. On December 4, 1951, the two of them flew wing to wing into enemy territory, just northwest of Chosin Reservoir, North Korea. Jesse's plane took enemy fire, lost oil, and began descent. Both Tom and Jesse looked for a possible level landing and zeroed in on what looked to be a pasture on top of a mountain. But upon closer inspection, the landing site came into clearer view. "The pasture was anything but smooth - small trees and boulders jutted from the snow." By the time Jesse's plane came to a stop, his legs were hopelessly trapped under the flight panel. All of the aviators had been adamantly instructed in no uncertain terms, if one of their fellow aviators went down, they were not to risk rescue. To do so meant facing a court - martial. The loss of one plane and pilot should not translate into the loss of two planes and two pilots. Tom disregarded those orders, and knowing that he would not be able to take off after landing, set his plane down in the same pasture. Tom's life was spared by rescue helicopters, but Jesse died before they arrived. Jesse and his plane were left there, but not before being incinerated with napalm by the rescue team.

Jesse Brown had been the first black Navy pilot in the history of the US military, and obviously, to die in the line of duty. Tom was not court-martialed, but was personally presented the Medal of Honor by Harry Truman, the first given to a Navy personnel since W.W. II. On the night before he died, Jesse had written his wife:

> Don't be discouraged, Angel, believe in God and believe in Him with all your might. And I know that things will work out alright. We need Him now like never before. Have faith with me, darling, and He'll see us thru and we'll be together again before long too. I want you to keep that pretty little chin up, Angel, Come on now, way up. I want you to also be confident in this: and that is, your husband loves his wife with all his heart and soul - no man never loved a woman more.[750]

Jack Twyman and Maurice Stokes were basketball teammates for the NBA Cincinnati Royals. During the 1959 — 60 season, Twyman and Wilt Chamberlain became the first two players in NBA history to average over 30 points per game. During his three seasons in the NBA, 1955 — 58, Maurice Stokes grabbed more rebounds than any other player, 3,492, standing only 6' 7". Tragically, his career was cut short by a fall to the floor, resulting in a head injury in the last game of the 1957 - 58 season. For 12 years, Stokes was a quadriplegic, eventually dying April 6, 1970.

Twyman became Stokes' legal guardian, going to see him each day, paying his bills, filing workman's compensation claims, and raising money through charity and exhibition basketball games. "Twyman communicated by going through the alphabet, letter by letter, until Stokes, who was mentally-alert, blinked in recognition. Slowly the process spelled out words." Twyman said of Stokes, "To see the way he conducted himself - I just stood in awe of him. It got so bad, and when

---

[750] Adam Makos. *Devotion: An Epic Story of Heroism, Friendship, and Sacrifice* (New York: Ballantine Books, 2015) 379.

I would be having a bad day myself, I would go to see Maurice, to say, I wanted to get pumped up, and he never failed to pump me up."[751] I forgot to mention that Twyman was white, and Stokes was black. What kind of influence did the Stokes-Twyman relationship have?

>After reading sportswriter Cliff Keene's story on Stokes in the Boston Globe, a Massachusetts family sent Twyman a check for $500, noting that this was their Christmas money. In a note accompanying the check, the father of the family wrote that they believed Stokes needed the money more than they needed gifts. Another family from Cincinnati did not exchange Christmas gifts for three years, sending the money that would have gone toward gifts to Maurice instead. A Wisconsin man sent Stokes five dollars along with a note: "I recently faced a number of setbacks myself, by being able to make a small contribution actually encourages me because it reminds me that there are such people as Maurice and Jack Twyman in the world."[752]

In 1997, John Lambert and Andy Boschma bowled together in a Yipsilanti, Michigan, bowling league. That was their only contact and the only avenue (lane) by which they knew each other. The 64-year-old Lambert, a retired employee of the University of Michigan Hospital, for three years had been on a waiting list for a kidney transplant. Boschma, a 33-year-old accountant donated one of his kidneys. Lambert said to Boschma, "I wouldn't hesitate to do this all over again." This story is strange enough in that the sacrificial gift was engendered by only a casual acquaintance; even more unbelievable is that Boschma is white and Lambert is African American.[753]

The Holiness Reality

Michael Lodahl when commenting on Christ's story about the "Good Samaritan" tells of a conversation with a Vietnam vet at a Nazarene prayer breakfast. The man used to be a Quaker, but was now a Nazarene. Lodahl asked, "Why the switch?" The man answered, "Well, you know they (Quakers) set up medical units during the war that

---

[751] Bob Carter, "Stokes' life a tale of tragedy and friendship."www.espn.com/classic/biography/s/Stokes_Maurice.html

[752] Pat Farabaugh. *An Unbreakable Bond: The Brotherhood of Maurice Stokess and Jack Twyman* (Haworth, New Jersey: Johann Press, 2014) 166.

[753] Putnam. *Bowling Alone*, 28.

helped the North Vietnamese." When Lodahl reminded him that Jesus would have us love our enemies, the vet responded, "That's where I draw the line." Lodahl later reflected, "It plagues me and I hope you, that this gentleman found it much easier to draw the line as a Nazarene than he had as a Quaker." Lodahl accurately summarizes our relationships, even for those of us who profess to be sanctified, to the other. "Our social and individual identities are typically formed by defining ourselves 'as opposed' to others, to those people over there beyond the line we have drawn, those who are not like us (and whom we do not like). National identities, ethnic identities, sports teams' identities, denominational identities, political party identities - the list of potential elements in the social construction of selfhood or identity is long indeed."[754]

The above is not the total story. I am confident that thousands of holiness types have been compelled by both a theology and experience of love to reach across racial barriers. Such was the case for Jesse C. Middendorf, who as a ten-year- old went fishing with his father, also named Jesse A. Middendorf, in the Catawba River just outside of Charlotte, North Carolina. Sitting in their small boat about one hundred feet from the shore, they observed four young white men, probably drinking, throwing large stones from a bluff onto two black fishermen down below. The senior Jesse ordered them to stop and when they did not, the Nazarene preacher rowed his boat ashore, and with paddle in hand ascended the steep bluff. When the four men were confronted, one of them grabbed the paddle and hit Middendorf, the father in the stomach with a loud "fap." The preacher wrestled the paddle from the belligerent troublemakers, and scattered the four rock throwers off the bluff. The ten-year-old boy, later to become a Nazarene Superintendent stood there wide-eyed, while the two black fishermen were amazed that a white man, a paddle-swinging Nazarene preacher, would risk life and limb to be their advocate and defender in racist North Carolina. The black men accompanied the two Jesses back to their car, helping them to load their boat, making sure there would be no retaliation from the red-neck racists. Needless to say, such a scenario witnessed by the son was worth a thousand sermons denouncing racism.

---

[754] Michael Lodahl, "On Being the Neighbor: How John Wesley's Reading of the Parable of the Good Samaritan May Cultivate Loving People," The Edwin Crawford Lectures: Northwest Nazarene University, Nampa, Idaho, February 5, 2009.

Our Present Racial Turmoil

In the seven-year period ending in 2012, a white officer killed a black person almost two times per week, or in that time period, approximately 700 black men were killed by white policemen in the United States.[755] I am aware, at least academically, of both sides of the problem. Thomas Sowell refers to my assessment of racial tension as given by an abstract person in an abstract world, and that police with everyday experience, rather than possessing only book knowledge, place their lives on the line every day. In other words, the people who make the law have not been in an actual situation which that law addresses. Sowell writes that,

> Many of the intelligentsia express not only surprise but outrage at the number of shots fired by the police in some confrontation with a criminal, even if many of these intellectuals have never fired a gun in their lives, much less faced life and death dangers, requiring split second decisions. Seldom, if ever, do the intelligentsia find it necessary to seek out information on the accuracy of pistols when fired under stress, before venting their feelings and demanding changes. In reality, a study by the New York City Police Department found that, even within a range of only six feet, just over half of the shots by the police missed completely. At distances of 16 to 25 yards - less than the distance from first base to second base on a baseball diamond, only 14% of the shots hit.[756]

This is not my area of expertise. I am not making a case for either white police officers or black men. I can only say with confidence, it is difficult to find anyone in our country who believes that race relations are improving. Also I know, I am grateful that I was not born Eric Garner, a black man in the inner city, with limited education, with limited skills, addicted to and dealing in crack cocaine, incarcerated multiple times, 100 pounds overweight, ultimately hustling cigarettes on the street, constantly hounded by police, arrested dozens of times, two wives, and five children he could not support. I am thankful that I do not live in a house with 29 city code violations, infested by rats, mice, bedbugs, and roaches. Garner was two and one-half times more likely to suffer

---

[755] Kevin Johnson, Meghan Hayer, and Brad Heath. "Local Police Involved in over Four Hundred Killings per Year," *USA Today*, (August 14, 2014).
[756] Thomas Sowell. *Intellectuals in Society* (New York: Basic Books, 2011) 29-30.

from asthma and five more times more likely to die from it than a white person of the same age.

I am unexplicably blessed that my life was not affected by the "broken window" philosophy, the "stop and frisk" philosophy, the "zero tolerance" philosophy, and the targeted "low quality of life" philosophy. I am glad that I am not counted in the bizarre statistic showing that 90 - 95% of all people in prison for drug offenses in New York City in the 90s were black and Hispanic, despite studies showing that 72% of all illegal drug users in the city were white."[757] I am grateful that my last words were not, "I can't breathe," as a policeman held me in a chokehold. Whatever the systemic and extenuating circumstances were in the killings of Trayvon Martin, Michael Brown, and Eric Garner, we know that perceptions vary widely between blacks and whites. Seventy-four percent of blacks polled perceive these individual events as a broader pattern of discrimination, racial profiling, and harassment, while only 29% of evangelical Protestants agree with some kind of trend or flaw within our national ethos. Particularly troublesome is that few white people have close friends who are black. Equally troublesome is that a child born in a black ghetto has a twenty-year shorter lifespan (ranking 230th in life expectancy, barely besting the country Yemen) than a child born in an upper-class white community.

I have provided little to no leadership integrating my community or the Church. No activity is more culturally formed and informed, than worship. Even my involvement with a Russian community, my same color of skin, leaves me alienated from the memories, traditions, and desires to save some remnant of their collective experience from the Motherland, even though I am physically present. In cultures other than my own, I am separated by my own liturgical convictions, and rituals that I am in some way convinced are essential to my spiritual welfare. On the other hand, I am not convinced that I should stay away from black churches because I am tone deaf with little sense of rhythm. Robert P. Jones concludes, "While not all forms of social separation need be lamented (for example, African American churches in a white-dominated society), the near absolute homogeneity that currently exists in churches and white core social networks, hinder our ability to begin

---

[757] Matt Taibbi. *I Can't Breathe: A Killing on Bay Street* (New York: Spiegel and Craw, 2017) 88.

to mend racial rifts. Moreover, this homogeneity thwarts our capacity to agree about something as basic as the reality of the problems that we face."[758]

Once again, if entire sanctification is defined as Holy love, that love as defined by Jesus means inclusiveness. The American holiness church has not modeled inclusiveness. But if I believe Mark Labberton, no theology, not even holiness theology, will bridge the chasm between ethnicities. "From conception onward, each of us gradually develops a mental frame that defines our more basic instincts, values, assumptions, habits, and choices." He further writes, "Context sets our life's terms and possibilities: it is this frame that defines, supports, and contradicts our values and actions."[759] And one might say contradicts our holiness theology and claims to "entire sanctification." Strange that in our age of enlightenment which boasts of the "global village," we cannot see more clearly than did John Woolman and Theodore Weld two centuries ago. But their theology was a little fuzzy.

Elizabeth Currid-Halkett charges that we live in a "structurally-flawed society," and much of our consumption, in particular where we send our children to college, and the neighborhoods in which we live, create an "us," and always involve leaving "others" out. Our status markers are particularly pernicious, in that they involve "frowning upon those who make inferior decisions on such matters, willfully ignorant that many of these decisions, veiled in morality, are practical and realistic outcomes of socio-economic conditions."[760]

Thus, my frowning on the family that entered the theatre is a particularly pernicious sin given the egalitarian efforts, claims, and life style of the historical Jesus. Currid-Halkett questions whether our consumptive choices do anything to advance society and concludes that for the aspirational class, "consumer gestalt reflects a frenzy and status-consicousness, that not only leaves many out, but also stresses us out. In all of our consuming - conspicuous and inconspicuous - we may be

---

[758] Robert P. Jones. *The End of White Christian America* (New York: Simon and Schuster, 2016) 194.

[759] Mark Labberton. "Still Evangelical?" *Still Evangelical? Insiders Reconsider Political, Social, and Theological Meaning*, ed. Mark Labberton (Downers Grove, Il: InterVarsity Press, 2018) 6,13.

[760] Currid-Halkett, *The Sum of Small Things*, 196.

missing out on living our lives entirely."[761] Christ suggested something like that when he said that "for whoever wants to save their life will lose it, but whoever loses their life for me will find it" (Matthew 16:25).

Other Kinds of Others

Within the American global village, issues of the "other" are exponentially multiplied. With mosques and Mormon temples as well as every other religious paradigm on the face of the Earth defining our neighborhoods, all of us will be faced at one time or another with interpreting or reinterpreting Christian love. Such was the case for Clarence Kinzler, a California Nazarene Superintendent in the 1990s, who recalled, "I was raised in Nampa, Idaho, and during my boyhood years saw 'the enemy' as the Roman Catholics and the Mormons."[762] One of his son's (Jim) friends was a Mormon boy. The father perceived the Holy Spirit breaking down his prejudice. God spoke (or he thought), "You preach and really believe the message of perfect love, don't you? Do you think if you laid My love in you against the love of a world religion, that my love would prevail?" About that time, an anti-Mormon film, "The God Makers," was shown in a local Nazarene church. The day after, Kinzler found himself standing between two Mormon fathers while watching Jim and his Mormon friends play soccer. After the game Clarence said to the dads, "See that big church down there (his church)? We will never do that to you because we love you too much for that." The Mormons put their arms around Clarence, walked him to his car and watched him drive away. The last meal that Clarence and his family had at their church before moving from Nampa to northern California was with several Mormon families. A group prayer led by Mormons sent the Nazarene and his family on their way.[763]

The "other" is presently moving beyond the racial and religious other into the political arena. A rigid, Republican fundamentalism (and there may be more than a few democratic fundamentalists) is displacing a holiness ethic and turning us into something other than biblical Christians. Christian righteousness is interpreted as righteous cause,

---

[761] Ibid., 197.

[762] Clarence Kinzler, "Articulating A Living, Christian Holiness in a Pluralistic World," Nazarene Theological Conference, February - March 1, 1992.

[763] Ibid., 6,7.

pre-empting a genuine Kingdom agenda. Such was the case for Randy Beckum, chaplain and professor at Mid-America Nazarene University. Randy spoke in chapel in February, 2015. He began with a confession that he was conflicted and troubled by a recent event. The movie *American Sniper* had garnered one hundred and four million dollars in its first four days of release, while the movie *Selma* depicting a critical event in the Civil Rights Movement had made only thirty million dollars during the entire time shown in theatres. Randy opined that we live in a nation that glorifies violence, via television, cinema, and video gaming. He then proceeded to quote from a plethora of biblical passages which called for a non-retaliatory and non-revengeful response to violence. Randy referenced Matthew 5, Luke 23, I Peter 3, as well as other passages.

Randy Beckum proclaimed that he was a patriot, but warned against equating God with patriotism. He reminded his chapel audience that the earliest creed of the Christian Church was "Jesus is Lord, Caesar is not." While Randy did not argue for pacifism, he challenged his listeners to put only "love at the top of the ladder; patriotism and nationalism do not belong there." The Old Testament law had been, "An eye for an eye and a tooth for a tooth," but Jesus had taught, "If someone slaps you on one cheek, turn to him the other cheek."

Randy challenged that the goal of Christianity is to become like Jesus, but confessed that "it is terribly difficult to follow in our American culture." He told the story of Peter drawing his sword on Malchus, and quoted Jesus that "All that live by the sword, will die by the sword." Randy's preaching style is casual, soft tone, conversational, and somewhat nonchalant. He was apologetic throughout the sermon, not desiring to impose his perspective on others. He closed his message by inviting the community at Mid-America to an ongoing cyberspace communication via email, Face Book, tweeting, etc.

Randy got more than he bargained for; he got fired from his administrative cabinet post, and finally forced from his employment altogether. Randy, a life-long Nazarene, and a son-in-law of one of the Church of the Nazarene's legendary figures, Paul Orjala, was not unaware of what he had done. He had trampled on a nationalistic, NRA advocating, Republican voting, hawkish, fundamentalist collective consciousness which defines the Church of the Nazarene. His twenty years of employment at Mid-America Nazarene University were over.

From my perspective, Randy could have said or have done some things differently. He could have pointed out the difference between nationalism and patriotism. He could have explained that pure pacifism is an impossibility and for the pacifists, there are multiple options for serving our country. He could have stated that Christianity has always had difficulty corresponding the personal/individual ethics of Jesus with a corporate/nationalistic ethic. (Less we forget, Dietrich Bonhoeffer was complicit and conflicted in a plot to assassinate Hitler.) Using a college chapel mainly attended by uninformed and non-critical thinking undergraduates, may have not been the best forum for leaving so many loose ends flapping in the wind.

Randy had not drawn a line in the sand, but perhaps unwisely opened conversation easily misinterpreted by the very conservative constituency supporting Mid-America Nazarene University, not able to rationally and non-emotionally process his ideas. What Randy had meant to be only suggestive and perhaps provocative, became a declaration, floating beyond the Mid-America Nazarene Campus, a full frontal assault on the prevailing fundamentalist culture paying the bills for the institution. And one would wonder if Randy discussed with any close friends or spiritual directors what he intended to do with his chapel sermon. Everybody lost, and nothing was solved.

It may have helped Randy as well as the rest of us, to have read James Davison Hunter's *To Change the World: The Irony, Tragedy, and Possibility of Christianity in the Late Modern World*. He would have realized that the Church of the Nazarene is so enculturated that it cannot be persuaded or changed by rational discourse. Hunter states, "[W]e now see that hearts and minds are only tangentially related to the movements of culture, that culture is much more complicated, and has life independent of individual mind, feeling, and will; indeed, it is not so much individual hearts and minds that move culture – but culture that ultimately shapes the hearts and minds and thus directs the lives of individuals."[764] The present DNA of the Church of the Nazarene has been generationally shaped by embracing a reactionary evangelicalism over

---

[764] Hunter, 45.

the last several decades for at least a half century. Hunter states, "Ideas do have consequences; not because those ideas are inherently truthful or obviously correct, rather because of the way they are embedded in very powerful institutions, networks, interests and symbols."[765] Changing this embedment with a chapel talk is akin to chipping away at a glacier with a BB gun.

Hunter further states, "In reality, culture as ideas and institutions is mixed together in the most complex ways imaginable with all other institutions not least of which in our own day are the market economy and the church."[766] I would add the church to the mix. Randy was involved in what Chuck Colson calls, "*A cosmic struggle between world views*, between the Christian world view and the various secular and spiritual world views arrayed against it."[767] To use Hunter's language, Beckum had attempted to "disentangle the life and identity of the church from the life and identity of American society."[768] A tall task for a chapel talk, but you can't blame Beckum for not trying.

If there is a uniqueness in holiness theology and its lifestyle, it has been lost or so marginalized that it cannot be heard. We really don't have a place at the table. Not even in American evangelicalism, much less, American Christianity in general. In Hunter's survey of evangelical Christianity, he references Pentecostals, but makes no mention of the "holiness movement" or any of its denominations. In identifying ourselves with the "Christian right," our voice has been lost or so amalgamated, that any distinctive such as those which belong to the Mennonites, or other Ana-baptist groups, are no longer identifiable. We have either stayed in the ghetto, such as smaller holiness groups, or if we escaped the ghetto, blotted out our collective memory as what it meant to be a unique and particular people. Problematically, what defined us as a unique people, a superficial exhibition of rules and regulations, was shed or blocked out as eagerly as the Warsaw Jews upon liberation, ripped off the Star of David. There is no evidence that Holiness denominations are prone to raise their voice against the present revival of nationalism and nativism. In fact, we may be part of the problem rather than solution. In

---

[765] Ibid., 44.
[766] Ibid., 39.
[767] Ibid., 25.
[768] Ibid., 184.

his latest book, *Christ in Crisis: Why We Need to Reclaim Jesus*, Jim Wallis states, "Many kinds of people are being 'othered,' and all of us by others of us. Yet, Jesus was quite clear about how we are to treat 'other.'" Clarity is never clear enough for those of us who do not take Jesus seriously.[769]

---

[769] Jim Wallis. *Christ in Crisis: Why We Need to Reclaim Jesus* (New York: HarperOne, 2019) 17.

Chapter 11:
The Animate

Being Consumed

The inanimate has become the animate. Things, human made things, grab my attention, assault my senses, and question my worthiness as a person, adequacy as a provider, my faithfulness as a citizen or a husband or as a father. Buying is an activity, an activity of being acted upon as much or more than acting. No society in the history of humankind has ever been more defined by individual ownership than present-day America: the unattached house, the one-driver car, the riding lawnmower only for my yard, the swimming pool only for my family, the bedroom for each person in the house. These are not the exceptions, but the norm in twenty-first century America, at least for the middle class. Voices, images, music, signs, symbols, logos, and above all curvaceous women, persuade me that if the above is not true, if I am not a voracious participant in the game of consumerism, I am not an adequate person. In a previous century, the word "personal" was used only for the rich: personal chauffeur, personal valet, and personal tailor. Now almost everyone has a personal computer, personal financial advisor, and possibly a personal physical trainer.

Havingness as the American way did not suddenly show up in the twenty-first century. From the very beginning of American settlement the amount of land one owned indicated one's worth. Who had rights to the land, the Whites or the Native Americans? Who should benefit from the produce acquired from the land, the British or the Americans? Who dictated the boundaries of the land, the present owner or the previous owner? Who would work the land, paid or slave labor? These questions were the primary reasons for thousands of endless lawsuits and ultimately, war. In his Pulitzer Prize-winning history of

Cooperstown, New York, Alan Taylor recounts how the famed author James Fennimore Cooper was reduced to poverty, having to sell all the furniture in his house because of faulty land deals inherited from his father, William Cooper.[770]

Ellen Elsinger, tracing the history of early Kentucky, points out the constant wrangle over property lines. A traveler in 1801 commented, "I never stopped at a house of a single inhabitant, who did not appear concerned of the validity of his own title, while he doubted that of his neighbor."[771] The problem was ubiquitous, with lawyers charging half of the value of the land to save the other half. This complicated calamity left hardly anyone unscathed. The legal tangle of land disputes was hopelessly confused by unscrupulous land dealers, initials carved into trees becoming obscured over time, creeks changing their course and landmarks being given various names.[772]

Over thirty years ago, I and my family on a brutally hot summer day, rolled across Colorado and Kansas in our Oldsmobile station wagon. We stopped to fill up at some small burg close to the state border. Upon leaving, my car vapor locked. (I had never heard of such a thing.) At that point we became an event; two people stopped to help, one who went to get gas to pour into the carburetor (no such thing as a carburetor today) and the other, who seemed to have all the time in the world, stayed to talk. "What do you do?" I asked. "Farm," he answered.. "How many acres?" I continued. "Twenty thousand," he responded. "Are they yours?" "Yep."

The man drove an old truck and dressed as if he did not own a penny other than buying the right kind of seed and using the right kind of fertilizer and owning gargantuan pieces of farm equipment. I suspect that a commodities culture had little effect on him, though he may have driven a Cadillac to church. I also suspect the farm has been split up or sold off and his children and grandchildren now have a much different relationship to things than my new-found friend.

---

[770] Alan Taylor. *William Cooper's Town: Power and Persuasion on the Frontier of the Early American Republic* (New York: Vintage, 1995).
[771] Ellen Elsinger. *Citizens of Zion: The Social Origins of Camp Meeting Revivalism* (Knoxville: The University of Tennessee Press, 1999) 63.
[772] Ibid., 64.

They are probably helping to carry the $3.827 trillion worth of revolving credit, mostly credit cards, weighing down on the American people. This does not count house mortgages, which may be the only thing worth paying interest on in the American economy.[773]

The above equals approximately $12,000 debt for each person in America. Since a child age 12 or under cannot own a credit card (not sure of this), the debt of the average adult is two to three times greater than this. And, since credit cards charge somewhere around 25% interest for carried over amounts, the result is enslavement. I consider financial bondage as one of our greatest social problems, a problem addressed by neither the evangelical left or right. The only attention given to it is by such persons as Dave Ramsey, who tells Christians how they can get rich while he is getting rich. An article in one of our recent denominational publications explained by putting a few dollars more in my retirement fund, I could have X number of dollars in my retirement. What the author failed to explain, is why I would want a few dollars more in my retirement.

We purchase what we believe to be freedom, but that freedom may be only an illusion. The communities in which we live both legitimate and dictate our spending. I have often reflected about how the lifestyle of a pastor validates the lifestyle of his/her parishioners. In order to be free we need sufficient information, and to be willing to face the hard reality of the information. Such information may contain where and how the item was made, how long it will last, what I will really pay for it, what are the harmful effects, etc. And for the Christian, how does this purchase reflect Christian stewardship?

In the total scheme of purchasing how does rationality stack up against emotion, impulse, escapism, competition, or some neurosis that turns me into a shopaholic? William Cavanaugh argues that, "Most contemporary marketing is not based on providing information, but on associating products with evocative images, and themes not directly related to the product itself."[774] Cavanaugh goes on to perceptively write, "Consumer culture is one of the most powerful systems of formation

---

[773] Terence Cullen, "The U.S. has more credit card debt than ever before," *New York Daily News* (January 9, 2018).

[774] William Cavanaugh. *Being Consumed: Economics and Christian Desire* (Grand Rapids: William B. Eerdman Publishing Company, 2008) 17.

in the contemporary world, arguably more powerful than Christianity. While a Christian may spend an hour per week in church she may spend twenty-five hours per week watching television, to say nothing of the hours spent on the internet, listening to the radio, shopping, looking at junk mail and other advertisements."[775]

Amazingly, I did not know the name of Herbert Buffum until writing this chapter. He wrote some ten thousand songs, one thousand of them actually published. *Ripley's Believe It Or Not* claimed that Buffum once wrote twelve songs in an hour.[776] No wonder he sold most of his songs for five dollars or less. He was a member of the Church of the Nazarene, but later left for a Pentecostal denomination. One of his verses from the explicitly holiness hymn "He Abides" has often played in my mind.

> There's no thirsting for the things
> Of the world — they've taken wings;
> Long ago I gave them up, and instantly
> All my night was turned to day,
> All my burdens rolled away;
> Now the Comforter abides with me.[777]

Buffum is to be blamed neither for his poetic exaggeration or his later defection to Pentecostalism. But at the same time one has to question his spiritual accuracy. Without doubt "No thirsting," "taken wings," and "instantly" were more possible for an early twentieth century Nazarene than a 2018 Nazarene. I can still hear the words reverberate from the cinder block walls of my childhood church. I do not know when and where I last heard this song. This is the only Buffum song out of his 10,000 songs to make the present Nazarene hymnal. The contemporary infrequency of this hymn being sung may be that the "wings" simply do not have enough lift for the vast array of commodities.

A Market-Driven Economy

With its scholastic energy spent on defining sanctification, assessing what is sin and what is not, there was not much left to define

---

[775] Ibid., 47.

[776] Herbert Buffum, cyberhymnal.org

[777] Herbert Buffum, "He Abides," *Sing to the Lord* (Kansas City: Lillenas Publishing Company, 1993) 315.

the reality and complexity of a market-driven economy much different in texture and methodology than the culture in which American holiness theology was conceived, systematized and applied. Our culture is constantly bombarding us with images of what it means to flourish, to succeed, to be happy, to be worthwhile, to be a person of significance. We are defined by what we desire more than by some spiritual crisis that we have experienced. The kingdom of the mall defines us more than does the kingdom of the Church. In fact, the pragmatic, utilitarian, marketing techniques of the church are more mall driven than anything that looks like the community described in Acts 2. James Smith writes, "In a culture whose civic religion prizes consumption as the height of human flourishing, marketing taps into our erotic religious nature and seeks to shape us in such a way that the passion and desire is directed to strange gods, alternative worship and another kingdom. And it does so by triggering and tapping into our erotic core - the heart."[778]

Holiness is a matter of the heart issuing in such practical matters as to how we spend our money and the material symbols that define us and more importantly to the American psyche, how these symbols define us to others. I have the distinct memory of going into the home of a well-known holiness preacher that was immaculately and richly decorated, far different than the Jim Walter home in which I lived. Spiritual appraisal needs to be tempered with aesthetic taste and creative abilities and may have little to do with monetary expenditures. What we tend to forget is that the early church was not shaped by prescriptions such as "You shall have all things in common." And "Be careful about using the personal pronoun 'mine.'" The economic consensus was not determined by the day of Pentecost, though it may have been enabled by such an event. Instead, there was a collective intuition that this is the way Christians relate to things, though alternative models would develop that equally represented and practiced kingdom living. In other words, it is not sufficient, nor are we epistemologically capable of completely forming Christian values by study of the Bible or so-called direct checks by the Holy Spirit, though I do believe in such.

---

[778] James K. A. Smith, *Desiring the Kingdom*. 75-76.

Communicating Christian Values

Christian values are best formed in family and discussed, because the route of becoming an authentic Christian in our society is not always fully clear. Communities speak much more profoundly than preachers, and communal practices are far more impressive than words. Thus, if an academic community lists its most distinguished alumni as business types or any type that has become "successful" in the secular community, or how it defines "making it in corporate ascension" or any kind of numerical quantifying, Christian moralizing in chapel, no matter how Jesus or biblical it sounds, falls on deaf ears. If you want to know what academic communities value, particularly those who claim to be Christian, just note their "alumni of the year" over the last quarter century. Unfortunately, it is often impossible to identify those most deserving honorific citation such as someone translating Scripture for a small New Guinea tribe, or ministering to rubber tree laborers in Guyana, South America.

The above was not much of an issue when we were all poor together. As discretionary income increased, made possible by two wage earners, it was noted that Oldsmobiles left the showroom floor just before Nazarene General Assembly. This was pointed out by the people who were not able to buy an Oldsmobile. Or as Freud said, "Righteous indignation is two percent righteous, forty-eight percent indignation, and fifty percent envy." Patterns of behavior give conversion and entire sanctification their content and are far more determinative than Sunday school lessons or catechism if such is practiced. For that reason, Paul Markham argues that our individualist and decisional concepts of conversion are inadequate. Quoting Allister McIntyre, "Hence the individual's search for his or her good is generally and characteristically conducted within a context defined by those traditions of which the individual's life is a part, and this is true both of those goods which are internal to practices and the goods of a single life."[779]

The narrative self is far more critical than the propositional self, the Bible-memorizing self, or the pursuit-of-theology self which is often the case in the academy. Our children's relationship to stuff will

---

[779] Paul Markham. *Rewired: Exploring Religious Conversion* (Eugene, Oregon: Penwick Publications, 2006) 160.

be more caught than taught. Testimonies to entire sanctification as an inward work of grace will be interpreted, not by the values we desire to portray, but by practices observed by those both closest to us and furthest from us. I suggest that Christian stewardship possibly means discussing all of our purchases within a Christian community or a small group. Does holiness require making my monthly credit card statement an "open book," at least, to trusted Christian friends? Obviously, our holiness ancestors did not have to answer this question. The issue was nonexistent.

Consumer Ethics is Tricky Business

Most of what we wear, drive, watch, listen to, boot up, and download is manufactured outside of the United States, simply because labor is cheaper. Recently in the world's most densely populated country, I was given a tour of a plant which exclusively manufactures men's pants and shorts. The manufacturing cost of making one pair of shorts is forty cents, which retails in the United States for $40.00, a ten-thousand percent mark-up. A sewer makes fifty cents per hour for the first forty hours and one dollar per hour for the next thirty. Of course, this forces all seamstresses to work seventy hours per week in order for their families to purchase the basic necessities for living, in a country where the average annual income per person is $521.00.[780]

The plant manager was rather proud that these women were given the extra hours for a possible fifty dollars per week wage. The worker should be grateful for the job, in that if she quits or gets fired, there are one hundred people lined up to take her place. A plant foreman is constantly supervising the quality and speed of her work. Immense pressure! The owner of the plant is building a much larger facility which will employ twice as many workers as the seven hundred whom he now employs. Will the additional workers rob the present workers of their overtime? I perceive the problem, but have no answer.

I have no evidence that the above employers maintain a lavish lifestyle, though they were able to educate their two sons in the United States. Capitalism rewards those who possess the creativity and take the

---

[780] Jason Mandryk. *Operation World: The Definitive Prayer Guide to Every Nation* (Colorado Springs: Biblica Publishing, 2010) 132.

risk to inaugurate a business venture. Rarely does it take into account that the founder begins with some kind of advantage, whether that advantage be inherited know-how or money. Vincent Miller, after reading about a woman who had literally worked herself to death for twelve cents per hour in a Chinese toy factory, wrote "A voiceless knot of grief forms in my throat. Did Chunmei work on any of the animals I'm tripping over this morning? The shell game of corporate outsourcing makes it impossible to know. I feel implicated but what to do? Divest? Participate in campaigns against such factories? Both are worthwhile but the quest for an adequate response (or even an inadequate one for that matter) only highlights the mindlessness of it all."[781]

Consumer ethics is tricky business. In the late 1970s, Mennonite Ron Sider spelled out his vision in *Rich Christians in an Age of Hunger*.[782] One of his prescriptions was, "Stop eating beef." Try playing this in Montana. I cast my kingdom vision in a large holiness church one Sunday morning. Some thought I had stopped preaching and gone to meddling. It was not well received. For the most part, consumer ethics is not part of the holiness agenda.

The Attention Merchants

Tim Wu traces the history of the four screens that have and continue to demand our attention, all with the purpose of selling us something: the silver screen (cinema), television, the computer, and the I phone. Rather than consuming, we are being consumed. Wu claims that, "All told, every second, our senses transmit an estimated eleven billion bits of information to our poor brains, as if a giant fiber-optic cable were plugged directly into them, firing information at full bore. In light of this, it is rather incredible that we are even capable of boredom."[783] All of these screens produce a celebrity culture, the allurement of the "rank and file," to bigger than life personalities who are utilized by the market economy to push and stream an endless supply of trinkets into the infinite void of American consciousness. The illusion is that we can become like these

---

[781] Vincent Miller. *Consuming Religion: Christian Faith and Practices in a Consumer Culture* (New York: Continuum, 2004) 16-17.

[782] Ronald J. Sider. *Rich Christians in an Age of Hunger: A Biblical Study* (Downers Grove, IL: InterVarsity Press, 1977).

[783] Tim Wu. *The Attention Merchants* (New York: Alfred A Knopf, 2016) 20.

cultural Gods if we acquire their accessories. Matthew McConaughey depicts this lie by driving a Lincoln: does he really pick his keys up with a swoop of his hand or in real life does he struggle to find his keys, like I do, in a basket full of keys? Does he really sit in the Lincoln amazed at the technology and craftsmanship of the interior, or is he like me, running late and can't get the car out of the garage fast enough? Is his life so empty that his highest moment of pleasure is driving around in the middle of the night? Borrowing language from Wu, "That perhaps explains why, for some, celebrity culture is so abominable; it is the ancient disgust with idol worship, triggering an atavistic emotional reaction, like the rage felt by Moses when he burned the golden calf, ground it into a powder, and scattering it on the water, forced his people to drink it."[784]

American consumers cannot comprehend that the people we worship don't give a damn about us, and have prostituted themselves in order to make prostitutes out of us. Wu reminds us, "Our deities are of course nothing like the God of Abraham, or even His saints. They are, rather, more like the pagan gods of old, prone to fits of anger and vindictiveness, petty jealousies, and embarrassing bouts of drunkenness. But this only lends to their illusion of accessibility, and at least for commercial purposes makes them more compelling to follow."[785]

The hold that particular celebrities have on the American psyche defies explanation other than the present zeitgeist is vacuous, ignorant, illiterate, and pathetically confused, grabbing on to anything that will give shallow existence, meaning, direction, or whatever. Wu summarizes the reasons for Oprah Winfrey's rise to stardom:

> Her substitution of spirituality for biblical Christianity, her promotion of forgiveness without atonement, and her references to a god "without labels" puts her at the epicenter of a seismic cultural earthquake. Perhaps not an earthquake: Oprah was not so far from the therapeutic deism that had long been the American religion. But her attentional reach made her a substantial danger to traditional faith — even perhaps to the nonreligious as well.[786]

---

[784] Ibid., 224.
[785] Ibid., 225.
[786] Ibid.

The above is not to deny Oprah's intelligence, initiative, charisma, creativity, and a genuine empathy for marginalized minorities with whom as a black woman she can communicate and identify. More mystifying are the Kardashians, who have none of Oprah's creativity but have managed to market their boring, tedious lives to the tune of 65 million dollars per year (2010), and Kim's alone 52.5 million by 2015.[787]

Maybe all of us can become the next Kardashians, and Face book has given us the perfect opportunity to market ourselves. Fame is no longer obtained by hard work, perseverance, creativity (which often demands isolated focus), but "the attention economy threw up its own mirage for the discontented masses, fame for everyone."[788] Wu observes, "In actuality, fame, or the hunger for it, would become something of a pandemic, swallowing up more and more people and leaving them with the scars of chronic attention – whoredom."[789]

The poorest of the poor, whether in Detroit or Calcutta, own a screen, a permanently attached appendage, that occupies a more prominent place in their self-understanding than the brain itself. The new social norm, for people in Los Angeles or Lagos is, "Never parting from one's device; standing and staring at it, as if paralyzed as the world goes by; of not looking up in the presence of others except when the urge to take a picture erupts at the strangest moment —*autre tech, autre moeurs*: it is probably the thing a visitor from a previous century would find the weirdest."[790]

Ancient wisdom has been traded for the distortion of reality whereby all of life becomes warped through a magnifying glass, promising bigger and better, hardly ever delivering more than a fleeting nanosecond of titillation, which should remind us of a preacher who three thousand years ago wrote in the midst of his own disillusionment, "Vanities of vanities, all is vanity." But alas, our increasing illiteracy makes it more improbable that as Americans, we would be able to identify Solomon, much less recall his wise counsel. For our society, the Simpsons have more to offer than does Solomon, and though we can access both with the appropriate app, the Simpsons are far more entertaining. We have

---

[787] Ibid., 248.

[788] Ibid., 307.

[789] Ibid.

[790] Ibid., 310.

chosen them or someone else equally inane for company: "Without expressed consent, most of us have passively opened ourselves up to the commercial exploitation of our attention just about anywhere and anytime. If there is to be some scheme of zoning to stem this sprawl, it will need to be mostly an act of will on the part of the individual."[791]

Yes, we need to be entirely sanctified, hearts purified, minds cleansed, filled with the Holy Spirit, forgiven, and constantly purged by the blood of Christ, equipped with the full armor of God. But believe it or not, we need more than that. We need a kingdom-filter, a Jesus sieve, a divinely-meshed strainer, an eschatological balance scale constantly asking, "What is wrong with this advertisement, where is the falsehood in this political claim, the skewed picture in this program, the trickery in this product, and the stifling debt if I buy this car?" What does acting on this urge, taking this trip, decorating with this furnishing, wearing these clothes or this jewelry say about my value system, my stewardship, and my commitment to life making the pronouncement, "Jesus is Lord."

There is no way to follow Christ without being counter-cultural — an angry response to a world that is attempting to sell me linear security, financial freedom for myself and my family, success that makes others envious, testosterone that transcends mortality, enough insurance to guarantee a nice funeral and ease for those I leave behind, enough military power to obliterate anyone who threatens our borders, all of which will remove the risk, dangers, and threats of life. All of this means is that there is nothing in my life worth dying for, and thus, in the end, I will have lived and died for nothing. Sebastian Junger in *Tribe* argues that soldiers are depressed and suicidal upon returning to the United States from Afghanistan and Iraq because they are no longer involved in the ultimate game, life and death.[792] Stanley Hauerwas and William Willimon simply state, "Our worst sins arise as our response to our innate fear that we are nobody."[793] Mark Edmundson sums up our present situation:

---

[791] Ibid., 343.

[792] Sebastian Junger. *Tribe: On Homecoming and Belonging* (New York: Hachette Book Group, 2016).

[793] Stanley Hauerwas and William H. Willimon. *Resident Aliens: Life in the Christian Colony* (Nashville: Abingdon Press, 1989) 67.

When the goals of the Self are the only goals a culture makes available, spirited men and women will address them with the energy that they would have applied to the aspirations of the Soul. The result is lives that are massively frustrating and not a little ridiculous. People become heroically dedicated to middle-class ends - getting a promotion, getting a raise, taking immeasurably interesting vacations, getting their children into the right college, finding the best retirement spot, and fattening their portfolios. Living without courage, contemplation, compassion, and imagination are lives sapped of significant meaning. In such lives, the Self cannot transcend itself.[794]

Americans may be the most idolatrous people in the world because we have to be a little faster, stronger, smarter, and more prosperous than everyone else. This is an exhausting race that earns me only six feet of land or an urn in the end. The American pastor is the one charged with informing all who will listen, that life's narrative doesn't have to be lived in and end in such foolish futility. We need holiness more than ever, but we need a holiness ethic that recognizes temptations, subtleties, deceptions, allurements, and possibilities for evil that our ancestors never faced. To be Christian is to be in the minority. And a more miniscule minority than we have been willing to confess or with whom we have been willing to participate. Christians are not in the majority in America or any other place. The Puritan Experiment has been overwhelmed with greed, selfishness, and "me first;" there is no theocracy. "Like an aging dowager, living in a decaying mansion on the edge of town, bankrupt and penniless, house decaying around her but acting as if her family still controlled the city, our theologians and church leaders continued to think and act as if we were in charge, as if the old arrangements were still valid."[795]

America's prevailing ethos promises a fixed ending; God says trust me for an open-ended ending, which only I know but will allow you to discover. The American teleosis is predicated on formulas for happiness as opposed to Jesus' chilling words to Peter, "When you are old, you will stretch out your hands, someone else will dress you, and lead you where you do not want to go" (John 21:18). This not-so-bliss prophecy

---

[794] Mark Edmundson. *Self and Soul: A Defense of Ideals* (Cambridge, MA: Harvard University Press, 2015) 50.
[795] Willimon and Hauerwas, 29.

is in direct contradiction to the world's constant bombardment with reminders that I need to control my destiny. Worse than blotting Jesus out of the picture, is proclaiming a Jesus who not only aligns himself with my desires, but promises that my desires will be fulfilled, as defined by, in my case, the American dream. In other words, in the American version of the Gospel, Jesus follows us rather than us following him with the promise, "I've got your back, wherever you want to go and whatever you want to do." As Chris Hedges puts it, "The gimmick of visualizing what we want and believing we can achieve it is not different from praying to a god or Jesus who we are told wants to make us wealthy and successful. For those who run into the bare walls of reality, the ideology has the pernicious effect of forcing the victim to blame him or herself for his or her pain or suffering."[796]

But there is a catch in the above: we still have to live in the world and identify with it, representing a delicate and even precarious task. As Kent Brower argues in his *Holiness in the Gospels*, Jesus came to reverse the separation motif which defined Jewish religion in the Old Testament. This was a major stumbling block for the Jews who observed a Messiah, who was without sin, being baptized for the remission of sins. Brower writes, "But Jesus shows that when separateness becomes the prime identity marker of the people, their attempt to preserve holiness becomes a barrier to engaging with God in His mission in the world."[797] He argues that holiness is contagious, outgoing, embracing, and joyous. Anything other comes across as snobbery, a condemning, judgmental attitude, concerned only with my own spiritual welfare. Personally, I observe how often I am tempted to pride (not always overcoming it) because I believe my values are better than someone else's. Thus, the very attempt to be Christian sends an unChristian message.

The above tendency leads to David Kinnaman's claim that to the non Christian world, particularly in America, "Modern-day Christianity no longer seems Christian."[798] We are seen by non Christians as hypocritical, focused on getting converts, anti-homosexual, sheltered,

---

[796] Chris Hedges. *Empire of Illusion: The End of Literacy and the Triumph of Spectacle* (New York, Nation Books, 2009)119.

[797] Kent Brower. *Holiness in the Gospels* (Kansas City: Beacon Hill Press of Kansas City, 2015) 129.

[798] David Kinnaman. *Unchristian: What a New Generation Thinks about Christianity and Why It Matters* (Grand Rapids: Baker Books, 2007) 29.

too political, and judgmental.[799] There would be some truth to responding with, "you are unfair," or these accusations are thin rationales for your own hedonism. I am reminded that about the only people Jesus condemned were the religious. As NTS President Jeren Rowell recalls, when he was preaching in the pastorate, he often said, "Whenever we read Pharisees in the Gospels, we can just go ahead and substitute our own names."[800]

A Holiness Lifestyle and Evangelism[801]

The pastor has made an appeal from the pulpit. The appeal may be for people to join an evangelistic team on Thursday evening, or to start a home Bible study in their neighborhood. Classes and training were offered to enable them to get started and provide the ongoing equipping and encouragement. Proportionate to the large congregation of evangelical and Bible-believing Christians, very few people responded. In regard to the dozen individuals who did begin participation in the Thursday evening evangelism sessions, the attrition rate was high and attendance sporadic. The pastor began to doubt his leadership abilities and teaching skills. Perhaps these people didn't have the 'gift' of evangelism anyway. Perhaps the church should depend on lifestyle evangelism and not try to force round people into square holes. Remember the ecclesiastical adage: "If it doesn't fly, prepare for a soft landing."

The problem with the alternate plan, lifestyle evangelism, is that it is the foremost reason why the church is not successful at evangelism. "Christians" do not possess the values, agendas, and orientation so essential to doing intentional or unintentional evangelism. Our privatized, individualistic, materialistic, hectic schedules effectively isolate us from many activities that call for a radically different orientation toward people and their eternal destiny. The fact is, people who are failing at relationships because of their quest for things, who are alienated from their neighbors because of their twelve-hour workdays, who are stressed out because of being dictated to by the world's definition of blessedness,

---

[799] Ibid., 29-30.

[800] Jeren Rowell. *Preaching Holiness: Pastoral Considerations* (Kansas City: The Foundry Publishing, 2018) 47.

[801] This section appeared in Darius Salter. *American Evangelism: Its Theology and Practice* (Grand Rapids: Baker Books, 1996) 342-346.

should not talk about doing evangelism, much less attempt it. Jack Bernard, in a perceptive article that calls for the Christian to enter a new culture, states, "Before we ever start asking questions about how to communicate the gospel, we need to deal with a much more important question, 'What kind of people ought we to be in order to be bearers of the words of life.'"[802]

Before one can penetrate the culture with an alternate worldview, one must be able not only to identify the culture, but make sure there is a differentiation between the penetrator and the penetrated. Thomas Oden defines the axial assumptions of modernity, the age and milieu in which Americans live, as "contempt for pre-modern wisdom, absolutized moral relativism, the adolescent refusal of parenting, idealization of autonomous individualism, and scientific empiricism as the final court of appeal in truth questions."[803] The practical results of these philosophical underpinnings have been narcissistic hedonism, minimal commitment to covenant responsibility, rampant consumerism, and a privatization of values that implicitly states, "You mind your own business, and I'll mind mine." There is a perception that we are free from external standards imposed by others, when we are really enslaved to the prevailing culture's criteria of what it means to be a person of significance in today's fast-paced society.

We have some vague notion that we are trapped on a treadmill that seems to be turning faster and faster. Commercialism tells us that we can control its rotation by purchasing computers, cellular phones, dictation devices, answering machines, calendar portfolios, elaborate filing systems, and endless credit and identification cards that will perform infinitely elaborate and detailed services. These only serve to grease the rollers of the treadmill. We are going nowhere fast, because we have not adequately defined where we need to go. Hence, it is difficult to entice people to go with us.

Vernard Eller defines the simple life as the "believer's inner relationship to God finding expression in his outward relationship to

---

[802] Jack Bernard. "I Found Jesus in My Wallet," *World Christian Magazine* (April 1990) 24.

[803] Thomas Oden. *After Modernity...What? Agenda for Theology* (Grand Rapids: Zondervan, 1990) 50.

'things.'"[804] The simple life is not a matter of volition, rules, prescriptions, egalitarianism, or even voluntary poverty. It is a total reorientation of the self-life to the center of all existence. We cannot map out a course of evangelism unless the polestar of our own lives has been examined and reconsidered. If pagans visit our churches, they are looking for people with a different polestar and the freedom of navigation that reference to that polestar brings. Unfortunately, seekers discover that the people housed in the edifice called a church are trapped in the very same anxieties and trivial pursuits that they are. The church has traded its eternal center for more temporal affairs, which is a frontal assault on the uniqueness of new creatures who are bound for the eschaton. Such blurred identity and amorphous description were not always true of those who call themselves Christians.

Richard Foster designates simplicity as the most outward expression of the Christian disciplines. Indeed, it probably more quintessentially represents what is popularly understood as lifestyle evangelism than any other one criterion. It is the *sine qua non* that enables the pagan world to hear a clear trumpet call by the would-be-evangelist. But the hedge of possessions obtained by restlessness and greed mutes the call or, at least, throws it off-pitch. Consider a recent poultry plant fire and the twenty-two employees who were consumed in that fire. Subsequent investigation revealed low wages, neglected safety precautions, slavish hours, and management that neglected the welfare of their workers in order to line their pocketbooks. No doubt, some individuals in the ownership and management team were professing Christians. All of us need to hear the words of Amos:

> Therefore, because you impose heavy rent on the poor and exact a tribute of grain from them, though you have built houses of well-hewn stone, yet you will not live in them; you have planted pleasant vineyards, yet you will not drink their wine (Amos 5:11).

Is there any escape from this unquenchable thirst to consume, quite often at the expense and exploitation of others? Foster suggests that we think of the misery that comes into our lives from the enormous greed that entraps us, that we practice a silence and solitude before God that dims the world's noise, and that we refuse to live beyond our means.

---

[804] Vennard Eller, *The Simple Life* (Grand Rapids: Eerdmans, 1973) 11.

People need to be motivated by a joy that doesn't take themselves too seriously and radically enables them to reschedule their priorities so that they have time to spend with their neighbors. Probably those who are the most effective evangelistically are families that have so radically restructured their existence that they have turned their large house, located next to a university, into a haven for students, or who have bought and renovated a structure that will serve as a hospice for AIDS patients, or transformed their gentleman's farm into a halfway house for unwed mothers. The list is endless as to how resources can be transformed into evangelistic tools.

Simplicity means that we make changes that enlarge our circumference of resources rather than diminish them. Widening one's circle of alternatives for being evangelistically effective may not necessarily mean moving to the inner city to start a mission for the homeless or a medical clinic for the destitute. But it will certainly mean heeding Foster's accurate advice that one should

> Stress the quality of the life above the quantity of life. Refuse to be seduced into defining life in terms of having rather than being. Cultivate solitude and silence. Learn to listen to God's speech in his wondrous, terrible, gentle, loving, all embracing silence. Develop close friendships and enjoy long evenings of serious and hilarious conversation. Such times are far more rewarding than the plastic entertainment that the commercial world tries to foist upon us.[805]

To be released from possessions to persons, from stress to simplicity, from consternation to contentment, is not a matter of resolution. Rather, it is what theologians have referred to as the expulsive power of a higher affection. It is holy obedience rooted in the eternal love of Jesus Christ. The expulsive power of holy love roots out the minor for the major, the temporal for the eternal, and the relative for the absolute. Holy love is able to visualize the greater cause; thus, "No soldier in active service entangles himself in the affairs of everyday life, so that he may please the one who enlisted him as a soldier" (2 Tim. 2:4).

That's it! We are too entangled in the affairs of this life to do the work of evangelism. There is a conflict of priorities, and only one thing

---

[805] Richard Foster. *Freedom of Simplicity* (San Francisco: Harper and Row, 1981) 123.

will solve the conflict — pleasing Him! Archbishop William Temple stated, "The spiritually minded man does not differ from the materially minded man chiefly in thinking about different things, but in thinking about the same things differently."[806] If we are going to begin to think differently about the souls of people, we will have to first think about things differently. That must have been what Jesus meant when He prayed for His disciples, "They are not of the world, even as I am not of the world. Sanctify them in the truth; your word is truth. As you sent me into the world, I also have sent them into the world" (John 17: 16-18).

If anyone knew about how to relate to both things and people under the canopy of pleasing God, it was Mother Teresa. She and the Sisters of Charity have ministered to 54,000 dying people from the streets of a metropolis whose squalid conditions are possibly the most despicable in the world. Claiming to be only a "pencil in the hand of God," she believed the poor were God's greatest gift to her because as she ministered to their needs, she was able to be with Jesus twenty-four hours a day. "We try to pray through our work by doing it with Jesus, for Jesus, to Jesus — that helps us put our whole heart and soul into it. The dying, the crippled, the mentally ill, the unwanted, the unloved — they are Jesus in disguise."[807]

Is it any wonder that the world is so attracted to her? They have never encountered anyone so radically free to be an angel of mercy, healing, and hope. Her serene confidence and single-minded direction was founded squarely on her philosophy of simplicity, which she revealed in the following statement:

> Take our congregation: we have very little, so we have nothing to be preoccupied with, The more you have, the more you are occupied, the less you give. But the less you have, the more free you are. Poverty for us is a freedom. There is no television here, no this, no that....I find the rich much poorer. Sometimes they are more lonely inside. They are never satisfied. They always need something more.[808]

---

[806] William Temple. *Nature, Man, and God* (London: Macmillan, 1934) 468.

[807] Edward Desmond, "A Pencil in the Hand of God," *Time*, (December 4, 1989) 11.

[808] Ibid.

Paul wrote, "Godliness with contentment is great gain." Contentment, if not our primary holiness witness, is one of the most critical messages to a world bent on accumulating stuff. Stuff obscures both our view of God and others.

Chapter 12:
The Mind

Harold Ockenga

Though Harold Ockenga's father was not a Christian, his Methodist mother instilled deep piety in her only son. Harold was industrious, athletic, handsome, winsome in personality, intellectually bright and spiritually sensitive. He was converted to Christ in high school, and under the tutelage and encouragement of a Mrs. Alice Plafman, he became convinced that he was called to ministry. Throwing aside his plans to attend the prestigious University of Chicago to become an attorney, he attended Taylor University in Upland, Indiana, founded in 1847, as Fort Wayne Female Seminary by the Methodist Episcopal Church. It was relocated to Upland, Indiana, in 1893 under Methodist auspices and assumed the name of William Taylor, the radical holiness missionary bishop of the Methodist Episcopal Church. By the time Ockenga arrived in 1923, Taylor University was not officially a Methodist institution. But there was enough influence from its heritage and its name sake that the doctrine of entire sanctification still "breathed" when Ockenga was a student.[809]

It was while on a gospel team ministry during the summer that conflict arose between the student members, and Ockenga realized he was a part of the problem. The issue of entire sanctification invaded his consciousness. The troubled young Christian rose early in the morning to pray about his spiritual deficiency, crying out to God, "Lord, if you don't do something for me, I'm not going to preach about something I do not have in my own life."[810] On the following Sunday, one of the team

---

[809] William Ringenberg. *Taylor University: The First 125 Years* (Grand Rapids: William B. Eerdmans Publishing Co., 1973).

[810] Harold Lindsell. *Park Street Prophet: A Life of Harold John Ockenga* (Wheaton: Van

members preached on Acts 1:8 and Ockenga fell under deep conviction. Though he had a strong urge to go forward when the invitation was given, his feet became immobilized. After the invitational hymn had finished, Harold stepped to the front of the church, and confessed his need. "I am going to the altar and ask Him to do something for me." Harold Lindsell described what happened to Ockenga that critical morning. "Something in Harold Ockenga died that day; it was not reduced; it was crucified. It was not hidden; it was brought forth to be slain. The self-life was dealt with just as his sins had been dealt with in salvation. The course of his life changed from that time onward. His one thought was to have the will of God for his life, pre-eminent in every decision. He now could say in simple sincerity, 'Not my will but thy will be done.'"[811]

Ironically, the Calvinist Lindsell had described the experience of entire sanctification in archtypical Wesleyan language. The question remained, how would this experience affect the ministry of perhaps the twentieth century's most influential Evangelical? For 33 years Ockenga pastored the highly visible Park Street Congregational Church in Boston, became the founding president of Fuller Theological Seminary, also founding president of Gordon Conwell Theological Seminary, and first board chair of the influential *Christianity Today*. Ockenga and Carl Henry were the two leading lights in organizing the National Association of Evangelicals, an endeavor seeking to disassociate itself from a more rigid fundamentalism.

In his Ph. D. dissertation on Ockenga, John Adams stresses the limited quality of academia at Taylor as opposed to its rich spiritual environment. This was not due to some intellectual aversion but simply the inability to attract Ph.D.s, and working faculty to their wit's end. One professor taught thirty-six hours per week. This was in all likelihood the case for almost all holiness schools. Thus, there was seemingly a two-stage development in Ockenga's academic trek, the spiritual first and then the intellectual. At Taylor, Ockenga served as the President of the Holiness League, for which he preached a sermon on Christ's understanding of holiness. Ten students responded to the "altar call," and the student newspaper recorded that "all of them prayed through to victory."[812]

Kampen Press, 1951)28.

[811] Ibid., 30.

[812] John Marion Adams. *The Making of a Neo-Evangelical Statesman: The Case of Harold*

Ockenga's Changed Theological Trajectory

Ockenga's professional and theological trajectory was determined not so much by his Methodist background, but by attending Princeton Theological Seminary, about the only theological graduate school with academic prestige not in the clutches of liberal theology. There Ockenga fell under the influence of J. Gresham Machen, scholastic rationalism's champion of orthodox theology. In 1929 Machen perceived himself as increasingly isolated from the Princeton theological faculty and founded the Presbyterian Westminster Seminary in Philadelphia, taking Ockenga with him.

Upon graduating from Westminster, Ockenga took a brief Methodist pastorate in Indiana. In 1931, he accepted a staff position with the arch conservative Clarence McCartney at First Presbyterian Church in Pittsburgh. He became pastor of the Point Breeze Presbyterian Church in the same city while completing a Ph.D. in Philosophy at the University of Pittsburgh. Due to the influence of Machen and McCartney, Ockenga adopted a Reformed theological position, though never becoming a five-point Calvinist. Due to the recommendation of his mentors, in 1936 Ockenga became the pastor of Park Street Church, one of America's most prestigious pulpits.

Ockenga's Holiness Theology

What happened to Ockenga's Methodist roots and sanctification encounter while a student at Taylor? It was not entirely forgotten. On Feb 4, 1940, Ockenga preached at Park Street a sermon titled "The Second Blessing: Sanctification and Holiness." He argued that there were two polarizing positions, each in error. Pentecostalism taught that the "Christian must seek a second blessing which is called a baptism of the Holy Spirit, which when received results in entire sanctification of the believer, the eradication of the sin nature and a life of sinlessness; all of which occur simultaneously which is attended by the manifestation of tongues."[813] Ockenga did not believe in a second baptism of the Holy Spirit. A believer is baptized with the Holy Spirit at salvation but filled

---

John Ockenga (unpublished Ph.D. dissertation, Baylor University, 1994) 116.

[813] Sermon by Ockenga, "The Second Blessing: Sanctification, and Holiness." Courtesy of Gordon Conwell Archives.

with the Holy Spirit at sanctification. Though he believed that there was a gift of tongues still operable, this gift was not the sign of being filled with the Spirit.

The other position with which Ockenga disagreed was dispensationalism, which limited Pentecost to a particular age of the Church. By believing that, "Pentecost was merely a manifestation of a dispensation change and had no experiential value for those who underwent it as a critical work of grace, they are shutting out a very great source of blessing from the Christian life."[814] What Ockenga did believe: first, the Bible definitely offers a second critical work of grace, but not in the sense usually imported to it from the Pentecostal movement. Second, the Bible demands the sanctified life on the part of the believer, but it does not demand the kind of life which is impossible of fulfillment. Third, the Bible requires holiness in the sense of a separated life, which alone is pleasing to the Lord.

For Ockenga, the key to this second crisis experience was consecration. Though Ockenga confessed that this full consecration and being filled with the Spirit may take place for some individuals at regeneration, this was not the norm. "That Spirit-filling does come, subsequent to one's conversion and regeneration, is the experience of most Christians whoever becomes Spirit-filled. This act of consecration, of giving over all unto God, of yielding oneself entirely to Him is as meaningful, as moving and as cataclysmic as in the experience of first accepting Christ as one's savior. It might quite legitimately be called a second work of grace."[815]

The biblical exposition which Ockenga gave, with one major exception, could have been taken straight from a holiness camp meeting (Ockenga as a child had attended the Des Plaines Holiness Camp, just outside of Chicago). Ockenga made reference to wrestling with Jacob, entering into Canaan, the Day of Pentecost, the Samaritan revival, and the house of Cornelius, all standard holiness texts. As to the exception, Ockenga was adamantly against either eradication or suppression theories of holiness but was unclear, or at least non-technical as to the alternative.

---

[814] Ibid., 3.

[815] Ibid., 6.

The word "eradication" has unfortunately been connected with the work. There is no such thing as eradication of inbred sin or of depravity. A man is a sinner after he is saved, although he may have been victorious he is a saved sinner. Nor does sanctification mean a suppression of the tendencies to sin, but it means the indwelling of the individual by the Holy Spirit who has control of his life. The Bible speaks of being sanctified through the inhabitation of the Spirit.[816]

Most interesting about the sermon is what Ockenga changed in the typewritten manuscript. In the title he crossed out "Blessing" and wrote in "Crisis," and seven other times he made this same change. Twice he changed "Holiness Movement" to "Pentecostal Movement." I can only conclude that Ockenga did not want to indict the Holiness Movement, or he possibly thought that his congregation would be more familiar with the Pentecostal Movement than the Holiness Movement. He did make one historical reference in keeping with his holiness heritage. "The title 'second blessing' was also given to this experience by John Wesley, and it forms one of the distinctive phases of the Methodist Revival and later preaching."[817] For the uninitiated, this statement was left without context and connection to the Holiness Movement.

As to an alternative trajectory of Ockenga's life, we are left only to speculate. What if he had attended Drew or Boston University and fallen under the spell of Edwin Lewis or Albert Knudsen before the former's conversion to evangelicalism? Would he have held onto his holiness theology? Would he have become a holiness exponent in Methodism or even became a member of the Holiness Movement? If so, he would have been condemned to marginality, if not irrelevancy. There were capable minds within the Holiness Movement, several who graduated from Harvard, such as Harold Kuhn, George Turner, and Timothy Smith, but none of them wrote, at least to the extent of Ockenga, who authored seven books just in the 1940s. Ockenga had gone to Boston, the citadel of New England theology, if not *all* of American theology. Lyman Beecher, Theodore Parker, Philips Brooks, Charles Chauncey, and William Ellery Channing had all pastored in Boston and Jonathan Edwards not far from there. Ockenga scholar Owen Strachan writes: "The young pastor was trained in Methodist and holiness circles that

---

[816] Ibid., 18.
[817] Ibid., 4.

challenged passionate young Christians like Ockenga to evangelize and pursue a sanctified life. Under the tutelage of Machen and others, Ockenga entered more fully into the confessional and intellectual tradition of historic Presbyterianism. Ockenga never lost his passion for evangelism and discipleship. But Machen's mentorship left Ockenga with a hunger for theological engagement."[818]

No crowd would offer more theological engagement than the 2,000 upper middleclass persons that gathered at Park Street each Sunday morning to hear the young pastor preach with both passion and theological depth. Ockenga was not a man plagued with self-doubt. He told a *Boston Herald* reporter that he "would rather live in Boston than any part of the United States of America, or of the world. Boston challenges me to do my best. I also feel that other systems of thought which have their centers in Boston and which compete with the system of thought which I advocate, are a profound challenge to my intellect and my ability."[819] Unfortunately, the Holiness Movement offered no such pulpit.

Timothy Smith

Just down the road, about ten miles south of downtown Boston stood Wollaston Church of the Nazarene. Wollaston is a small burg between Quincy and Quincy Bay. The church served as the unofficial college church for Eastern Nazarene College. Thus, the school's three-times-a-week chapels were held at the church, a functioning basement facility serving both students and congregation until the completion of the sanctuary in 1980. Before the completion, the edifice was facetiously referred to as the "topless church." From 1971-1975, Timothy L. Smith served as its minister, and weekly commuted from his teaching post at Johns Hopkins University in Baltimore to his pastorate. This four-year endeavor was seen by his Hopkins colleagues as puzzling. Yet, Smith not only did nothing to camouflage his devout Christian commitment, but proclaimed his theological persuasion, Wesleyan Holiness, in writing and speech whenever he thought appropriate. Often, when others deemed it inappropriate.

---

[818] Owen Strachan. *Awakening The Evangelical Mind: An Intellectual History of the Neo-Evangelical Movement* (Grand Rapids: Zondervan, 2015) 43.
[819] Ibid., 57

No one in the American Holiness Movement during the twentieth century surpassed the academic stature of Timothy Smith. In 1955, Smith completed his Ph.D. at Harvard, having written a dissertation, *Popular Protestantism in Nineteenth Century America*, under the direction of Arthur Schlesinger, Sr. The dissertation won Harvard's highest academic award and was published under the title *Revivalism and Social Reform in Mid-Nineteenth Century America*.[820] This work is the most seminal project ever completed by an individual within an American holiness denomination. There are few general or even specialized works on American Church history which do not reference the book. Robert T. Handy praised Smith's *Revivalism* as a "brilliant study," and Martin Marty assessed that Smith pushed "a defensible thesis very hard and documents it with almost numbing efficiency."[821] This academic achievement was even more remarkable in that Smith pastored the Cliftondale Church of the Nazarene during the entire duration of his residential studies at Harvard. The downside of Smith's accomplishment is that his dissertation was the high point of his scholarly realization.

Smith's parents were unique. They were both pious and intellectual. His father, Lester B. Smith, attended Vanderbilt and subsequently taught at the Pilgrim Holiness College in Frankfort, Indiana, and also served as president of John Wesley College in Greensboro, North Carolina. When he preached, he had only the Greek New Testament before him. In spite of his father's intellectual acuity, Smith assessed his mother as the more capable preacher of the two. Dolores Smith, along with her husband, founded the Newport News, Virginia, Church of the Nazarene, and Dolores pastored the church after her husband's death in 1954, for another 12 years, retiring at age 75.

Smith's Linking the American Holiness Movement with Wesley

In 1955, the Church of the Nazarene commissioned Smith to write its denominational history. The academic dexterity and detail with which Smith completed the project would have made a much larger denomination proud. The strength of the book is a very astute

---

[820] Timothy L. Smith. *Revivalism and Social Reform in Mid-Nineteenth Century America* (Nashville: Abingdon Press, 1957).

[821] Floyd Cunningham, "Common Ground: The Perspectives of Timothy L. Smith on American Religious History," *Fides et Historia* 44.2 (Summer/Fall 2012) 23.

analysis of "come-outism," the confluence of very diverse groups, all of them adhering to what they believed to be John Wesley's understanding of "entire sanctification," coming together under one umbrella. The downside of Smith's analysis is an issue that would become increasingly controversial within Wesleyan holiness scholarship: Smith drew a straight theological line between John Wesley's societies and Phoebe Palmer's parlor. This was particularly problematic since so many Wesleyans, Congregationalists, Baptists, Quakers, and Presbyterians, as well as others bought into the more amorphous "higher life movement."

Smith made clear that the Methodist leadership, with their vaguely defined doctrinal edges, had distanced themselves from Wesley, as opposed to the holiness crowd who gravitated around the National Camp Meeting Association for the Promotion of Holiness. Smith wrote, "The strength of their propaganda in fact lay in their constant appeals to the meaning of Wesley, Fletcher, and the first American Bishop, Francis Asbury. So successful were they in identifying sanctification with Methodist orthodoxy, that opponents were hard pressed to find ground upon which to stand without laying themselves open to the charge of heresy."[822] Smith further stated, "In earlier decades, critics of the 'second blessing' had professed great respect for the founder. They contented themselves with publishing fragments of his writings which seemed to prove that Wesley questioned the idea of an instantaneous second experience, or that he discouraged testimony to it and left undefined the precise nature of 'sin in believers' which it eradicated. The holiness specialists managed by the 1880s pretty well to demolish these arguments and to make the veneration of Wesley their most powerful weapon."[823]

If nothing else, Timothy Smith was firm in his convictions and was not intimidated by his colleagues at Johns Hopkins or any place else. He wore his theological beliefs on his shirt-sleeve, and though he could defend his position with the best minds, he may have not done some of us with a little less intellectual acuity, and who desire to proclaim Wesleyan holiness, any favors. Even Smith's former student, defender and biographer Floyd Cunningham admits that

---

[822] Timothy L. Smith. *The Church of the Nazarene: The Formative Years* (Kansas City: Nazarene Publishing House, 1962) 21.
[823] Ibid., 42.

Through his writing, frequent lectures on Christian college campuses, acerbic comments in learned society meetings and advice given to younger proteges, Smith demonstrated that one could be both a warm-hearted believer and a hard-headed empiricist with no patience for unsubstantiated statements of supposed fact. At the same time, though he was a graduate of the University of Virginia and Harvard, Smith's evangelicalism made him an outsider with the academy and as an unapologetic Wesleyan, even an outsider to other evangelicals. He embraced that outsider status with a certain aplomb that could be interpreted as pugnacity.[824]

One wonders if Smith himself held to some "unsubstantiated statements" and if such "pugnacity" was necessary in order for him to be simultaneously recognized as an honest scholar within a particular confession of the Christian faith.

H. Orton Wiley

Molly Worthen argues that while Carl Henry, Ockenga and others were attempting to construct a worldview under which a broad band of evangelicals could gather, "The Nazarenes and Mennonites argued about 'worldliness' and abandonment of older customs and styles of dress."[825] She exalts H. Orton Wiley as gifted with a subtle, theological touch as "comfortable in ancient, neo-platonic philosophy and medieval scholastism as he was in the pages of John Wesley's sermons."[826] He attempted to lift his denomination above petty ethical issues and rigid understandings of Scripture which characterized the increasingly recalcitrant and retreating fundamentalists. Wiley was raised in a Nebraska sod house, spent his youth raising hogs and collecting rattlesnake skins. The family moved to Oregon, and after his father died, he worked in a drug store, later attending Berkeley and Pacific Theological Seminary. He fell in with the California Nazarenes and at age thirty-six became president of their college at Pasadena.

Wiley attempted to guide the Church of the Nazarene into a reverential interpretation of Scripture that revealed Christ, rather than the fundamentalistic literalism, a pseudo-scientific method of reading the

[824] Cunningham, 26
[825] Worthen, 38.
[826] Ibid., 40.

Bible.[827] But in dismay, "Wiley watched first-hand as the fundamentalist spell bewitched Wesleyan Holiness churches and transformed their views of Christian earthly obligations."[828] Though the Church of the Nazarene had been conceived by a strong social conscience which it put into practice, it increasingly abandoned this practice for an anti-worldly stance for personal sanctification and an imminent apocalypse. Nazarenes as well as other holiness denominations attempted to stem the fundamentalist tide, but only intensified internal bickering, which in Worthen's assessment, "Did not make for effective public theology."[829] According to Worthen, Wiley and Harold Bender, a capable Mennonite theologian, "remained church theologians little known outside their respective traditions. The neo-evangelicals Henry and Ockenga paid almost no heed to their efforts."[830] Wesleyans were not unique, but representative of the majority of American Evangelicals who prioritized "piety over critical thinking and were always suspect of academia even as they touted training for their ministers."[831]

The Reformed Theology Fusillade Against the Holiness – Pentecostal Movements

At this point we double back to Hunter's thesis that great minds need great money, and Nelson Bell, who had to leave his missionary work in China with the outbreak of World War II, persuaded oil magnate J. Howard Pew to float a new magazine *Christianity Today*, which by 1958 had become "the most widely and regularly read Protestant magazine," according to Carl Henry, its editor. Henry would emerge as the most influential neo-evangelical in America. After the publication of Smith's *Revivalism and Social Reform*, Henry criticized the Wesleyan for "spanking the Calvinists whenever there is an opportunity."[832] This sniper's bullet was part of a larger fusillade of artillery to obliterate theological traditions that were not safely within the Reformed fortress. John Howard Yoder, like Wiley and Bender, was on the outside as were Nazarenes Rob Staples and Mildred Wynkoop. The latter two

---

[827] Ibid.

[828] Ibid., 41.

[829] Ibid., 42.

[830] Ibid., 45.

[831] Ibid., 50.

[832] Ibid., 66.

complained about the "inerrancy statement" that had crept into the Wesleyan Theological Society's "Statement of Faith," and Staples cried foul regarding *Christianity Today's* treatment of Wesleyans. Wynkoop's *Theology of Love* drew praise from Wesleyan scholars Donald Dayton and Howard Snyder, but drew little attention from the evangelical mainstream.

To the Wesleyans' credit they did not argue for rigid creation science any more than they did for predicting the rapture. Wesleyans did not buy into the sensational aspects of looking either backwards or forwards. They transcended the sensationalism of Pat Robertson, Tim LaHaye, Hal Lindsey, Jerry Falwell, and in particular, those reactionary fundamentalists who claimed that the rise and fall of Christendom hinged on the word "inerrancy." Unfortunately, many holiness folk on the lay level bought into all of these popular theologies and knew nothing of Timothy Smith's argument in The *Christian Century* that "Wesleyans, Lutherans, and Calvinists, who questioned inerrancy were not caving in to modern biblical scholarship 'drawing upon the writings of the Reformers themselves to affirm our conviction that the meanings, not the words of biblical passages are authoritative and that understanding these meanings requires close and critical study of the texts rather than incantation of supposedly inerrant words.'"[833] Worthen may be overly optimistic when she claims, "Evangelicals in a variety of traditions, particularly Wesleyan Holiness Christians and Anabaptists, have decoupled Christianity from conservative politics and called for believers to invest their resources into social justice, international relief, and environmentalism."[834]

Nazarenes as well as other holiness types should be grateful for Worthen's treatment of Wiley, in that she carefully parses out Wiley's thinking from the broader band of fundamentalism and even neo-evangelicalism. Regretfully, Mark Noll, supposedly the Dean of evangelical historians, in his *Scandal of the Evangelical Mind*, lumps dispensationalists, Pentecostals, and the Holiness Movement all together. Treatments of the Holiness Movement fall under such subtitles as "theological innovations" and "a new surge of anti-intellectualism."

---

[833] Timothy L. Smith, "Reader's Response: Determining Biblical Authority's Base, *The Christian Century* (March 2, 1977) 198.
[834] Worthen, 254.

Making no distinction between the American Holiness Movement and the British Keswick Movement (and there certainly was a degree of continuity) Noll quotes Martin Lloyd Jones: "If you want to be holy and righteous we are told the intellect is dangerous and it is thought generally unlikely that a good theologian is likely to be a holy person.... You ask me to diagnose the reason for the present weakness and I am doing it....If you teach that sanctification consists of 'letting go' and letting the Holy Spirit do all of the work then don't blame me if you have no scholars."[835] Jones should have known that his characterization was a caricature, especially if he had made any concerted attempt to read his British ancestor, John Wesley.

Noll interpreted the Holiness Movement as well as Pentecostalism and dispensationalism as representing "patterns of thinking" antithetical to intellectual development. According to Noll, these three movements treated under his subtitle "The Intellectual Disaster of Fundamentalism," would continue by the 1950s to leave American conservatives "moribund."[836]

In Defense of Holiness Academia, in Particular by Donald Dayton

Three critical responses are worth noting. Pentecostal scholar Cheryl Bridges-Johns suggested that we are not called to be the great universities of Europe or the next Harvard of America. Such an approach accepts the so-called centrist reading of reality and offers explanation after explanation, rebuttal after rebuttal, with the hope of convincing critics that we are more like the really learned of the world. She argues that Wesleyan Pentecostals are not called to a rationalistic, enlightenment form of knowledge but rather, "love knowledge." This knowledge is received as a gift, a response that involves a complex form of life which was the quest of John Wesley. Johns writes, "We have the opportunity to manifest the scandal of love's knowledge, a knowing which is not grasping but a letting go, a knowing which is not grounded in its own self presence but in the presence of the source of all knowing."[837]

---

[835] Mark A. Noll. *Scandal of the Evangelical Mind* (Grand Rapids: William B. Eerdmans Publishing, 1994) 124.

[836] Ibid., 110.

[837] Cheryl Bridge-Johns, "Partners in Scandal: Wesleyan and Pentecostal Scholarship," *Pneuma* Vol. 21, No. 2 (Fall 1999) 197.

Wesleyan scholar David Bundy noted the strong pre-millenial accent which precluded long-term education on a short-term planet. I can personally verify this, because once I asked Paul Rees if he had any regrets. "Yes," he responded. "I wish I would have earned a Ph.D. The emphasis was so much on the 'second coming,' that one better get out and start preaching." Bundy blames not an intellectual deficiency in Wesleyan Pentecostal schools, but larger cultural forces which have marginalized much of evangelicalism. (Remember Hunter's argument that ideas have to be harnessed to power, mainly money, such as John D. Rockefeller's underwriting the University of Chicago and James Buchanan Duke endowing Duke University.) Bundy writes that, "Because of the expensive traditions of the scholarly guilds, the unavailability of significant government funds, the lack of financial resources available within the tradition and with the resultant heavy teaching loads, a Wesleyan Holiness institution devoted to scholarly pursuits within their tradition seems a distant dream."[838]

No one has challenged Mark Noll's and George Marsden's Reformed Presbyterian interpretation of American evangelicalism more than Donald Dayton. Dayton argued for a Holiness-Pentecostal formation of American evangelicalism, rather than its eruption from the fundamentalist-modernist controversy of the early twentieth century. Dayton began his argument with *Discovering an Evangelical Heritage* in 1976.[839] The book could have been titled *Discovering a Holiness Heritage*, as almost all the main actors which he noted were "second blessing" exponents. According to Dayton, American evangelicalism evolved through such reformers as Charles Finney, the Lane rebels, Jonathan Blanchard, Theodore Weld, Orange Scott, Luther Lee, A. B. Simpson and many others, who found their spiritual energy and motivation in themes of sanctification.

In the late 1980s, Dayton found himself in a running debate with George Marsden, who in his *Reforming Fundamentalism: Fuller Seminary and the New Evangelicalism*, according to Dayton, had neglected the Wesleyan- Pentecostal side of things. Dayton accused

---

[838] David Bundy. "Blaming the Victim: The Wesleyan Holiness Movement in American Culture," *Wesleyan Theological Journal*. No. 32 (Spring 1997) 177.

[839] Donald W. Dayton. *Discovering An Evangelical Heritage* (New York: Harper & Row Publishers, 1976).

Marsden of adopting a theologically-oriented "conservative/liberal" paradigm, in which evangelicalism is seen primarily as a conservative or traditional reaction against liberalism. Instead, Dayton wanted consideration for holiness churches in shaping evangelicalism, not so much as a conservative movement, but as a "radicalization of the Methodist pull-away from Anglicanism in the direction of revivalism and low-church piety."[840]

The rightness or wrongness of Marsden and Dayton is beyond the scope of our investigation. But a comment by Marsden provides a critical insight for the demise of the Holiness Movement. "Militant anti-modernism is at least one prominent dimension of that movement (fundamentalism), though there are other dimensions as well. Neo-evangelicals, such as those who founded Fuller Seminary, inherited that militancy against modernism. This was evidenced in their concern for apologetics and their emphasis on the inerrancy of Scripture."[841] These polemical and apologetical concerns called for a written defense of the faith, and founded the publishing houses of Zondervan, Baker, and Eerdmans, not coincidentally located in the Calvinistic stronghold of Grand Rapids, Michigan. The Wesleyan Holiness Movement was unable to produce a cooperative publishing venture among its several denominations (other than the failed attempt by the Francis Asbury Society discussed in Chapter 7).

Joel Carpenter interprets Marsden as insisting that, "It would be impossible to be true to the story of early Fuller Seminary, if he did not stress the professors' militant orthodoxy. They possessed a passion for theological intellectuality, and their primary concern was to use it in defense of the fundamentals of the faith."[842] Holiness folk neither exhibited nor exercised such militant orthodoxy or passion for theological respectability. They chose between a pure heart and a clear mind, experiential piety as opposed to theological rectitude. If history has consequences, and history is the biography of persons, then the

---

[840] Donald W. Dayton. "The Search for the Historical Evangelicalism: George Marsden's History of Fuller Seminary as a Case Study," *Christian Scholars Review* 23, No. 1 (1993) 17.

[841] George Marsden. "Response to Don Dayton," *Christian Scholars Review*, 23, No. 1(1993) 37.

[842] Joel Carpenter. "The Scope of American Evangelicalism: Some Comments on the Dayton-Marsden Exchange," *Christian Scholars Review*, 23, No. 1(1993) 58.

lineages of Francis Asbury and Jonathan Edwards are not difficult to trace. They were pure anti-types, one the doer and the other, the thinker. As to who was most important in shaping the early Republic, it will be subjectively decided by those of us who claim one or the other as our ancestor.

Spirituality and Anti-Intellectualism in the Holiness Movement

But nobody is entirely wrong, not even Mark Noll, working from the perspective of his Reformed bias and having flown from one lofty perch, Wheaton College, to another, Notre Dame University, which seems to be the goal of any serious scholar. Unfortunately, there is historical evidence for his indictment. Russell V. DeLong, as the Dean of Nazarene Theological Seminary in a 1966 commencement address, warned that "the scholarly drive for excellence may supplant the spiritual."[843] He then contradicted himself by stating, "There should be no conflict. Truth is one."[844] If DeLong did not fear that the quest for academic excellence would supplant spiritual primacy, why did he raise the issue? Even the more perceptive minds, the leading thinkers of the Church of the Nazarene, did not shrug off the issue. Westlake T. Purkheiser believed that "Nazarenes had difficulty in maintaining a balance between warm hearts and cool heads, a deep devotion and high professional ideals."[845] William Greathouse took a divergent perspective, warning the Church of the Nazarene against a "neo-gnosticism," an ideology that sought to create a division between the secular and the sacred which would lead to anti-intellectualism.[846]

There is no reason to believe that the Nazarenes are unique at this point from other holiness denominations or even the wider evangelical movement. Course loads, committee assignments and advisory responsibilities all mitigate against writing as opposed to a professor at a major research institution who teaches only one course per semester. Under a quarter of the professors teaching at a school within the "Council for Christian Colleges and Universities" (96 member schools, 22 of them

---

[843] Oran Randall Spindell. *An Analysis of Higher Education In The Church of The Nazarene, 1945-1978.* (Unpublished Ph.D. Dissertation, Oklahoma State University, 1981).

[844] Ibid., 291.

[845] Ibid., 30.

[846] Ibid., 308.

having some connection to the Wesleyan Holiness movement) have published a book and less than two-thirds have "published an article in a peer-reviewed journal."[847]

The tension between academic freedom and constituency fear is not entirely unfounded. Eli Knapp, a professor at Houghton College, a Wesleyan school, describes the delicate balancing act of trying to interpret the biblical creation account in light of scientific paradigms. It seems the best methodology is to tacitly imply that there are competing claims and even varying interpretations of Genesis 1 and 2, somewhat but not entirely accommodating to Darwin. If students want to pursue further investigation or have unanswered questions, Knapp makes himself available for lunch or a stroll across the campus. "It seems more and more of today's students, the so-called millennial generation, crave sincerity and beg for discussion. They do not want the easy stuff; they want the controversial. Gray areas are attractive and intellectual honesty trumps all. The sturdier students noticed my evolutionary evasiveness in class, if they did not call me out on this in class, they called me out after it."[848]

The Wider Evangelical Issue

Interestingly, William C. Ringenberg, considered by many to have written the standard history of Christian colleges in America, spent his entire life teaching at a holiness college, Taylor University. Noll wrote the introduction to the 2006 edition *The Christian College: The History of Protestant Higher Education in America.* Though he did not single out the Holiness Movement, Noll remained somewhat pessimistic about the intellectual vigor of American Evangelicals as a whole. "In an age, finally, demanding forceful Christian responses to powerful secular ideologies, careful Christian probing of complex intellectual issues, and creative Christian initiatives for pressing contemporary problems, much of evangelicalism still retains a stultifying 19th century suspicion of all

---

[847] Dan Russ. "Fear Not: Security, Risk and Academic Freedom" in *The Christian College Phenomenon: Inside America's Fastest Growing Institutions of Higher Learning,* eds. Samuel Joeckel and Thomas Chesnes (Abilene, TX: Abilene Christian University Press, 2012), 174.

[848] Eli J. Knapp. "Intelligently Designed Discussion: My Journey through Intellectual Fear in Higher Education," *Christian Scholar's Review,* XLVI, No. 2 (Winter 2017) 145-53.

thinking that does not rest on mythic views of America's past, egalitarian common sense, or popular interpretations of the Bible."[849] He further stated, "The tendency has ever been present for Christian academics to drift into the secularism of the wider culture or to relapse into the obscurantism of cultic sectarianism."[850]

A couple of Ringenberg's observations are important to us. Of the twenty-one largest accredited Bible schools in the 1990s, only one holiness institution made the cut, Nazarene Bible College in Colorado Springs with Biola and Moody leading the way. He indicts Henry Clay Morrison, founder of Asbury Theological Seminary and twice president of Asbury College. "By 1920, Asbury's leader thought it necessary to preach against modernism as well as for holiness, with a result that they sounded increasingly like the more Calvinist fundamentalists. Morrison, a crusading religious orator in the style of Bryan, attacked the Protestant liberals for claiming what their theology was not rather than what they did believe."[851] Ringenberg is correct as I have already demonstrated.

Another Ringenberg observation is that SAT scores for Christian college applicants are no indicator of the number of students sent on to professional schools and Calvin College ranked highest for students entering post-graduate education. Ringenberg noted Indiana Wesleyan University, that by 2005 boasted of more than 9,000 students on its nine regional campuses and 70 total program centers, while maintaining a high graduation rate (80%). One wonders if Wesleyan Keith Drury, a former IWU professor, would be in agreement with former President Mark Smith's claim for "Exemplariness in quality control, the facilitation of student success, and a faith and learning integration emphasis commiserate with that of the traditional program."[852]

For George Marsden, Nathan Hatch, and others, the problem of academic marginalization and lack of scholarly prowess are to be

---

[849] William C. Ringenberg. *The Christian College: A History of Protestant Higher Education in America* (Grand Rapids: Baker Academic, 2006) 34-35.

[850] Ibid., 35.

[851] Ibid., 172.

[852] Ibid., 221. Obviously, these statistics are outdated. IWU now has some 14,000 students at 15 regional sites, with the main campus located at Marion, Indiana. Statistics courtesy of Karen Roorbach, Senior Counsel to the President of Indiana Wesleyan University, Marion, Indiana.

found in the wider cultural issues of evangelicalism. Marsden, while referencing the attempts of Oral Roberts, Pat Robertson, and Jerry Falwell, who founded major universities, refers to them as "embarrassing misnomers both in scope and scholarly production. They hardly compare to modestly scaled secular universities, much less to a Princeton or a Johns Hopkins."[853] Hatch maintains that for most evangelical schools, instead of abstract thinking, intensive reading and careful research one finds "ideological traditionalism that orients thinking around a set of principal ideas and practices rather than around institutions or creeds."[854] Unfortunately, holiness theology was often world-negating rather than world encompassing. Alliteration allowed conservative holiness folk to easily catalogue their enemies as Communist, Catholic, charismatic, and Calvinist. In the 60s, at least a minority of conservatives within the Holiness Movement were likely to be members of the John Birch Society and to read John Stormer's anti-Communist tract, *None Dare Call It Treason*. Hatch further states: "Evangelical academicians are often children of reaction against the stern parent of fundamentalism – its inbred suspicion of intellectualism, its retreat from liberal arts education, its hostility to aesthetics, its inability to confront modern science in constructive ways, its legalism, and most importantly, its parochial religious vision."[855]

Children of Reaction in the Church of the Nazarene

The "children of reaction" scenario was played out when a coterie of students left the Church of the Nazarene in the early 1960s; three of them were children of well-known people in the denomination, G. B. Williamson, Albert Harper, and Ralph Earle. These three students had distinguished careers. Charles Harper became a well-known poet and pastor in the Congregational Church. Joseph Williamson, a Harvard Ph.D., became Dean of the Chapel at Princeton University. Eastern

---

[853] George Marsden. "Why No Major Evangelical University," in *Making Higher Education Christian: The History and Mission of Evangelical Colleges in America*. eds. Joel Carpenter and Kenneth W. Shipps. (Grand Rapids: William B. Erdman's Publishing Company. 1987) 299.

[854] Nathan O. Hatch. "Evangelical Colleges and the Challenge of Christian Thinking," in *Making Higher Education Christian: The History and Mission of Evangelical Colleges in America*. eds. Joel Carpenter and Kenneth W. Shipps (Grand Rapids: William B. Eerdman's Publishing Co. 1987) 161.

[855] Ibid., 165.

Nazarene College named him alumnus of the year in 2004, and in 2002, he was honored with a lifetime achievement award for distinguished leadership and service by the Association of College and University Affairs.[856] Ralph Earle, Jr., established a nationally-known counseling center in Las Vegas, Nevada.

A fourth student, Thomas Starnes, did not have an aristocratic heritage in the Church of the Nazarene, and became pastor of one of United Methodism's most prestigious pulpits, Capitol Hill United Methodist Church in Washington, D.C. Starnes never forgot his debt to the Church of the Nazarene. When A. E. Kelly, an obscure Nazarene evangelist died, Starnes wrote the *Herald of Holiness* recounting how his dad, an alcoholic and father of eight children, had been saved under Kelly's ministry. "Life was never the same again. He quit drinking. He got a good job. He became a faithful member of Christ's holy church. And two of his sons are in the ministry, as are two of his granddaughters. I wish I had told A.E. Kelly that."[857]

Some of these students found themselves in a perfect intellectual storm. They were in a Doctrine of Holiness class, taught by someone incapable of answering their questions. This person, with little academic preparation, had been appointed by the General Superintendents, often referred to as just "Generals." Almost every day after class the despairing professor told Ken Grider that he was going to quit, but Grider encouraged him to continue.[858] Unfortunately, he continued. Chuck Harper would write, "Well before coming to New Haven, I knew I was no longer an evangelical, as that theological stance was expressed in the Church of the Nazarene."[859] Starnes wrote, "For good or ill, I could not preach the Church of the Nazarene's cardinal doctrine that claimed that one could be free of sin in this life. Neither could I withhold membership in the body of Christ for those that might dance, play bridge, go to the picture show."[860]

The 1960s walkout of some of the Church of the Nazarene's brightest students was not limited to NTS, but played out on other

---

[856] Nazarene Archives. Joseph Williamson file.

[857] Nazarene Archives. Thomas Stearns file.

[858] Phone conversation with Paul Bassett, Summer 2018.

[859] Nazarene Archives, Chuck Harper file, "How My Mind Is Changing."

[860] Thomas Starnes, "Kelly's Trombone," Thomas Starnes file, Nazarene Archives.

Nazarene campuses as well, none more so than Bethany Nazarene College in Oklahoma City. Prescott Johnson, a Kierkegaard scholar, held sway over a coterie of intellectual students, including Gary Hartpence, later to be known as Gary Hart. Gary, the most popular student on campus, was also known for his deep Christian devotion and academic acuity. Few of Johnson's students remained Nazarenes. Pulitzer Prize-winning historian Garry Wills states that, "The barriers that holiness doctrine reared against the world stood in the way of their sampling the cultural explosion in the 1960s."[861] Johnson headed for a distinguished career at the University of Oklahoma and Hart, along with Chuck Harper, to Yale Divinity School. Harper was Hart's college roommate and referred to Hart as the sharpest student he had ever known.[862] Wills designated Hart as a "would-be rake and moralist, spy and philosopher king."[863] The rest is history.

One of the most intellectual faculty members of Nazarene Theological Seminary, my colleague, once said, "All of my teaching assistants seem to become Episcopalians." I do not know that he reflected on the "why."[864] The answer may have been given by Nathan Hatch: "The problem simply put is that the tradition of faith in which many of us were raised has been powerful enough to maintain their hold, but not powerful enough either intellectually or spiritually to provide an orienting vision for all of life."[865] Unfortunately, the Holiness Movement has continued to operate in a worldview, which no longer fits the realities of today's overwhelming complexity. In many ways, Wesleyan holiness exponents are not to be blamed, as the rules of engagement changed. They were faced with a "catch 22" dilemma: Do we maintain our identity through isolation, or do we broaden our concerns while our ideology withers away? Starnes must have asked himself, "Would my father have been instantaneously saved from alcohol, in a church representing a broader societal venue and a higher socio-economic standing in the community?"

---

[861] Garry Wills. *Under God: Religion in American Politics* (New York: Simon and Schuster, 1990) 47.

[862] Phone conversation with Chuck Harper, Summer 2018.

[863] Ibid., 50.

[864] H. Orten Wiley's two sons became Episcopalian priests. Wiley often attended both an Episcopal Church and a Nazarene Church on Sunday morning.

[865] Hatch, "Evangelical Colleges," 164.

Whatever the success or failure of the Wesleyan Holiness mind, no blame can be laid at the feet of John or Charles Wesley the latter who wrote:

> Come Father, Son and Holy Ghost,
> Unite the pair so long disjoined,
> Knowledge and vital piety,
> Learning and holiness combined,
> And truth and love, let all men see.
> In those whom up to thee we give,
> Thine, wholly thine, to die and live.[866]

---

[866] Charles Wesley hymn, "Come Father, Son, and Holy Ghost" verse 5. https://www.ccel.org/w/wesley/hymn/jwg04/jwg0473.html

Chapter 13:
Moving Forward

A Robust Pneumatology

The Wesleyan Holiness Movement has been characterized by a robust theology of the Holy Spirit. We need to get beyond the arguments as to whether our pneumatology is Wesleyan, Palmerian, Finneyan, Mahanan, and Keswickian, or most representative of the 19th century Holiness Movement as propagated by the National Camp Meeting Association for the Promotion of Holiness. We also need to get beyond the power-purity question; both were stressed by our holiness ancestors. We need to again confess that our only hope is to be found in the power and presence of the Holy Spirit.

Christ's last will and testament was, "And I will ask the Father and he will give you another counselor to be with you forever - the Spirit of truth. The world cannot accept him, because it neither sees him nor knows him. But you know him, for he lives with you and will be in you" (John 14:16-17). Christ's last command to his disciples was, "Do not leave Jerusalem, but wait for the gift my father promised, which you have heard me speak about. For John baptized with water, but in a few days you will be baptized with the Holy Spirit" (Acts 1: 4-5). The Wesleyan Holiness Movement, though it believed the biblical promise of receiving the Holy Spirit was central to the doctrine of holiness, it did not have a corner on this truth. Denominations and individuals across the whole spectrum of Christianity have laid claim to the necessity of receiving the Holy Spirit for purity, power and service.

Charles Finney

Charles Finney's testimony is impressive. After returning from the woods to his attorney's office, Finney observed that the fire he had previously lit in the fireplace was about to go out. "But as I turned and was about to take a seat by the fire, I received a mighty baptism of the Holy Spirit. Without any expectation of it, without ever having the thought in my mind that I had ever heard the thing being mentioned by any person in the world, the Holy Spirit descended upon me in a manner that seemed to go through me, body and soul. I could feel the impression, like a wave of electricity, going through and through me. Indeed, it seemed to come in waves and waves of liquid fire; for I could not express it in any other way. It seemed like the very breath of God. I could recollect distinctly that it seemed to fan me, like immense wings."[867] This "baptism" took place on the night of Finney's conversion, not some time after as a "second work of grace."

Dwight L. Moody

In 1871 after the Chicago fire in which Dwight Moody's home and preaching tabernacle burned to the ground, the renowned evangelist made a trip to New York to beg funds for his church and others who had been wiped out by the conflagration. Shortly before the fire, two Free Methodist women approached Moody suggesting that he "needed the power of the Spirit." Moody responded, "I thought I had power. I had the largest congregation in Chicago and there were many conversions." The women continued to pray for Moody and insist that he be filled with the Holy Spirit. Moody recalled, "I began to cry out as I never did before. I really felt that I did not want to live if I could not have this power for service." Moody's prayer was answered. While on his begging tour of New York City, "I was crying all the time, that God would fill me with his Spirit. Well, one day in the city of New York — Oh what a day! — I cannot describe it. I seldom refer to it; it is almost too sacred an experience to name. Paul had an experience of which he never spoke for fourteen years. I can only say that God revealed himself to me, and I had such an experience of his love that I had to ask God to stay his hand."[868]

---

[867] H. Shelton Smith, et al. *American Christianity: An Historical Interpretation with Representative Documents* vol. II (New York: Charles Scribners' Sons, 1963) 22.
[868] William R. Moody. *The Life of Dwight L. Moody.* (New York: Fleming Revell, 1900)

John Sung

One of the most stirring and challenging episodes in the history of Christendom is the revival in China and Indonesia led by John Sung in the two decades preceding World War II. He earned a Ph.D. in chemistry at Ohio State University. With a faint conviction that he was called to preach, he then enrolled at Union Theological Seminary in New York City. Even though he had been a committed Christian, his commitment faded when confronted with liberal theology, and the confused Sung turned to Taoism and Buddhism. But he also read Christian biographies and began seeking the baptism of the Holy Spirit. The Holy Spirit came! Forgetting that it was midnight and that others were sleeping, he rushed out into the halls of the dormitory shouting and praising God for deliverance. Convinced that the Holy Spirit, the heavenly Guest, had moved into the cleansed room of his heart, Sung started witnessing to everyone he met.

Sung's behavior was so abnormal that the Union Theological Seminary administration had him committed to the White Plains New York Mental Asylum. He was told that the stay would only be for six weeks. Instead, he was there for over six months, exactly 193 days.[869] On his trip back to China he threw all of his diplomas, medals and fraternity keys overboard, saving only his Ph.D. diploma to show his father. Wherever Sung went, revival broke out. The following description was typical: "The closing testimony meeting went on for hours. No one could stop it. Pastors of leading churches testified with shame to fruitless lives, to indifference to the condition of those without Christ, and a lack of real interest in God's work."[870] Sung, having been raised the son of a

---

146-149.

[869] Daryl Ireland did his Boston University Ph. D. dissertation on Sung, and with careful investigation, beyond the scope of our inquiry, argues that Sung needed hospitalization as he suffered from hallucinations, catatonic states, and possibly other psychotic episodes. Sung used his autobiography to paint Union Theological Seminary as anti-authentic Christianity and having treated him unfairly. Ireland convincingly demonstrates that Sung's narrative is filled with inaccuracies and exaggerations, but serve the purpose of vindicating fundamentalism, as compared with modernist Union Theological Seminary. See Daryl R. Ireland, "John Sung's Malleable Conversion Narrative," *Fides Et Historia* 45:1 (Winter-Spring 2013) 48-75. I have used Ireland's spelling of Sung's name, rather than Lyall's, which is probably due to a translation resolved with an arbitrary preference.

[870] Leslie T. Lyall. *John Song: Flame for God in the Far East* (Chicago: Moody Press,

Methodist pastor, stated, "I had previously read John Wesley's biography and how, every time he preached people were converted and came to Christ, had often longed for the same experience. Now I had begun to witness something like it."[871] Daryl Ireland assesses that, "Sung traveled tens of thousands of miles throughout China and Southeast Asia, and was instrumental in the conversion of perhaps 100,000 people – nearly 20 % of all Protestants in China at the time."[872]

Sung brought revival to Thailand, Vietnam, Singapore, Malaysia, Indonesia, Borneo, and Taiwan. When someone asked him about the success of his ministry the 5'2" evangelist responded, "Be careful about money. Be careful about women. Be careful to follow where God leads; when the Lord calls He will open the door."[873] Sung died of cancer and pneumonia at the age of 42, August 18, 1941. His biographer, Leslie T. Lyall had the following told to him by a lady in Taiwan, who at the age of 12 was converted under Sung's ministry.

> After preaching four times a day for at least two hours each time he "would go to his room" and study the Bible, his pen writing down continuously the thoughts that would come to him. He could hardly tear himself away to eat. And late at night he would sometimes fall back on his bed fully dressed and utterly tired out. The old pastor would then come and remove his shoes and cover him over very early in the morning. Dr. Sung would be awake to give two or three hours to prayer before the days' ministry began.[874]

When John Sung was a nine-year-old boy, revival had come to his father's church and became known as the Hingha Pentecost. According to Lyall, "After he became a famous preacher himself, it was always his prayer that the Holy Spirit of Pentecost might so rest on him that wherever he went the parched soil of many hearts might become like gardens in spring time after the refreshing showers, just as in those memorable days."[875]

1964) 81.

[871] Ibid., 72.

[872] Ireland, 48.

[873] Ibid., 136.

[874] Ibid., 159.

[875] Ibid., 11.

Lela G. McConnell

Lela G. McConnell was born into a Methodist home, in Honey Brook, PA, in 1886. The youngest of seven children, Lela was told by her mother, "How the Lord came upon her in a marked way all during my prenatal days. She read the Bible and prayed and sang and rejoiced in the Lord as never before."[876] As a child Lela was spiritually precocious, loving revivals, class meetings and Sunday night praise services. As a public school teacher, after whipping a large boy for misbehavior, she was convicted over her anger. That summer she attended a holiness camp meeting in Delano, New Jersey. For eight services straight she went to the altar seeking to be entirely sanctified. "One day later I was sitting by a tent, discouraged and tempted to leave the camp and go home. The Devil was trying his best to defeat me. I was reading a little pamphlet 'Heaven or Hell, Which?' I cried to the Lord and groaned in my spirit, 'Oh, God! I must have the blessing now! Instantly the Holy Spirit applied the blood of Jesus to my carnal heart and cleansed it, and then he came to abide. Sweet rest and assurance was mine. His glory filled my soul. The work was done and the Comforter, the Holy Ghost had come.'"[877]

Eventually Lela McConnell founded Mount Carmel High School, Kentucky Mountain Bible Institute, and a score of churches in "bloody Breathitt County" in eastern Kentucky. The conditions were brutal. She rode her horse over mountainous terrain, held dozens of store front revivals, trudged through ankle deep mud, caught a raft down the river for transportation, thought she would freeze and starve to death in the winter, stared down drunken ruffians holstered with pistols, and helped clear the ground where her churches and schools were built. Having founded Mount Carmel in 1924, by 1941 she had students from 14 counties. One of the students recalled, "To get to my home from Mount Carmel was to go through War Creek, Bloody Creek then to Devil's Creek; beyond that is Hell Creek and still farther on is Hell-Fer-Sortin' Creek, but it was Devils' Creek where Jesus found me."[878]

---

[876] Lela G. McConnell. *The Pauline Ministry in the Kentucky Mountains* (Louisville: Pentecostal Publishing Company 1942) 7.

[877] Ibid., 18.

[878] Ibid., 82.

On July 4, 1939, sixteen inches of rain fell over a four-hour period, turning Frozen Creek on which Kentucky Mountain Bible Institute was located into a raging torrent. The rushing water swept the Bible School away, drowning sixteen of its occupants including Horace Myers and his three children. Left behind was his wife, Nettie Myers who continued to teach at the school for another forty years. I was her student almost three decades after she had lost her family. Lela McConnell wrote, "The gracious seasoning of the Holy Ghost power that had been accumulating in the hearts and lives of our workers through the years was well-appropriated in these severe tests and sorrows."[879] The "workers," over 100 faculty and staff at the high school and Bible school, worked without salary, exhibiting sacrifice and commitment. They invested in me and thousands of others. Outside of that investment and their belief in holiness of heart and life calling for radical obedience, I would not be writing this book.

Dean Smith

Dean Smith made a terrible start as a head basketball coach at the University of North Carolina. The short man with the big nose, who had played for the University of Kansas, but hardly ever got off the bench, had followed Frank McGuire. McGuire was tall, suave, good-looking and in 1957 had pulled off a huge upset of Kansas and Wilt Chamberlain, in what is still the only three overtime game for a National Championship. Smith did not inherit much player talent from McGuire, and in the 1961-2 season went 8 and 9. For the next season North Carolina went 18 and 6. Perhaps Smith thought he was off and running, but for the 1964-5 season his record was a measly 500, 12 and 12. The criticisms mounted and what really hurt was after an away loss at Wake Forrest, upon returning to campus, Smith saw himself hung in effigy. "A dummy hung from a noose in front of the gym. I could tell it was me because of the long nose." In spite of beating Duke at the next game, Smith was again hung in effigy on the North Carolina campus, this time burned. "Who needs this? I would be happy coaching High School and teaching math."[880]

---

[879] Ibid., 117.

[880] Dean Smith. *A Coach's Life* (New York: Random House, 1999) 77.

After losing to Maryland the next week he came home and began reading a book written by Catherine Marshall, *Beyond Ourselves*. After midnight he came to the chapter "The Power of Helplessness." He reflected "Having been raised by two parents who are professing Christians, I had heard all of my life about the Holy Spirit, an inner counselor in every human being....I had always been aware of the Holy Spirit, I realize, but I had never truly given myself over to it. So often in my life I thought I was self-sufficient."[881] When Smith closed the book, he thought to himself "I give up. You take over." "As soon as the words formed in my mind, I immediately felt a letting go and a peace."[882] After thirty years as the head basketball coach at the University of North Carolina, Dean Smith retired with the most wins in the history of Division I NCAA basketball. What is even more impressive was that Smith was never the subject of a single NCAA Investigation, and out of the 245 young men who earned a varsity letter under Dean Smith, 237 of them earned a college degree. Even more important, almost everyone who ever met the North Carolina coach found him to be a humble and gracious man. They liked him.

Finding God at Harvard

A resume could have hardly been more impressive: a Ph.D. in Economics from MIT, a professor of Economics and Policy at Harvard's Kennedy School of Government, and having been published in the *Wall Street Journal*, the *New York Times* and the *New Republic*. Glenn Loury was accomplished, but miserable, turning to drugs and alcohol. "I was dead in spirit despite the fact that I had professional success as a tenured professor at Harvard....my achievements gave me no sense of fulfillment."[883] He ended up in a substance abuse program in a psychiatric hospital. Immediately after being released Loury attended an Easter service. Not instantaneously, but gradually, he became a Christian.

Relationships, especially parenting and marriage, took on a new meaning. Loury testified to a further dramatic change, "With my

---

[881] Ibid., 79.

[882] Ibid.

[883] Glenn Loury, "A Professor Under Construction," in *Finding God at Harvard: Spiritual Journeys of Christian Thinkers*, ed. Kelly K. Monroe (Grand Rapids: Zondervan Publishing House, 1996) 74.

spiritual growth has come an appreciation of the joy of worship and praise, and an ability to share the gospel and minister to people. This was made possible when I received the baptism of the Holy Spirit - The power that the Lord has made available to all of us who believe. These spiritual gifts seemed at first embarrassing to me. Emotionalism in worship grated against my intellectual style; it seemed archaic, characteristic of something primitive. Yet in due course there I was, full of joy and prepared to worship, not passively but openly."[884] Loury is convinced that God transformed him for the purpose of encouraging those in academia to have a relationship with God. "Ours can be a spiritually barren landscape. Declarations of faith are rare on campus and those who make them are often marginalized."[885] A life that at one time had been self-centered, vacuous and hedonistic was now focused on the welfare of others; not just those around him but the marginalized of society. "The knowledge of God's unconditional love for humankind provides moral grounding for my work in cultural and racial reconciliation, economics and justice."[886]

Finding God at the DMV

This past week I went to the Department of Motor Vehicles to renew my driver's license. The DMV is the closest one can get to visiting a third world country without leaving the U.S.A. Why we have not placed this particular phase of life in efficiency mode is beyond my understanding. I grabbed a number and plopped down in a metal chair and opened a book, attempting to make others think that I was making good use of my time. Not only am I neurotically attached to a book, but also making sociological appraisals of the people around me. No better group than the crowd at the DMV.

The lady sitting to my right has had a hard life, so I thought. I was correct: a baby out of wedlock, a son in prison, failed marriages. And her latest husband of seven years good for nothing! Her live-in boyfriend was now fixing up her house, "really in bad shape." I asked her where she went to church, "A charismatic church." "Do you speak in tongues, I asked?" "Yes," was the reply. "What does that do for you?"

---

[884] Ibid.

[885] Ibid., 75.

[886] Ibid., 76.

She answered, "It gives me assurance, hope, and peace. A reason to keep going." She asked me where I went to church, "Nazarene. Have you ever been to a Church of the Nazarene?" "Yes," she answered. "What did you think?" I asked. Her answer, "They were too quiet." I did not tell her that Nazarenes used to be called "Noiserenes."

Crisis Spiritual Experience, The Altar Call and Spiritual Formation

I offer the above vignettes to emphasize that no two experiences with the Holy Spirit are alike. Of the above people, the only classical Wesleyan Holiness "Baptism with the Holy Spirit" took place in the life of Lela McConnell. I am grateful for the two Free Methodist ladies who told Dwight Moody he needed "something more." I am glad, not just because I'm from North Carolina, that Catherine Marshall wrote a chapter "The Power of Helplessness" in her book *Beyond Ourselves*, and Dean Smith kept reading. I was enriched by the lady at the DMV who I thought didn't have much to offer. She is the kind of person who used to visit the Church of the Nazarene and continue to come because she had found help in the midst of helplessness. We used to give altar calls for remedying helplessness and people were filled with the Holy Spirit, completely and instantaneously. My prayer is that this possibility is more than a distinct memory.

In 1994, Nazarene Theological Seminary began a curriculum in "Spiritual Formation," at that time, the freshest item on the Academy's theological. Morris Weigelt and Dee Freeborn served as the primary, if not only professors for a number of courses such as prayer and scripture reading. In that same year, Beacon Hill Press of Kansas City (NPH) published a book *The Upward Call*, the denomination's publishing effort on spiritual formation written by Wes Tracy, Dee Freeborn, Morris Weigelt, and Janine Tartaglia. The chapters were titled with the normative content for a curriculum in spiritual formation: "Meeting God in Worship," "Meeting God in the Word," "Meeting God in Prayer," etc. What makes the book unique for a spiritual formation text is Weigelt's explicit challenge to entire sanctification as a second work of grace. In answering his own question, how do I find sanctifying grace, he wrote,

D. Expect Sanctifying Grace Instantaneously by Faith
It sounds like a gradual process of growth at first, and it does require time for God to prepare the believer's heart. But

the testimony of God's people throughout the centuries almost always declares that sanctifying grace comes instantaneously, after the believer has once and for all made consecration complete and opened the very depths of his heart to the purging fire of the Spirit.[887]

But one is tempted to ask if Weigelt was giving token salute to his denomination's distinctive creed. If he was engaged in wishful thinking that he and his colleagues could hold on to a heritage, which was quite different than the faith structures propagated by Duke, Drew, Candler, and just about any other ATS seminary, and which NTS was buying into. I certainly would not blame Weigelt for naivete or unawareness, as he is one of the brightest and most articulate people I have ever known. And if God does have an audible voice, it would sound like Morris Weigelt's.

In November of 1992, Asbury Theological Seminary professor Stephen Harper was on the NTS campus lecturing on spiritual formation. On the evening which the faculty hosted the guest lecturer for dinner, New Testament professor, Alex Deasley, asked Harper, "If we have entire sanctification, why do we need spiritual formation?" I do not remember Harper's answer, but I will never forget the question. I suspect that Deasley was investigating the possibility of conflicting paradigms though he gave no hint that he believed them to be mutually exclusive.

In 2018, Doug Hardy, Professor of Spiritual Formation at NTS, and Derek Davis, director of Academic Programs at NTS, wrote an article for the *Journal of Spiritual Formation and Soul Care*, tracing the history and development of the spiritual formation curriculum at NTS. The authors give full credence to the denomination's and the seminary's commitment to entire sanctification. For the capstone of a seminarian's completion of his or her training at NTS, the degree candidate is administered what could be defined as an exit interview over five areas: **1)** knowledge of God/self, **2)** self-description, **3)** identification of practices and discipline strategy, **4)** able to articulate a philosophy/theology of ministry, **5)** ministerial identity, and **6)** practical skills for ministry. The most extensive part of the assessment evaluates a student's knowledge of God and self. The assessment of his or her answers can fall into one of five categories: **a.** no awareness, **b.** minimal awareness, **c.** able to receive

---

[887] Wes Tracy et al. *The Upward Call: Spiritual Formation and the Holy Life* (Kansas City: Beacon Hill Press of Kansas City, 1994) 46.

feedback, **d.** able to articulate his/her personal strengths and weaknesses with minimal defenses, **e.** adds to "**d**" "without defensiveness," and is able to appropriately evaluate his/her own contributions to the SIS process."[888]

What I find curious in the above assessment is that nowhere is the issue of entire sanctification mentioned. David Wilson, for twelve years General Secretary of the Church of the Nazarene, assures me that every candidate for "Elder," a fully-credentialed minister, is asked by a "District Committee on Ministerial Credentials," to not only articulate the doctrine of entire sanctification, but to testify to the experience of entire sanctification. I can only conclude that there is a disconnect between spiritual and academic preparation for ministry as provided and assessed by Nazarene Theological Seminary and the expectations of its parent denomination, though that may not be totally true. I can more confidently suggest that there has been a paradigm shift in the Church of the Nazarene of which Alex Deasley was prescient.

I am not an in depth student of "spiritual formation" as it has been defined by the Academy over the past quarter of a century. But I have no doubt that it has been a needed corrective to quote "once done" or even "twice done" spirituality, but I wince when I read the following: "*Doing is the only way we can change our being.*" On any given day, we cannot choose to have a new character. However, over the course of time, our character is chosen—little by little by our freely chosen *actions* (our doing)."[889] I know thousands of people who have no inclination for character transformation that come through and from virtuous practices and habits. Outside of transforming grace, there is no inclination to choose virtuous habits. In the Wesleyan/Edwardian scheme radical spiritual transformation yields Christian virtues and not vice versa.

In the Wesleyan Holiness tradition the infilling of the Holy Spirit was enabled by the "altar call." As the spiritual formation movement gained ascendance, the altar call, an invitation to come forward to

---

[888] Douglas S. Hardy and Derek L. Davis, "Re-Engaging the Wesleyan-Holiness Tradition in Response to Diversification and Fragmentation in Theological Education: Christian Spiritual Formation Teaching and Practice at Nazarene Theological Seminary," *Journal of Spiritual Formation & Soul Care*, Vol. II (2018) 157.

[889] Rick Langer, "Points of Unease with the Spiritual Formation Movement," *Journal of Spiritual Formation and Soul Care*, Vol. 5, No. 2 (2012) 198.

receive the baptism of the Holy Spirit has almost gone out of existence. The Holiness Movement's crisis theology was vitally linked to crisis worship. Almost all worship services ended with an invitation, the high point of the liturgy. The worth of the worship service was measured by the number of people who came forward. Obviously, there are serious theological problems with this kind of pragmatic assessment. Nonetheless, in keeping with Phoebe Palmer's altar theology, the altar call became the primary sacrament in Wesleyan Holiness worship, the foremost means for both justification and entire sanctification.

Does the above mean that the altar call is obsolete, and is no longer a means for a person to consecrate themselves to God and believe for entire sanctification? Can the spiritual formation model and the crisis model coexist? Can the conversionary, decisional, evangelistic, invitational mode of worship exist alongside a sacramental, symbolical, nurturing model? I would hope so, but I think I'm in the minority. None of the ten Nazarene churches which I visited to find some evidence of a Wesleyan Holiness emphasis ended with an invitation for either justification or entire sanctification. One reason for this is the fading camp meeting influence on Wesleyan Holiness worship. The camp meeting was given to spontaneity, testimonies, physical demonstration and above all, decisional preaching to a verdict, a call for individuals to come forward and to make marked measurable progress on the *ordo salutis*. Much of the camp meeting style of worship carried over into the Sunday morning worship of the local church.

The Church of the Nazarene, and I suspect other holiness denominations, have gone through a paradigm shift. In 1979, the Church of the Nazarene registered 198 commissioned evangelists (A commissioned scheduled evangelist is an elder in the Church of the Nazarene who gives him or herself to preaching revivals rather than pastoring a church.) As of the writing of this book, in 2019, that number has shrunk to 27, hardly any of them full-time and none of them able to earn a living with free-will offerings. The only way an evangelist can stay on the road is to create an administrative board which supplements his/her income. Norman Moore, who believes himself to be the only full-time Nazarene evangelist west of the Mississippi, has written, "Our best analysis from pastors, district superintendents, global ministries leaders, and evangelists, reveals that a majority of our churches do not have any specifically scheduled revival services each year. Further inquiry indicates that revivals are fewer and shorter among those churches that still schedule them."[890]

Revival as a scheduled four-day event is not a permanent institution. Revival as renewal by the Holy Spirit is an absolute must. Holy convocation, waiting on God, prayer preparation before and during a planned event, are patterns for God visiting his people throughout Scripture. These patterns are not optional for the vitality of God's Church. While preaching a camp meeting, I had really stumbled and struggled one night. Both the preacher and the congregation were dull and flat. The next night two people separated themselves from the congregation, and prayed for me while I preached. (I did not know this until afterwards.) God came, the Holy Spirit enabled, I soared, and scores sought God. To entirely write off this possibility, is to reduce ourselves to routinization.

I find some irony in the above. When Charles Finney, Dwight Moody, H.C. Morrison, Phineas Bresee and Uncle Bud Robinson as well as others were "baptized" with the Holy Spirit, none of them were in a church setting. There seems to be something sovereign about God pouring out his Spirit as in Acts 4, or the Asbury College Revival. Another irony is that in praying with scores of seekers at the altar, rarely have I encountered someone seeking to be filled with the Holy Spirit. The seeker is most often dealing with an existential or practical issue, such as a troubled marriage, or a wayward child, or the vague sense that they are not measuring up spiritually.

Part of the above is due to the worshipper setting the agenda rather than God and the "word," and the "word" determining what needs to happen in the life of the believer. This personal agenda was amplified by the practice of inviting congregants to come and kneel at the altar during the pastoral prayer, presenting before God whatever burdens one may be carrying, whatever the seeker deems to be the need of the moment. This form of liturgy is hard to argue with, but we must recognize that there is a vast difference between God coddling us and God consuming us with his cleansing fire. To not preach on the

---

[890] Norman Moore, "Let's Think Revival," *Grace and Peace*, Issue 18 (Fall 2018) 39.

baptism of the Holy Spirit and to not give an invitation to be filled with the Holy Spirit is a profound transition in holiness worship. As I've argued in other places, either there are identifying markers and practices in holiness worship or there are not. Once again, we need to recognize there is a vital relationship between *lex credendi* and *lex orandi*, the law of belief and the law of prayer. Historically for the Holiness Movement, its ideology has dictated its worship practices and vice versa; to lose one is to lose the other.

Rediscovering Jesus

Our understanding of Jesus and who and what he represented has been truncated, if not reduced to a dualism: the Holiness Movement has focused on the Christological Jesus rather than the historical Jesus, the ascetic Jesus as opposed to the social Jesus, the divine Jesus at the expense of the human Jesus, the other-worldly Jesus rather than the world-embracing Jesus, the exclusive Jesus, rather than the inclusive Savior, the American Jesus exalted above the egalitarian Jesus, the kingdom of Jesus in heaven rather than the kingdom of Jesus on earth and above all a Jesus shaped in our own image rather than God's image. The social gospel was so enmeshed in liberal theology that its much needed emphasis on Christ and his kingdom was dismissed by conservatives. Carl Henry warned fundamentalists, which by this time included the Holiness Movement, that "fundamentalism in revolting against the Social Gospel seemed to also revolt against the Christian social imperative."[891] He described fundamentalism's lost social conscience:

> But, almost unawares, Fundamentalism became increasingly absorbed in resistance to non-evangelical humanism as a deceptive competitor for the commitment of multitudes, and because of its prophetic cheerlessness about the present age came more and more to narrow its message for the "faithful remnant" that would be called out of the godless world context. The die was cast, not so much because God had made present world conditions inevitable as because of the foreseen hardness of men's hearts, so that the nonsupernaturalistic idealisms could all be abandoned to future disillusionment. Whereas once the redemptive gospel was a world-changing message, now it was narrowed to a world

---

[891] Carl F. H. Henry. *The Uneasy Conscience of Modern Fundamentalism* (Grand Rapids, William B. Eerdmans Publishing Company, 1947) 32.

resisting message. Out of twentieth century Fundamentalism of this sort there could come no contemporary version of Augustine's *The City of God*.[892]

Knowing Jesus, at least better knowing him, is a lifelong process. I'm still surprised, after about a half century of marriage, by what I don't know about my wife and what she does not know about me. I haven't really been paying close enough attention. The analogy fails in that both of us are changing. The constant rediscovery of Jesus is not demanded by his changing, but by the quickly passing seasons of my own life. The Jesus understood in the bright days of summer is different, at least from my perspective, than the Jesus I worship and attempt to follow through the dark cold days of winter. Leander Keck writes that, "The vindication of Jesus- the Jesus whose life does not end with manifest proof of his validity- meaning that he who reconstructures his understanding of God and of himself on the basis of Jesus can come to terms with his own incompleteness, with the non-validated character of his own existence."[893]

Unfortunately, for some "entire sanctification" pre-empted the need for constant restructuring. Jesus was the parable of God, and like the parables he told, there are layers of meaning, some of them available only through the prism of mature spirituality where God in his sovereign wisdom grants illumination for the need of the moment beyond my comprehension. I encouraged (made) all of my four daughters read *The Narnia Chronicles* somewhere around the second grade. I suspect should they as adults choose to read them now, their insights and interpretations would be different from their earlier attempts to understand some rather profound symbolism. Not only is there the written word that needs to be absorbed, but a second grader would hardly ask what exactly was in C.S. Lewis' mind when he wrote *The Lion, The Witch* and *The Wardrobe*.

Keck claims that the kingdom of God is "not simply the extension of anyone's present into the future where it is consummated, but is rather the future's claim to restructure everyone's present, including present understandings of God."[894] Keck further writes that, "Jesus does not have a doctrine of original sin; but he sees that no one can assume that he

[892] Ibid., 30.

[893] Leander Keck. *A Future for The Historical Jesus: The Place of Jesus in Preaching and Theology* (Nashville: Abingdon Press, 1971) 240.

[894] Ibid., 225.

stands in right relation to the God of the kingdom and that each must reorder his life if he trusts the God who comes."[895] Thus, my life needs to be reordered and reordered and reordered. It needs to be reordered in light of my diminishing powers, my increasing dementia, taking into my home my divorced daughter and grandson, the system that tries to place me on a shelf when I still have something to offer but am not sure exactly what that might be. The bottom line is to serve a Jesus who enables constant transitioning often unwelcomed transitions such as from public life to private life, from preaching in a church of 2,000 with my images magnified on two gargantuan video screens behind me to a life of isolated reflection. This is the moment that I need a dose of Brennan Manning's "ruthless trust" without which I become a complaining, whining, accusing, ungrateful soul. Without being able to genuinely affirm that Christ is trustworthy, I live in the constant agony of demanding the respect of others without simply being content that God considers me sufficiently worthwhile to not only die for me but to elect me for the vocation of proclaiming His word. I identify with Manning's confession:

> In preaching the gospel I have been graced to speak fearlessly in the knowledge and conviction that the Word of God must not be fettered, compromised, or watered down, but in my personal life, my fears and insecurities continue to lead me voraciously to seek the approval of others, to assume a defensive posture when I'm unjustly accused, to feel guilty over refusing any request to doggedly live up to others' expectations, to be all things to all people in a way that would make St. Paul shudder.[896]

There should be no dichotomy between Jesus' atonement for humanity and his oneness with all human kind. While I trust Christ for victory over sin and purification from sin I am called to extend these benefits as far as I can, to as many as I can, whenever I can. I must sincerely beseech God to open appropriate avenues at appropriate times and at appropriate places. Two weeks ago I sat on an international flight and fell into conversation with a couple from India, now living in Northern Oklahoma. He has a Ph.D. in agriculture, doing what with it, I was not intelligent enough to comprehend. They were returning to New Dehli

---

[895] Ibid.

[896] Brennan Manning. *A Glimpse of Jesus: The Stranger to Self Hatred* (San Francisco: HarperCollins Publishers, 2003) 43.

(I could tell them I had recently been in New Dehli) to visit the dying mother of the wife after a seven year absence. After mumbling something about what I do (which I always manage in any conversation) they requested "Give us some words to say." Wow, here was an opportunity to shoot them with the "gospel gun," a captive audience, unable to jump off the plane at 33,000 feet. I felt restrained, dropping the barrel of my gun, and said, "I don't know what your faith paradigm is, but I know there is a loving, just God who is ministering to your mother and who will be with you and I will be praying for you. And even though your mother seems to be unconscious she may well comprehend far more than you know." These people could not have lived in Oklahoma and not know that as a Christian preacher, as a travelling missionary, as someone who visits refugee camps, that I in some way represent Jesus Christ. I could not help but recall my Hindu guide at the Taj Mahal who informed me that there are 33 gods in every cow. And I might assume of the Indian couple that like Gandhi they might be more Christ-like than I am. And that Christ-likeness at various times and places has little to do with a formal profession of faith in Christ.

If You Have to Choose One or the Other, Do Right Rather Than Believe Right

As I am writing this, hundreds of Syrian refugees are fleeing across the Mediterranean, traversing Europe, evading border guards and entering whatever country will accept them. Journalist Patrick Kingsley informs us: "As news spreads of how refugees are being treated on arrival in Hungary, dozens of ordinary Austrians and Hungarians are descending on the area near the Roszka Railroad. Their aim is to rescue refugee families who have managed to evade the Hungarian border guards and then drive them from southern Hungary to Eastern Austria where they can continue their journey as normal."[897] One thousand refugees land daily on the Greek island of Lesvos where Eric and Philippa Kempson live on the North coast. Each morning Eric looks through his binoculars, identifying refugees on rubber rafts. "Once they are identified they scoop down to the likely landing point and hand out water, dry clothes and food to the most vulnerable arrivals. And there are a lot of them: pregnant women, paralyzed people in wheelchairs, a man

---

[897] Patrick Kingsley. *The New Odyssey: The Story of Europe's Refugee Crisis* (London: The Guardian, 2017) 270.

with burn wounds so recent that flesh was 'hanging off his hands.'"[898] Eric's religion is a little nebulous; he makes a scant living selling "new age" trinkets such as bracelets, ornate grottos and macabre sculptures. He also meditates in a circle of stones laid out in his garden.[899]

The Holiness Movement may have to confess that what people do is more important than what they believe, though there is *always* a connection between practice and belief. As others have said, what we believe does not really matter; it is what we believe enough to do. Holiness allows not only for prevenient grace, but coterminous and eschatological Christic grace beyond comprehension. I do not agree with Albert Schweitzer's argument that Jesus misunderstood the timing of the Kingdom's fulfillment and expected an apocalyptic consummation in his own lifetime or, at least, before the death of his disciples that never occurred. This theological miscue did not prevent Schweitzer from mastering the organ and piano, becoming perhaps the world's foremost authority on Johann Sebastian Bach, completing a dissertation for a Ph.D. on *The Religious Philosophy of Kant* at the Sorbonne (he was proficient in French, German, and English), and attaining a medical degree at the University of Strasbourg in 1913.

In 1913, Schweitzer and his wife, an anesthesiologist, established a hospital in a chicken coop at Lambarene, in French Equitorial Africa, now Gabon, some fourteen days up river by raft. He took his piano with him. During the first nine months, the couple saw some 2,000 patients, plagued with a range of diseases from malaria to leprosy. Eventually, Schweitzer built a hospital where he spent most of the next half century. Holiness for Schweitzer was "reverence for life," which he thought to be his greatest contribution and for which he is best known. He wrote in his *My Life and Thought*, "The one important thing is that we shall be as thoroughly dominated by the Kingdom of Jesus, as Jesus requested his followers to be....Anyone who ventures to look the historical Jesus straight in the face and to listen for what he may have to teach him in His powerful sayings soon ceases to ask what this strange-seeming Jesus can still be to him. He learns to know Him as One who claims authority over him."[900]

---

[898] Ibid., 182.

[899] Ibid., 180.

[900] As included in Gregory W. Dawe's *The Historical Jesus Quest: Landmarks in the*

Whatever the flaws and contradictions in the life of Albert Schweitzer, no one can accuse him of not giving sufficient attention to the historical Jesus.

The Year of Living like Jesus

In 2008, Edward C. Dobson, former senior pastor at Calvary Church, Grand Rapids, Michigan, and one time 1st Lieutenant of Jerry Falwell's Moral Majority, decided to live like Jesus. Reading his account reveals a valiant effort.[901] Most surprising to me, was how much effort Dobson gave to being Jewish because Jesus was a Jew: growing an untrimmed beard, strictly observing the Sabbath, wearing a tasseled t-shirt under his regular shirt, observing the "Ten Days of Repentance" between Rosh Hashanah and Yom Kippur, and eating only kosher food. Less convincing was praying the Rosary, focusing on icons (a life-size crucifix seemed to come alive) actually praying in a closet, utilizing the Episcopal prayer beads, and praying through the Eastern Orthodox prayer rope.

What could have been predicted was Dobson picking up hitchhikers, giving money to strangers even though he was convinced he was being taken, giving away eight of his twelve personally tailored suits, listening to a complete reading of the Gospels some thirty-five times, and regularly drinking a beer at a bar. "I discovered that having a beer in my hand disarms people. They're much more likely to listen to what I have to say about the Bible if I am sipping beer while I am talking."[902]

But what most surprised Dobson and most represented a radical departure from his past, was that he voted for Barack Obama. This was a betrayal of his Bob Jones University education and his Moral Majority leadership. Though he did not agree with Obama's stance on abortion, he did after careful reflection and study, decide that Obama more faithfully represented the teachings of Jesus than did John McCain, and that "pro-life," was a wider concern than one issue.

Search for the Jesus of History (Louisville: John Knox Press, 1999) 208-209.

[901] Ed Dobson. *The Year of Living Like Jesus: My Journey of Discovering What Jesus Would Really Do* (Grand Rapids: Zondervan, 2009).

[902] Ibid., 166.

Being pro-life means being concerned about those who are dying of HIV/AIDS.

Being pro-life means being concerned about those who are living in poverty.

Being pro-life means being concerned about those who lack adequate healthcare - especially children.

Being pro-life means being concerned about those in our communities who are into gangs and drugs and will ultimately end up in prison.

Being pro-life means being concerned about those innocent civilians who are being killed in Afghanistan, Iraq, the Gaza Strip, Israel, and places all over the world.

Being pro-life means being all of these and a whole lot more.[903]

Dobson gave the above an extensive amount of energy and time, while his bodily strength was being sapped by ALS (Lou Gehrig's disease). Two observations: First, I think Dobson at times failed to separate the cultural Jesus from the Savior of the World. Second, and more importantly, I was left asking myself, how a serious attempt to incorporate in everyday life the biblically revealed and narrated Jesus, would preempt or radically transform my traditional holiness theology and lifestyle. I might become more concerned about what Jesus thinks about me than about how others esteem me. But I may not have that much to lose. The following from Jesus only tangentially applies to me, if at all: "Woe to you when everyone speaks well of you" (Luke 6:26). Though I covet popularity, I don't seem to be overwhelmed by throngs of people hanging on my every word and deed. Even if I tweeted more, I'd be way behind the Kardashians. (And you thought I was totally void of pop culture - well almost, according to my daughters.)

Where Have You Gone, Walter Cronkite?

Growing up during the 60s I listened to Chet Huntley and David Brinkley bring the NBC evening news. Even though they were part of the same news team, they reported from different locations, one Washington and the other New York. Most of all, I remember their signature signoff: "Good night, Chet, Good night, David, and Good night for NBC news." In spite of the Cold War, nuclear threat, and whatever negative events that may have happened in the world on that particular day, I was somehow

---

[903] Ibid., 243-244.

left with the impression and the assurance that it was a "good night." And had I listened to Edwin Newman on ABC, or Walter Cronkite on CBS, I would have been left with the same kind of certitude. I'm not quite certain as to how Americans in those days chose their favorite newscaster – the content of what they reported and the rhetoric with which they addressed a national audience had more in common than in variation. Their comportment was genteel and their emotions so subdued that those who gathered in front of the one TV in the house, would wonder if the newscasters had deeply held opinions about anything. It was as if the critical criterion of news casting was neutrality, and all the reporters had taken a course in conflict management, in how to be a divested arbiter for the purpose of reconciliation among all Americans, if not all of humankind. When Dan Rather replaced Walter Cronkite as CBS anchor, the big question was whether he would exude the avuncular warmth and grandfatherly compassion that made Cronkite perhaps the most beloved newscaster in the history of television.

Is there a Walter Cronkite anywhere in the world? Allow me to be clear that I do not think that Cronkite and his contemporaries were completely objective. But I am just as certain that they were not at each other's throats with an intentional script to contradict, counter attack, and question the credibility of their Neilson-rated competitors. I am thinking they could have played a round of golf together without their blood pressure rising. One gets the idea that if Glen Beck and Chris Matthews played golf together, they might use the clubs for something other than driving or putting.

Not As Bad As It Seems (Well Almost)

Allow me to demythologize certain beliefs that currently divide us. Myth #1: This is not the most vituperative, vociferous, belligerent and malicious era of American politics. Certainly the Civil War was the apex of animosity. But that was such an atypical event that comparisons with our era do not really count. No presidential election has ever exceeded the 1801 Jefferson –Adams standoff for invective. Bernard Weisberger states "Readers and viewers of the year 2000 (we would say 2016) outraged by the slither of political debate into a cesspool of 'negative' and 'attack' ads may find it almost reassuring that two hundred years ago, campaign tactics were not a bit purer."[904]

The newspapers slung accusations and slander far more readily than reporting the weather, in that they had no reliable means to predict the latter. None exceeded Benjamin Bache, grandson of Benjamin Franklin, and editor of the *Philadelphia Aurora*, who had the temerity to claim, "If ever a nation was debouched by a man, the American nation has been debouched by Washington. If ever a nation has ever been deceived by a man, the American nation has been deceived by Washington."[905] The opposing Philadelphia daily was *The Porcupine Gazette* published by William Cobbett, who launched into Bache with, "You are a liar and an infamous scoundrel."[906] But Cobbett was polite compared to John Fenno, Jr., publisher of the *Gazette of the United States*. When the two of them met on the street, Fenno tried to bite off Bache's finger, as Bache walloped him with his cane. This kind of belligerence was not left to the newspapers. It seems that one of the qualifications for being a leader in the early Republic was an acerbic tongue, and no one outdid the pious John Adams. With neurotic hatred for Alexander Hamilton he labeled his nemesis as, "That bastard brat of a Scottish peddler! His ambition, his restlessness and all his grandiose schemes come, I'm convinced, from a superabundance of secretions, which he couldn't find enough whores to absorb!"[907]

The members of today's United States Congress are models of decorum and civility compared to the eruptions that took place between the founding of the Republic and the Civil War. In 1797, Vermont Representative Matthew Lyon spat in the face of Connecticut Representative Roger Griswold. Two weeks later, the two of them squared off in the House with a hickory cane and a pair of fireplace tongs.[908] The event did not quite live up to the violence inflicted on Charles Sumner by Preston Brooks in 1856. Because Sumner, on the Senate floor, had accused Brooks' cousin, Andrew Butler, Senator from South Carolina,

---

[904] Bernard A. Weisberger. *America Afire: Jefferson–Adams and the Revolutionary Election of 1800* (New York: HarperCollins, 2000) 201.

[905] Ibid., 205.

[906] Ibid., 208.

[907] Mark Mancini. "Mental Floss: 7 of John Adams' Greatest Insults." Website: mentalfloss.com/51899/7-john-adams-greatest-insults

[908] Weisberger, 185.

of polluting himself with the "harlot slavery," and Sumner's using such infuriating language as rape and virgin, Brooks, some days later, stepped into the Senate chamber, and rained down about 30 blows on Sumner's head with a "gutta percha" cane, almost killing him. "Sumner was as senseless as a corpse."[909] And it took three years for him to return to the Senate.

Myth #2: Donald Trump is the worst President we have ever had. Though I am not sympathetic with many of Trump's actions, attitudes, and careless language, he is far from the worst. Franklin Pierce, James Buchanan, and Warren G. Harding top the list of worst Presidents. Harding spent more time drinking, carousing, card playing, and womanizing than he did governing. Trump is one of the most energetic, proactive, and combative Presidents we have ever had. He puts in long hours, is articulate, and is possibly the most astute business man (and maybe most unethical) we have had sit in the Oval Office. If impeached, he is unlikely to be convicted. The stock market may be at an all time high by the time he finishes his first term.

Myth #3: America is a Christian nation. Never has been and never will be. National policy is formulated and enacted on the basis of economic prosperity and national security. "America first" is hardly a Christian motto. Imperialism, exceptionalism, ethnocentricity, and nativism all feed into nationalism, an attitude that unfortunately disadvantages others in order to confer prosperity on five percent of the world's population, Americans. The hypocrisy, the dishonesty, and rationalization of American policy often cover up motives that cause others to view us much differently than we view ourselves. Reinhold Niebuhr claimed that in worshipping our nation as God, "There is always an element of perversity, as well as of ignorance in this worship. For other nations and cultures are perversely debased and become merely the instruments or tools, the victims or allies of the nation of one's worship....The culture which elaborates this scheme of meaning, makes its own destiny into the false center of the total human destiny."[910]

---

[909] Stephen Puleo. *The Caning: The Assault that Drove America to Civil War* (Yardley PA: Washington Publishing, 2013) 57.
[910] Reinhold Niebuhr. *Faith and History: A Comparison of Christian and Modern Views of History* (New York: Charles Scribner's Sons, 1949) 114-115.

Trump's campaign rhetoric included building a wall between Mexico and the U.S.A., increasing military spending, racist remarks about Muslims, disengagement from the North Atlantic Treaty Organization, economically advantaging ourselves with higher tariffs, particularly on China, and pulling out of the Paris Climate Control Accord. David Brooks interpreted his Inaugural Address as offering, "A Zero Sum, Ethnically Pure, Backward-looking, Brutalistic Nationalism."[911] Trump's fellow Republican, George W. Bush, who claims to be a born again Christian, was a little less prosaic about Trump's inaugural speech. He immediately assessed, "That was some weird s—t."[912]

Trump is the most populist president since Andrew Jackson. Populism denotes the politics of resentment, and to a certain extent, paranoia. These are institutional traits which fuel choices with the passions of revenge and animosity, a passion which spins out negative rhetoric, "a barbaric childish yawp coming out of democratic man."[913] Jonah Goldberg points out, "Demagoguery appeals to the gut instincts of the mob or the crowd — is an ancient form of rhetoric." He further writes, "In primitive societies where strangers are perceived to be enemies and where survival requires inflaming a zealous defensiveness of the group and demonizing hatred for the other, the ability to see the world in black-and-white is a competitive advantage."[914] If nothing else Trump is competitive, competitive enough to self-righteously announce that he was going to clean up the "cesspool in Washington" with Barack Obama and George W. Bush sitting behind him on the inaugural platform. One is reminded of Willie Stark in Robert Penn Warren's *All the King's Men*.

> If they had politicians back in those days, they said, Gimme, just like all of us politicians do. Gimme, gimme, my name's Jimmie. But I'm not a politician today. I'm taking the day off. I'm not even going to ask you to vote for me. To tell

---

[911] David Brooks, "After the Women's March" article included in *The Kansas City Star* (January 26, 2017).

[912] George W. Bush on Donald Trump: https://nypost.com/2017/03/29/bush-trump-iminous-inaugural-speech-was-some-wierd-sh-t/

[913] Jonah Goldberg. *Suicide of the West: How the Rebirth of Tribalism, Populism, Nationalism, and Identity Politics is Destroying American Politics* (New York: Crown Forum, 2018) 296.

[914] Ibid., 298.

the God's unvarnished and unbuckled truth, I don't have to ask you.[915]

Identity Politics

Politics feeds on group loyalty. The human inclination to find identity in a group, a group that promotes my values, secures my goals and provides for my needs as I define those needs. Political opinions function as "badges of social membership." They are like the array of bumper stickers that people put on their cars showing the political causes, universities and sports teams that they support. Many, if not most, people live within a motif: dress like a cowboy, wear the jacket of a race car driver, or the same kind of basketball shoes as Michael Jordan. Lebron James had a $95 million shoe contract with Nike before he even finished high school; Nike could not have made a safer bet.

At this point it should become clear that the social cohesion which politics requires and even demands is problematic for the Christian. If our primary identity is found in Jesus Christ, then that identity should shape everything we say or do. I felt for Mike Pence, when as a Christian the only way he could respond to Trump's sexual immorality was to completely skirt the question when asked about it by a reporter. Thus, any sincere Christian with a Christian identity beyond nominality finds him or herself with a severe conflict of conscience. How can I play in a game when its rules are often contrary to whatever I have learned about decency, honesty, justice and fairness?

Unfortunately to be a member of a given group often equates to having derogatory attitudes and even expressing them about other groups. As Jonathan Haidt writes, "Most people turn out to have negative implicit associations with many social groups, such as black people, immigrants, obese people and the elderly."[916] As a Jew living in New York, Joseph Heller, the author of *Catch 22*, told of informing some of his fellow white Brooklynites that Jesus was a Jew: "The immediate and united stiffening of the entire circle of white faces was an instantaneous warning that they had never been told this before and did not want to be

---

[915] Robert Penn Warren. *All The King's Men* (New York: Harcourt, 1946), 11.
[916] Haidt., 68.

told forever."[917] The present renewal of nativism should assault Christian sensitivity rather than being affirmed by a fresh wave of "Christian" nationalism.

Identity politics is a beguiling and not so subtle betrayal of the Kingdom of God. Dick Meyer states, "The need to make others wrong has turned into an addiction. The argument culture has ceded to a belligerent culture."[918] We need to meditate on Hebrews 12:14: "Follow peace with all men and holiness, without which no one shall see the kingdom of God." Any partisan politics that lessens our love or respect for a fellow Christian is a sin. The war between evangelical conservatives and the liberal media is making us the laughing stock of, as well as muting, our Christian testimony to the world. To be an active agent co-opted by the present political culture is diametrically opposed to being an agent of reconciliation. "Blessed are the peace makers for they shall be called the children of God" (Matt 5:9).

As I write this during the Christmas season of 2018, Americans will once again watch Jimmy Stewart in *It's a Wonderful Life*. Produced by Frank Capra, its good feeling denouement as in all Capra's films such as "Mr. Smith Goes to Washington" coined the phrase a "Capranesque ending." This would be all the more meaningful if Americans knew Frank Capra's story. As a Sicilian immigrant, Capra escaped the peonage of a sugar cane field on a Pacific island, when in a row boat he was picked up by an Australian liner and delivered to his family in California. But he felt himself no less miserable: "I hated being poor. Hated being a peasant. Hated being a scrounging news kid trapped in a Sicilian ghetto of Los Angeles. My family could not read or write. I wanted out. A quick out."[919] The American military provided the "out" and the rest is history.

I suppose that Jesus' stance against the Jewish political parties Pharisees, Sadducees, and Zealots was not simply their ostentation, hypocrisy, and lack of genuine interiority, but their exclusion of others. Holiness for Jesus meant not only separation from evil, but separation from others who find their distinction in separation. Elie Wiesel in

---

[917] Nell Irwin Painter. *The History of White People* (New York: W. W. Norton & Co., 2010) 360.

[918] Dick Meyer. *Why We Hate Us: Discontent in the New Millennium* (New York: Crown Publishers, 2008) 44.

[919] Painter, 362.

his book *The Oath* claimed that the primary trait of Jewishness is "distinction." At the end of each Sabbath an Jew Orthodox prays the prayer of dictinction. "Blessed are You, LORD our God, King of the universe, who distinguishes between the sacred and the secular, between light and dark, between Israel and the nations, between the seventh day and the six days of labor. Blessed are You, LORD, who distinguishes between the sacred and the secular."[920]

We need good government. Our forefathers wisely foresaw that the good could only be preserved by a check on evil, a skepticism with even a healthy dose of cynicism, that calls for radical accountability. We call it a system of checks and balances. I do not believe that there is a deep state, a conspiratorial, unidentifiable group of people beyond the power of the electorate. Paradoxically, American democracy demands Christian participation without submersion, concern without consumption, conviction without absolutism, and above all humility that allows for the free expression of those who see things differently. It allows above all gratitude for debate about the proper tension between socialism and capitalism, law enforcement and the rights of individuals, free industry and inconvenient regulation, and social welfare that does not guarantee entitlement.

The issue is not whether we will ever perfectly answer the above questions, but whether we will continue to have an enlightened public that can rationally process such questions in an informed manner. Democracy demands of the Christian to be a responsible citizen participating in the process, being grateful for government and even more grateful that Washington is not the ultimate answer to our problems. For the Christian the sovereign state is always less than sovereign; the joy of getting one's candidate elected has to be muted by the reality that the winner will exhibit contradictions and imperfections and never live up to the promises he or she has proffered. As I write this we are burying George Herbert Walker Bush, # 41, one of the best men who ever sat in the White House, but was forever haunted by six simple words, "Read my lips. No new taxes." His imperfection was the imperfection of democracy; one can never be elected without telling people what they want to hear rather than the plain truth of what they need to hear.

---

[920] Retrieved from: https: //en.wikipedia.org/wiki/List_of_Jewish_prayers_and_ blessings#Havdalah_(%22Separation%22_ceremony)

The Church as a Holiness Corporation

Though the Holiness Movement practiced corporate prayer and believed in the guidance of the Holy Spirit, little thought was given as to how God operated by providing every day oversight of temporal issues. As the pastor increasingly took on the identity of a CEO, the Church's affairs were run like any other corporate entity, by majority vote. A careful reading of the book of Acts will reveal how much more than today's Church, the early Church relied on God for moving forward. Casting lots, as recorded in Acts 1, to choose a twelfth disciple may seem arcane, if not irresponsibly mystical, unless one considers that the eleven apostles took the decision out of their own hands and placed it in God's hands. But notice that they prayed before the casting of lots: "Show us which of these two you have chosen to take over this apostolic ministry" (verse 24). Quakers and other sects still do not vote, but wait on God for a consensus, "a sense of the meeting," giving full credence to the belief that running God's Church is a supernatural business. They operate much as did the early Church as evidenced in Acts 15:28, "It seemed good to us and the Holy Spirit." Current decision making in the American church would be more akin to corporations such as Microsoft and McDonalds than the communal exercises directed by the Holy Spirit recorded by the New Testament Church.

The above is not to paint the early believers as a pristine community easily transcending its problems, making conflict reconciliation superfluous because there really was no conflict. Contrary to this view, the New Testament church was conflicted and typical of "Christians" at any time and place attempting to blend nationalities and temperaments. The complaining of the Hellenistic Jews in Acts 6:6 for not getting their fair share of the pie was certainly cause for a church split or at least censure in some form. The Apostles could have sided with their kin, real Jewish Jews, but instead granted believers authority to select "seven men from among you who are known to be full of the Spirit and wisdom" (Acts 6:3). By now, if we are honest, it should be clear that the Church as Luke describes and narrates it in Acts "deemed Holy Spirit enabled gifts and graces far more important than trained and innate ability. The spontaneous and charismatic administration evidenced in Acts is largely absent from the normative practices of the 21st Century American church, which operates with a blend of both autocracy and democracy."[921] Inagrace Dietterich contrasts the normative Robert's *Rules of Order*, win-lose debate, shareholder-in-control methodology prevailing in today's church as opposed to a process that will discern the mind and will of God:

> It is the role of the Spirit to correct, convince, and lead those who profess faith in Jesus Christ into God's truth. Discernment requires this guidance because God acts, speaks in, and through the ambiguous circumstances of worldly life....As the ecclesia of God, a people gathered and sent to be about God's business, the church is called to a way of making decisions that articulates and correlates with listening, hearing, testing, planning, and obeying together in the power of the Holy Spirit.[922]

Nowhere is Dietterich's observation more apparent than in Acts 13, when Simeon, Lucian, and Manaen laid hands on Saul and Barnabas' commissioning the Church's first missionary envoy: "While they were worshipping the Lord and fasting the Holy Spirit said, Set apart for me Barnabas and Saul for the work for which I have called them" (Acts 13:22). Leadership in the book of Acts often depended on a direct line to God. Visions were often God's medium of choice in guiding the church and setting the agenda. It would have taken nothing less than a vision for Ananias to affirm and accept Saul, the Pharisee hit man who may have been headed to Damascus with Ananias as his target. A vision, which was divine instruction for Peter to trash most of the theology he had ever learned, sent the very prejudiced apostle to the house of Cornelius. A vision sent Paul to Athens, a city saturated with gods, and pseudo-intellectuals. Not a place to peddle the "foolishness of the cross."

I'm not exactly sure where dreams and visions fit into God's leadership paradigm for today's church. Like most moderns I see the danger in such individualistic mysticism, practices that could lead to cultic delusions. But we may need to give renewed credence to and

---

[921] Darius Salter, "Foundations of Administration: The Book of Acts as Case Study," in *Foundations of Church Administration,* ed. Bruce L. Petersen, et.al (Kansas City: Beacon Hill Press of Kansas City, 2010) 14. Much of this section is derived from this article.

[922] Inagrace T. Dietterich, "Missional Community: Cultivating Communities of the Holy Spirit," in *Missional Church: A Vision for a Sending of the Church in North America,* ed. Darrell L. Guder (Grand Rapids: Eerdmans Publishing Company, 1998) 172-173.

confidence in Joel's promise that in the last days (and there are no days more last than these) "your old men will dream dreams and your young men will see visions" (Joel 2:28). This may be a bit much to ask for a mega church full of corporate executives, but it is not optional that the body of Christ find direction through prayer, fasting and honest dialogue. These means are the only assurance of God's reign. And if God doesn't reign over a corporate body of believers, where does He reign? As I have previously written, "The over-arching theme for administration is that it seeks the guidance of the Holy Spirit for both the community's eternal life and missional outreach....Administration in the Book of Acts is spiritual authority grounded in relationship with God and a loving identity with those who are in the household of faith."[923] The Holy Spirit is the only hope for the Church to become holy, holiness bestowed on both its individual members and corporate identity.

Distracted, Distracted, Distracted

The movie *The Doctor* starring William Hurt, opens with a group of physicians performing open heart surgery while they sway, swing, and sing to rock music. Not that farfetched. According to Matt Richtel, "A neurosurgeon in Denver was accused of making personal calls during surgery and, owing to distraction, left the patient partially paralyzed."[924] In fact, a survey done by *Perfusion*, a medical journal, found that fifty-five percent of the technicians monitoring the bypass machines had talked on their cell phones during cardiopulmonary bypass surgery.[925]

God is never distracted, but evidently he did not include that quality in humankind at creation, because Eve was distracted. She was distracted from God when there wasn't much to distract her, just a snake. Our snake is the Digital Age which includes iPods, iPads, iPhones, television, Xbox, Game Boy, Play Station, email, radio, DVDs, audiotapes, movies, what Dick Meyer refers to as "a gargantuan daily data dump,"[926] and a multiplicity of screens beyond my comprehension. One cartoon, captioned "patient-centered medicine" depicted a group of

---

[923] Ibid., 23.

[924] Matt Richtel. *A Deadly Wandering: A Mystery, A Landmark Investigation, and the Astonishing Science of Attention in the Digital Age* (New York: HarperCollins Publishers, 2014) 283-384.

[925] Ibid., 384.

[926] Meyer, 87.

doctors, all with their backs to the patient, reading a computer screen.[927] One of the traditional practices for God reflection is "centering down," (a Quaker term) — an intense focus on God with elimination of all peripheral concerns. How does God focus figure in our increasing need for Face book interaction, Instagram, fact finding, information gathering, ego amplifying, and GPS technology? The average Smartphone user checks his phone 150 times per day.[928] A 2014 study discovered that in every minute in every day, "3 billion Internet users in the world send 204 million emails, uploaded 72 hours of new YouTube videos, made over 4 million Google searches, shared 2,460,000 pieces of facebook content, downloaded 48,000 Apple apps, spent $83,000 on Amazon, tweeted 277,000 messages, and posted 216,000 new Instagram photos."[929]

I am alien to the world of technology, but as estranged as I am, have nonetheless discovered a multitude of its advantages. I can resource digitized books and articles; I can illustrate a sermon with a movie clip; my wife can find me a hotel in a majority-world country; pastors can disciple their congregations by posting each day a verse of Scripture with commentary, and shut-ins can worship with their home church online. But it deserves to be asked, how does electronic discipling and pastoring compete with the exponentially increasing messages that we are receiving each day? Neuroscientists are almost universally agreed on one of the foremost characteristics of modernity: our attention spans cannot keep up with the attention grabbing. According to Dr. Paul Atchley, a neuroscientist from the University of Kansas, "When you add it all up, the social lure of information, receiving and disclosing the intermittent delivery mechanism, the stimulation of inner activity, and the neurochemicals associated with reward, you wind up with something powerful to the point of being overpowering. To some researchers, it feels like a process of neurological hijacking."[930] Meyer argues, "The massive delivery of content we face taxes the brain so much it has become more difficult to like the world. The soul is next. We're soaked in media.

---

[927] Allen Frances. *Twilight of American Sanity: A Psychiatrist Analyzes the Age of Trump* (New York: HarperCollins Publishers, 2017) 31.

[928] Eric Andrew-Gee, "Your Smartphone Is Making You Stupid, Antisocial, and Unhealthy. So Why Don't You Put It Down?," www.theglobeandmail.com/techonology/ your-smartphone-is-making-you-stupid/article37511900.

[929] Quoted in Craig N. Gay. *Modern Technology and the Human Future: A Christian Appraisal* (Downers Grove: InterVarsity Press, 2018) 47.

[930] Richtel, 215.

We're pickled and pruny. Our nervous systems are over stimulated, our psyches malnourished. What we face is not media as conventionally understood. It is OmniMedia."[931]

The more we live in cyberspace, the less we live in real space; the more we live in our own creation, the less we live in God's creation, the more we live in virtual reality, the less we live in reality; the more we are on the world's frequency, the less we are on God's frequency. In answering the question, "Is God in Cyberspace?" Thomas Friedman answers that the "Internet is an open sewer of untreated, unfiltered information, where they need to bring skepticism, and critical thinking to everything they read and basic civic decency in everything they write."[932] Friedman further notes that a November 22, 2016 study published by the Stanford Graduate School of Education found "a dismaying inability by students to reason about information they see on the Internet.... Students, for example, had a hard time distinguishing advertisements from news articles, or identifying where information came from."[933] And more critical is the inability to differentiate the important from the unimportant. Meyer states, "This points out an important failing of OmniMedia. It trivializes the important and inflates the trivial. The DWI arrests of starlets get far more coverage than the genocide in Darfur: It's not even a close call."[934]

My Addiction to Fastness

Whatever holiness is, it is focus on God: sustained, patient, non-distracted focus at odds with all efficiency and measurement models for life's processes. There is no "bottom line" for holiness other than God likeness. Worship is giving God his due, as opposed to my favorite sport's team and the stock market, both of which I can quickly access on my iPhone. The key word in the Digital Age is faster: faster networking, faster iPhones, faster computers, and faster delivery systems of all kinds (why didn't I invent Amazon.com?.) But the faster I can obtain what I want, the faster I want it. Faster is never fast enough, not fast food, not the

---

[931] Meyer, 88.

[932] Thomas L. Friedman. *Thank You for Being Late: An Optimist's Guide to Thriving in an Age of Accelerations* (New York: Picador, 2016) 378.

[933] Ibid., 378.

[934] Meyer, 89.

microwave, not jet travel, and certainly not my questions about airline miles which direct me through what seems a thousand computerized questions before I get to an incarnated voice. Thus, I want to offer Salter's Law; hopefully it will rank with Metcalf's Law, Murphy's Law, etc. The faster the world becomes, the more impatient I become. My impatience is directly proportionate to the speed with which the object or destination of my desire is delivered. Or my patience is disproportionate to the speed of delivery. If that be so, I am in for a lot of impatience. Friedman writes,

> Intel's main workhorse microprocessor is that 14-nanometer chip it introduced in 2014. It packs a mind-boggling 37.5 million transistors per square millimeter. By the end of 2017, explained Mark Bohr, Intel Senior Fellow For Technology and Manufacturing, Intel will begin producing and distributing a 10mm chip that will pack "100 million transistors per square millimeter — more than double the previous density with less heat and power usage." When you multiply these vastly more powerful chips over multiple motherboards and multiple racks in multiple servers and multiple server farms, well, if you think the world is fast now just wait a year.[935]

I am addicted to time. How much accomplishment can I cram into a time container? Thus, multi-tasking is an ever present temptation, though I know because of narrow escapes that talking on a cell phone while I am driving endangers me and others. This past Christmas 2018, I gave a copy of *A Deadly Wandering* to each of my four daughters, a riveting account of Reggie Shaw's responsibility for killing two men because he was texting. Experiment after experiment has shown drivers are more accident prone, even when listening to the radio, much less talking on a cell phone or navigating their built-in computer screens, which are becoming standard equipment on all cars. Screens are addictive and escapist, connected to something beyond our present reality, the task and situation of the moment, which according to Craig Gay, minimizes "the importance of ordinary reality."[936] Gay states, "While it has often been the case, there are technologies that have empowered us to become more of ourselves, modern, automated machine technology seems rather

---

[935] Ibid., 46.
[936] Gay, 157.

to allow us to become less, diminishing us even as it proposes to deliver 'more' and 'better,' 'faster' and 'easier,' 'new' and 'improved.'"[937]

Note how incongruous some of the above words sound in the pursuit of holiness. Is there a faster, easier way to God in the 21st Century than in the 1st century? Each morning I pray Isaiah's promise, "They that wait upon the Lord shall renew their strength, and they shall mount up with wings as eagles. They shall run and not be weary, they shall walk and not faint" (Isaiah 40:31 KJV). But often as the day progresses, my impatience takes over my waiting, trusting, and submitting. My impatience often makes several statements at least implicitly, "I am more important than you are." "My time is more important than your time." "My only worth is in doing." "Tasks are more important than people." "I am not grateful for the particular impasse in which I find myself."

Patience is at the heart of holiness because it demonstrates respect for God's will and the people he has placed in my path. Peter maps out the painstaking steps to holiness:

> For this very reason, make every effort to add to your faith goodness; and to goodness, knowledge; and to knowledge, self-control; and to self-control, perseverance; and to perseverance, godliness; and to godliness, brotherly kindness; and to brotherly kindness, love. For if you possess these qualities in increasing measure, they will keep you from being ineffective and unproductive in your knowledge of our Lord Jesus Christ (2 Peter 1:5-8).

The Greek word, *upomones,* can be translated as patience, endurance, or perseverance. Trusting God through difficulty is the only route to God likeness. Cruciform theology dircctly contradicts technology. The only way we can run the race is not to find better running shoes or the latest technology, but to lay aside whatever hinders us (which may mean that which is captivating our attention) and to run with patience "the race marked out for us, fixing our eyes on Jesus, the author and perfecter of our faith, who for the joy set before him, enduring the cross, scorning the shame, sat down at the right hand of the throne of God" (Hebrews 12:2). This ancient formula for God connection may cause us in the West to question our dependence on technology that has pushed us into a hurry up mode. Therefore, I think that the African

---

[937] Ibid., 26.

couple in the mud brick home, even though there is no electricity or running water, are happier and more content than I am. Since they do not have Wi-Fi or television, or even electricity to dispel the darkness, they are free from most of the things that Americans cannot do without. They have reached what psychiatrist Allen Frances designates as the "happiness set point," which has little to do with circumstances, and after enough food, clothes, and shelter to sustain us, nothing to do with stuff. "Homeostasis is one of the most valuable concepts in all of science – it helps explain why some people are naturally so much happier than others. And why an individual's happiness remains so stable in spite of seemingly large changes in external circumstances."[938]

The above African village has the feeling of tranquility. As I watched a group of girls playing a game with their feet, tossing a hand-made rag ball not allowing it to hit the ground, they may have been enjoying the moment more than my daughters who played competitive softball with all the expensive equipment and trips. Heidi Campbell and Stephen Garner sum up technology in the West: "Within Western society there is the expectation that technology especially information technology, is not just something added to everyday life but an expected necessity or even a human right. Whether studying, working, shopping, socializing, or dealing with providers of essential services and government departments, Westerners are hard-pressed to function without some sort of investment, both financial and ideological, in technology."[939] From my perspective, technology often fails to become a means to an end, but becomes an end in itself.

Technology – The Antithesis of Community

One consistent theme emerges in theological critiques of technology. It is an atomistic, individualistic, and often voyeuristic enterprise with little community accountability. Community tradition and discernment count for less and less. Campbell and Garner note that "researchers...have found that the Internet may encourage a hyper-autonomy, which we have described above in terms of networked individualism, a movement toward personalized networks facilitated by

---

[938] Frances, 241.

[939] Campbell, Heidi, and Garner, Stephen. *Networked Theology: Negotiating Faith in Digital Culture* (Grand Rapids: Baker Academics, 2016) 129.

the social structures of network societies."[940] According to Gay, what we have in Internet communication, and in particular, Internet religion, is a disembodied gospel, bypassing traditional sources of both Church and family. He asks, "Are our technologies enhancing ordinary embodied face-to-face relations, for example, by creating and/or protecting time and space for them?"[941] My answer is an emphatic "no!" I have watched perfectly sane and otherwise civil human beings be totally occupied with and absorbed by their Smart phones at a small social gathering of family which they have not seen for a long time or will not see for a long time. And why someone desires to pipe artificial noise into their brain while jogging, cutting themselves off from God's creation which includes both nature and his children, is beyond me.

All of the societal and spiritual problems of television have been intensified and amplified in the age of the Internet. In his sociological critique of television, Robert Putnam notes that in 1950 ten percent of homes had television, rising to ninety percent by 1959, the "fastest diffusion of a technological innovation ever recorded."[942] Putnam argues and demonstrates that more television watching means less of virtually every form of civic participation and social involvement.[943] Putnam lists the major casualties caused by watching TV: "religious participation, social visiting, shopping, parties, sports, and organizational participation."[944] Television increasingly attempts to disgust, startle, shock, and scare with graphic imagery, deadening us to reality and the severity of a suicide bomber or mass shooting. While television, which unlike the Internet still has some self-imposed and governmental regulations, the Cyberspace line between reality and artificiality becomes blurred. Putnam argues that the public spectacle of television "leaves us at that arrested stage of development rarely moving beyond parallel attentiveness to the same external stimulation."[945] Putnam's following summary is helpful:

> People who say that TV is their "primary form of entertainment" volunteer and work on community projects less often, attend fewer dinner parties and fewer club meetings,

---

[940] Ibid., 73.
[941] Gay, 177.
[942] Putnam, 221.
[943] Ibid., 228.
[944] Ibid., 237.
[945] Ibid., 244.

spend less time visiting friends, entertain at home less, picnic less, are less interested in politics, give blood less often, write friends less regularly, make fewer long-distance calls, send fewer greeting cards and less e-mail, and express more road rage than demographically matched people who differ only in saying that TV is not their primary form of entertainment.[946]

At least the computer has a social connection component. But the communication is often unfiltered, ungoverned by the community standards of Church or State. Unfortunately, Trump will be remembered more for his tweets, for which I am not sure he seeks advice from close friends or family, much less his Cabinet, than he will be remembered for his "State of the Union" addresses. It's fast draw, shoot from the hip, verbal carnage and any collateral impact is ignored. No, Trump is not our worst president ever. But in a day of unfiltered communication, speak before you think, vociferate without counsel, I am not sure anyone fulfilling the highest office in the world ever better fit the analogy of "loose cannon."

We need pastors who stand in the pulpit and say, "Get off the computer. Turn off the television. Disbelieve the advertisements. Don't spend your money on gadgets, and know that Satan more than ever has found the perfect devices to deceive you." He is much better equipped than he was in the garden, but through the power of the Holy Spirit to overcome media addiction, he can be beaten. Never before has "the prince of the power of the air" been of greater influence, but no less true is "greater is he who is in us, than he who is in the world" (I John 4:4).

Holiness is Becoming More Christian

Is holiness something other than being more Christian? I often think of Dennis Kinlaw's statement, "The world doesn't need more Christians; it needs more Christians who are more Christian than they already are." Thus, "entire sanctification" entails not simply a one-time experience but a total Christian makeover. How do I spend my time? To whom and to what do I listen? How do I spend my money? To what am I addicted making me less loving, less patient, and less concerned about my neighbor, both next door and on the other side of the world?

---

[946] Ibid., 231.

This transformation will not take place by more rules handed down by the church. It will only take place by patient honesty before God and those with whom I am most intimate. I am sorry, Phoebe Palmer, and my other holiness ancestors, though I am indebted to you, there really isn't a "shorter way."

Conclusion

In 1705, Dionysius Papin, a French physicist and mathematician, built the world's first steamboat. This invention was a threat to a "guild of boatsmen" who made their living transferring goods in small crafts, powered by hands on oars. When Papin arrived at the city of Munden, Germany with his prized boat, local water tradesmen boarded it with, I suppose axes and sledgehammers, smashing the boat to smithereens. Papin died a pauper, dumped in a grave, never to be found. Daron Acemoglu and James A. Robinson, refer to Papin's newly minted steamboat as "creative destruction." Before reading their *Why Nations Fail*, I had never heard of Papin. Perhaps you hadn't either.[947]

Acemoglu and Robinson cite dozens of "creative destruction" events throughout history. For instance, when William Lee invented the stocking frame knitting machine in 1589, he failed to obtain a patent in both France and England. His machine would have thrown thousands of "hand knitters" out of work and upset the entire economic order. When the printing press reached the Ottoman Empire (Turkey) in the early nineteenth century, only about 2 % of the people could read, which was just fine for the power elite, who held the illiterate population under submission. The sultan rejected the dissemination of knowledge through books. "Books spread ideas and make the population much harder to control. Some of these ideas may be valuable new ways to increase economic growth, but others may be subversive and challenge the existing political and social status quo."[948]

I suspect that God may be in the "creative destruction" business. Reading between the lines in Acts 7, leads me to believe that Stephen was

---

[947] Daron Acemoglu and James A. Robinson. *Why Nations Fail: The Origins of Power, Prosperity, and Poverty* (New York: Currency of Crown Publishing Group, 2012) 202-203.
[948] Ibid., 215.

stoned because he was emptying out the synagogue of the "Freedmen." Each Sabbath there were fewer people in the synagogue and more people out on the street listening to Stephen, who's preaching was accompanied with "signs and wonders." Of course, his death was the beginning of the modern missionary movement as recorded in Acts 8:1.

Stephen's story was to be repeated almost ad infinitum thoughout the history of the Church. Martin Luther, John Wesley, George Whitefield, Charles Finney, B. T. Roberts, and Henry Clay Morrison were all involved in and accused of "creative destruction." Lyman Beecher warned Charles Finney that he would fight him all the way if he tried to cross the state line from New York to Connecticut.[949] Henry Clay Morrison was suspended from the ministry of the Methodist Episcopal Church South for preaching without permission in the Dublin District of the Northwest Texas Conference. Morrison, who would endure a church trial and be acquitted, had the last laugh: "The amusing feature about it all was that the wife of one of the local preachers came to the tent while the committee was at work, and while her husband was preparing charges, she was most gloriously sanctified. She shouted and testified with great joy.[950] When Randy Clark visited Wilmore, Kentucky, in February of 1995, God may have been doing some creative destruction.

Phoebe Palmer was a spiritual giant, a creative destructor, working outside of the boundaries of the Methodist Episcopal Church. Her love for God, intensity of devotion, spiritual practices, Christ-like attitudes, evangelistic influence, and her model as both a wife and mother, rank her with Madame Guyon and Catherine Adorna, as well as other French and Spanish mystics. She, even more than Wesley, conceived and formulated the American Holiness Movement. I would loved to have been a fly on the wall in her Tuesday afternoon parlor meetings especially when Thomas Upham and Nathan Bangs were in attendance. It could be that Phoebe Palmer had more spiritual influence on nineteenth century America than any other woman. But reading Phoebe Palmer's best-known book which explicates her holiness theology, *The Way of Holiness: Notes by the Way*, while challenging and edifying, raises some critical issues.

---

[949] Sydney Ahlstrom. *A Religious History of the American People* (New Haven: Yale University Press, 1972) 461.
[950] Percival A. Wesche. *The Life, Theology, and Influence of Henry Clay Morrison* (unpublished Ph.D. dissertation, The University of Oklahoma, 1954) 127.

Palmer lived a gentrified, upper-class existence. Married to a physician, Walter, she had servants to do her domestic work. Thus, she practiced a spiritual elitism, not available to most 21st century American women, who juggled a hectic life of vocational and domestic responsibilities. This is not to discredit Palmer because there are still many women of leisure in our society, who exhibit little of the spiritual relish and discipline which Palmer practiced.

Palmer's theology is a dizzying and bewildering epistemological trip, a search for certitude that seems to never be resolved. Palmer is known best for her altar theology, i.e., believe one is entirely sanctified on the basis of trusting the promises of Scripture. However, we find the following quotes in chronological order. Certitude was anything but certain. The reader is left to interpret: "She (Palmer often referred to herself in the third person) had withdrawn her attention, as far as possible, from everything that might divide its purposes, and centered it in the aim to get an assurance that she was a child of God, in some such *luminous* or *extraordinary* manner that there never might be a shade of plausibility in the temptation to doubt."[951] Later she wrote: "*I received the assurance that God the Father, through the atoning Lamb, accepted the sacrifice; my heart was emptied of self, and cleansed of all idols, from all filthiness of the flesh, and spirit, and I realized that I dwelt in God and felt that, He had become the portion of my soul, my All in All.*"[952] Afterwards, she then recorded, "And now, in condescension to my constitutional infirmities, my proneness to reason O give me this blessing in some such tangible form, that the enemy of my soul may never be successful with the temptation, that I believe merely because I will believe. Thou knowest that I would not believe, without a proper foundation for my faith; and now let me have this blessing in some *tangible* form, that I may know the precise ground upon which I *obtained*, and also upon which I may *retain* it."[953] She later observed, "And yet in the early career of the believer, how anxious he generally is to get an experience in minutia like others, and how prone to dissatisfaction when this is not attained!"[954] Concerning Palmer's last statement, I ask: "Doesn't Palmer's formula encourage the dissatisfaction which Mildred Wynkoop experienced?" How does

---

[951] Ibid., 73.

[952] Ibid., 82.

[953] Ibid., 86-87.

[954] Ibid., 112.

one gain a clear understanding of assurance for the experience of entre sanctification? Palmer provides little to no help with these questions. This confusion may have been one of the reasons Hannah Whitall Smith wrote:

> My first introduction to fanaticism, if I leave out all that I got from the Quakers to start with, which was a good deal, came through the Methodist doctrine of entire sanctification. That doctrine has been one of the greatest blessings of my life, but it also introduced me into an emotional region where common sense has no chance, and where everything goes by feelings and voices and impressions.[955]

Like much of American spirituality, Palmer's holiness theology was quite individualistic. With little understanding of corporate holiness, thus lacking an ecclesiology, this may have been her most serious departure from Wesley. She wrote, "...I think I should not need any other skill or weapon than the word of God, the sword of the Spirit. Furnished with them, every man is invested with the power not only to fight his own battle, but to plead his own cause."[956]

There is an unsound rationalism in Palmer's theology, which Randy Maddox and Harold Raser have pointed out, and I would add, a circumventing of sovereign grace. Palmer wrote, "For a long time past, it as been a solemn, settled, conviction with me, that the reason why more sincerely pious persons do not attain the witness that the blood of Jesus cleanseth, is for want of bringing the matter to a point, and then deciding with energy and perseverance, I *must* and *will* have it *now*"[957] (italics hers).

Unfortunately like many holiness exponents, Palmer made exaggerated claims. "The proper principle of humility has thus, by this trial, been brought with such tangibility within my grasp, has to leave a continual and blessed certainty on my mind, that God has indeed given me the grace of perfect humility."[958] Palmer further made this claim for herself, "She never afterward saw it necessary to enter heart and soul

---

[955] Ray Strachey. *Religious Fanaticism: Extracts from the Papers of Hannah Whitall Smith* (London: Faber and Gwyer, 1928) 203.

[956] Ibid., 129.

[957] Ibid., 140.

[958] Ibid.,110. (Doesn't this claim to humility, invalidate humility?)

into the otherwise vexatious cares with which the mother of every family is surrounded, but found, after having chosen with her whole soul 'the better part,' that she could ever sing — 'Lo, I come with joy to do My blessed Master's will, Him in outward works pursue, And serve his pleasure still.'"[959]

More important than inconsistencies or consistencies in Palmer's theology, was her influence as a person. She was a charismatic, spiritually-inclined, articulate author, living in America's largest city, the seat of the powerful Methodist Episcopal publishing house. She was a personal friend of Abel Stevens, Nathan Bangs, and Timothy Merritt, and others who were not only versed in Wesley but also through their writings on American Methodism, protected and remained true to its unique theological commitments. More important than Palmer's *The Way of Holiness* was her book *The Promise of the Father,* the first full-length treatise written in America on the ministerial and spiritual prerogatives of women, based on Joel 2. She had theological and biblical authority, in her own mind and in the perspective of many others, to exert spiritual leadership. Charles Edwin Jones sums up her influence:

> Mrs. Palmer's Tuesday Meeting for the Promotion of Holiness (so popular that it outlived her thirty years), influenced a dedicated core of the Methodist ecclesiastical elite, as well as prominent members of other communions. Her following included not only Methodists such as Stephen Olin, president of the Wesleyan University in Connecticut, Nathan Bangs, editor of the New York *Christian Advocate*; and bishops Edmund Janes, Leonidas Hamline, and Jesse Peck; but Congregationalists, Thomas C. Upham, professor at Bowdoin, and Asa Mahan, president of Oberlin; Episcopalian Charles Cullis, a physician of Boston; Baptists E. M. Levy and A. B. Earle, ministers in Philadelphia and Boston respectively; and Friends Hannah Whitall Smith, author of the popular *A Christian's Secret to a Happy Life*, and David S. Updegraff, leader in the Ohio Yearly Meeting.[960]

Attending Phoebe Palmer's Tuesday afternoon meetings was similar to the hundreds who came to Wilmore for the 1970 Asbury College Revival, or the thousands who came to Toronto in 1994 out of

---

[959] Ibid., 61.

[960] Charles Edwin Jones, *Perfectionist Persuasion: The Holiness Movement and American Methodism, 1867-1936* (Metuchen, NJ: Press, Inc., 1974) 2-3.

curiosity or spiritual hunger. For all of them, there were cultural forces at play, which did not eliminate the possibility of God's presence. Thomas Kuhn wrote, "To be accepted as a Paradigm, a theory must seem better than its competition, but it need not, and in fact never does, explain all the facts with which it can be confronted."[961] Note that Kuhn did not say "be better," but "seem better." He also wrote, "An apparently arbitrary element compounded of personal and historical accident, is always a formative ingredient of the beliefs espoused by a given scientific community at a given time."[962] For our purposes, we pluralize accident(s) and change scientific community to religious community. Hence, we offer the excellent summary paragraph from Melvin Dieter:

> The newness then, essentially was a change in emphasis resulting from a simple, literal Biblical faith and the prevailing mood of revivalism combined with an impatient, American pragmatism that always seeks to make a reality at the moment whatever is considered at all possible in the future. Edwards' "immediateness" and Finney's "directness" joined with Wesley's claim to full release from sin to create a powerful logic for the new perfectionist movement's challenge to Methodism and the whole Christian Church.[963]

Of course the above confluence of factors no longer exists. As I informed my preaching students, you will preach in a time, place, and setting on Sunday morning that will and can never be repeated. The next Sunday there will be a different group of people, if only by a few, who having had their lives impacted by personal events familially, vocationally, nationally, etc., that they have never exactly experienced and will never be exactly repeated. If that is true on a weekly basis, how much more true by the year, the decade, or the century.

Think back on all the perceptual instruments we have employed in our examination, none of them available to Palmer and her immediate descendants: sociology, psychology, cultural history, immediate and long distance communication, qualitative research, conversation with dozens of people, almost two centuries of historical distance, not to speak of the power of being incarnationally present in almost any other culture

---

[961] Thomas S. Kuhn. *The Structure of Scientific Revolutions* (Chicago: The University of Chicago Press, 2012) 18.

[962] Ibid., 4.

[963] Melvin E. Dieter, *The Holiness Revival of the Nineteenth Century* (Metuchen, NJ: The Scarecrow Press, Inc., 1980) 31.

on the globe within 36 hours. For these and other reasons beyond our understanding to those who have been raised within the traditional holiness paradigm, that way no longer "seems better." Competing spiritual and theological claims are more prevalent and available than ever before. In light of these competing spiritual voices and bombardment of humanistic and often godless disciplines of learning, it should not amaze us that the influence of the theology, if not conceived, at least incubated in Phoebe Palmer's parlor, has dwindled. What is more amazing is that the unique niche within the two thousand year history of the Church continues to have a life-changing impact on persons around the globe to this day. Its longevity is due to its inherent truth, though no truth represents the full truth, and its workability. Thousands, if not millions, have sought 'entire sanctification" and found exactly that for which they were looking. Perhaps an equal number were disappointed and turned away.

There is a certain amount of control that can be exercised in a Victorian parlor, or even on a small Christian college campus, a control that is demolished or preempted in a state university or behemoth corporation. Excluding variables and experimenting with, teaching with, and administrating with the same constants guarantees if not the same products, similar results. Of course, such environmental sheltering and protection are often shattered given the complexities and realities that all of us run in to, producing frightening alarm when we find out that the equipment with which we have been endowed, perhaps foisted on us, doesn't work. Put another way, the paradigm operative in one community may not function so well in another. Unfortunately, for second blessing holiness to work, there was often but not always a biosphere element surrounding it, hardly available to a hedge-fund broker on Wall Street or a running back in the NFL. Thus if a theological perspective is truly Christian, a proposition truly orthodox, it should be good for all times, all places, and all people. Or to state in a bit more sophisticated manner, *sempre ubique ab omnibus*, the faith which is proclaimed "always, everywhere, by everyone." Or to be more practical according to Richard Langer, any spiritual regiment must pass the "soccer mom" test. In other words, are these spiritual disciplines possible for a person living in a normative early twenty-first century context? He does not deny that a family needs to be less involved in secular or even religious activities. I know of parents who allow their children to be involved in only one sport per year. In short, Langer does not perceive monasticism as possible for parents who have an array of obligations to their children.

> If the spiritual formation movement (or for our purposes the Holiness Movement) wants to become the normal path of discipleship for evangelical congregations, it must craft a vision of discipleship that can be practiced by a soccer mom, not a soccer mom on a three-month sabbatical—because a soccer mom never gets a sabbatical. We must find tools that allow one to go deeper without going elsewhere. We must find practices for an *embedded* spirituality not an *extracted* spirituality.[964]

As Palmer's theology filtered down to the National Camp Meeting Association, and thousands gathered to seek the holiness of God, formulated as "entire sanctification," "a second work of grace," they had reason to believe that heaven had come down to earth. They probably thought "This will never end." But it did. Only historians are able to peer back to those tabernacles, tents, and brush arbors, and imagine the sights, sounds, smells, and even to participate in the spiritual intensity and eternally-binding fellowship, that is almost unknown to an American society often unable to differentiate technological stimulation from Holy Spirit inspiration.

As we have hinted, Wesley Biblical Seminary was the last best hope for an accredited graduate school within the American Holiness tradition. Its founder and first president, Ivan Howard, who had done his graduate wok in early American Methodism, was aware of contradictions within both Wesley's and Palmer's doctrine of entire sanctification. Palmer's name-it claim-it altar theology was vehemently attacked by such Methodist heavyweights as Nathan Bangs and Randolph Foster, the latter who charged that Palmer's position led to "delusion and to spurious though sincere professions."[965]

There was little agreement between prominent theologians such as Miner Raymond and John Miley, as well as popular preachers such as Brengle, Carradine, and Joseph Smith. Howard states, "To make bad

---

[964] Langler, 201.

[965] Ivan Howard. "Wesley versus Phoebe Palmer: An Extended Controversy," *Wesleyan Theological Journal*, Vol. 6, No. 1 (Spring 1971) 36.

matter worse, Wesley's views and Mrs. Palmer's views are combined at times in preaching in such a way that the seeker is assured of the immediate witness of the Spirit if he comes and seeks, and after a brief season of seeking he is told to take it by faith."[966] If there was this much deviation disagreement in the origin of the doctrine of instantaneous entire sanctification, the confusion and controversy would only intensify as time went on. Thus lacking a plausible foundation, it is not surprising that a quarter of a millennium-old edifice has begun to crumble, if not at least in the view of some, been completely demolished.

But none of the above is to say that God is inactive, much less dead in our world. I hope that this narrative has demonstrated that God's miraculous transforming power is more visible than ever in our world. Just because the millennials who sway to rock music magnified by psychedelic lights with hands up-raised, looking at graphic images of the love of God in Jesus in sanctuaries that look nothing like the steepled, colonial churches fit for a Currier and Ives calendar, have never heard of Phoebe Palmer, is no reason to despair. We holiness types, who have been caught in a generational gap between what was and what is, are not called to mourn, but to rejoice. When God creatively destroys, He always builds a new edifice. God never ceases to do a new thing! He is always up to date. Holiness will always take care of itself, if we fix our eyes upon Jesus, the author and finisher of our faith.

At the heart of holiness theology is crucifixion, a self-denial that does not play all that well in a culture of Christian cruises, Christian spas, and Christian entertainment. There is a basic incongruity between the agenda of American Christianity and the commitments of our holiness ancestors, an ever increasing chasm that has been explored by this investigation. Of course, the chasm is hardly detectable to a Christianity that promotes the desires of the self, rarely calling into question much of the selfist theology which envelopes the American church. Mark Edmundson has argued that the ideals of previous generations have been bartered for a "Self" defined by the "wants of certain and precise and particular objects. His life is determined by wants. He could almost write his autobiography based on his desire for this or that object and

---

[966] Ibid., 37.

his success or failure in obtaining it."[967] Edmundson begins this astute cultural analysis with the following:

> It is no secret: culture in the West has become progressively more practical, materially oriented, and skeptical. When I look out at my students, about to graduate, I see people who are in the process of choosing a way to make money, a way to succeed, a strategy for getting on in life. (Or they are, in a few instances, rejecting the materially based life, though often with no cogent alternative to pursue in its stead.) It's no news: we're more and more a worldly culture, a money-based culture geared to the life of getting and spending, trying and succeeding, and reaching for more and more. We are a pragmatic people. We do not seek perfection in thought or art, war or faith. The profound stories about heroes and saints are passing from our minds. We are anything but idealists. From the halls of academe, where a debunking realism is the order of the day, to the floor of the market, where a debunking realism is also the order of the day, nothing is in worse repute than the ideal. Unfettered capitalism runs amok; Nature is ravaged, the rich gorge; prisons are full to bursting; the poor cry out in their misery and no one seems to hear. Lust of Self rules the day.[968]

Whatever can be said for holiness theology and its exponents, it was a worthwhile ideal. Whether that ideal was obtained, is not for the historian or even the psychologist to give a definitive answer. As has been suggested by others, the very profession of holiness provided the inner motivation to live as if the profession could match both an inward and outward reality. And if one believes that a particular religious experience or relationship is obtainable, there is a correlating probability that the attainment will be sought and even realized. I agree with my seminary colleague who said, "I'll take holiness however I can get it."

This "expectation of the ideal" raises several critical questions. Is the ideal subjectively and psychologically defined as opposed to theologically and biblically defined? How likely is one to pursue a particular vision of holiness outside of the participant's community and methodology for becoming a holy person? How inclined are the "sanctified" to express spirituality in terms not defined, utilized, and framed by the individual's immediate social context? In Thomas Kuhn's

---

[967] Edmundson, 96-97.
[968] Ibid., 1.

words, "To the extent, of course, that individuals belong to the same groups and thus share education, language, experience, and culture, we have good reason to suppose that the sensations are the same."[969] Another Kuhn observation is important: Rarely is a person or group persuaded that the paradigm which they have held onto for most or all of their lives, is wrong. The group simply dies off, and a new generation renders a slightly, if not radically different version of scientific beliefs, religious beliefs, political beliefs, etc., than their ancestors.

This book has suggested several paradigm shifts. Crisis to process, holiness purity to Pentecostal power, individual to corporate spirituality, world retreating to world embracing, and altar crisis spirituality to spiritual formation. These shifts should not automatically be interpreted as progress. Historians have correctly interpreted Rome's embracement of Christianity as in some ways disastrous. Rome may have changed Christianity more than Christianity changed Rome. Often there is a pendulum swing, a counter-shift in revolutionary change. We needed Luther's justification by faith, but we did not need Zwingli's iconoclasm or his memorialist definition of the Eucharist. Thus who knows, but that a future generation will discover a second work of grace, quite similar to Phoebe Palmer's altar theology, which early twenty-first century holiness descendents discarded?

I observe a significant number of holiness descendents, that though their theology may be blurred, their vision is not. They have refocused and reinterpreted in ways their holiness parents never envisioned. Emily Hays who along with her husband Chris, pastor an inner-city Church of the Nazarene in Nashville, Tennessee. They have imaginably constructed a holiness code quite different than the rules and regulations that provided the ethical scaffolding for older Nazarenes.

- How our food is grown matters.
- If workers are paid a fair wage matters.
- Saving endangered species matters.
- It matters if we fill up landfills with billions of dirty diapers.
- How we spend our money matters.
- What you do with your body matters.

---

[969] Kuhn, 192.

- It matters if you use a sword (aka gun) or a plowshare.
- The example you set for others matters.
- What bank you call your own matters.
- How you treat your neighbors matters.
- What you do with your time matters.
- Freeing slaves and rehabilitating prisoners matters.[970]

Jamie Gates, director of the Center for Justice and Reconciliation at Point Loma University pointed out the need for holiness "weirdoes" but weirdoes quite different than weirdoes who were once defined as holy rollers. Raised by Nazarene missionaries in South Africa, Jamie realized when he got to college, "I was good at abstaining from personal sins on the top ten list of holiness no nos, my holiness theology at that time did not prepare me to understand let alone to resist the ways I was caught up in the social sins of our time."[971] Jamie has decided to continue to be a weirdo, but a much different kind of weirdo as defined by the holiness distinctives of past generations. "I find my holiness commitments calling me to draw back from my overconsumption of entertainment and information overload. I struggle to be released from the unholy images of others and myself misshaped by millions of advertising images over the years, and so we keep the Sabbath in part by turning off our TVs and other screens off on Sunday."[972] (Oh, come on, Jamie…that's when the Chiefs play!) He further writes, "We live in a world where sex-saturated images, music, conversations and relationships are so ubiquitous, that we are numbed to the realities of sex trafficking in our midst while many in our churches actively join in the softer side of the sex industry that fuels exploitation."[973] The bottom line for Jamie: "I am thinking holiness churches need to be weird."[974]

The Gates and Hays essays were the result of a questionnaire created by Thomas Oord and Josh Broward, focusing on generation Xers and Millennials between the ages of 15 and 55. Oord categorized the

---

[970] Josh Broward and Thomas J. Oord, eds. *Renovating Holiness* (Nampa, ID: SacraSage Press, 2015) 83-84.
[971] Ibid., 339.
[972] Ibid., 342.
[973] Ibid.
[974] Ibid.

responses of the one-hundred contributors into ten dominant themes regarding holiness.

1. Diversity reigns.
2. The Bible still matters.
3. What is entire sanctification and what role does it play?
4. The issues of love are paramount.
5. Community counts; relationships are relevant.
6. It is more about process than crisis.
7. Other Christians are holy too.
8. There is still a creditability gap.
9. Being holy means engaging culture.
10. Hospitality is the way of holiness.[975]

Radical Holiness Exemplified

Stewart Royster, age 25, died from a poisonous snake bite in the jungles of Columbia, South America on November 24, 1973. He was attempting to evacuate four Motilon Indians to medical facilities. On the trip he lost his glasses, which left him almost blind while fording some dozen raging rivers and crawling on hands and knees over trails he could barely identify. Stewart had been raised in a conservative holiness home, his parents, Asbury College graduates. He did not simply live within the Christian paradigm handed down to him. Stewart was extremely bright and adventuresome, but he was far more than a soldier of fortune. Doing academic work in anthropology he was empathetic with other cultures and particularly critical of American values. Having been thrown into a room with another aspiring missionary while studying linguistics at Wycliffe Translators, Stewart left the following self-revealing portrait:

> My roommate is very different from me. He became a Christian through the witness of a Campus Crusade boy in his fraternity, and he looks like the early '60s — clean cut, sweet smelling, football fan, fraternity jock. It is next to impossible for us to come to an agreement on what sort of music to play. His tastes and interests seem to belong to a world I vaguely remember at the University of Denver. Yet, we have come to accept each other and realize that we are both loved and

---

[975] Ibid., 479-485.

saved by the same Christ. We have even had some good times in the Scripture together. It's strange, but I believe it is much easier for me to accept dirty, drunken Indians than this sort of line-toeing man of the American System. God knows that, and is teaching me to overcome my prejudice and ridicule. I realize I don't have to like nor close my eyes to warped values, but I have to *love*. I'm sure that living with me has been a big strain on him, and God is freeing him of prejudice as well. Breaking prejudice and ethnocentrism is apparently a big part of God's work in the world today. He is demanding acceptance and unity regardless of sect and cultural barriers. Christians all over the world are being shown without equivocation that we must live "with all lowliness and meekness, with long suffering, forbearing one another in love" (Eph: 4:2).[976]

Royster's hometown newspaper, the *Louisville Courier Journal* dubbed him a "diplomat to the jungles." If that be so, he was a diplomat without the accouterments and privileges afforded a governmental ambassador residing in an embassy. He was not immune to or unmindful of the daily contrast to the American middle-class comforts in which he had been raised. On August 1, 1970, he penned: "Got to brooding over the fact that there is never quite enough food, that the bugs cause a constant fight on my part to keep from being eaten alive, and without enumerating any more discomforts, that physically I was not adapted to this hostile tropical jungle, and never could be."[977] The 95 degree heat compounded by the 99 % humidity made persevering through any given day a genuine challenge. "It always amazes me how fantastic little things like soap, a dry hammock, and wild turkey can be, when one has suffered a few discomforts....I know that pain is necessary for growth and it is clear the work Christians must do is never easy."[978]

Stewart had a genuine empathy and respect for the Multilon Indians. Hesitating to call himself a missionary, he discovered that the Indians had as much to teach him as they to learn from him. "These people seem to always be happy, continually joking and playing, children and adults all joining together. When hunting and fishing they retain the

---

[976] Robert Stewart Royster. *Unquiet Pilgrimage: The Journal of Robert Stewart Royster* (Louisville, KY: Operation Appreciation, 1979) 40.
[977] Ibid., 29.
[978] Ibid.

excitement and thrill of their first trip up the river or expedition in the mountains."[979]

The jocularity and joyousness of the Indians did not entirely release Stewart from an almost constant depression and melancholy caused by the suffocating physical environment. "Once in the jungle there is no escape to parties, to movies, to social gatherings, to a plush car. The jungle has no favorites; all must answer to its laws. The snake bites the rich or poor; the insects plague man and beast alike."[980] God alone provided stamina for the daily challenge. "At present I feel overwhelmed at all that has to be done and at the same time I'm tired —psychologically and spiritually tired…but God has proved himself helpful and faithful in the past and I am sure he will now."[981] Stewart discovered the one answer for sustainability: "I came into another fellowship of believers who made me realize that the power source of Christianity is the Holy Spirit, and for this one must open himself up and receive. With their help one night I received, not in any dramatic way, but I left the room realizing it had been done. The gift was a gift of faith."[982]

Paul Rees, missionary statesman and holiness preacher extraordinaire wrote of Stewart Royster: "Reflective, subjective, empathetic, moody, vulnerable, articulate, incredibly tough yet immeasurably tender — *that* was Stewart Royster, whose bared soul and brave record now lie remarkably before you."[983] Dennis Kinlaw preached Stewart's funeral at his home church in Louisville, Kentucky, from the words of Jesus, "Except a corn of wheat fall and die it abideth alone, but if it die, it bringeth forth much fruit." Royster's story is extreme and exotic, but one wonders how many times it would be multiplied, if our Nazarene, Wesleyan, and Free Methodist youth, were enabled to "not be conformed to the world but be transformed so that they might prove what is the good and acceptable will of God."

Stewart did not go to Columbia outside of models that propelled him. His parents had been missionaries to Honduras, and his mother Helene (pronounced He-laine) had founded "Operation-Appreciation"

---

[979] Ibid., 75.
[980] Ibid., 26.
[981] Ibid., 38.
[982] Ibid., 33.
[983] Ibid., from Foreword, no page.

in Louisville, Kentucky, a ministry to soldiers from nearby Fort Knox. Though Stewart did not buy into many of the holiness mores of his parents, and was skeptical about the theological formulas that had shaped them, he still acknowledged the influence of his parents. On May 1, 1973, he wrote, "Mother, I just remembered Mother's Day; I have no card and no gift. Please forgive and accept my bare appreciation for your huge investment in my life."[984] We all make investments in our children, but what kind of investments do we make? After all the vacation Bible schools, Bible quizzing, ski trips, lock ins, Christian rock concerts (the list is endless), are our adolescents entering adulthood more inclined to do something radical with their lives or are they better prepared to live the American dream?

Does "radical" obedience equate to the ministries of Stewart Royster and Nick Ripken, placing one's self in imminent danger? Not necessarily. Allow me to introduce you to Harold Hepner who attends my church, Kansas City Church of the Nazarene. When he was an Asbury College student, he lost his left arm in a car accident. Though it only hung by the skin, surgeons managed to save it as a shorter version. Each Christmas Harold rings a bell for the Salvation Army, standing with a kettle in front of Target, Wal-Mart, or wherever. Over the last thirty years, Harold has raised approximately $1,000,000 and has persevered in spite of a series of back surgeries. For six days per week, some 40 — twelve hour days beginning before Thanksgiving and ending after New Years, Harold stands on cold concrete taking only bathroom breaks. I know something of Harold's sacrifice. As an Asbury College student, I rang bells for the Salvation Army one Christmas in Pittsburgh, and one Christmas in Washington, DC, but I rang two hours on and two hours off, and could hardly stand the soreness in my back and shoulders. I was 21-years-old, and Harold is 80, having endured recent neck surgery for deteriorating discs. This past Christmas, 2018, Harold raised $28,000.

Neither Royster nor Hepner are fulfilling a mandate of an institutional church at a given location. Though they were both shaped by a local church, the two of them transcend sectarian identity. Neither of them was, nor are, commissioned by an institution. I am not even sure as to how their common Wesleyan holiness heritage motivated or motivates either of them. I have no evidence that either of them would

[984] Ibid., 41.

link their Christian commitment to a definitive second work of grace known as entire sanctification. I am convinced that they have prayed either consciously or unconsciously the same prayer which John Inskip prayed before he became president of the National Camp Meeting Association for the Promotion of Holiness, "Wholly and Forever Thine, O Lord." That is holiness.

Many of the institutions that once made holiness their paramount objective are now dead and gone: Western Evangelical Seminary, Cascade College, Vennard College, Owosso College, Allentown Pilgrim College, Kernersville College, and the Christian Holiness Association, to name a few. But "holiness" is alive and well. It is alive because God is alive. It is self-sustaining because God is self-sustaining. No one can honestly and sincerely seek God without being confronted with his holiness. Without hearing his requirement and his provision, "Be ye holy because I am holy!" Holiness is the essence of who God is, and it is his delight to pour his nature into us. His unchanging character is determined to change our character. Making mere mortals holy has been and will continue to be God's greatest miracle.

God has not forsaken the Churches who have historically identified themselves with the Wesleyan Holiness Movement. Neither is he partial to the Church of the Nazarene, The Wesleyan Church, The Free Methodist Church, The Salvation Army, and the dozens of other denominations, who place themselves under the holiness umbrella. God still shows up wherever his presence is sincerely desired whether the church be Wesleyan Arminian, or five- point Calvinist. To believe that God favors a particular denominational label or brand is fatal. To believe that God is faithful to those who diligently and honestly seek Him with all their heart is the beginning of revival and renewal. There is evidence of this happening throughout Christendom around the world. May all of us who claim to follow Christ, hear the life-giving words of Isaiah:

> See, I am doing a new thing!
>   Now it springs up; do you not perceive it?
> I am making a way in the desert
>   and streams in the wasteland.
> The wild animals honor me,

The jackals and the owls,
because I provide water in the desert
and streams in the wasteland,
to give drink to my people, my chosen,
the people I formed for myself
that they may proclaim my praise. Isaiah 43: 19-21

BIBLIOGRAPHY

Primary

Asbury, Francis. *The Journal and Letters of Francis Asbury*, Vol. II, eds. Elmer Clark, J. Manning Potts, and Jacob S. Payton (London: Epworth Press, 1958).

Bartleman, Frank. *Azusa Street: The Roots of Modern-day Pentecost* (Plainfield, NJ: Logos International, 1980).

Boehm, Henry. *Reminiscences, Historical and Biographical of Sixty-four Years in the Ministry* (New York: Carlton and Porter, 1866).

Brooks, David. *The Second Mountain: The Quest for a Moral Life* (New York: Random House, 2019).

Buffum, Herbert, "He Abides," *Sing to the Lord* (Kansas City: Lillenas Publishing Company, 1993).

Cattell, Everett. *The Spirit of Holiness* (Grand Rapids: William B. Eerdmans Publishing Company, 1963).

Chambers, Oswald. *My Utmost for His Highest* (Grand Rapids: Oswald Chambers Publications, 1982) February 21.

Church of The Nazarene Manual, 2013-17, Article 903.10 (Kansas City: Nazarene Publishing House, 2013).

Curnock, Nehemiah, ed. *The Journal of the Rev. John Wesley* Vol. VI (London: The Epworth Press, 1938).

Dunning, H. Ray. *Grace, Faith and Holiness* (Kansas City: Beacon Hill Press of Kansas City, 1988).

Finley, James B. *Autobiography of James B. Finley* (Cincinnati: Methodist Book Concern, 1872).

Firth, John. *The Experience and Gospel Labors of the Reverend Benjamin Abbott* (Philadelphia: D. & S. Neall, 1825).

Fosdick, Harry Emerson, "A Fundamentalist Sermon by a Modernist Preacher," in *20 Centuries of Great Preaching* Vol. IX, eds. Clyde E. Fant and William M. Pinson (Waco, TX: Word Books, 1971) 41-48.

_____. *As I See Religion* (New York: Harper & Brothers, 1931).

Foster, Randolph. *Christian Purity or the Heritage of Faith* (New York: Eaton & Mains, 1897).

Francis Asbury Society Executive Committee Meeting Minutes," April 27, 1995, Recorder, Al Coppedge, Courtesy of Mark Nysewander.

Gill, Frederick. *Selected Letters of John Wesley* (New York: Philosophical Library, Incorporated, 1956).

Glendinning, William. *The Life of William Glendinning* (Philadelphia: W. W. Woodward, 1795).

Greathouse, William. *Wholeness in Christ: Toward a Biblical Theology of Holiness* (Kansas City: Beacon Hill Press of Kansas City, 1998).

Grider, J. Kenneth. *A Wesleyan Holiness Theology* (Kansas City: Beacon Hill Press of Kansas City, 1994).

Harris, Merne and Richard S. Taylor. "The Dual Nature of Sin," *The Word and the Doctrine*, ed. *Kenneth E. Geiger* (Kansas City: Beacon Hill Press of Kansas City, 1966) 89-118.

Hawley, Zerah. *A Journal of a Tour* (New Haven: S. Converse, 1822).

Heitzenrater, Richard. *The Elusive Mr. Wesley: John Wesley His Own Biographer*, Vol. I (Nashville: Abingdon Press, 1984).

Hills, A.M. *Holiness and Power* (Cincinnati: Revivalist Office, 1897).

James, William. "A Definition of Faith" in *Readings in the Psychology of Religion*, ed. Orlo Strunk, Jr. (Nashville: Abingdon Press, 1959) 196-197.

Jones, Charles Edwin. *A Guide to the Study of the Holiness Movement* (Metuchen, NJ: The Scarecrow Press, 1947).

Kinlaw, Dennis F. *How Every Christian Can Have the Mind of Christ* (Nappanee, IN: Evangel Publishing House, 1998).

_____. *Let's Start with Jesus: A New Way of Doing Theology* (Grand Rapids: Zondevan, 2005).

_____. *Preaching in the Spirit* (Grand Rapids: Zondervan, 1985).

Kohlberg, Lawrence, "A Cognitive Developmental Approach to Moral Education," *The Humanist*, ed. Paul Kurtz (Buffalo: Hoffman Printing Company, 1972) 13-16.

Lewis, C. S. *Mere Christianity* (New York: HarperCollins Publishers, 1980).

_____. *The Screwtape Letters and Screwtape Proposes a Toast* (New York: The Macmillan Company, 1961) Preface.

Lillenas, Haldor. *Down Melody Lane: An Autobiography* (Kansas City: Beacon Hill Press, 1953).

_____. "Glorious Freedom," *Sing to the Lord* (Kansas City: Lillenas Publishing Company, 1993).

Maxwell, John. *Be All You Can Be: A Challenge to Stretch to Your God-Given Potential* (Nashville: David C. Cook, 2007).

_____. *Developing the Leader within You 2.0* (New York: HarperCollins Leadership, 2018).

McConnell, Lela G. *The Pauline Ministry in the Kentucky Mountains* (Louisville: Pentecostal Publishing Company 1942).

McDonald, William. *The Double Cure, or Echoes from the National Camp Meetings* (Boston: The Christian Witness Co., 1894).

Morris, Leila, "Holiness unto the Lord," in *Sing to the Lord*.

Morrison, Henry Clay. *Is the World Growing Better or Is the World Growing Worse?* (Louisville: The Pentecostal Publishing Company, 1932).

_____. *Some Chapters of My Life Story* (Louisville: Pentecostal Publishing Company, 1941).

_____. *The Follies of Fosdick* (Louisville: Pentecostal Publishing Company, 1936).

_____. *The Second Coming of Christ* (Louisville: The Pentecostal Publishing Company, 1914).

_____. *The World War in Prophecy: The Downfall of the Kaiser and the End of the Dispensation* (Louisville: The Pentecostal Publishing Company, 1917).

Oswalt, John N. "A revised copy of a paper presented to a forum of the faculty of Asbury Theological Seminary in April 1995." Courtesy of Oswalt to this author.

Purkiser, W. T., Richard S. Taylor and Willard H. Taylor. *God, Man, and Salvation* (Kansas City: Beacon Hill Press of Kansas City, 1977).

Royster, Robert Stewart. *Unquiet Pilgrimage: The Journal of Robert Stewart Royster* (Louisville, KY: Operation Appreciation, 1979).

Smith, Dean. *A Coach's Life* (New York: Random House, 1999).

Staples, Rob L., "The Current Wesleyan Debate on the Baptism of the Holy Spirit," (unpublished paper presented to Nazarene

Theological Seminary Breakfast Club, 1979) available at Nazarene Theological Seminary Library.

Staples, Rob L., "My Ordeal by Fire: The Record of a Crisis I Faced as Professor of Theology at Nazarene Theological Seminary." Courtesy of Steve McCormick, available in Nazarene Archives.

Strachey, Ray. *Religious Fanaticism: Extracts from the Papers of Hannah Whitall Smith*. (London: Faber and Gwyer, 1928).

Taylor, Richard S. *God's Integrity and the Cross* (Nappanee, IN: Francis Asbury Press, 1999).

_____. *The Main Issue: The Why and How of Holiness Preaching* (Salem, OH: Schmul Publishing Company, 2006).

_____. *Understanding Ourselves: Acquiring a Christian Mind: Biblical Studies in the Psychology of Holiness* (Salem, OH: Schmul Publishing Company, 1997).

_____. *A Right Conception of Sin: Its Relation to Right Thinking and Right Living* (Kansas City: Beacon Hill Press of Kansas City, 1945).

_____. *Life in the Spirit: Christian Holiness in Doctrine, Experience and Life* (Kansas City: Beacon Hill Press, 1966).

_____. *The Disciplined Life* (Kansas City: Beacon Hill Press, 1962).

_____. *A Return to Christian Culture or Why Avoid the Cult of the Slob?* (Salem, OH: Schmul Publishing Company, 2004).

Telford, John, ed. *The Letters of the Rev. John Wesley*, Vol. VI (London: The Epworth Press, 1960).

Tracy, Wes et al. *The Upward Call: Spiritual Formation and the Holy Life* (Kansas City: Beacon Hill Press of Kansas City, 1994).

Wallis, Jim. *Christ in Crisis: Why We Need to Reclaim Jesus* (New York: HarperOne, 2019).

Wesley, Charles, "Love Divine, All Loves Excelling," *Sing to the Lord* (Kansas City: Lillenas Publishing Company, 1993).

Wesley, John and Charles Wesley. *John and Charles Wesley: Selected Prayers, Hymns, Journal Notes, Sermons, Letters, and Treatises in The Classics of Western Spirituality*, ed. Richard J. Payne and Frank Whaling (Mahwah, NJ: Paulist Press, 1981).

Wesley, John, "Salvation by Faith," *Wesley's Standard Sermons*, Vol. I, ed. Edward Sugden (Grand Rapids: Francis Asbury Press, 1955) 35-52.

_____. "The Repentance of Believers," *Sermons*, Vol. II, 379-397.

_____. "On Sin in Believers," *Sermons*, Vol. II (Grand Rapids: Francis Asbury Press, 1995) 360-397.

_____. "Catholic Spirit," *Sermons*, Vol. II, 126-146.

_____. *A Plain Account of Christian Perfection* (Kansas City: Beacon Hill Press of Kansas City, 1971).

_____. "Earnest Appeal to Men of Reason and Religion," *The Works of John Wesley*. Third edition, Vol. 8 (London: Wesleyan Methodist Book Room, 1872) 3-45.

_____. *Works*, "Thoughts upon Liberty," Vol. XI, 34-46.

_____. *Works*, "Brief Thoughts on Christian Perfection," Vol. XI, 446.

_____. *Works*, "The Spirit of Bondage and Adoption," Vol. V, 98-111.

_____. *Works*, "The First Fruits of the Spirit," Vol. I, 87-97.

_____. *Wesley's Notes on the Bible* (Grand Rapids: Francis Asbury Press, 1987).

White, James F. ed. Intro: *John Wesley's Sunday Service of the Methodists in North America,* (Nashville: The United Methodist Publishing House, The United Methodist Board of Higher Education, 1984).

Wiley, H. Orton. *Christian Theology,* Vol. II (Kansas City: Beacon Hill Press of Kansas City, 1969).

Wood, J. A. *Perfect Love* (South Pasadena, CA: published by the author, 1891).

Wynkoop, Mildred, "An Existential Interpretation of the Doctrine of Holiness," a message presented in Chapel Service, Western Evangelical Seminary, Portland, Oregon, November 3, 1955.

_____. *A Theology of Love* (Kansas City: Beacon Hill Press of Kansas City, 2015).

_____. *Foundations of Wesleyan Arminian Theology* (Kansas City: Beacon Hill Press of Kansas City, 1967).

Secondary

Acemoglu, Daron and James A. Robinson. *Why Nations Fail: The Origins of Power, Prosperity, and Poverty* (New York: Currency of Crown Publishing Group, 2012).

Adeney, Miriam. *Kingdom Without Borders: The Untold Story of Global Christianity* (Downers Grove, IL: InterVarsity Press, 2009).

Ahlstrom, Sydney. *A Religious History of the American People* Vol. I (Garden City, NY: Image Books, 1975).

Anderson, Alan. *To The Ends of the Earth: Pentecostalism and the Transformation of World Christianity* (New York: Oxford University Press, 2013).

Arndt, William F. and F. Wilbur Gingrich. *A Greek-English Lexicon of the New Testament and Other Early Christian Literature* (Chicago: The University of Chicago Press, 1957).

Baker, Frank. *John Wesley and the Church of England* (London: Epworth Press, 1970).

Bangs, Carl. *Phineas Bresee: His Life in Methodism, the Holiness Movement, and the Church of the Nazarene* (Kansas City: Beacon Hill Press, 1995).

Beals, Ivan A. *A Racist Legacy: Will the Church Resolve the Conflict?* (Notre Dame, IN: Crossroads Books, 1997).

Beard, Steve. *Thunderstruck: John Wesley and the "Toronto Blessing"* The entire book was downloaded and sent by Beard to this author, January 22, 2019.

Beverley, James A. *Holy Laughter & The Toronto Blessing: An Investigative Report* (Grand Rapids: Zondervan Publishing House, 1995).

Birkirts, Swen. *The Gutenberg Elegies: The Fate of Reading in an Electronic Age* (Boston: Faber and Faber, 1994).

Biser, Samuel K. *Genetic Miracles: For People with an Inherited Disease - Who Need a Miracle to Stay on Earth,* Version 2 (Waynesboro, VA: Sam Biser Press, Inc., 2012-2016).

Brailsford, Mabel. *A Tale of Two Brothers, John and Charles Wesley* (New York: Oxford Unversity Press, 1954).

Brands, H. W. *Traitor to His Class: The Privileged Life and Radical Presidency of Franklin Delano Roosevelt* (New York: Anchor Books, 2008).

Brereton, Virginia. *Training God's Army: The American Bible School, 1880-1940* (Bloomington: Indiana Press, 1990).

Brooks, David. *Bobos in Paradise: The New Upper Class and How They Got There* (New York: Simon and Schuster, 2000).

_____. *The Road to Character* (New York: Random House, 2016).

Broward, Josh and Thomas J. Oord, eds. *Renovating Holiness* (Nampa, ID: SacraSage Press, 2015).

Brower, Kent. *Holiness in the Gospels* (Kansas City: Beacon Hill Press of Kansas City, 2015).

Brown, Candy Gunther, "Global Awakenings: Divine Healing Networks and Global Community in North America, Brazil, Mozambique and Beyond," in *Global Pentecostal and Charismatic Healing*, ed. Candy Gunther Brown (New York: Oxford University Press, 2011) 351-378.

Brown, Kenneth O. *Inskip, McDonald, Fowler: "Wholly And Forever Thine"* (Hazelton, PA: Holiness Archives, 1999).

Brown, Kenneth O., and P. Lewis Brevard. *History of the Churches of Christ in Christian Union* (Circleville, OH: Circle Press, Inc., 1980).

Caldwell, Tommy. *The Push: A Climber's Search for the Path* (New York: Penguin Publishing Group, 2017).

Campbell, Heidi, and Stephen Garner. *Networked Theology: Negotiating Faith in a Digital Culture* (Grand Rapids: Baker Academics, 2016).

Cary, W. W. *Story of the National Holiness Missionary Society* (Chicago: National Holiness Missionary Society, 1940).

Cavanaugh, William. *Being Consumed: Economics and Christian Desire* (Grand Rapids: William B. Eerdman Publishing Company, 2008).

Cohen, Lizabeth. *A Consumer's Republic* (New York: Random House, 2003).

Collins, Kenneth J. "Why The Holiness Movement is Dead," in *Counterpoint: Dialogue with Drury on the Holiness Movement,* ed. D. Curtis Hale (Salem, OH: Schmul Publishing Company, 2005) 56-72.

Cox, Harvey. *Fire From Heaven: The Rise of Pentecostal Spirituality and the Reshaping of Religion in the Twenty-first Century* (New York: Addison Wesley Publishing Company, 1995).

Crooks, George. *The Life of Matthew Simpson of the Methodist Episcopal Church* (New York: Harper Brothers, 1890).

Crossan, John Dominic. *The Historical Jesus: The Life of a Mediterranean Jewish Peasant* (San Francisco: Harper Collins, 1991).

Cunningham, Floyd, ed. *Our Watchword and Song: The Centennial History of the Church of the Nazarene* (Kansas City: Beacon Hill Press of Kansas City, 2009).

Currid-Halkett, Elizabeth. *The Sum of Small Things: A Theory of the Aspirational Class* (Princeton: Princeton University Press, 2017).

Davies, Nole and Martin Conway. *World Christianity in the Twentieth Century* (London: SCM Press, 2008).

Dawe, Gregory W., *The Historical Jesus Quest: Landmarks in the Search for the Jesus of History* (Louisville: John Knox Press, 1999).

Dayton, Donald W. *Discovering an Evangelical Heritage* (New York: Harper & Row Publishers, 1976).

_____. *Theological Roots of Pentecostalism* (Metuchen, New Jersey: The Scarecrow Press, 1987).

DeYoung, Curtis Paul, Michael O. Emerson, George Yancey, and Karen Chai Kim. *United by Faith: The Multi-racial Congregation as an Answer to the Problem of Race* (New York: Oxford, 2003).

Dieter, Melvin E. *The Holiness Revival of the Nineteenth Century* (Metuchen, NJ: The Scarecrow Press, Inc., 1980).

Dietterich, Inagrace T., "Missional Community: Cultivating Communities of the Holy Spirit," in *Missional Church: A Vision for a Sending of the Church in North America*, ed. Darrell L. Guder (Grand Rapids: Eerdmans Publishing Company, 1998).

Dillard, Annie. *Pilgrim at Tinkercreek* (New York: Harper & Row, 1974).

Dobson, Ed. *The Year of Living Like Jesus: My Journey of Discovering What Jesus Would Really Do* (Grand Rapids: Zondervan, 2009).

Drury, Keith. "The Holiness Movement is Dead, A Retrospective," in *Counterpoint: Dialogue with Drury on the Holiness Movement*. ed. D. Curtis Hale (Salem, OH; Schmul Publishing, 2005) 17-35.

Easterbrook, Gregg. *The Progress Paradox: How Life Gets Better While People Feel Worse* (New York: Random House, 2003).

Edmundson, Mark. *Self and Soul: A Defense of Ideals* (Cambridge, MA: Harvard University Press, 2015).

Eller, Vennard. *The Simple Life* (Grand Rapids: Eerdmans, 1973).

Ellul, Jacques. *The Subversion of Christianity* (Grand Rapids: William B. Eerdman Publishing Company, 1984).

_____. *To Will and to Do* (Philadelphia: The United Church Press, 1969).

Elsinger, Ellen. *Citizens of Zion: The Social Origins of Camp Meeting Revivalism* (Knoxville: The University of Tennessee Press, 1999).

Emerson, Michael O., and Christian Smith. *Divided by Faith: Evangelical Religion and the Problem of Race in America* (New York: Oxford, 2000).

Epstein, David. *The Sports Gene: Inside the Science of Extraordinary Athletic Performance* (New York: Portfolio/Penguin, 2014).

Erikson, Erik H. *Childhood and Society* (New York: W. W. Norton & Company, Inc., 1978).

_____. *Gandhi's Truth: On the Origins of Militant Non-violence* (New York: W. W. Norton and Company, 1969).

_____. *Identity: Youth and Crisis* (New York: W.W. Norton & Company, 1968).

Farabaugh, Pat. *An Unbreakable Bond: The Brotherhood of Maurice Stokes and Jack Twyman* (Haworth, New Jersey: Johann Press, 2014).

Ferguson, John. *Pelagius: A Historical and Theological Study* (Cambridge: W. Heffer and Sons, 1956).

Flew, R. Newton. *The Idea of Perfection* (London, Oxford University Press, 1934).

Foster, Richard. *Freedom of Simplicity* (San Francisco: Harper and Row, 1981).

Frances, Allen. *Twilight of American Sanity: A Psychiatrist Analyzes the Age of Trump* (New York: HarperCollins Publishers, 2017).

Freud, Sigmund. *Civilization and Its Discontents* (London: Penguin, 2002).

Friedman, Edwin. *Generation to Generation: Family Process in Church and Synagogue* (New York: The Gilford Press, 1985).

Friedman, Thomas L. *Thank You for Being Late: An Optimist's Guide to Thriving in an Age of Accelerations* (New: York: Picador, 2016).

Furlong, Monica. *Merton: A Biography* (San Francisco: Harper and Row Publishers, 1980).

Gay, Craig N. *Modern Technology and the Human Future: A Christian Appraisal* (Downers Grove: InterVarsity Press, 2018).

Goldberg, Jonah. *Suicide of the West: How the Rebirth of Tribalism, Populism, Nationalism, and Identity Politics is Destroying American Politics* (New York: Crown Forum, 2018).

Goodwin, Doris Kearns. *No Ordinary Time: Franklin and Eleanor Roosevelt: The Home Front in World War II* (New York: Simon and Schuster, 1994).

Gray, L. Jack, "Revival in Our Nation: An Interpretation," in *One Divine Moment: The Asbury Revival*, ed. Robert E. Coleman (Old Tappan, NJ: Fleming H. Revell Company, 1970) 113-118.

Green, V. H. *The Young Mr. Wesley* (London: Edward Arnold, 1961).

Gresham, Loren P. and L. Paul Gresham. *From Many Came One in Jesus' Name: Southern Nazarene University Looks Back on a Century* (Virginia Beach, VA: The Donning Company Publishers, 1998).

Gunter, Stephen. *The Limits of Love Divine: John Wesley's Response to Antinomianism and Enthusiasm* (Nashville: Abingdon, 1989).

Hammond, Geordan. *John Wesley in America: Restoring Primitive Christianity* (Oxford: Oxford University Press, 2014).

Haidt, Jonathan. *The Righteous Mind: Why Good People are Divided Between Politics and Religion* (Vintage Books: New York, 2012).

Haroutunian, Joseph. *Piety versus Moralism: The Passing of the New England Theology* (New York: Henry Holt and Company, 1932).

Hatch, Nathan O. "Evangelical Colleges and the Challenge of Christian Thinking," in *Making Higher Education Christian: The History and Mission of Evangelical Colleges in America*. eds. Joel Carpenter and Kenneth W. Shipps (Grand Rapids: William B. Eerdman's Publishing Co. 1987) 155-171.

_____. "The Puzzle of American Methodism," in *Methodism and the Shaping of American Culture*, eds. Nathan O. Hatch and John H.Wigger (Nashville: Kingswood Books, 2001) 23-40.

Hauerwas, Stanley and William H. Willimon. *Resident Aliens: Life in the Christian Colony* (Nashville: Abingdon Press, 1989).

Hays, Richard B. *The Moral Vision of the New Testament: A Contemporary Introduction to New Testament Ethics* (San Francisco: HarperSanFrancisco, 1996) 215-290.

Hedges, Chris. *Empire of Illusion: The End of Literacy and the Triumph of Spectacle* (New York: Nation Books, 2009).

Henry, Carl F. H. *The Uneasy Conscience of Modern Fundamentalism.* (Grand Rapids: William B. Eerdmans Publishing Company, 1947).

Holifield, E. Brooks. *A History of Pastoral Care in America: From Salvation to Self-Realization* (Nashville: Abingdon Press, 1983).

Howard, Martha M., "A First-hand View of the First Ten Years of Wesley Biblical Seminary and of Its Founding President," (July 1994) unpublished and furnished by Wesley Biblical Seminary, Jackson, Mississippi.

Hughes, T. Walt. *Wilmore, Kentucky* (Compton, CA: M. and A. Books, 1965).

Humble, R. G. *Sergeant Alvin C. York: A Christian Patriot* (Circleville, Ohio: Churches of Christ in Christian Union, 1966).

Hunter, James Davison. *To Change the World: The Irony, Tragedy, and Possibility of Christianity in the Late Modern World* (New York: Oxford, 2010).

Jackall, Robert. *Moral Mazes: The World of Corporate Managers* (New York: Oxford University Press, 2010).

James, Henry. "Campus Demonstrations," in *One Divine Moment*, 55-67.

John, Perry. *Sgt. York: His Life, Legend and Legacy* (Nashville: B. and H, Publishing, 1997) No page number. E-book retrieved online from Mid-Continent Public Library, Kansas City, MO, unpaginated.

Jones, Charles Edwin. *Perfectionist Persuasion: The Holiness Movement and American Methodism, 1867-1936* (Metuchen, NJ: Press, Inc., 1974).

Jones, Robert P. *The End of White Christian America* (New York: Simon and Schuster, 2016).

Junger, Sebastian. *Tribe: On Homecoming and Belonging* (New York: Hachette Book Group, 2016).

Keck, Leander. *A Future for the Historical Jesus: The Place of Jesus in Preaching and Theology* (Nashville: Abingdon Press, 1971).

Kelly, Dean. *Why Conservative Churches Are Growing* (New York: Harper and Row, 1972).

Kinghorn, Kenneth Cain. *The Story of Asbury Theological Seminary* (Lexington, KY: Emeth Press, 2010).

Kingsley, Patrick. *The New Odyssey: The Story of Europe's Refugee Crisis* (London: The Guardian, 2017).

Kinlaw, Dennis F., "Campus Roots for Revival," in *One Divine Moment*, 107-111.

Kinnaman, David. *Unchristian: What a New Generation Thinks about Christianity and Why It Matters* (Grand Rapids: Baker Books, 2007).

Kuhn, Thomas S. *The Structure of Scientific Revolutions* (Chicago: The University of Chicago Press, 2012).

Labberton, Mark, "Still Evangelical?" in *Still Evangelical? Insiders Reconsider Political, Social, and Theological Meaning*, ed. Mark Labberton (Downers Grove, IL: InterVarsity Press, 2018).

LeRoy, Daniel E.. *Rediscovering Our Holiness Heritage: How the Wesleyan Church Can Get Back What We Gave Away* (Kernersville, NC: Old Blue Truck Publishing Company, 2018).

Lindsell, Harold. *The Holy Spirit in the Latter Days* (Nashville: Thomas Nelson, 1983).

Lindsell, Harold. *Park Street Prophet: A Life of Harold John Ockenga* (Wheaton: Van Kampen Press, 1951).

Loury, Glenn, "A Professor under Construction," in *Finding God at Harvard: Spiritual Journeys of Christian Thinkers*, ed. Kelly K. Monroe (Grand Rapids: Zondervan Publishing House, 1996) 68-76.

Lyall, Leslie T. *John Song: Flame for God in the Far East* (Chicago: Moody Press, 1964).

Makos, Adam. *Devotion: An Epic Story of Heroism, Friendship, and Sacrifice* (New York: Ballantine Books, 2015).

Mandryk, Jason. *Operation World: The Definitive Prayer Guide to Every Nation* (Colorado Springs: Biblica Publishing, 2010).

Manning, Brennan. *A Glimpse of Jesus: The Stranger to Self Hatred* (San Francisco: Harper Collins Publishers, 2003).

Markham, Paul. *Rewired: Exploring Religious Conversion* (Eugene, Oregon: Penwick Publications, 2006).

Marsden, George. "Why No Major Evangelical University," in *Making Higher Education Christian: The History and Mission of Evangelical Colleges in America*, eds. Joel Carpenter and Kenneth W. Shipps (Grand Rapids: William B. Erdman Publishing Company. 1987) 294-304.

_____. *Jonathan Edwards: A Life* (New Haven: Yale University Press, 2003).

Martin, David. *Pentecostalism: The World Their Parish* (Malden, Massachusetts: Blackwell Publishers, 2002).

Mastriano, Douglas V. *Alvin York: A New Biography of the Hero of the Argonne* (Lexington: University of Kentucky Press, 2014).

Merriam Webster's Collegiate Dictionary (Springfield, MA: Merriam Webster Inc, 2004).

Meyer, Dick. *Why We Hate Us: Discontent in the New Millennium* (New York: Crown Publishers, 2008).

Millard, Candace. *Hero of the Empire: The Boer War: A Daring Escape and the Making of Winston Churchill* (New York: Anchor Books, 2016).

Miller, Robert. *Harry Emerson Fosdick: Preacher, Pastor, Prophet* (New York: Oxford University Press, 1985).

Miller, Vincent. *Consuming Religion: Christian Faith and Practices in a Consumer Culture* (New York: Continuum, 2004).

Moody, William R. *The Life of Dwight L. Moody* (New York: Fleming Revell, 1900).

Moore, Robert L. *John Wesley and Authority: A Psychological Perspective* (Missoula, MT: Scholars Press, 1979).

Niebuhr, Reinhold. *Faith and History: A Comparison of Christian and Modern Views of History* (New York: Charles Scribner's Sons, 1949).

Noll, Mark A. *Scandal of the Evangelical Mind* (Grand Rapids: William B. Eerdmans Publishing, 1994).

Oden, Thomas. *After Modernity... What? Agenda for Theology* (Grand Rapids: Zondervan, 1990).

Oropeza, B. J. *A Time To Laugh* (Peabody, MA: Hendrickson Publishers, 1995).

Oswalt, John N. *Called to Be Holy: A Biblical Perspective* (Anderson, IN: Francis Asbury Press, 1999).

Otto, Rudolph. *The Idea of the Holy* (New York: Oxford University Press, 1923).

Outler, Albert. "Biblical Primitivism in Early American Methodism" in *The Wesleyan Theological Heritage,* eds. Thomas Oden and Leicester Longden (Grand Rapids: Zondervan, 1991) 145-159.

Packer, J. I. *Knowing God* (Downers Grove, IL: InterVarsity Press, 1973).

Painter, Nell Irwin. *The History of White People* (New York: W. W. Norton & Co., 2010).

Peck, M. Scott. *A World Waiting to be Born: Civility Rediscovered* (New York: Bantam Books, 1994).

Peters, John L. *Christian Perfection and American Methodism* (Grand Rapids: Francis Asbury Press of Zondervan Publishing House, 1985).

Pfaff, Donald W. *The Altruistic Brain: How We are Naturally Good* (New York: Oxford University Press, 2015).

Pietsch, B. M., "Reference Bibles and Interpretive Authority " in *The Bible in American Life,* eds. Philip Goff, et. al. (New York: Oxford, 2017) 119-126.

Polk, Thad A., "The Addictive Brain," *The Great Courses* (Chantilly, VA: The Great Courses, 2015) 26-29.

Powell, Samuel M., "A Contribution to a Wesleyan Understanding of Holiness and Community," in *Embodied Holiness: Toward a Corporate Theology of Spiritual Growth,* eds. Samuel M. Powell and Michael Lodahl (Downers Grove, IL: InterVarsity Press, 1999) 166-189.

Puleo, Stephen. *The Caning: The Assault that Drove America to Civil War* (Yardley PA: Washington Publishing, 2013).

Putnam, Robert D. *Bowling Alone: The Collapse and Revival of American Community* (New York: Simon and Schuster Paperbacks, 2000).

Quanstrom, Mark. *A Century of Holiness Theology* (Kansas City: Beacon Hill Press, 2004).

Rack, Henry. *Reasonable Enthusiast: John Wesley and the Rise of Methodism* (London: Epworth Press, 2002).

Raser, Harold. *More Preachers and Better Preachers: The First Fifty Years of Nazarene Theological Seminary* (Kansas City: Nazarene Publishing House, 1995).

Richtel, Matt. *A Deadly Wandering: A Mystery, A Landmark Investigation, and the Astonishing Science of Attention in the Digital Age* (New York: HarperCollins Publishers, 2014).

Ringenberg, William C. *The Christian College: A History of Protestant Higher Education in America* (Grand Rapids: Baker Academic, 2006).

_____. *Taylor University: The First 125 Years* (Grand Rapids: William B. Eerdmans Publishing Co., 1973).

Ripken, Nik with Gregg Lewis. *The Insanity of God: A True Story of Faith Resurrected* (Nashville, BNH Publishing Group, 2013).

Robb, Edmund W. *The Spirit Who Will Not Be Tamed: The Wesleyan Message and The Charismatic Experience* (Anderson, IN: Bristol House Ltd., 1997).

Roberts, Gary Leland. *Massacre at Sand Creek: How Methodists Were Involved in an American Tragedy* (Nashville: Abingdon Press, 2016).

Roberts, Robert C. *Taking the Word to Heart: Self and Other in An Age of Therapies* (Grand Rapids: William B. Eerdmans Publishing Company, 1993).

Rowell, Jeren. *Preaching Holiness: Pastoral Considerations* (Kansas City: The Foundry Publishing, 2018).

Russ, Dan. "Fear Not: Security, Risk and Academic Freedom" in *The Christian College Phenomenon: Inside America's Fastest Growing Institutions of Higher Learning*, eds. Samuel Joeckel and Thomas Chesnes (Abilene, TX: Abilene Christian University Press, 2012) 171-181.

Salter, Darius L. *America's Bishop: The Life of Francis Asbury* (Nappanee, IN: The Francis Asbury Press, 2003).

_____. "Foundations of Administration: The Book of Acts as Case Study," in *Foundations of Church Administration*, ed. Bruce L. Petersen, et.al (Kansas City: Beacon Hill Press of Kansas City, 2010) 9-23.

_____. *What Really Matters in Ministry* (Grand Rapids: Baker Book House, 1990).

_____. *"God Cannot Do Without America:" Matthew Simpson and the Apotheosis of Protestant Nationalism* (Wilmore, Kentucky: First Fruits Press, 2017).

_____. *American Evangelism: Its Theology and Practice* (Grand Rapids: Baker Books, 1996).

_____. *Deep and Wide* (Charleston, SC: Create Space, 2012).

Sangster, W. E. *The Path to Perfection: An Examination and Restatement of John Wesley's Doctrine of Christian Perfection* (Nashville; Abingdon Cokesbury Press, 1943).

Schmidt, Corwin E. "The Continuing Distinctive Role of the Bible in American Lives: A Comparative Analysis," in *The Bible in American Life*, eds. Phillip Goff, et.al. (New York: Oxford University Press, 2017) 203-222.

Seamands, John T., "Churches Come Alive," *One Divine Moment*, 69-81.

Shelton, H., Robert T. Handy, Lefferts A. Loetcher. *American Christianity: A Historical Interpretation with Representative Documents*, Vol. II (New York: Charles Scribner's Sons, 1963).

Shenk, Joshua. *Lincoln's Melancholy: How Depression Challenged and Fueled His Greatness* (New York: Houghton-Mifflin Company, 2005).

Sholl, Doug, "The Contributions of Lawrence Kohlberg to Religious and Moral Education," in *Religious Education*, ed. Randolph Miller (New York: The Religious Education Association, 1971) 364-372.

Smith, James K. A. *Desiring the Kingdom: Worship, Worldview, and Cultural Formation* (Grand Rapids: Baker Academics, 2009).

Smith, Timothy L. *Called Unto Holiness-The Story of the Nazarenes: The Formative Years* (Kansas City: Nazarene Publishing House, 1962).

_____. *Revivalism and Social Reform in Mid-Nineteenth Century America* (Nashville: Abingdon Press, 1957).

_____. *Speaking the Truth in Love: Some Honest Questions for Pentecostals* (Kansas City: Beacon Hill Press, 1977).

_____. "The Theology and Practices of Methodism, 1887–1919," in *The History of American Methodism* Vol. II, ed. Emory Bucke (Nashville: Abingdon, 1958) 608-659.

Snyder, Howard. *The Divided Flame: Wesleyans and the Charismatic Renewal* (Grand Rapids, Francis Asbury Press, 1986).

Sowell, Thomas. *Intellectuals in Society* (New York: Basic Books, 2011).

Stanley, Susie. *Holy Boldness: Women Preachers' Autobiographies and the Sanctified Life* (Knoxville: The University of Tennessee Press, 2002).

Stearns, Richard. *The Hole in Our Gospel: What Does God Expect of Us? The Answer That Changed My Life and Might Just Change the World* (Nashville: Thomas Nelson, Inc., 2009).

Steele, Richard. *"Gracious Affections" and "True Virtue" According to Jonathan Edwards and John Wesley* (Metuchen, NJ: The Scarecrow Press, 1994).

Stone, Bryan P. *Evangelism after Christendom: The Theology and Practice of Christian Witness* (Grand Rapids, Brazos Press, 2007).

Strachan, Owen. *Awakening The Evangelical Mind: An Intellectual History of the Neo-Evangelical Movement* (Grand Rapids: Zondervan, 2015).

Taibbi, Matt. *I Can't Breathe: A Killing on Bay Street* (New York: Spiegel and Craw, 2017).

Taves, Ann. *Fits, Trances, and Visions: Experiencing Religion and Explaining Experience from Wesley to James* (Princeton: Princeton University Press, 1999).

Taylor, Alan. *William Cooper's Town: Power and Persuasion on the Frontier of the Early American Republic* (New York: Vintage, 1995).

Temple, William. *Nature, Man, and God* (London: Macmillan, 1934).

Tennent, Timothy. *Invitation to World Missions* (Grand Rapids: Kregel, 2010).

Thacker, Jr., Joseph A. *Asbury College: Vision and Miracle* (Nappanee, IN: Evangel Press, 1990).

Thornton, Wallace. *A Response to Keith Drury's "The Holiness Movement is Dead,"* (Somerset, KY: Self-published, 1999).

_____. *Radical Righteousness: Personal Ethics and the Development of the Holiness Movement* (Salem, OH: Schmul Publishing Company, 1998).

Tredoux, Johan. *Mildred Bangs Wynkoop: Her Life and Thought* (Kansas City: Foundry Publishing, 2017).

Trueblood, Elton. *Abraham Lincoln; Theologian of American Anguish* (New York: Harper and Row Publishers, 1953).

Tucker, Karen B. Westerfield. *The Sunday Service of the Methodists: Twentieth-Century Worship in Worldwide Methodism* (Nashville: Abingdon Press, 1996).

Turner, George Allen. *The More Excellent Way* (Winona Lake, IN: Light and Life Press, 1952).

Turner, James. "Secularization and Sacralization: Speculations on some Religious Origins of the Secular Humanities Curriculum, 1850-1900," in *The Secularization of the Academy*, eds. George M. Marsden and Bradley J. Longfield (New York: Oxford University Press, 1992) 74-106.

Vance, J. D. *Hillbilly Elegy: A Memoir of a Family and Culture in Crisis* (New York: Harper Collins, 2016).

Vickers, John. *Thomas Coke: Apostle of Methodism* (New York: Abingdon Press, 1969).

Warren, Robert Penn. *All The King's Men* (New York: Harcourt, 1946).

Weisberger, Bernard A. *America Afire: Jefferson–Adams and the Revolutionary Election of 1800* (New York: Harper Collins, 2000).

Wells, David. *No Place for Truth or Whatever Happened to Evangelical Theology?* (Grand Rapids: William B. Eerdmans Publishing Company, 1993).

Willard, Dallas. *The Spirit of the Disciplines: Understanding How God Changes Lives* (San Francisco: HarperCollins, 1988).

Williamson, Glen. *Born for Such a Day: The Amazing Story of Western Evangelical Seminary* (Portland, OR: LaSabre Press, 1974).

Wills, Garry. *Under God: Religion in American Politics* (New York: Simon and Schuster, 1990).

Wood, J. A. *Perfect Love* (South Pasadena, CA: published by the author, 1891).

Worthen, Molly. *Apostles of Reason: The Crisis of Authority in American Evangelicalism* (New York: Oxford University Press, 2013).

Wright, N. T. *The Challenge of Jesus: Understanding Who Jesus Was and Is* (Downers Grove: Inter Varsity Press, 1999).

Wu, Tim. *The Attention Merchants* (New York: Alfred A Knopf, 2016).

Yancey, Phillip. *The Jesus I Never Knew* (Grand Rapids: Zondervan, 1995).

Journals

Arnett, William M., "Entire Sanctification," *The Asbury Seminarian* Vol. XXX (October, 1975) 24-49.

_____, "The Role of the Holy Spirit in Entire Sanctification in the Writings of John Wesley," *Wesleyan Theological Journal*, Vol. 14, No. 2 (Fall 1979) 15-30.

Bridge-Johns, Cheryl, "Partners in Scandal: Wesleyan and Pentecostal Scholarship," *Pneuma: The Journal of the Society for Pentecostal Studies*, Vol. 21, No. 2 (Fall 1999) 183-197.

Bundy, David, "Blaming the Victim: The Wesleyan Holiness Movement in American Culture," *Wesleyan Theological Journal*, No. 32 (Spring 1997) 161-178.

Carpenter, Joel, "The Scope of American Evangelicalism: Some Comments on the Dayton-Marsden Exchange," *Christian Scholars Review*, 23, No. 1(1993) 53-61.

Clapper, Gregory S., "True Religion and the Affections: A Study of John Wesley's Abridgement of Jonathan Edwards' Treatise on Religious Affections," *Wesleyan Theological Journal,* Vol. 19, No. 2 (Fall 1984) 77-89.

Collins, Kenneth, "John Wesley's Topography of the Heart: Dispositions, Tempers and Affections," *Methodist History* Vol. XXXVI, No. 3 (April 1998) 162-175.

Cunningham, Floyd, "Common Ground: The Perspectives of Timothy L. Smith on American Religious History," *Fides et Historia* 44.2(Summer/Fall 2012) 21-55.

Dayton, Donald W., "The Search for the Historical Evangelicalism: George Marsden's History of Fuller Seminary as a Case Study," *Christian Scholars Review* 23, No. 1 (1993) 12-33.

Deasley, Alex R. G., "Entire Sanctification and the Baptism with the Holy Spirit: Perspectives on the Biblical View of the Relationship," *Wesleyan Theological Journal,* Vol. 14, No. 1 (Spring 1979) 27-44.

Dieter, Melvin E., "The Wesleyan Holiness and Pentecostal Movement: Commonalities, Confrontation and Dialogue," *Pneuma: The Journal of the Society for Pentecostal Studies*, vol. 12, number 1, (Spring 1990) 4-13.

Dunning, H. Ray, "Holiness, Technology and Personhood," *Wesleyan Theological Journal,* Vol. 21, nos. l and 2, (Spring -Fall, 1986) 177-185.

Grider, J. Kenneth, "Spirit Baptism: The Means of Entire Sanctification," *Wesleyan Theological Journal*, Vol. 14, No. 2 (Fall 1979) 31-50.

Hynson, Leon, "The Wesleyan Quadrilateral in the American Holiness Tradition," *Wesleyan Theological Journal*, Vol. 20, No. 1 (Spring 1985) 19-33.

Jones, Charles Edwin, "Tongues Speaking and the Wesleyan-Holiness Quest for Assurance of Sanctificaation," *Wesleyan Theological Journal*, Vol. 22, Issue 2 (Fall 1987) 117-124.

Joy, Donald, "Human Development and Christian Holiness," *The Asbury Seminarian*, Vol. 31 (1976) 15-28.

Kinlaw, Dennis F., "Charles Williams' Concept of Imagery Applied to the Song of Songs," *Wesleyan Theological Journal*, Vol. 16, No. 1 (Spring, 1981) 85-92.

Kisker, Scott, "The Claude Thompson Controversy at Asbury Theological Seminary: Holiness Theology in Transition," *Wesleyan Theological Journal*, Vol. 33, No 2 (Fall 1998) 230-247.

Knapp, Eli. "Intelligently Designed Discussion: My Journey through Intellectual Fear in Higher Education," *Christian Scholar's Review*, XLVI, No. 2 (Winter 2017) 145-53.

Kurschner, Mathias J., "The Enthusiasm of The Rev. John Wesley," *Wesleyan Theological Journal*, Vol. 35, No. 2 (Fall 2000) 114-137.

Lyon, Robert W., "Baptism and Spirit-Baptism in the New Testament," *Wesleyan Theological Journal*, Vol. 14, No. 1 (Spring 1979) 14-26.

_____. "The Baptism of the Spirit–Continued," *Wesleyan Theological Journal*, Vol. 15, No. 2 (Fall 1980) 70-79.

Maddox, Randy, "The Use of the Aorist Tense in Holiness Exegesis," *Wesleyan Theological Journal*, Vol. 6, No. 2 (Fall 1981) 106-118.

Marsden, George. "Response to Don Dayton," *Christian Scholars Review*, 23, No. 1(1993) 35-40

Maser, Frank. "John Wesley's Only Marriage: An Examination of Dr. Frank Baker's Article 'John Wesley's First Marriage,'" *Methodist History* 16, No. 1 (October 1977) 33-41.

Merritt, John G. "Fellowship in Ferment: A History of the Wesleyan Theological Society, 1965-84." *Wesleyan Theological Journal,* Vol. XXI, No. 12 (Spring/Fall, 1986) 186-204.

Olson, Mark, "Strange Bedfellows: A Reappraisal of Mildred Wynkoop's *A Theology of Love,*" *Wesleyan Theological Journal,* Vol. 42, No. 2 (Fall 2010) 196-217.

Poloma, Margaret M., "Inspecting the Fruit of the 'Toronto Blessing,'" *Pneuma: The Journal of the Society for Pentecostal Studies,* Volume 20, No. 1 (Spring 1998) 43-70.

Smith, Timothy L. "A Wesleyan Response to the New Perfectionism," *The Asbury Seminarian,* (July 1971) 26-36.

Thompson, David L., "Kuhn, Kohlberg, and Kinlaw: Reflections for Over-serious Theologians," *Wesleyan Theological Journal* Vol. 19, No. 1 (Spring 1984) 7-25

Turner, George Allen, "The Baptism of the Holy Spirit in the Wesleyan Tradition," *Wesleyan Theological Journal,* Vol. 14, No. 1 (Spring 1979) 60-76.

Wacker, Grant, "Travail of a Broken Family: Evangelical Responses to Pentecostalism," *The Journal of Ecclesiastical History,* Vol. 47, No. 3 (July 1996) 515-528.

Wynkoop, Mildred Bangs, "John Wesley - Mentor or Guru?" *Wesleyan Theological Journal,* Vol. X (Spring 1975) 5-14.

_____, "Wesleyan Theology and Christian Development," *The Asbury Seminarian,* Vol. 31, (1976) 35-41.

Archives (Letters, Cassettes, CDs)

Asbury College Archives, "When God Comes" DVD, produced by Asbury College.

Bangs, Carl, Letter from Carl Bangs to Mildred Bangs Wynkoop, March 19, 1958, Wynkoop Collection, Nazarene Archives.

Board of General Superintendents Statement, December 2, 2002, Nazarene Archives

Cunningham, Paul, Letter from Paul Cunningham to Rob Staples, April 13, 1984, included in "My Ordeal."

Cunningham, Paul, Letter from Paul Cunningham to Rob Staples, April 27, 1984, included in "My Ordeal."

Greathouse, William, Letter from William Greathouse to Paul Cunningham, March 2, 1984, included in "My Ordeal."

Harper, Chuck, "How My Mind Is Changing," Harper file. Nazarene Archives.

Ingersol, Stan, "The Woman Behind the Words: Mildred Wynkoop and Authentic Faith," Wynkoop Collection, Nazarene Archives.

Kinlaw, Dennis F., CHA Seminar, "Holiness and the Hope for the 21st Century," DVD, April 1985. In this author's possession, also available on cassette in the CHA files, Asbury Theological Seminary Archives.

Ockenga, Harold, "The Second Blessing: Sanctification, and Holiness," Courtesy Gordon Conwell Archives.

Palmer, Phoebe, Letter from Phoebe Palmer to Matthew Simpson, no date, Simpson papers, Container 13, Library of Congress.

"Something Additional," unidentified newspaper, Crooks' papers, United Methodist Archives, Drew University.

Staples, Rob L., Letter from Rob Staples to Paul Cunningham, March 8, 1984, included in "My Ordeal."

Starnes, Thomas. "Kelly's Trombone," Starnes file, Nazarene Archives.

Taylor, Richard, Letter from Richard Taylor to William Greathouse, March 7, 1987, Taylor Collection, Nazarene Archives.

_____, "Personal Resume," 1984, Taylor Collection, Nazarene Archives.

Walter, Vic, Letter from Vic Walter to Mildred Wynkoop, May 19, 1959, Wynkoop Collection, Nazarene Archives.

Wynkoop, Mildred, Letter from Mildred Wynkoop to John Riley, February 16, 1958, Wynkoop Collection, Nazarene Archives.

_____, Letter from Mildred Wynkoop to Dear Mother, May 19, 1959, Wynkoop Collection, Nazarene Archives.

_____, Letter from Mildred Wynkoop to Dear Mother, May 23, 1959, Wynkoop Collection, Nazarene Archives.

_____, Letter from Mildred Wynkoop to Stephen Nease, May 6, 1979, Nease Collection, Nazarene Archives.

_____, "My Life," February, 16, 1984, Wynkoop Collection, File 1427-2, Nazarene Archives.

_____, "What Holiness Means to Me," Wynkoop Collection, File 2227-14, Nazarene Archives.

Unpublished Dissertations

Adams, John Marion. *The Making of a Neo-Evangelical Statesman: The Case of Harold John Ockenga* (unpublished Ph. D. dissertation, Baylor University, 1994).

Benefiel, Ron. *The Church of the Nazarene: A Religious Organization in Change and Conflict* (unpublished Ph. D. dissertation, University of Southern California, 1986).

Brown, Kenneth O. *Leadership in the National Holiness Association with Special Reference to Eschatology, 1867-1919* (unpublished Ph. D. dissertation, Drew University, 1988).

Debord, David. *A Pastoral Theological Reconstruction of Self-Regard, Self-Sacrifice, and Sanctification in the Wesleyan-Holiness Tradition* (unpublished Ph. D. dissertation, Iliff School of Theology, 1997).

Johnson, Steve. *John Wesley's Liturgical Theology: His Sources, Unique Contributions and Synthetic Practices* (unpublished Ph. D. dissertation, The University of Manchester, 2016).

Kirkemo, William. *Substantialist and Relational Understandings of Entire Sanctification Among Church of the Nazarene Clergy* (unpublished D. Min. dissertation, Asbury Theological Seminary, 2008).

Lennox, Stephen. *Biblical Interpretation in the American Holiness Movement, 1875-1920* (unpublished Ph. D. dissertation, Drew University, 1992).

Quanstrom, Mark. *A Century of Holiness Theology: The Doctrine of Entire Sanctification in the Church of the Nazarene: From Extravagant Hope to Limited Expectation* (unpublished Ph. D. dissertation, St. Louis University, 2000).

Smith, Ronald E. *"Old Path Methodism" in Modern World: Henry Clay Morrison's Campaign for the Evangelical Option in the Modern Period* (unpublished Ph. D. dissertation, Drew University, 2005).

Spindell, Oran Randall. *An Analysis of Higher Education in the Church of The Nazarene, 1945-1978* (unpublished Ph. D. Dissertation, Oklahoma State University, 1981).

Staples, Rob. L. *John Wesley's Doctrine of Christian Perfection: a Reinterpretation* (unpublished Ph. D. dissertation, Pacific School of Religion, 1963).

Wesche, Percival A. *The Life, Theology and Influence of Henry Clay Morrison* (unpublished Ph. D. dissertation, University of Oklahoma, 1954).

Magazines

Albertson, Cricket, "A Pivotal Impact," *The High Calling* (July–August, 2017) 3, 6-7.

Bernard, Jack. "I Found Jesus in My Wallet," *World Christian Magazine* (April 1990).

Desmond, Edward. "A Pencil in the Hand of God," *Time* (December 4, 1989).

Moore, Norman, "Let's Think Revival," *Grace and Peace*, Issue 18 (Fall 2018) 38-40.

Morrison, Henry Clay, "Letter to Fosdick," *Pentecostal Herald* (December 13, 1922).

Oswalt, John N., "In Memory of Dr. Dennis F. Kinlaw," *The High Calling* (July – August, 2017) 10-11.

Oswalt, John, "Maintaining the Witness: An Interview with Dr. Kinlaw," *The High Calling* (September-October, 2013) 10-15.

"Position of the Church of the Nazarene on Speaking in Tongues," *Herald of Holiness* Volume 65 Number 20 (October 15, 1976) 4-5.

Smith, Larry D., "Sergeant Alvin C. York: Christian Hero of World War I," *God's Revivalist and Bible Advocate* (November 2018) 8-9.

Smith, Ronald E., "A Vision for Ministry: Where the Rubber Meets the Road," *The High Calling* (September/October 2013) 3, 8-9.

Stanger, Frank Bateman, "The Inaugural Address of Dr. Frank Bateman Stanger," *The Herald* (October 17, 1962) 18-19.

Taylor, Richard S., "Why the Holiness Movement Died," *God's Revivalist and Bible Advocate* (March 1999) 17-27.

Vincent, J. Paul, "A Kind of Answer: Leadership in the Kingdom," *The High Calling* (September/October, 2013) 4-5, 19.

Newspapers

Brooks, David, "After the Women's March" article included in *The Kansas City Star* (January 26, 2017).

Cullen, Terence, "The U.S. has more credit card debt than ever before," *New York Daily News* (January 9, 2018).

Johnson, Kevin, Meghan Hayer, and Brad Heath. "Local Police Involved in over Four Hundred Killings per Year," *USA Today*, (August 14, 2014).

Nicely, Steve, "TV Church May Set the Stage for Religious Conflict" *The Kansas City Times* (Tuesday, February 19, 1980).

Salter, Darius, "Atlantic High School Class of 1965: More Than Meets the Eye" *The News Times*, Morehead City, NC, May 27, 2015.

Starnes, Thomas, "Leaving Nazarenes Just As Gary Hart Did Wasn't Easy," *Ann Arbor News* (June 1, 1987) Starnes file. Nazarene Archives.

Websites

Andrew-Gee, Eric, "Your Smartphone Is Making You Stupid, Antisocial, and Unhealthy. So Why Don't You Put It Down?," www.theglobeandmail.com/techonology/your-smartphone-is-making-you-stupid/article37511900. 27.

Carter, Bob. "Stokes' life a tale of tragedy and friendship."www.espn.
com/classic/biography/s/Stokes_Maurice.html

Charles Wesley hymn, "Come Father, Son, and Holy Ghost" verse 5.
https://www.ccel.org/w/wesley/hymn/jwg04/jwg0473.html

George W. Bush on Donald Trump: https://nypost.com/2017/03/29/
bush-trump-iminous-inaugural-speech-was-some-wierd-sh-t/

Herbert Buffum, cyberhymnal.org

https://en.wikipedia.org/wiki/List_of_Jewish_prayers_and_
blessings#Havdalah_(%22Separation%22_ceremony)

https://en.wikisource.org/w/index.php?title=We_shall_fight_on_the_
beaches&oldid=6803077

https://www.ccel.org/w/wesley/hymn/jwg04/jwg0473.html

Hunter, James Davison, "To Change the World," retrieved at https://
www.disciplinations.org/media/to-change-the-world_Hunter.

JonathanEdwards.www.ntslibrary.com/PDF%20Books/
Jonathan%Edwards%20Freedom%of%20the Wil.pdf

King, David A. "McLuhan's Still Current Theory Deeply Rooted
in Catholicism," *The Georgia Bulletin*, (October 24,
2013). http://georgiabulletin.org/column//david-a-king/
commentary/2013/10/mcluhans-still-current-media-theory-
deeply-rooted-in-catholism/

Mancini, Mark. "Mental Floss: 7 of John Adams' Greatest Insults."
Website: mentalfloss.com/51899/7-john-adams-greatest-insults

Quotesinvestigator.com

Rev. Dr. Joseph Williamson, Archivist, Pastor, and Scholar, dies at 75.
https://macucc.org/obituary/detail/94876

SIR_2018_WesleyMS.pdf. Strategic Information Report Wesley Biblical
Seminary, 2017-18.

Tennent, Timothy, posted in blog: "Conversion through faith in Jesus Christ: Why I am a Methodist and an Evangelical."

"Top 50 Leadership and Management Experts" (http://www.inc.com/ jeff-haden/the-top-50-leadership-and-management-experts-mon.html) Inc. Magazine.

Treatise on Religious Affections, 6. www.jonathan-edwards.org/ Religious Affections. Pdf

Wesley, Susannah. (Letter, June 8, 1725) Home. Snu.edu

Conferences

Kinzler, Clarence, "Articulating A Living, Christian Holiness in a Pluralistic World," Nazarene Theological Conference, February -March 1, 1992.

Lodahl, Michael, "On Being the Neighbor: How John Wesley's Reading of the Parable of the Good Samaritan May Cultivate Loving People," The Edwin Crawford Lectures: Northwest Nazarene University, Nampa, Idaho, February 5, 2009.

Stowe, Eugene, "Higher Education and Our Holiness Heritage," at Nazarene Theological Conference: Nazarene Theological Seminary, Kansas City, MO (Nazarene Archives, December 1982) 17.

Motion Pictures

The Darkest Hour, Dir., Joe E. Wright. Perf. Gary Oldman, Kristin Scott Thomas, Lily James, Stephen Dillane, Ronald Pickup, and Ben Mendelsohn. Focus Features-Universal Pictures, 2017.

INDEX

CPSIA information can be obtained
at www.ICGtesting.com
Printed in the USA
LVHW051602021221
705096LV00012B/960

9 781621 719403